W. Gregory Walker

The Law and Practice relating to the Administration of the Estates

of deceased Persons

W. Gregory Walker

The Law and Practice relating to the Administration of the Estates of deceased Persons

ISBN/EAN: 9783337159368

Printed in Europe, USA, Canada, Australia, Japan

Cover: Foto ©ninafisch / pixelio.de

More available books at **www.hansebooks.com**

THE LAW AND PRACTICE

RELATING TO THE

ADMINISTRATION OF THE ESTATES OF DECEASED PERSONS.

ADDENDA.

REFERENCES TO THE RULES OF COURT, 1883, AND THE STATUTES OF 1883.

Page 1. All the sections of the Chancery Procedure Act and of 15 & 16 Vict. c. 80 referred to in this work are repealed by 46 & 47 Vict. c. 49, with a proviso (sec. 6 (c)) that the enactments relating to the making of Rules of Court contained in the Judicature Act, 1875, and the Acts amending it, shall be deemed to extend and apply to the matters contained in and regulated by the repealed Acts. Under this power, new Rules of Court have recently been made, regulating the practice of administration actions. Most of these are merely re-enactments of old Rules and Orders; those that are new are particularly mentioned below.

(c). For Form of Summons, see App. L., 25.

Pages 2, 30. By Ord. LV. ii. r. 3, it is now expressly provided that an assignee of a person entitled to apply may himself take out the summons.

Page 7. Under Ord. LV. ii. r. 4, an order may be made on summons for the administration of the real estate, whether there is or is not a trust for or power of sale.

Page 8. There is now no power for the plaintiff to choose the Judge; see Ord. V. r. 9.

Page 11.	Chapters II. and III. must now be read subject to the provision in Ord. LV. ii. r. 10, that it shall not be obligatory on the Court or a Judge to make an order for the administration of the estate, if the questions between the parties can be properly determined without; and in *Lane* v. *Lane* (W. N. 1883, 171) a reference to chambers was ordered to inquire whether general administration was necessary.
Page 21.	As to delivering statement of claim, see now Ord. XIX. r. 2, and Ord. XX. r. 1 (*c*), and the Forms in App. C. II., Nos. 1, 2; D. II. If more prolix forms are used without justification, the parties using them will have to pay the costs; see Ord. II. r. 2.
Pages 31, 37.	As to actions by infants, lunatics, and married women, see now Ord. XVI. iii. rr. 16—21.
Page 36 (*x*).	This case was affirmed by the House of Lords (W. N. 1883, 200), but seems likely to lead to a remarkable conflict of jurisdiction, for a decree for administration of the whole estate *in Scotland* has since been obtained from the Court of Session, including an injunction against removing any part of the estate out of the jurisdiction of the Scotch Court.
Page 40.	Add to note (*z*), " see also Ord. XVI. r. 11."
Page 41.	For Ord. XVI. r. 12, *read* Ord. XVI. r. 11 ; but see now Ord. XVI. rr. 33—40.
Page 45.	By Ord. IX. r. 3, husband and wife must both be served, *unless the Court or a Judge shall otherwise order.*
Page 47 (*h*).	For Form of indorsement, see App. G., 28.

ADDENDA.   liii

Page 48.   Persons served with notice of the judgment now appear
             as defendants, without any order of course: Ord. XVI. r.
             41. As to service on infants and persons of unsound
             mind, being defendants to an action, see Ord. IX. rr. 4, 5.

Page 51.   For Forms of executors' and trustees' affidavit of the
             testator's estate, see App. L., 11—13.

Page 54.   Chapter V. must now be read subject to Ord. LV. r. 12,
             which provides that the issue of a summons under r. 2 of
             the same Order for the determination of any question in
             the administration shall not interfere with or control any
             power or discretion vested in any executor, adminis-
             trator, or trustee, except so far as such interference or
             control may necessarily be involved in the particular
             relief sought.

Page 60.   As to payment into Court, see App. M.

Page 91.   As to examination of witnesses, see Ord. XXXVII. ii.;
             subpœna, Ord. XXXVII. iii.; and examination before a
             chief clerk, Ord. LV. rr. 16, 17.

Page 95.   For the procedure on sales, and Forms, see Ord. LI. i.
             and ii., (which gives a much wider power of sale); and
             App. L., 15, 16, 23.

Page 96.   For directions as to taking accounts, and Form of chief
             clerk's certificate, see Ord. XXXIII. r. 7, and App. L., 10,
             17—20.

Page 99.   Under Ord. LV. r. 71, the Judge may, if the special
             circumstances require it, discharge or vary the certificate
             at any time.

Page 102 (c).   For Form of advertisement, see App. L., 3.

Page 103 (i). For Form of notice, see App. L., 8.

Page 104. For Form of executor's affidavit, see *Ibid.*, 5, 6.

(*l*). For Form of notice, see *Ibid.*, 4.

Page 112. For Form of notice to creditors of claims allowed or disallowed, see *Ibid.*, 7, 8.

Page 118 (z). For Form of advertisement, see *Ibid.*, 2.

Page 128. For Form of request to set down an action for further consideration, see *Ibid.* 26.

Page 129. For Form of notice of so setting down, see *Ibid.* 27.

Page 134. For Form of notice that cheques may be received, see *Ibid.* 9.

Page 138. Add to note (*p*) a reference to Ord. XXXIV.; but it is suggested that such a question should now be decided by summons under LV. ii. rr. 3, 5.

Pages 141–144. As to costs of executors and trustees who unreasonably institute or carry on or resist any proceedings, see now Ord. LXV. r. 1.

Pages 168–173. This must be read subject to sec. 125 of the Bankruptcy Act, 1883, which provides that any creditor whose debt would have been sufficient to support a bankruptcy petition may on the decease of the debtor apply to the Bankruptcy Court by petition for an order for the administration in bankruptcy of the debtor's estate; but such order is not to be granted without the concurrence of the personal representatives, until the expiration of two months from the grant of probate or letters of administration, unless the debtor shall have committed an act of bankruptcy within three months of his decease. The petition

ADDENDA.   lv

is not to be presented after proceedings for administration have been commenced in any other Court, but that Court may transfer such proceedings to the Bankruptcy Court, on proof that the estate is insolvent. After the order is made, the estate vests in the official receiver, who will realise and distribute it, as in bankruptcy, but proper funeral and testamentary expenses are to be paid first, and everything done "in good faith" by the personal representative, before the order, is of course not to be upset; but as between him and the official receiver, notice of the presentation of the petition is equivalent to notice of an act of bankruptcy, and no payment or transfer of property by the personal representative after such notice will be a good discharge to him. See also Rules 200—202.

Page 169.   Section 168 of the Act of 1883 defines "secured creditor" in practically the same terms.

Sections 45 and 46 of the new Act correspond to sec. 87 of the old Act.

Page 171 (*q*).   The right of a secured creditor to realise his security is still preserved; sec. 9 (2).

The rules as to proof by secured creditors are now contained in Schedule II. of the Act, rr. 9—17, and the provisions for taking accounts of mortgaged property and the sale thereof, in the Rules of 1883, rr. 65—69. The practice will be much the same as it has hitherto been, but under r. 12 (c) of the Rules in Schedule II. the creditor can call upon the trustee to elect within six months whether the property shall or shall not be realised, and if he does not exercise the option, the equity of redemption vests in the creditor, and the valuation will be unimpeachable. Rules 13 and 14 provide for rectification of the valuation, and consequent adjustment of accounts between the creditor and the trustee.

Page 172.   The debts and liabilities provable are, under sec. 37 of the new Act, the same as before, except that unliquidated demands arising by reason of a breach of trust are now provable, and the Court has power to order any debt or liability which is incapable of being fairly estimated to be deemed a debt *not* provable.

Section 40 of the new Act corresponds to sec. 32 of the old Act, but it may be mentioned that though by 46 & 47 Vict. c. 28 the rule laid down in the cases referred to in note (c) is substituted for that which eventually prevailed, so far as relates to wages, yet, as the Act does not refer to the administration of estates of deceased persons, the practice in administration will remain unaltered.

Section 42 of the new Act re-enacts the provisions with regard to distress for rent contained in sec. 34 of the old Act, but provides also that where an order is made for the administration in bankruptcy of the estate of a person dying insolvent, the landlord's rights are limited as in the case of bankruptcy.

Page 173.   It would seem that voluntary bonds are still payable *pari passu* with other debts ; sec. 40 (4).

For r. 77, is now substituted r. 20 of Schedule II.

As to valuation of annuities and future and contingent liabilities, see now sec. 37.

(*g*).   See now sec. 38 of new Act.

Page 181.   The limit of value up to which applications may be made in chambers by summons instead of petition has been much extended by Ord. LV. i. ; and by sub-sec. 16 of r. 2 of this Order, applications for orders on the

ADDENDA. lvii

further consideration of any cause or matter, where the order to be made is for the distribution of an insolvent estate or for the distribution of the estate of an intestate, or of a fund among creditors or debenture holders, are to be made by summons in chambers.

Page 189. The motion on an appeal under 38 & 39 Vict. c. 50, s. 6, must now be made upon two clear days' notice to the other side; Ord. LIII. rr. 2, 3, 5; *Re a County Court appeal*, Q. B. D. Nov. 9, 1883.

Page 193. See now App. L., 25.

Page 195. For Form of indorsement, see App. G., 28.

For usual administration order, see App. L., 28.

For Form of advertisement, see *Ibid*. 3.

Page 200. For Form of notice, see *Ibid*. 8.

Page 201. For Form of notice to produce documents, see *Ibid*. 4.

For Form of advertisement, see *Ibid*. 2.

INDEX :—

	Old Reference to Rules or Orders.	Page.	Reference to Rules of Court, 1883.
Page 227	Cons. Ord. VII. r. 1	13, 194	O. XVI. r. 45.
	r. 5	45	See now O. XVI. r. 44.
	rr. 6, 7	49	See O. XVI. r. 41, and O. LV. r. 27.
	XXI. r. 10	128, 129	O. XXXVI. r. 21.
	XXIII. r. 9	181	{ Not provided for; see Chancery Funds Rules, 1874, r. 14.
	r. 14	51	O. XXXIII. r. 6.
	r. 18	49	O. XVI. r. 40.
	r. 19	46	O. XVI. r. 42.
	r. 20	47, 195	O. XVI. r. 43.
	XXXV. r. 7	3	O. LIV. r. 4.
	rr. 8, 9	3	O. LV. rr. 22, 23.
	r. 13	96	O. LI. r. 3.
	r. 15	86	O. LV. r. 28.

Old Reference to Rules or Orders.	Page.	Reference to Rules of Court, 1883.
Page 227 Cons. Ord. XXXV. r. 16	87, 93	O. LV. r. 33.
r. 18	45	O. LV. r. 35.
r. 19	52, 53	See now O. XXXIII. r. 2.
r. 20	94	O. LV. r. 40.
r. 22	86, 123	{ O. LV. r. 32, and see O. XXXIII. r. 9.
r. 23	124	O. XXXIII. r. 9.
r. 26	90	O. LV. r. 37.
rr. 27, 28	90	O. XXXVIII. rr. 20, 21.
r. 29	91	O. XXXVII. r. 28.
r. 30	92	See O. XXXVIII. ii.
rr. 33, 34	90	O. XXXIII. rr. 4, 5.
rr. 35, 36	103	O. LV. rr. 45, 46.
r. 37	118	O. LV. r. 47.
r. 38	118	Not provided for.
r. 39	103, 118	O. LV. r. 48.
r. 40	103, 118	O. LV. r. 54.
r. 41	118	{ Not provided for, but see O. LV. r. 57.
228 rr. 43, 44	119	O. LV. rr. 57, 59.
r. 45	100	O. LV. r. 18.
rr. 46, 48	97	O. LV. rr. 68, 67.
r. 49	88, 100	See O. LV. r. 69.
r. 50	88, 100	Abrogated; see O. LV. r. 69.
r. 51	98, 100	Abrogated; see O. LV. r. 65.
rr. 52, 53	98, 100	O. LV. r. 70.
r. 54	100	{ See now O. L. ii. and App. L. Nos. 14, 22.
r. 55	98	O. LV. r. 70.
r. 56	100	See now O. LV. r. 65.
XXXVII. r. 10	49	O. LXIV. r. 1.
XL. rr. 24, 25	111	{ O. LV. rr. 51, 58, and O. LXV. r. 27, § 26.
XLII. rr. 9—11	110, 119	O. LV. rr. 62—64.
Sched. K., No. II.	193	App. L., No. 25.
Sched. L.	201	App. L., No. 2.
Ord. May 27, 1865, rr. 1, 2, 3, 5, 6, 7, 8	Ch. IX.	O. LV. rr. 47, 49, 50, 52, 53, 55, 56.
r. 9	113	{ Not provided for, but see O. LV. r. 57.
rr. 10, 12, 13	Ch. IX.	O. LV. rr. 57, 60, 61.
Regulations, August 8, 1857, r. 5	86	See LV. r. 28.
r. 6	86	O. LV. r. 30.
r. 7	45	Obsolete.
r. 13	96	O. LI. r. 4.

ADDENDA. lix

	Old Reference to Rules or Orders.	Page.	Reference to Rules of Court, 1883.
Page 228	Rules of the Supreme Court, 1875, Ord. I. r. 1	8	O. I. r. 1.
	Ord. II. r. 1	8	O. II. r. 1.
	III. r. 2	8	O. III. r. 2, and O. XX. r. 4.
	r. 4	9	O. III. r. 4, and App. A. III. vii.
	r. 8	8, 22	O. III. r. 8.
	V. r. 4	8	O. V. r. 4.
	r. 4a	8	O. V. r. 9.
	IX. rr. 4, 5	45	O. IX. rr. 4, 5.
	XI. r. 1	36	O. XI. r. 1 (but jurisdiction limited).
	r. 1a	36	O. XI. r. 2, and see r. 4.
	XII. r. 4	190	O. XII. r. 6.
	XIII. r. 9	22	See O. XIII. r. 12.
229	XV. rr. 1, 2	8, 22, 23, 191	O. XV. rr. 1, 2.
	XVI. r. 7	43	O. XVI. r. 8.
	r. 9	44	O. XVI. r. 9.
	r. 9a	44	O. XVI. 32.
	r. 11	41	See O. XVI. rr. 33—40.
	r. 12a	45	O. XVI. r. 44.
	r. 12b	93	O. XVI. r. 47.
	r. 17	116	See O. XVI. rr. 48—55.
	XVII. r. 2	29	O. XVIII. r. 2.
	XXIX. rr. 10, 11	19, 20	O. XXVII. rr. 11, 12.
	XXXIII.	23, 52	O. XXXIII. r. 2.
	XXXV. rr.1,4,11,12,13	191	O. XXXV. rr. 1, 2; 6; 13; 14; 16,17.
	XL. r. 1	21	O. XL. r. 1.
	r. 11	18, 66, 68	O. XXXII. r. 6.
	L. r. 4	46	O. XVII. r. 4.
	Ll. rr. 1, 2a, 3, 4.	77, 84, 77, 79	O. XLIX. rr. 1, 5, 7, 8.
	LII. r. 6a	124	O. L. r. 10.
	LIII. r. 4	19, 20	O. LII. r. 5.
	LVIII. r. 15	88	O. LVIII. r. 15.
	r. 19	188	O. LIX. r. 4.
	App. A. II. s. 1	9	App. A. III. ss. 1, 2.
	Add. Rules, 12 August, 1875, Ord. VI. 1	135	O. LXV. r. 8, and App. N.
	Add. Rules, 1875 (Costs), r. 21	95	O. LXV. r. 27, § 23.
231	15 & 16 Vict. c. 80, s. 26	126	O. LV. r. 2.
	s. 30	91	O. LV. r. 16.
	s. 33	88	See now O. LV. rr. 67—69.
	s. 34	98	See now O. LV. r. 70.
	c. 86. s. 42, r. 1	24	O. XVI. r. 33.
	rr. 2, 3	29	O. XVI. rr. 34, 35.
	r. 6	26	O. XVI. r. 38.
	r. 8	40, 44, 47—49	O. XVI. r. 40.

	Old Reference to Rules or Orders.	Page.	Reference to Rules of Court, 1883.
Page 231	15 & 16 Vict. c. 86, s. 42, r. 9	40, 43	O. XVI. r. 8.
	s. 44	34	O. XV. r. 46.
	s. 45	1, 193	O. LV. rr. 3—5, but see r. 10.
	s. 46	3	O. LV. r. 20.
	s. 47	7, 193	Extended by O. LV. rr. 3—5, but see r. 10.
	s. 52	46	O. XVII.
	s. 54	75	O. XXXIII. r. 3.
	s. 55	95	O. LI. r. 1.
	s. 57	182	O. L. r. 9.

THE

LAW AND PRACTICE

RELATING TO THE

ADMINISTRATION OF THE ESTATES OF DECEASED PERSONS

BY THE

Chancery Division of the High Court of Justice.

WITH AN

APPENDIX OF ORDERS AND FORMS,

ANNOTATED BY REFERENCES TO THE TEXT.

BY

W. GREGORY WALKER, B.A.,

AUTHOR OF "THE PARTITION ACTS, 1868 AND 1876; A MANUAL OF THE LAW OF PARTITION AND OF SALE IN LIEU OF PARTITION," "A COMPENDIUM OF THE LAW OF EXECUTORS AND ADMINISTRATORS,"

AND

EDGAR J. ELGOOD, B.C.L., M.A.,

BOTH OF LINCOLN'S INN, BARRISTERS-AT-LAW, AND LATE SCHOLARS OF EXETER COLLEGE, OXFORD.

LONDON:

STEVENS AND HAYNES,

Law Publishers,

BELL YARD, TEMPLE BAR.

1883.

LONDON:
BRADBURY, AGNEW, & CO., PRINTERS, WHITEFRIARS.

PREFACE.

This Treatise was planned and commenced by Mr. Gregory Walker as a companion volume to his "Compendium of the Law of Executors and Administrators," but, after writing rather more than one-half of the book, he decided to relinquish the English Bar for that of New South Wales, and placed his manuscript and materials in my hands for completion. Before he left England we discussed together the general plan of the unfinished part of the work, but as he gave me full discretion to revise and add to what he had written, it follows that the responsibility for any deficiencies should more properly rest upon myself.

I believe the arrangement of the Table of Cases to be entirely new, and I hope that I have attained the double object of not burdening the text or notes with references to contemporary Reports, while sparing those who do not possess the authorised Reports considerable trouble, when referring to the Law Journal, Law Times, Weekly Reporter, or Jurist, as the case may be.

The references to Daniell's Chancery Practice are to the 5th edition throughout; where possible, a reference has been added in brackets to the 6th edition, of which the first volume only is as yet published. The Rules and Orders of the Supreme Court are cited as " O.," the Consolidated Orders of the Court of Chancery as " Cons. Ord." These latter have been verbally altered in accordance with the nomenclature of the present practice, " action," " statement of claim," and " judgment " being substituted for " suit," " bill," and " decree ;" but I have not thought it necessary to call attention to this in the text.

In the Appendix will be found references to the text, as in the Compendium of Executors.

My thanks are due to Mr. Pemberton for kindly permitting me to insert in the Appendix some of the more ordinary Administration Judgments from the 3rd edition of his " Judgments and Orders," to which, as also to the 4th edition of Seton's Decrees, frequent reference has been made ; also to my friends Mr. W. T. Langford and Mr. J. W. Brodie-Innes, both of Lincoln's Inn, for many valuable suggestions ; and to Mr. Langford and my brother E. Crawshaw Elgood (of the Common-Law Bar) for very considerable assistance in the laborious and uninteresting task of filling in the references to contemporary Reports.

E. J. E.

LINCOLN'S INN,
April, 1883.

CONTENTS.

CHAPTER I.
INSTITUTION OF PROCEEDINGS FOR ADMINISTRATION.

A. ADMINISTRATION SUMMONS.

(a) *Personal Estate.*

                                PAGE

Assignees may obtain the summons.—Representatives of the accounting representative may be defendants.—Upon whom it must be served.—Copy to be filed.—Extension of time for appearance.—Appearance to be entered.—Court may make order *ex parte* in default of appearance.—Summons by executor against co-executor.—Discretion of Judge to refuse order for administration upon summons.—The jurisdiction only exercised in simple cases.—Only the *usual* order can be made ; *e.g.*, no account for wilful default.—Questions arising out of usual order *may* be determined ; but an administration action will generally be directed.—Administration of property appointed by will of *feme covert*.—Service of summons out of jurisdiction.—Appointment of guardian *ad litem* to lunatic defendant 1

(b) *Real Estate.*

Jurisdiction where executors have only power of sale, or sale is conditionally directed to be postponed.—No jurisdiction in case of intestacy . . 7

B. ADMINISTRATION ACTION.

Title of writ.—Indorsements on writ ; claiming that accounts be taken ; for a receiver ; showing representative capacity of parties.—Special indorsement *necessary* in creditors' actions for administration of real and personal estate ; *optional* in case of personal estate only 8

CHAPTER II.
HOW JUDGMENT FOR ADMINISTRATION MAY BE OBTAINED.

Judgment for administration.—I. In proceedings by summons.—II. In administration actions :—(1) At the trial.—As a short cause after notice.— Evidence.— Plaintiff's right to sue must be proved or admitted.—Creditor plaintiff.—Holder of a bill of exchange.—Title of legal personal representatives ; of devisees ; of heir of an intestate.—Evidence required for *common* judgment ; for *special* judgment, *e.g.*, wilful default,—at the hearing upon special case made; in a proper case on further consideration; or in a fresh action after leave of the Court obtained; generally before judgment, after amendment of the pleadings, if necessary.—Lord Eldon's rule that one act of wilful default must be proved before inquiry directed, still the rule of the Court.—(2) On motion for judgment; (*a*) upon admissions in the pleadings; but only in simple cases, and subject to the discretion of the Court to order the action to go into the general paper.—Motion on admissions combined with motion in default of pleading.—(*b*) In default of defendant pleading; either as short causes or in their regular turn in the general paper.—Notice of motion.—(*c*) Where there are no pleadings.—In what cases statement of claim should be delivered.—(*d*) In default of appearance.—(3) Upon summons for accounts and inquiries, either after statement of claim, or when none intended to be delivered 11

CHAPTER III.

OF THE PARTIES TO ADMINISTRATION ACTIONS.

I. WHO MAY MAINTAIN ACTIONS AS PLAINTIFFS.

A. PERSONAL ESTATE.

(1 & 2) Beneficiaries, although their interest contingent, if present or existing; *secus*, if an expectancy only.—(3) Creditors, including voluntary covenantees.—But the debt must be *debitum in presenti*.—(4) Legal personal representatives, or one of them, sufficient if one at least has proved the will.—Executor may even commence action before probate, and deliver pleadings, but must produce probate before motion made, for right of action is not *dependent* on probate.—So, also, in the case of plaintiff taking out administration after action brought.—This right not to be used oppressively.—Proceedings when plaintiff's title as legal personal representative lost after judgment 24

B. REAL AND PERSONAL ESTATE.

(1) Legatee, when legacy charged on land.—(2) Persons interested in proceeds of sale of realty.—(3) Residuary devisee or heir.—(4) Creditor. —(5) Trustee, but not executor or administrator *as such*.—Assignees of persons who might have been plaintiffs may sue both as to real and personal estate, including mortgagees, legal personal representatives, trustees in bankruptcy, and *semble*, since the Judicature Act, voluntary assignees of a debt due from a testator.—Infant or lunatic plaintiff, and *feme covert* 29

II. WHO ARE NECESSARY OR PROPER DEFENDANTS.

A. In administration of *personal* estate at suit of beneficiaries or creditors, all executors proving or acting must be defendants.—Any proving or acting afterwards must be added as defendants.—Relief in actions against executors before probate generally confined to appointment of a receiver.—Person named executor, but not proving or acting except as agent of other executors.—Appointment of administrator *ad litem* by Chancery Division insufficient to enable administration judgment to be obtained.—Full personal representative necessary.—So, as to administrator *ad litem* appointed by Probate Division.—Where testator died out of the jurisdiction. — Married woman defendant.—Representatives of deceased executors.—When administrator *durante minore œtate* a necessary party.—Executor *de son tort* cannot be sued for administration; nor for an account, unless legal personal representative be before the Court; at least before the hearing 31

B. In administration of real estate, *all* the trustees must be parties.—Practice where one of two trustees dies insolvent after judgment . . 39

III. PERSONS SERVED WITH NOTICE OF THE JUDGMENT.

All who would formerly have been necessary parties.—Trustees represent their *cestuis que trustent*.—Reason for bringing all interested parties before the Court.—All interested in personalty alone represented by the executor.—In general, all residuary devisees and legatees must be before the Court.—How far trustees represent their *cestuis que trustent*.—One or more of a class in same interest allowed or appointed to sue or be sued on behalf of or for all.—Service upon infants, &c.—Service dispensed with, or substituted service allowed.—Birth of infant beneficiary after action brought.—Entry of memorandum of service.—Title and endorsement of notice.—Service out of the jurisdiction.—Service of a copy.—Persons served bound by the proceedings, but cannot be made to account till made parties.—Nor can they be treated as co-plaintiffs, and obtain inquiries as such.—Parties served may obtain order of course to attend the proceedings.—Infants.—Persons served may apply to add to the judgment 40

CHAPTER IV.

THE JUDGMENT, AND ADDITIONS MADE TO IT.

Administration judgment moulded to enable the Court to deal with the whole action on further consideration.—Less extensive in creditors' actions.—Further accounts or inquiries may be ordered; but formerly, not so as to charge defendants with wilful default; otherwise under the new practice.—How application made to add to judgment . . . 50

CHAPTER V.

THE EFFECT OF JUDGMENT FOR ADMINISTRATION ON POWERS AND DISCRETIONS OF TRUSTEES AND EXECUTORS.

After judgment, new trustee cannot be appointed without approval of the Court; nor investments made, nor powers of management exercised.—Nor may one creditor be preferred to another.—But an executor may exercise his right of retainer.—Executor may mortgage assets after judgment.—*Before* judgment, trustees may exercise discretion.—And the Court will not interfere with "absolute" or "uncontrolled" discretion of trustee.—Payment of debts.—Sale of real and leasehold estate . . . 54

CHAPTER VI.

AS TO SECURING TRUST FUNDS BY ORDERING THEM INTO COURT.

Funds admitted to be in hand ordered to be paid into Court upon interlocutory motion; even though applicant may show only a *primâ facie* title.—In what cases the application refused.—The Court will exercise discretion to prevent needless payment in and out.—Debts admitted to be due from executor to the testator regarded as in his hands.—So, as to moneys in the hands of executor's partner.—What moneys may be deducted by executor.—What amounts to an admission by executor.—At what stage in the action money will be ordered to be paid into Court.—Immaterial in what manner the money is admitted to be in his hands.—Motion under Order XL., r. 11.—Investment of money in Court 60

CHAPTER VII.

CONCURRENT ACTIONS FOR ADMINISTRATION—STAY—TRANSFER—CONSOLIDATION.

One of two concurrent administration actions will be stayed, when judgment obtained in the other.—Upon whose application.—Mode of applying for stay.—Principles on which order will be made.—When relief claimed is co-extensive, which action will be stayed.—Action of residuary legatee preferred to that of a creditor; tenant for life to remainderman.—Two actions by same infant.—The Court may interfere *ex mero motu*.—Consolidation of concurrent administration actions.—Palatine Court.—Where relief claimed is not co-extensive.—One action may be *partially* stayed; or accounts in one ordered to be used in the other; or one stayed, the judgment in the other being added to.—Costs of applications to stay proceedings.—Transfer of one of two concurrent actions from one branch of Chancery Division to another.—Which action will be transferred.—As to consent of plaintiff in second action.—Consolidation.—Staying proceedings after foreign judgment has been obtained.—Staying creditors' actions in Queen's Bench Division after judgment for administration in Chancery Division.—Actions not in the High Court may still be restrained by Chancery Division.—Transfer to Chancery Division, after judgment for administration, of actions against executors or administrators 69

CHAPTER VIII.

PROCEEDINGS IN CHAMBERS.

Prosecution of judgment.—Directions by the Judge.—Adjournment to the Judge.—Appeal from Judge.—Suitor's right to be heard by Judge himself.—How qualified.—Rehearing by Judge in Court.—Time limited for re-hearing.—Evidence.—Affidavits.—Notice of amount and particulars of charge beyond amount admitted.—Cross-examination.—Powers of chief clerk.—Examiner.—Mode of examining witness before chief clerk.—Practice where witness refuses to answer.—Persons having liberty to attend the proceedings.—Their right to costs determined by the Judge.—Sale under judgment or order.—The chief clerk's certificate.—Certificates either *general* or *separate*.—Time for signature of certificate by Judge.—Certificate, &c., signed and adopted by Judge, to be filed, and be binding on all parties, unless discharged or varied within eight clear days.—Applications to discharge or vary certificate.—Exceptions as regards certificates to be acted upon by Paymaster-General without further order, and certificates on passing receivers' accounts.—Certificate may be referred back 86

CHAPTER IX.

PROOF OF CLAIMS IN CHAMBERS.

A. Advertisements for creditors.—Peremptory.—In what papers inserted.—By whom prepared.—Creditor need not make affidavit or attend, unless required; but party prosecuting cause to take office copies of affidavits, if any.—Notice to creditor to produce security or other evidence.—Notice by post sufficient.—Claims to be examined and result verified by affidavit of executor or other person appointed by Judge.—Such affidavit may be postponed.—Adjudication on the claims.—Plaintiff must prove his debt in chambers, unless assets admitted.—Evidence.—Claims for unliquidated damages.—Contingent liabilities, &c.—Cross-examination of creditor.—Right of creditor to affidavit of documents by executors.—The Statute of Limitations.—The rule in *Sterndale* v. *Hankinson, semble*, no longer prevails.—Interest on debts.—Costs of creditors establishing claims; and failing to establish them.—Notice to creditors of claims allowed or disallowed.—New claims before adjourned adjudication.—Special leave to make claims after time fixed by advertisement; even after certificate.—As to claims after apportionment.—Creditor may obtain proportion only of his claim; and may be obliged to sue legatees 102
B. Advertisements for claimants *not named* in will.—Claims book.—Adjournment; closing further evidence.—Claims heard on adjournment day.—Admitting further claims.—List of claims allowed.—Interest on legacies. -Costs of next of kin.—Refunding 117

CHAPTER X.

THE CONDUCT OF ADMINISTRATION ACTIONS AND OF PROCEEDINGS ARISING THEREOUT.

Plaintiff has *primâ facie* right to conduct of proceedings.—Practice when plaintiff guilty of delay.—Conduct of different inquiries given to different persons; *e.g.*, conduct of sale given to trustees.—Plaintiff in creditors' action found to be a debtor to estate.—Death of creditor plaintiff.—Application for conduct to be made in chambers.—Conduct of proceedings arising out of the administration action 122

CHAPTER XI.

FURTHER CONSIDERATION.

When and how actions set down on further consideration.—Short cause.—Notice of setting down, and appearances, and costs of persons unnecessarily appearing.—Declaration of title, and distribution of fund.—Inquiry as to damages.—Costs of action dealt with.—Evidence.—Questions cannot generally be raised on further consideration which have not been pleaded.—Interest on balances or debts.—Certificate cannot be varied, unless on regular application, except where error apparent 123

CHAPTER XII.

COSTS OF ADMINISTRATION ACTIONS.

Costs and debts first provided for on further consideration.—Costs.—Principles on which costs are allowed out of the estate.—Costs of plaintiffs.—Mere pecuniary legatee.—Rule in *Wilson* v. *Squire*.—Legatee plaintiff generally allowed his costs.—Concurrent actions.—Annuitant.—Residuary legatees or next of kin.—Where executors have overpaid some of the residuary legatees, and the others obtain administration judgment.—Costs of residuary legatee not allowed as between solicitor and client, except by consent, and should never be allowed where infants interested.—Appeal for costs.—Creditor generally allowed his costs.—When ordered to pay the costs, or deprived of his costs.—Costs in chambers.—Executor or administrator.—General rule as to costs of trustees and executors.—Strong case required to deprive them of costs; still stronger to make them pay them.—Executors may lose, or have to pay, costs of parts of the action.—When ordered to pay all the costs; except of the accounts.—Sometimes allowed costs upon making restitution.—Executor's costs when improperly bringing administration action.—Costs of insolvent executor or trustee.—Costs set off against debt to estate.—So as to legacy or share of residue; except where debtor bankrupt before death of creditor.—Bankruptcy of one of two co-executors.—Where innocent executor ordered to pay costs jointly with guilty executor.—Trustees should not generally sever in their defence.—Costs of an executor who is a solicitor.—Executors or trustees may appeal for costs.—Their costs are payable as between solicitor and client.—Real Estate.—Costs of persons attending the proceedings.—Plaintiff not succeeding may be allowed his costs; but not from the defendants *personally*.—Costs of assignees or mortgagees of beneficiaries.—Rules where fund deficient.—Costs of executor paid in priority.—When heir regarded as trustee for creditors.—Costs of disclaiming trustees as between party and party only.—Executors, *as such*, not entitled to costs out of real estate.—Creditor plaintiff, when entitled to solicitor and client costs.—No contribution now ordered from creditors towards plaintiff's costs.—Costs of mortgagee, plaintiff in an administration action.—Costs of legatee plaintiff, where fund deficient.—When paid in priority to debts, but as between party and party only; except as to costs of getting in and realization.—Next of kin plaintiffs have no priority.—Executor's right of retainer paramount to right to costs of all other persons.—The general personalty the primary fund for costs; then the pecuniary legacies, next the undisposed of realty, lastly specific gifts.—What costs included.—Costs of administration of real estate only.—Apportionment between real and personal estate.—Apportionment between pure and impure personalty.—Adjustment after payment of costs out of a fund not chargeable therewith.—Marshalling of assets by testator.—Costs of administration action included in "testamentary expenses."—Apportionment between legal and equitable assets 135

CHAPTER XIII.

OF THE ORDER IN WHICH ASSETS ARE ADMINISTERED.

The old law not here discussed.—The Act of 1869, and the Judicature Act, 1875.—The Act of 1869.—Specialty creditors have no priority over simple contract creditors.—The Judicature Act, 1875, imports the rules of Bankruptcy in administering insolvent estates.—What debts still have priority.—Costs and debts payable out of the same fund . . 161
Order in which assets are resorted to.—1. The general residuary personalty. —2. Real estate devised in trust to pay debts.—3. Real estate descended. —4. Specific devises and bequests charged with debts.—5. General pecuniary legacies.—6. Specific devises and bequests.—7. Real or personal estate appointed.—Adjustment when debts paid out of property not chargeable therewith.—Alienation by heir or devisee.—Retainer by executor for his own debt, out of legal assets only.—Rule of hotchpot where part of debt retained or paid out of legal assets in priority to other creditors.—Marshalling 164
The Judicature Act, 1875, and the rules in Bankruptcy.—1. As to secured and unsecured creditors.—Mortgagees.—Object of the enactment.—Courses open to secured creditors.—Redemption by executor at creditor's valuation.—2. Debts and liabilities provable.—No priority for rates, or wages, or rent.—*Semble*, right to distrain unaffected.—Mutual credits.—Statute-barred debts.—Voluntary bonds.—No interest on debts from date of administration judgment.—3. Valuation of annuities and future and contingent liabilities.—Locke King's Act.—Mortgaged estate now taken by devisee *cum onere*.—Specific legatee of mortgaged personal estate, other than leaseholds, may have it redeemed.—Marshalling; against devisees of mortgaged estates; against real estate in favour of legatees having no charge upon it.—No marshalling in favour of charities; except by direction of testator.—Priority between legatees; none in general; but widow has priority, if entitled to dower, and given a legacy in satisfaction thereof.—Annuities, whether payable out of capital or income only.—Abatement of legacies and annuities . . 168

CHAPTER XIV.

PROCEEDINGS AFTER FURTHER CONSIDERATION.

PAGE

Assets generally distributed on further consideration.—If not, shares usually carried over to separate accounts.—Subsequent application for payment out.—Payment of duty.—Payment out to trustees.—Payment out on security being given to refund, or when woman past child-bearing.—Payment out pending inquiries.—Chattels bequeathed for life.—Legatees now not called upon to give security to refund.—No assets now retained to meet claims in respect of leaseholds.—Executors liable for distributing assets out of Court with notice of contingent claims.—Stay of payment out pending an appeal 180

CHAPTER XV.

OF THE JURISDICTION OF COUNTY COURTS AND DISTRICT REGISTRARS.

Concurrent jurisdiction of County Courts up to £500.—In what Court proceedings to be commenced.—Transfer to Chancery Division.—Provisions for a re-transfer.—When action transferred and when dismissed.—Counter-claim.—Costs.—Transfer to County Court.—Appeals.—Appeal by motion.—District registries.—Limitation of authority of District registrars 184

APPENDIX.

Form of administration summons under 15 & 16 Vict. c. 86, ss. 45, 47 . 193
Cons. Ord. vii. r. 1 194
Probate Act, 1857 (20 & 21 Vict. c. 77), s. 64 194
Form of indorsement on notice of judgment or order 195
Minutes of ordinary administration judgments ;
    I.—IV. Creditors' actions . . . . . . 195—197
    V.—VIII. Actions by next of kin, trustees, executors or beneficiaries . . . . . . 197—199
Form of advertisement for creditors 200
Notice to creditor to prove his claim 200
Notice to creditor to produce documents 201
Form of advertisement for claimants, other than creditors . . 201

INDEX 203

TABLE OF CASES.

NAMES OF CASES.	AUTHORISED REPORTS.	LAW JOURNAL. (New Series unless otherwise stated.)	LAW TIMES. (New Series unless otherwise stated.)	WEEKLY REPORTER.	JURIST. (Old Series unless otherwise stated.)	PAGE.
ACASTER v. Anderson	19 Be. 161	24 Ch. 437	24, O.S., 249	3, 156	...	5
Adair v. Young	11 C. D. 136	...	40, 598	...	...	183
Adams v. Claxton	6 Ves. 226	...	...	...	...	134
— v. Waller	W. N. '66, 200	35 Ch. 727	14, 727	14, 789	...	109
Agriculturist, &c., Co., Re	3 DeG.F.&J.194	30 Ch. 619	4, 430	9, 682	7, N.S., 590	88
— —	—	—	...	11, 330	...	87
Albion Steel & Wire Co., Re	7 C. D. 547	47 Ch. 229	38, 207	26, 348	...	172
Alcock v. Gill	W. N. '69, 270	...	21, 704	...	...	87
Aldrich v. Cooper	8 Ves. 308	...	...	...	...	175
Aldridge v. Westbrook	4 Be. 212	10 Ch. 363	...	...	...	147
— v. —	5 Be. 188	...	...	...	...	154
Alison's Trusts, Re	8 C. D. 1	47 Ch. 755	38, 304	26, 450	...	72
Alison v. Alison	...	50 Ch. 574	44, 547	29, 732	...	60
Alston v. Trollope	{ 35 Be. 466 { 2 Eq. 205	...	14, 451	14, 722	...	109
Alvanley(Ld.) v. Kinnaird	...	13 Ch. 65	2, O.S., 206	...	8, 114	123
Ambler v. Lindsay	3 C. D. 198	45 Ch. 768	35, 93	24, 982	...	38
Ancaster (D.) v. Mayer	1 Bro. C. C. 454	...	...	...	...	164, 174
Anderson v. Butler's Wharf Co.	21 C. D. 131	51 Ch. 694	...	30, 723	...	89
Angell v. Haddon	1 Madd. 529	...	...	...	...	114
Annesley v. Ashurst	3 P. Wms. 282	...	...	...	...	59
Anon.	...	...	...	...	17, 435	12
—	4 Sim. 359	...	...	...	...	63
— v. Robarts	1 J. & W. 251	...	...	...	...	54
Anson v. Towgood	6 Madd. 374	...	...	...	...	74
Armstrong v. Armstrong	12 Eq. 614	...	25, 199	19, 971	...	93, 146
— v. Storer	9 Be. 277	...	...	...	...	10
— v. —	14 Be. 535	...	...	...	...	154
Arthur v. Hughes	4 Be. 506	...	...	...	...	36
Ashburner v. Macguire	2 Bro. C. C. 108	...	...	...	...	179
Ashley v. Ashley	4 C. D. 757	46 Ch. 322	36, 200	25, 356	...	103
— v. Sewell	{ 10 Ha. App. 66 { 3DeG.M.&G.933	22 Ch. 659	21, O.S., 39	1, 260	17, 269	4, 6, 35
Ashton v. Wood	8DeG.M.&G.698	26 Ch. 275	28, O.S., 228	5, 271	3, N.S., 146	99
Ashworth, Ex parte	18 Eq. 705	43 Bk. 142	30, 906	22, 925	...	171
Aspinall v. Bourne	29 Be. 462	...	...	...	...	134
Association of Land Financiers, Re	16 C. D. 373	50 Ch. 201	43, 753	29, 277	...	172
Att.-Gen. v. Clack	1 Be. 467	...	...	...	...	57
— v. Lawes	8 Ha. 32	19 Ch. 300	...	14, 77	...	137, 157

TABLE OF CASES.

NAMES OF CASES.	AUTHORISED REPORTS.	LAW JOURNAL. (New Series unless otherwise stated.)	LAW TIMES. (New Series unless otherwise stated.)	WEEKLY REPORTER.	JURIST. (Old Series unless otherwise stated.)	PAGE.
Austen v. Haines	4 Ch. 445	38 Ch. 385	20, 152	17, 900	...	46
Aylmer v. Winterbotham	...	...	...	...	4, N.S., 19	137
Bagot v. Legge	2 Dr. & Sm. 259	34 Ch. 156	11, 263	13, 1	10, N.S., 1092	158
Bagshaw, Ex parte	13 C. D. 304	...	41, 743	28, 403	...	171
Bailey v. Bailey	12 C. D. 268	48 Ch. 628	41, 157	27, 909	...	164
Baillie v. Baillie	5 Eq. 175	37 Ch. 225	17, 376	16, 272	...	82
Bain v. Sadler	12 Eq. 570	40 Ch. 791	25, 202	19, 1077	...	108
Baker v. Baker	6 H. L. C. 616	27 Ch. 417	31, O.S., 62	6, 410	4, N.S., 491	178
— v. Martin	8 Sim. 25	...	...	...	...	55
— v. —	5 Sim. 380	...	...	...	...	106
— v. Wait	9 Eq. 103	39 Ch. 204	21, 632	18, 185	...	185
Ballard v. Marsden	14 C. D. 374	49 Ch. 614	42, 763	28, 914	...	146
Bank of Turkey v. Ottoman Bank	2 Eq. 366	...	14, 884	...	...	60
Barber v. Mackrell	12 C. D. 534	...	41, 201	27, 894	...	52
Barker v. Rogers	7 Ha. 19	...	...	...	...	43, 114, 117
Barnard v. Wieland	W. N. '82, 103	...	...	30, 947	...	19
Barnewell v. Iremonger	1 Dr. & Sm. 255	...	...	8, 740	...	158
Barraclough v. Greenhough	L. R. 2 Q. B. 612	36 Q. B. 251	14, 899	4, 934	...	14
Bartlett v. Bartlett	4 Ha. 631	...	...	...	...	61
— v. Wood	...	30 Ch. 614	4, 692	9, 817	...	136
Barton v. Barton	3 K. & J. 512	...	...	...	3, N.S., 808	128
— v. Cooke	5 Ves. 461	...	...	...	...	138
Basevi v. Serra	14 Ves. 313	...	...	...	...	150
Bateman v. Margerison	6 Ha. 496	...	...	...	...	39
— v. —	...	...	...	2, 607	...	131
Bates v. Eley	1 C. D. 473	45 Ch. 270	34, 50	24, 424	...	91
Bath v. Bell	...	...	39, 422	...	...	23, 139
Bayliss v. Watkins	...	32 Ch. 106	...	...	9, N.S., 570	99
Beaney v. Elliott	W. N. '80, 99	...	...	...	...	131
Bear v. Smith	5 De G. & Sm. 92	21 Ch. 176	...	...	16, 708	132
Beardmore v. Gregory	2 H. & M. 491	34 Ch. 392	12, 264	13, 674	11, N.S., 363	39
Beauchamp (Earl) v. Marq. of Huntley	Jac. 546	...	...	...	...	82, 84
Beaumont v. Oliveira	4 Ch. 309	38 Ch. 239	20, 53	17, 269	...	176
Bedford v. Leigh	2 Dick. 707	...	...	...	...	9
Belcher v. Belcher	2 Dr. & Sm. 444	...	...	13, 913	...	71
Bell v. Alexander	6 Ha. 543	...	...	...	...	37
— v. Bell	...	33 Ch. 384	9, 643	12, 230	10, N.S., 14	126
— v. Turner	2 C. D. 409	45 Ch. 681	...	24, 451	...	129
Bennett v. Baxter	10 Sim. 417	9 Ch. 137	...	...	4, 50	126
— v. Bowen	20 C. D. 538	51 Ch. 825	47, 114	...	...	22, 191
— v. Moore	1 C. D. 692	45 Ch. 275	...	24, 690	...	18, 68
Bentall v. Sharp	(Seton, 320)	...	...	...	...	77
Bentley v. Bentley	1 N. R. 390	...	7, 819	...	...	112
Berkeley v. Mason	19 Eq. 467	44 Ch. 554	...	23, 687	...	3, 6, 35, 41
Berry v. Gaukroger	W. N. '82, 64	...	...	...	...	99
— v. Gibbons	15 Eq. 150	42 Ch. 231	...	...	...	96
— v. —	3 Ch. 747	42 Ch. 89	19, 88	21, 754	...	56, 58
— v. Hebblethwaite	1 K. & J. 80	...	42, O.S., 9	...	...	154
Bestwick, Ex parte	2 C. D. 485	15 Bk. 148	34, 784	24, 938	...	172

TABLE OF CASES.

NAMES OF CASES.	AUTHORISED REPORTS.	LAW JOURNAL. (New Series unless otherwise stated.)	LAW TIMES. (New Series unless otherwise stated.)	WEEKLY REPORTER.	JURIST. (Old Series unless otherwise stated.)	PAGE.
Beswick v. Orpen	16 C. D. 202	50 Ch. 25	43, 728	29, 467	...	146
Betagh v. Concannon	2 Moll. 559	...	...	...	...	62
Bethell v. Abraham	17 Eq. 24	43 Ch. 180	29, 715	22, 179	...	54, 56
Beynon v. Beynon	W. N. '73, 186	...	...	...	...	50
Bick v. Motley	2 M. & K. 312	...	...	...	...	97
Birkett, Re	9 C. D. 576	47 Ch. 846	39, 418	27, 164	...	138
Birks v. Micklethwait	...	34 Ch. 362	13, 31	...	...	144
— v. Silverwood	14 Eq. 101	41 Ch. 638	27, 18	...	...	186
Birt v. Burt	22 C. D. 604	...	48, 67	31, 334	...	58
Blackett v. Blackett	...	...	24, 276	19, 559	...	33
Blake v. Blake	2 Sch. & L. 26	...	...	...	...	60
Blakeley v. Blakeley	...	...	24, O.S., 322	3, 288	1, N.S., 368	5
Bland v. Daniell	W. N. '67, 169	...	...	...	...	157
Blaun v. Bell	7 C. D. 382	47 Ch. 120	...	26, 165	...	157
Blewitt v. Blewitt	Younge, 541	...	...	...	...	32, 33
Bluett v. Jessop	Jac. 240	...	...	...	...	140
Boatwright v. Boatwright	17 Eq. 71	43 Ch. 12	29, 603	22, 147	...	108
Bolton v. Powell	{ 14 Be. 275 2 De G. M. & G. 1 }	...	...	...	16, 24	26
— v. Stannard	...	27 Ch. 845	31, O.S., 310	6, 570	4, N.S., 576	43
Bond v. Barnes	2 De G. F. & J. 387	...	...	...	...	77
— v. Graham	1 Ha. 482	11 Ch. 306	...	...	6, 620	35
Booth v. Hutchinson	15 Eq. 30	42 Ch. 492	27, 600	21, 116	...	173
— v. Leycester	3 M. & Cr. 459	...	...	...	...	82
Bootle v. Blundell	1 Mer. 193	...	...	...	...	164
Boswell v. Gurney	13 C. D. 136	...	...	27, 865	...	{ 107, 111, 173
Bothamley v. Sherson	20 Eq. 304	44 Ch. 589	33, 150	23, 848	...	174
Bourne v. Mole	8 Be. 177	...	...	...	...	64, 66
Bowen v. Bowen	...	...	...	24, 246	...	20
Bowyer v. Griffin	9 Eq. 340	39 Ch. 159	...	18, 227	...	144, 145
Boyes v. Cook	W. N. '76, 28	...	33, 778	...	...	21
Brackenbury, Re	2 P. D. 272	46 P. D. 42	36, 744	25, 698	...	168
Bradford v. Nettleship	...	...	...	10, 264	...	181
Bradley v. Stelfox	3 De G. J. & S. 402	...	...	...	...	73, 74
Braithwaite v. Wallis	21 C. D. 121	52 Ch. 15	...	31, 180	...	61, 181
Brandon v. Brandon	3 N. R. 287	...	...	...	...	42
Branwhite, Ex parte	...	48 Ch. 463	40, 652	27, 646	...	173
Bray v. Tofield	18 C. D. 551	50 Ch. 817	45, 464	30, 55	...	9, 110
— v. West	9 Sim. 429	...	...	...	...	152
Breton v. Mockett	W. N. '75, 255	...	33, 684	...	...	21
Brett v. Carmichael	{ 35 Be. 340 W. N. '66, 103 }	} 35 Ch. 369	14, 247	14, 507	...	114
Brewer v. Yorke	20 C. D. 669	...	46, 289	31, 109	...	183
Briant v. Tibbut	...	...	20, 62	17, 274	...	99
Bridges v. Hinxman	16 Sim. 71	...	...	...	...	13
Bridgwater Engineering Co., Re	12 C. D. 181	48 Ch. 389	...	...	...	172
Bridson v. Smith	...	...	...	24, 392	...	19
Briggs v. Wilson	5 De G. M. & G. 12	...	23, O.S., 136	...	...	109
British M. Investment Co. v. Smart	10 Ch. 507	44 Ch. 695	32, 849	23, 800	...	166
Brook v. Badley	4 Eq. 106	37 Ch. 884	16, 762	16, 947	...	130
Brookes v. Stroud	1 Salk. 3	...	...	...	...	27

TABLE OF CASES.

NAMES OF CASES.	AUTHORISED REPORTS.	LAW JOURNAL. (New Series unless otherwise stated.)	LAW TIMES. (New Series unless otherwise stated.)	WEEKLY REPORTER.	JURIST. (Old Series unless otherwise stated.)	PAGE.
Brooks v. Reynolds ...	1 Bro. C. C. 183 / 2 Dick. 603	...		...	...	81
Broughton v. Broughton	5 DeG.M.&G.160	25 Ch. 250	...	3, 602	1, N.S., 965	147, 148
Brown v. Brown	1 Kc. 275	...	...	...	...	177
— v. De Tastet	4 Russ. 126	...	...	...	...	66
— v. Lake	2 Coll. 620	...	...	...	...	125
— v. —	1 DeG.&Sm.144	...	...	...	...	114
— v. Pittman	Gilb. 75	...	...	...	...	32
— v. Rye	17 Eq. 343	43 Ch. 228	29, 872	...	...	187
— v. Shaw	1 Ex. D. 425	...	...	...	...	189
— v. Stone	...	...	...	30, 923	...	117
Browne v. Collins	12 Eq. 586	...	...	...	...	89
Bruff v. Cobbold	7 Ch. 217	41 Ch. 402	26, 223	20, 284	...	49
Budgen v. Sage	3 M. & Cr. 683	...	...	...	...	72
Buller v. Withers	1 J. & H. 332	...	...	...	...	181
Bunting v. Marriott	...	...	...	9, 264	7, N.S., 565	183
Burch v. Coney	...	...	...	...	14, 1009	25, 106
Burrell v. Smith	9 Eq. 443	39 Ch. 544	22, 263	...	...	155, 167
Burton v. Roberts	6 H. & N. 93	29 Ex. 484	...	...	...	81
Bush v. Watkins	14 Bc. 33	...	...	...	...	132
Butlin v. Arnold	1 H. & M. 715	...	10, 95	12, 571	...	125
Button v. Woolwich Building Society ...	5 Q. B. D. 88	49 Q. B. 249	42, 54	28, 136	...	189
CAFE v. Bent	3 Ha. 245	13 Ch. 169	...	...	8, 141	56
— v. —	5 Ha. 24	...	...	...	...	30, 136
Campbell v. Campbell ...	16 C. D. 198	...	43, 727	29, 233	...	56
Capps v. Capps	4 Ch. 1	...	...	...	...	46
Cardell v. Hawke	6 Eq. 464	...	19, 47	...	...	107
Carmichael v. Gee	5 App. Cas. 588	49 Ch. 829	43, 227	29, 293	...	178
Carne v. Brancker	...	...	20, 797	17, 342, 837	...	131
Carr v. Henderson	11 Bc. 415	18 Ch. 39	12, O.S., 529	...	...	154
— v. Ingleby	1 DeG.&Sm.362	...	...	...	...	178
Carron Iron Co. v. Maclaren	5 H. L. C. 416	...	...	3, 597	...	83
Carter v. Sanders	2 Dr. 248	23 Ch. 679	...	2, 325	...	30
Cary v. Hills	15 Eq. 79	42 Ch. 100	28, 6	21, 106	...	32, 33
Cash v. Parker	12 C. D. 293	48 Ch. 691	40, 878	27, 835	...	32
Cast v. Poyser	3 Sm. & Gif. 369	26 Ch. 93, 353	28, O.S., 118, 197	...	3, N.S., 38	92, 103
Catherwood v. Chabaud	1 B. & C. 150	1, O.S., K.B., 16	...	...	...	14
Catley v. Sampson	33 Bc. 551	34 Ch. 96	10, 519	12, 927	...	30
Cattell v. Simons	8 Bc. 243	14 Ch. 138	...	...	9, 418	114
Chaffers v. Headlam	...	22 Ch. 1038	...	...	17, 754	62
Chalmers v. Laurie	10 Ha. App. 27	...	...	1, 265	...	45, 47
Chapman v. Chapman ...	1 Be. 34	20 Ch. 465	...	...	15, 265	9
— v. Knight	5 C. P. D. 308	49 C. P. 425	42, 538	28, 919	...	190
— v. Mason	W. N. '79, 93	...	40, 678	...	...	84
Charter v. Charter	3 C. D. 218	45 Ch. 705	34, 412	24, 874	...	152
Cheetham v. Crook ...	McCl. & Y. 307	...	...	...	...	72
Chester v. Phillips	4 C. D. 230	46 Ch. 95	35, 501	25, 211	...	44
— v. Rolfe	4DeG.M.&G.798	23 Ch. 233	22, O.S., 298	...	18, 114	26

NAMES OF CASES.	AUTHORISED REPORTS.	LAW JOURNAL. (New Series unless otherwise stated.)	LAW TIMES. (New Series unless otherwise stated.)	WEEKLY REPORTER.	JURIST. (Old Series unless otherwise stated.)	PAGE.
Chilton v. Corp. of London	7 C. D. 735	47 Ch. 433	38, 498	26, 474	...	19
Chissum v. Dewes	5 Russ. 29	...	...	...	...	156
Christian v. Adamson	W. N. '69, 208	...	...	...	...	142
— v. Foster	2 Ph. 161	16 Ch. 119	...	...	...	158
Chubb v. Carter	W. N. '67, 179	...	...	...	...	182
Clare v. Clare	21 C. D. 865	51 Ch. 553	46, 851	30, 789	...	145
Clark v. Phillips	...	...	...	2, 331	...	53
Clarke v. Clarke	9 Ha. App. 13	...	20, O.S., 88	1, 48	...	45
Clarkson v. Musgrave	9 Q. B. D. 386	51 Q. B. 525	...	...	...	190
Clegg v. Rowland	3 Eq. 368	36 Ch. 137	15, 385	15, 251	...	4, 37
Clough v. Dixon	10 Sim. 564	...	...	...	...	34
Clowes v. Hilliard	4 C. D. 413	46 Ch. 271	...	25, 224	...	25
Coal Consumers' Association, Re	4 C. D. 625	46 Ch. 501	35, 729	25, 300	...	172
Coates v. Coates	3 N. R. 355	...	...	...	10, N.S., 532	150, 158
Cobbold v. Pryke	4 Ex. D. 315	49 Ex. 9	...	28, 259	...	80, 184
Cockburn v. Thompson	16 Ves. 321	...	...	...	...	44
Cocq v. Hunasgeria Coffee Co.	4 Ch. 415	...	20, 207	17, 509	...	78
Cohen v. Alcan	1 DeG.J.&S.398	...	10, 284	12, 678	10, N.S., 531	6
Colebourne v. Colebourne	1 C. D. 690	45 Ch. 749	...	24, 235	...	8
Collinson v. Ballard	2 Ha. 119	...	...	...	...	51
Collis v. Collis	2 Sim. 365	...	...	...	...	63
— v. Robins	1 DeG.&Sm.131	16 Ch. 251	9, O.S., 121	...	11, 362	152
Colman v. Turner	10 Eq. 230	39 Ch. 776	22, 836	18, 963	...	7
Colyer v. Colyer	...	...	...	11, 355	9, N.S., 294	44
— v. —	...	32 Ch. 101	7, 522	11, 79	...	143
Concannon v. Cruise	1 Moll. 332	...	...	...	...	14
Consterdine v. Consterdine	31 Be. 330	31 Ch. 807	...	10, 727	3, N.S., 906	58
Cook v. Bolton	5 Russ. 282	...	...	...	...	123
— v. Gregson	2 Dr. 286	23 Ch. 734	23, O.S., 86	2, 401	...	167
Cooke v. Gittings	21 Be. 497	...	26, O.S., 268	4, 268	...	39
Coombs v. Coombs	L. R. 1 P. & M. 193, 288	35 P.&M.78 36 P.&M.21	14, 635 15, 329	14, 975 15, 286	...	168
Coope v. Carter	2DeG.M.&G.292	21 Ch. 570	19, O.S., 119	...	...	17, 52
Cooper v. Blissett	1 C. D. 691	45 Ch. 272	...	24, 235	...	9
— v. Cooper	L. R. 7 H. L. 53	44 Ch. 6	30, 409	22, 713	...	95
Coote v. Whittington	16 Eq. 534	42 Ch. 846	29, 206	21, 837	...	38
Cope's Trusts, Re	W. N. '77, 87	...	36, 437	...	...	181
Corser v. Cartwright	L. R. 7 H. L. 731	45 Ch. 605	29, 596	...	...	166
Costa Rica, Rep. of, v. Strousberg	16 C. D. 8	50 Ch. 7	43, 399	29, 170	...	92
Coster v. Coster	1 Ke. 199	...	...	...	...	182
Cotterell v. Stratton	8 Ch. 295	42 Ch. 417	28, 218	21, 234	...	149
Couldery v. Bartrum	19 C. D. 394	51 Ch. 265	45, 689	30, 141	...	171
Courtenay v. Williams	3 Ha. 539	13 Ch. 461 15 Ch. 204	6, O.S., 517	...	3, 844	146
Cousins v. Lombard Bank	1 Ex. D. 404	45 Ex. 573	35, 484	25, 116	...	189
Cowslad v. Cely	Prec. Ch. 83	...	...	...	...	32
Cox v. Allingham	Jac. 514	...	...	...	...	14
— v. King	9 Be. 530	...	8, O.S., 1	...	10, 236	106
Cradock v. Owen	2 Sm. & G. 241	...	23, O.S., 19	2, 319	...	134
— v. Piper	1 Mac. & G. 664 1 H. & Tw. 617	19 Ch.107	15, O.S., 61	...	14, 97	147
Creak v. Capell	6 Madd. 114	...	...	...	...	65

TABLE OF CASES.

NAMES OF CASES.	Authorised Reports.	Law Journal. (New Series unless otherwise stated.)	Law Times. (New Series unless otherwise stated.)	Weekly Reporter.	Jurist. (Old Series unless otherwise stated.)	Page.
Creasor v. Robinson	14 Be. 589	21 Ch. 64	18, O.S., 82	...	...	39
Cresswell v. Parker	11 C. D. 601	...	40, 599	27, 897	...	36
Crofton v. Crofton	15 C. D. 591	49 Ch. 689	...	29, 169	...	82, 83
Croggan v. Allen	22 C. D. 101	...	47, 437	31, 319	...	136
Crompton v. Huber	...	...	25, O.S., 43	3, 347	1, N.S., 465	100
Cross v. Kennington	11 Be. 89	...	...	...	...	156
— v. Maltby	...	...	...	8, 646	...	99
Crowder v. Stewart	16 C. D. 368	50 Ch. 136	...	29, 331	...	56, 163, 166
Crowle v. Russell	4 C. P. D. 186	48 C. P. 76	39, 320	27, 84	...	81
Croxton v. May	9 C. D. 388	...	39, 461	27, 325	...	182
Crumlin Viaduct Works Co., Re	11 C. D. 755	48 Ch. 537	...	27, 722	...	170
Cumberland v. Clark	4 Ch. 412	...	...	17, 524	...	76
Cumming, Re	5 DeG. M.&G. 30	23 Ch. 261	22, O.S., 312	2, 248	18, 181	26
— v. Slater	1 Y. & C. C. 484	...	...	...	...	72
Cummins v. Bromfield	...	...	...	...	3, N.S., 657	147
— v. Cummins	3 Jo. & L. 64	...	...	...	...	26
Curling v. Austin	2 Dr. & Sm. 129	...	...	10, 682	...	131
Cuthbert v. Harmby	13 Eq. 202	41 Ch. 216	...	...	...	46
— v. — sub nom. Wharmby	W. N. '69, 12	...	...	...	...	102
Danby v. Danby	...	...	32, O.S., 348	...	5, N.S., 54	60, 61
— v. Poole	...	...	7, 240	10, 515	...	15
Daubney v. Leake	35 Be. 311 / 1 Eq. 495	35 Ch. 347	...	14, 413	...	95, 130
Davenport v. Stafford	14 Be. 319 / 2 DeG.M.&G.901	...	...	...	...	51, 132
Davey v. Plestow	...	19 Ch. 491	...	...	14, 388	76
— v. Ward	7 C. D. 754	47 Ch. 335	...	26, 390	...	57
David v. Dalton	W. N. '79, 86	...	...	...	...	21
— v. Frowd	1 M. & K. 200	2 Ch. 68	...	...	...	113, 120
Davies v. Topp	1 Bro. C. C. 525	...	...	...	...	168
— v. Williams	13 C. D. 550	49 Ch. 352	42, 469	...	...	187
Davis v. Angel	31 Be. 223 / 4 DeG.F.&J.524	31 Ch. 613	6, 850, 880	10, 685, 722	8, N.S., 709, 1024	24, 25
— v. Davis	2 Atk. 21	...	...	...	...	99
— v. —	...	48 Ch. 40	...	28, 345	...	77, 78
— v. Flagstaff Mining Co.	3 C. P. D. 228	47 C.P. 503	38, 769	26, 431	...	187
Dawkins v. Morton	1 Jo. & H. 339	...	6, 214	10, 339	...	88, 90
Dawson v. Kearton	3 Sm. & G. 186	25 Ch. 166	26, O.S., 256	4, 222	2, N.S., 113	173
Day v Batty	21 C. D. 830	...	...	...	...	93, 95
— v. Day	31 Be. 270	31 Ch. 806	...	10, 728	8, N.S., 1166	196
— v. Whittaker	6 C. D. 734	46 Ch. 680	36, 683	25, 767	...	192
Dean v. Morris	...	...	...	5, 345	...	158
— v. Wilson	10 C. D. 136	48 Ch. 148	...	27, 377	...	124
— v. Wright	21 C. D. 581	...	47, 501	31, 174	...	28
De Balinhard v. Bullock	9 Ha. App. 13	...	20, O.S., 189	...	...	44
De Feuchères v. Dawes	5 Be. 110	...	...	...	...	32, 33
De La Salle v. Moorat	11 Eq. 8	40 Ch. 44	23, 479	19, 88	...	7
Delevante v. Childe	...	...	1, 397	...	6, N.S., 118	5
Densem v. Elworthy	9 Ha. App. 42	...	20, O.S., 217	...	...	43

NAMES OF CASES.	AUTHORISED REPORTS.	LAW JOURNAL. (New Series unless otherwise stated.)	LAW TIMES. (New Series unless otherwise stated.)	WEEKLY REPORTER.	JURIST. (Old Series unless otherwise stated.)	PAGE.
Dewdney, Ex parte	15 Ves. 479	...	...	...	...	109, 173
Dickenson v. Teasdale	1 De G. J. & S. 52	32 Ch. 37	7, 655	...	9, N.S., 60, 237	165
Dickins v. Harris	W. N. '66, 93	...	14, 98	...	...	37
Dicks v. Yates	18 C. D. 76	50 Ch. 809	44, 660	...	...	150
Dickson v. Harrison	9 C. D. 243	47 Ch. 761	38, 794	26, 730	...	90
Dighton v. Withers	31 Be. 423	...	...	...	...	155
Dilkes v. Broadmead	2 De G. F. & J. 566	30 Ch. 268	3, 605	9, 238	7, N.S., 56	166
Dimsdale v. Dudding	1 Y. & C. C. 265	...	...	...	...	137
Dixon v. Dixon	3 Bro. C. C. 509	...	...	...	...	97
— v. Wyatt	4 Madd. 392	...	...	...	...	125
Doe d. Bassett v. Mew	7 Ad. & El. 240	...	...	...	...	14
— d. Ashburnham v. Michael	16 Q. B. 620	20 Q. B. 480	...	...	15, 677	15
Donald v. Bather	16 Be. 26	...	...	...	...	36
Donne v. Lewis	2 Bro. C. C. 257	...	...	...	...	164, 165
Doody v. Higgins	9 Ha. App. 32	...	...	1, 30	...	42, 43, 47
Dorrett v. Meux	15 C. B. 142	23 C. P. 221	23, O.S., 144	2, 480	...	14
Douglas v. Forrest	4 Bing. 686	{ 6, O.S., C.P. 157 }	...	...	...	32
Douthwaite v. Spensley	18 Be. 74	...	...	...	...	66
Dove v. Everard	1 R. & M. 231	...	...	...	...	33, 34
Dowbiggin v. Trotter	W. N. '72, 150	...	27, 731	20, 1024	...	71, 122
Dowd v. Hawtin	19 C. D. 61	...	...	30, 601	...	127
Dowdeswell v. Dowdeswell	9 C. D. 294	48 Ch. 23	38, 828	27, 241	...	34, 35
Down v. Ellis	5 Be. 578	...	...	...	...	105
Drever v. Maudesley	5 Russ. 11	...	...	...	...	113
Drewry v. Thacker	3 Sw. 538	...	...	...	...	80
Dryden v. Foster	6 Be. 146	12 Ch. 189	...	...	...	74
Duignan v. Croome	W. N. '79, 206	...	41, 672	...	...	167
Duncan v. Watts	16 Be. 204	...	...	...	...	177
Dymond v. Croft	3 C. D. 512	45 Ch. 612	35, 27	24, 700	...	21
Dyson v. Pickles	W. N. '79, 12	...	...	27, 376	...	192
Eames v. Hacon	18 C. D. 347	50 Ch. 740	45, 196	29, 877	...	36
Earle v. Sidebottom	W. N. '68, 121	37 Ch. 503	...	24, 39	...	122
Eccles v. Eccles	...	...	33, 338	...	...	190
Edmunds v. Acland	5 Madd. 31	...	...	...	...	123
Edwards v. Edwards	10 Ha. App. 63	...	21, O.S., 263	1, 504	...	61
Eglin v. Sanderson	3 Giff. 434	...	6, 151	...	8, N.S., 329	142, 143
Egremont v. Thompson	4 Ch. 448	...	...	17, 900	...	46
Eiffe v. Hilliard	L. R. 7 H. L. 39	...	...	...	...	127
Electric T. Co. of Ireland, Re	24 Be. 137	26 Ch. 614	...	...	...	91
Ellis v. Ellis	1 Sch. & Lef. 1	...	...	...	...	119
Elmslie v. McAnlay	3 Bro. C. C. 624	...	...	...	...	26
Eltoft v. Brown	2 Ha. 621	...	...	...	...	22
Esgair, &c., Co. Re	...	...	2, 744	8, 660	...	92
European Assurance Co. v. Radcliffe	7 C. D. 733	...	...	24, 417	...	58
Eustace v. Lloyd	W. N. '76, 299	...	35, 900	25, 211	...	82
Evans v. Lewis	...	...	2, 559	...	...	131
— , Ex parte	13 C. D. 252	49 Bk. 7	41, 565	28, 127	...	169
Eyre v. Cox	...	46 Ch. 316	...	24, 317	...	8, 9
— v. Marsden	4 M. & Cr. 231	...	...	...	2, 583	158

NAMES OF CASES.	AUTHORISED REPORTS.	LAW JOURNAL. (New Series unless otherwise stated.)	LAW TIMES. (New Series unless otherwise stated.)	WEEKLY REPORTER.	JURIST. (Old Series unless otherwise stated.)	PAGE.
Fallows v. Lord Dillon.	...	...	23, O.S., 154	2, 507	...	131, 157
Farquharson v. Floyer	3 C. D. 109	45 Ch. 750	35, 355	...	...	165
Farrell v. Smith	2 B. & B. 337	...	...	...	...	37
Farrow v. Austin	18 C. D. 58	...	45, 227	30, 50	...	140, 149
Fearnside v. Flint	22 C. D. 579	...	48, 154	31, 318	...	165
Fenner v. Taylor	6 Madd. 3	...	...	...	...	139
Fenton v. Wills	7 C. D. 33	47 Ch. 191	37, 373	26, 139	...	157
Ferguson v. Gibson	14 Eq. 379	41 Ch. 640	...	...	...	{ 55, 152, 166
Field v. Titmuss	1 Sim., N.S., 218	20 Ch. 328	...	...	15, 121	105
Finlay v. Davis	12 C. D. 735	...	39, 662	27, 352	...	192
Fisher v. Fisher	2 Ke. 610	7 Ch. 176	...	...	...	158, 165
— v. Shirley	W. N. '79, 103	...	...	...	...	163
Fleming v. Buchanan	3 DeG.M.&G.976	22 Ch. 886	22, O.S., 8	...	...	165
— v. East	Kay, App. 52	...	23, O.S., 252	2, 643	18, 1112	131
— v. Prior	5 Madd. 423	...	...	...	...	123
Flintoff v. Haynes	4 Ha. 309	...	...	...	...	111, 133
Flood v. Patterson	29 Be. 295	30 Ch. 486	4, 78	9, 294	7, N.S., 324	35
Foley v. Burnell	1 Bro. C. C. 274	...	...	...	...	182
Ford v. Bryant	9 Be. 410	15 Ch. 261	...	...	10, 484	16
Fordham v. Clagett	20 C. D. 134	51 Ch. 461	46, 70	30, 374	...	88
— v. Wallis	10 Ha. 217	22 Ch. 548	21, O.S., 190	1, 118	17, 228	175
Forrest v. Prescott	10 Eq. 545	...	...	18, 1065	...	164
Foster v. Handley	1 Sim., N.S., 200	...	...	...	15, 73	167
Fowler v. Reynal	3 Mac. & G. 500	21 Ch. 121	18, O.S., 113	...	15, 1019	132
— v. Roberts	2 Giff. 226	...	2, 368	8, 492	6, N.S., 1189	81
Fraser v. Dowbiggin	(Bacon, V.-C.'82)	...	...	...	...	37
Freeman v. Cox	8 C. D. 148	47 Ch. 560	...	26, 689	...	68
— v. Fairlie	3 Mer. 29	...	...	...	...	64
— v. Pennington	3 DeG. F.&J.295	31 Ch. 216	5, 514	10, 184	...	30, 42
Freme v. Clement	18 C. D. 499	50 Ch. 801	44, 398	30, 1	...	165
Frost v. Ward	2 De G. J. & S. 70	...	9, 668	12, 285	...	71
Frowd v. Baker	4 Be. 76	...	...	...	...	71, 76
Fryer v. Royle	5 C. D. 540	...	36, 441	25, 528	...	9
— , Re	3 K. & J. 317	26 Ch. 398	...	5, 552	3, N.S., 485	5
Fuller v. Green	24 Be. 217	...	...	...	...	140
— v. Redman	26 Be. 600	29 Ch. 324	...	...	5, N.S., 1046	109
Furze v. Hennet	2 De G. & J. 125	...	...	...	...	19, 71
Gage v. Rutland	W. N. '82, 92	...	46, 848	...	...	144
Gardner v. Beaumont	...	48 Ch. 644	41, 82	...	...	124
— v. Garrett	20 Be. 469	...	...	...	...	76, 84
Garland v. Littlewood	1 Be. 527	8 Ch. 369	...	...	...	52
Garrett v. Noble	6 Sim. 504	3 Ch. 159	...	...	...	18
Gaskell v. Holmes	3 Ha. 438	...	...	...	8, 396	130
Gatti v. Webster	12 C. D. 771	48 Ch. 763	41, 18	27, 935	...	23
Gaunt v. Taylor	2 Be. 346	7 Ch. 2	...	...	4, 166	147
— v. —	2 Ha. 413	...	...	...	...	151
Gawthorpe v. Gawthorpe	W. N. '78, 91	...	...	...	...	59
Gee v. Mahood	W. N. '74, 207	...	...	23, 71	...	150
— v. —	11 C. D. 891	48 Ch. 657	40, 663	27, 843	...	178
General Rolling Stock Co., Re }	7 Ch. 646	41 Ch. 732	27, 88	20, 762	...	108
Gibbons v. Dawley	2 Ch. Cas. 198	...	...	...	...	24

TABLE OF CASES.

NAMES OF CASES.	AUTHORISED REPORTS.	LAW JOURNAL. (New Series unless otherwise stated.)	LAW TIMES. (New Series unless otherwise stated.)	WEEKLY REPORT
Gilbert v. Lee	34 Be. 574	...	12, 818	13, 10?
— v. Smith	2 C. D. 686	45 Ch. 514	35, 43	24, 56?
Gillespie v. Alexander	3 Russ. 130	...	...	...
Gill's Case	12 C. D. 755	48 Ch. 774	41, 21	27, 93
Gisborne v. Gisborne	2 App. Cas. 300	46 Ch. 556	36, 564	25, 51(
Glass v. Oxenham	2 Atk. 121	...	...	...
Gledhill v. Hunter	14 C. D. 492	49 Ch. 333	43, 392	28, 53(
Glover v. Ellison	W. N. '72, 34	41 Ch. 288	26, 234	20, 408
Godfrey v. Harben	13 C. D. 216	49 Ch. 3	...	28, 73
Golden v. Newton	Johns. 720	...	1, 541	8, 256
Golder v. Golder	9 Ha. 276	22 Ch. 154	...	...
Goldsmid v. Stonehewer	9 Ha. App. 38	22 Ch. 109	20, O.S., 202	...
Good, Ex parte	14 C. D. 82	49 Bk. 49	42, 450	28, 55?
Goodchild v. Terrett	5 Be. 398	...	...	...
Goodrich v. Marsh	W. N. '78, 186	...	...	...
Gough v. Bult	16 Sim. 323	17 Ch. 486	...	...
Gouldsmith v. Luntley	W. N. '75, 97	...	32, 535	...
Governesses' B. Inst. v. Rusbridger	18 Be. 467	...	...	...
Gowan v. Broughton	19 Eq. 77	44 Ch. 275	31, 533	23, 33?
Grace v. Terrington	1 Coll. 3	...	...	...
Graham v. Keble	2 Dow, 17	...	...	...
— v. Maxwell	{ 1 Mac. & G. 71 1 H. & Tw. 247 }	18 Ch. 225	...	...
Grant v. Grant	34 Be. 623	34 Ch. 641	12, 721	13, 10?
Graves v. Hicks	11 Sim. 551	10 Ch. 185	...	...
— v. Wright	{ 1 C. & L. 267 2 Dr. & W. 77 }			
Gray v. Gray	13 Ir. Ch. 404	...	...	...
Great Britain Mutual Life Ass. Soc., Re	19 C. D. 39	51 Ch. 7	45, 554	30, 145
Greedy v. Lavender	11 Be. 417	18 Ch. 62	12, O.S., 266	...
Green v. Badley	7 Be. 274	...	...	...
— v. Coleby	1 C. D. 693	45 Ch. 303	...	24, 240
— v. Measures	W. N. '66, 122	...	...	...
Greenwood v. Penny	12 Be. 403	...	...	...
Greig v. Somerville	1 R. & M. 338	...	...	...
Gresham v. Price	35 Be. 47	...	...	...
Griffiths v. Hamilton	12 Ves. 298	...	...	...
Groves v. Groves	Kay, App. 19	23 Ch. 199	22, O.S., 184	2, 86
— v. Lane	...	...	...	...
Guidici v. Kinton	6 Be. 517	...	...	...
Gunnell v. Whitear	10 Eq. 664	39 Ch. 869	22, 645	18, 883
Guthrie v. Walrond	W. N. '74, 99	...	29, 377	22, 723
Gwyer v. Petersen	26 Be. 83	...	...	...
HAGELL v. Currie	2 Ch. 449	36 Ch. 448	16, 307	15, 605
Haldane v. Eckford	W. N. '66, 50	...	14, 14	14, 306
— v. —	W. N. '79, 80	...	...	...
Hales v. Morris	(Kay, J., 1882)	...	...	...
Hall v. Austin	2 Coll. 570	15 Ch. 384	7, O.S., 279	...
— v. Hallet	1 Cox, 134	...	...	...
Halliley v. Henderson	...	...	31, O.S., 9	...

NAMES OF CASES.	AUTHORISED REPORTS.	LAW JOURNAL. (New Series unless otherwise stated.)	LAW TIMES. (New Series unless otherwise stated.)	WEEKLY REPORTER.	JURIST. (Old Series unless otherwise stated.)	PAGE.
Ialy v. Barry	3 Ch. 452	37 Ch. 723	18, 491	16, 654	...	81
Immond v. Walker	...	...	...	...	3, N.S., 686	60, 62
Iamp v. Robinson	3 De G. J. & S. 97	...	...	...	...	37
Iandford v. Handford	5 Ha. 212	...	...	...	...	90
— v. Storie	2 S. & S. 196	3, O.S., Ch. 110	...	...	...	10
Iandley v. Davis	...	28 Ch. 873	32, O.S., 330	...	5, N.S., 190	157
Iankin v. Kilburn	2 C. D. 628	...	...	24, 1031	...	178
— v. Turner	10 C. D. 372	...	39, 285	27, 20	...	120
Iannay v. Basham	W. N. '83, 7	...	...	...	...	145
Ianson v. Stubbs	8 C. D. 154	17 Ch. 671	...	26, 736	...	163
Iarbin v. Darby	28 Be. 325	29 Ch. 622	2, 531	8, 512	6, N.S., 906	148
Iares v. Lea	10 Eq. 683	...	22, 776	18, 1083	...	186
Iargraves v. White	...	22 Ch. 640	...	...	17, 436	12
Iarloe v. Harloe	20 Eq. 471	44 Ch. 512	33, 247	23, 789	...	159
Iarmer v. Harris	1 Russ. 155	...	...	...	...	145
Iarmood v. Oglander	8 Ves. 106	...	...	...	...	164, 165
Iarris v. Gandy	1 De G. F. & J. 13	29 Ch. 38	...	...	...	70
— v. Lightfoot	...	...	...	10, 31	...	70, 71
Iarrison v. Graham	1 P. Wms. 241	...	...	...	...	33
— v. Gurney	2 J. & W. 563	...	...	...	...	82
— v. Richards	1 Ch. 473	35 Ch. 677	15, 137	14, 823	12, N.S., 871	126
Iartwell v. Colvin	16 Be. 140	...	...	...	...	113
Iarvey v. Bradley	4 Eq. 13	...	...	15, 527	...	16
— v. Coxwell	W. N. '75, 22	...	32, 52	...	...	122
— v. Harvey	4 Be. 215	...	...	...	...	44
— v. Wilde	14 Eq. 438	41 Ch. 608	27, 471	...	...	164
Iatch v. Searles	2 Sm. & G. 147	24 Ch. 22	22, O.S., 280	2, 242	...	112
Iatton v. May	3 C. D. 148	...	...	...	...	178
Iawkes v. Barrett	5 Madd. 17	...	...	...	...	70
Iayward v. Hayward or Price	Kay, App. 31	23 Ch. 549	22, O.S., 345	2, 332	...	88, 92
Heatley v. Newton	19 C. D. 326	51 Ch. 225	45, 455	30, 72	...	90
Heighington v. Grant	1 Ph. 600	11 Ch. 171	...	...	10, 21	143
Henderson v. Dodds	2 Eq. 532	...	14, 752	14, 908	...	152, 153, 154
Henley & Co., Re	9 C. D. 469	48 Ch. 147	39, 53	26, 885	...	163
Henshaw v. Angell	9 Eq. 451	39 Ch. 524	21, 784	...	...	99
Hensman v. Fryer	3 Ch. 420	37 Ch. 97	17, 394	16, 162	...	157, 165
Hepworth v. Heslop	3 Ha. 485	...	...	...	...	154
Hertford, M. of, v. De Zichy	9 Be. 11	15 Ch. 58	...	...	...	42
Hetherington v. Longrigg	10 C. D. 162	48 Ch. 171	...	27, 303	...	18, 68
Heugh v. Scard	W. N. '75, 186	...	33, 659	24, 51	...	142
Hewett v. Foster	7 Be. 348	...	...	...	...	144
Heyn v. Heyn	Jac. 49	...	...	...	...	22
Hicks v. May	13 C. D. 236	49 Ch. 192	42, 383	28, 499	...	114
Hill v. Binney	6 Ves. 738	...	...	...	...	13
— v. Bridges	17 C. D. 342	50 Ch. 470	44, 730	...	...	107, 173
— v. King	1 N. R. 341	...	8, 220	...	9, N.S., 527	97
— v. Perssé	...	...	...	25, 275	...	190
— v. Walker	4 K. & J. 166	...	32, O.S., 71	...	...	55
Hilliard v. Fulford	4 C. D. 389	46 Ch. 43	35, 750	25, 161	...	139
Hinde v. Blake	4 Be. 597	...	...	...	...	64
Hinsley v. Ickeringill	17 C. D. 151	50 Ch. 364	...	29, 500	...	165

TABLE OF CASES.

NAMES OF CASES.	AUTHORISED REPORTS.	LAW JOURNAL. (New Series unless otherwise stated.)	LAW TIMES. (New Series unless otherwise stated.)	WEEKLY REPORTER.	JURIST. (Old Series unless otherwise stated.)	PAGE.
Hipkins v. Hildick	...	...	44, 547	29, 733	...	169
Hirst, Ex parte	11 C. D. 278	...	...	...	...	171
Hitchen v. Birks	10 Eq. 471	...	23, 335	18, 1015	...	34
Hoe v. Nelthorpe or Nathorp	3 Salk. 154 / 1 Ld. Ray. 154	...	...	...	...	13
Hollingsworth v. Brodrick	4 Ad. & E. 646	...	...	...	...	79
— v. Shakeshaft	14 Be. 492	21 Ch. 722	...	...	...	16, 133
Holloway v. Cheston	19 C. D. 516	51 Ch. 208	...	30, 120	...	89
Home Counties, &c., Co., Re	...	...	6, 374	10, 457	...	88
Hooper v. Smart	1 C. D. 90	45 Ch. 99	33, 499	24, 152	...	16
Hope v. Carnegie	1 Ch. 320	...	14, 117	14, 489	12, N.S., 284	82
Horner v. Horner	...	23 Ch. 10	22, O.S., 115	2, 47	...	27, 39
Hoskins' Trusts, Re	6 C. D. 281	46 Ch. 817	35, 925	25, 779	...	149
— v. Campbell	2 H. & M. 43	...	10, 93	12, 546	...	72
Houseman v. Houseman	1 C. D. 535	...	34, 633	24, 592	...	28, 48, 125, 142, 149
Howard v. Chaffers	2 Dr. & Sm. 236	32 Ch. 686	...	11, 585	9, N.S., 634	132
— v. Easton	...	...	45, 136	29, 885	...	142
Howell v. Kightley	8 DeG.M.&G.325	25 Ch. 341	27, O.S., 61	...	...	99
Howells v. Jenkins	1 DeG.J.&S.617	32 Ch. 788	9, 184	11, 1050	...	175
Hubbard v. Latham	W. N. '66, 105	35 Ch. 402	14, 616	14, 553	...	93, 95, 119, 130
Hudson v Carmichael	...	...	...	...	18, 851	100
Hughes v. Eades	1 Ha. 486	11 Ch. 297	...	6, 455	...	13
— v. Key	20 Be. 395	...	...	...	...	147
— v. Wynne	T. & R. 307	...	...	...	...	165
Hull v. Falconer	...	...	11, 761	...	11, N.S., 151	114
Humble v. Shore	3 Ha. 119	...	...	...	...	12, 42
Hume v. Rundell	6 Madd. 331	...	...	...	...	14
Humphreys v. Ingledon	1 P. Wms. 752	...	...	...	...	27
— v. Humphreys	3 P. Wms. 349	...	...	...	...	39
Hunt v. Chambers	20 C. D. 365	51 Ch. 683	46, 399	30, 527	...	50
— v. Stevens	3 Taunt. 113	...	...	...	...	13, 27
Hunter v. Baxter	3 Giff. 214	31 Ch. 432	5, 46	...	...	109
— v. Young	4 Ex. D. 256	48 Ex. 689	41, 142	27, 637	...	37, 116
Hutchinson v. Ward	6 C. D. 692	...	36, 178	25, 452	...	191, 192
Hutley, Re	1 C. D. 11	45 Ch. 79	33, 337	...	...	77
INDERSON v. Warth	...	...	25, O.S., 43	...	1, N.S., 440	181
Inchley v. Allsop	...	...	...	9, 649	7, N.S., 1181	125
Ingle v. Partridge	32 Be. 661	32 Ch. 813	9, 361	12, 65	...	65
Irby v. Irby	24 Be. 525	...	...	...	3, N.S., 1314	55, 158
— v. ——	25 Be. 632	...	32, O.S., 141	6, 853	...	146
Isaacs v. Weatherstone	10 Ha. App. 30	...	...	...	...	68
JACKSON v. Leaf	1 J. & W. 229	...	...	...	...	76
— v. Pease	19 Eq. 96	...	...	23, 43	...	157
Jacobs v. Rylance	17 Eq. 341	43 Ch. 280	...	...	...	146
James v. Aston	...	25 Ch. 343	27, O.S., 33	4, 401	2, N.S., 224	34
— v. Gwynne	...	...	...	...	2, N.S., 436	124

TABLE OF CASES.

Authorised Reports.	Law Journal. (New Series unless otherwise stated.)	Law Times. (New Series unless otherwise stated.)	Weekly Reporter.	Jurist. (Old Series unless otherwise stated.)	Page.
...	...	...	10, 640	...	90
5 Be. 28	...	18, O.S., 82	...	...	42
1 Ves. 738	...	...	...	...	67
8 Eq. 18	...	...	...	...	117
1DeG.M.&G.609	26 Ch. 63	28, O.S., 134	5, 56	2, N.S., 1125	39
1 Russ. 283	...	...	...	...	125
1 C. D. 562	...	...	26, 206	...	16, 53
1 K. & J. 458	...	...	...	...	30
1 S. & S. 73	...	...	...	...	63
14 Be. 498	...	...	6, 120	...	125
1 C. P. D. 258	...	...	27, 941	...	9
18 Be. 480	...	...	...	...	133
...	...	12, 822	...	11, N.S., 777	38, 48, 49
1 Bro. C. C. 25	...	...	...	...	130
1 C. D. 492	47 Ch. 583	38, 494	26, 595	...	131, 149
...	...	...	10, 55	...	35
1 Ha. 267	17 Ch. 369	...	...	14, 145	43
N. N. '82, 6	...	...	...	...	73
1 Ves. 518	...	...	...	...	55
1 Sim. N.S. 241	21 Ch. 630	20, O.S., 30	...	...	16, 52
1 C. D. 327	47 Bk. 91	38, 661	26, 645	...	169
N. N. '75, 4	...	...	23, 225	...	93, 153
Y. & C. C. 437	...	...	...	...	13
...	...	19, O.S., 252	...	16, 605	71
1 Ir. Eq. 399	...	...	...	...	54
15 Be. 300	...	...	...	...	72
1 Ch. 379	43 Bk. 102	30, 620	22, 350	...	160
...	...	...	2, 316	18, 348	49
1 Be. 460	...	...	...	...	140
1 M. & Cr. 191	7 Ch. 167	...	...	2, 106	22
...	11 Ch. 14	...	...	5, 1052	141
14 Be. 10	34 Ch. 195	9, 832	...	10, N.S., 762	76
1 Ha. 692	22 Ch. 157	19, O.S., 19	...	16, 237	26
W. N. '76, 225	...	...	24, 901	...	29
...	...	...	28, 411	...	145
18 C. D. 300	50 Ch. 629	43, 25	30, 395	...	146
1 M. & K. 358	...	...	...	...	174
16 Be. 358	...	...	...	...	182
1 C. D. 549n.	...	...	...	...	170
16 Be. 77	...	...	...	16, 752	144, 158
27 Be. 33	...	...	...	...	124
1 DeG.&Sm.291	...	...	...	...	76
18 Be. 7	23 Ch. 170	22, O.S., 150	2, 82	17, 1044	110
...	29 Ch. 286	1, 290	8, 111	6, N.S., 61	134
10 C. D. 715	48 Ch. 196	40, 33	27, 226	...	16
10 Ch. 136	44 Ch. 203	31, 813	23, 223	...	112, 157, 165
W. N. '72, 210	...	-	21, 135	...	4
...	24 Ch. 625	...	...	1, N.S., 1078	196

TABLE OF CASES.

NAMES OF CASES.	AUTHORISED REPORTS.	LAW JOURNAL. (New Series unless otherwise stated.)	LAW TIMES. (New Series unless otherwise stated.)	WEEKLY REPORTER.	JURIST. (Old Series unless otherwise stated.)	PAGE.
Large v. Large	W. N. '77, 198	...	...	...	...	9
Lashley v. Hogg	11 Ves. 602	...	...	...	...	10, 113
Latch v. Latch	10 Ch. 464	44 Ch. 445	...	23, 686	...	26, 32, 39
Law v. Hunter	1 Russ. 100	...	...	...	...	15, 16
Lawrence v. Bowle	2 Ph. 140 / 1 C. P. Coop. 241	...	...	...	...	147
Lechmere v. Brazier	1 Russ. 72	4, O.S., Ch. 95	...	...	...	133, 153, 154
Lee v. Nuttall	12 C. D. 61	48 Ch. 616	41, 363	27, 805	...	55, 56, 163, 170
— v. Sturrock	W. N. '76, 226	...	...	...	...	47
— v. Willcock	6 Ves. 605	...	...	...	...	97
Leeds v. Lewis	...	...	...	...	3, N.S., 1290	87
Lees v. Lees	15 Eq. 151	42 Ch. 319	27, 743	21, 215	...	95
Leigh v. Turner	...	...	14, 8	14, 361	...	134
Lenton v. Brudenell	...	...	...	12, 1127	...	108
Leonino v. Leonino	10 C. D. 460	48 Ch. 217	40, 359	27, 388	...	174
Levy v. Lovell	14 C. D. 234	49 Ch. 305	42, 242	28, 602	...	170
Lewellin v. Cobbold	1 Sm. & G. 572	...	22, O.S., 131	...	17, 1111	61
Lewis v. Trask	21 C. D. 862	...	...	...	...	144, 145
Lilford (Ld.) v. Powys-Keck	1 Eq. 347	35 Ch. 302	...	14, 240	...	175
Lincoln v. Windsor	9 Ha. 158	20 Ch. 531	18, O.S., 39	...	15, 765	148
Linford v. Gudgeon	6 Ch. 359	40 Ch. 514	...	19, 577	...	185, 188
Littlewood v. Collins	1 N. R. 457	...	8, 265	11, 387	...	72
Livesey v. Harding	1 Be. 343	...	...	...	...	196
Lloyd v. Cross	W. N. '71, 101	...	...	...	...	47
Lockhart v. Hardy	5 Be. 305	...	...	...	...	106
— v. Reilly	1 De G. & J. 464	27 Ch. 54	...	...	...	147
Lodge v. Pritchard	4 Giff. 294	32 Ch. 775	9, 107	11, 532	9, N.S., 982	151
London & County Ass. Co., Re	...	...	...	5, 794	...	88, 92
London & Prov. Bk. v. Bogle	7 C. D. 773	47 Ch. 301	37, 780	26, 573	...	166
London Syndicate v. Lord	8 C. D. 84	48 Ch. 57	38, 329	26, 427	...	66, 67
Longbourne v. Fisher	...	47 Ch. 379	40, 124	27, 405	...	127
Longdendale Cotton S. Co., Re	8 C. D. 150	48 Ch. 54	38, 776	26, 491	...	73
Loomes v. Stotherd	1 S. & S. 458	1, O.S., Ch. 220	...	...	...	166, 167
Lord v. Lord	2 Eq. 605	35 Ch. 683	...	...	...	91
Lovat v. Fraser	L. R., 1 H. L. Sc. 24	...	...	...	...	164
Low v. Carter	1 Be. 426	...	...	...	...	142
Lowe v. Farlie	2 Madd. 101	...	...	...	...	36
Lowes v. Lowes	2 DeG.,M.&G.784	22 Ch. 179	20, O.S., 196	1, 27	16, 991	125
Lowis v. Rumney	1 Eq. 451	...	...	...	...	108
Lowry v. Fulton	9 Sim. 115	8 Ch. 314	...	...	...	33
Lucas v. Siggers	7 Ch. 517	41 Ch. 364	26, 651	20, 458, 478	...	78, 79
— v. Williams	...	...	...	10, 606	8, N.S., 207	82
Luckraft v. Pridham	...	48 Ch. 636	...	...	...	157
Luke v. Tonkin	21 C. D. 757	...	46, 684	30, 874	...	17, 53

TABLE OF CASES.

NAMES OF CASES.	AUTHORISED REPORTS.	LAW JOURNAL. (New Series unless otherwise stated.)	LAW TIMES. (New Series unless otherwise stated.)	WEEKLY REPORTER.	JURIST. (Old Series unless otherwise stated.)	PAGE.
Lyall v. Weldhen	9 Ch. 287	...	30, 146	22, 633	...	78, 79
Lyttleton v. Cross	3 B. & C. 317	...	...	...	...	55
MACARTHUR v. Dudgeon	15 Eq. 102	42 Ch. 263	...	21, 166	...	91
Macdonald v. Foster	6 C. D. 193	...	37, 296	25, 602	...	192
Macfarlane's Claim	17 C. D. 337	50 Ch. 273	44, 299	...	...	173
McHardy v. Hitchcock	...	...	...	...	12, 781	69
McHenry v. Lewis	22 C. D. 397	52 Ch. 16	47, 549	31, 305	...	79
Mackenzie v. Taylor	7 Be. 467	...	...	...	...	139
Mackie v. Darling	12 Eq. 319	...	...	19, 796	...	30, 62
Maclaren v. Stainton	...	26 Ch. 332	26, O.S., 191	...	2, N.S., 49	79
Maclean v. Dawson	1 Sw. & Tr. 425	...	34, O.S., 53	...	...	34
— v. —	{ 27 Be. 21 / 4 DeG.&J.150 }	28 Ch. 742	33, O.S., 158	...	5, N.S., 1091	34
McMurray v. Matthew	W. N. '76, 47	...	33, 804	...	...	70
McVeagh v. Croall	1 DeG.J.&S.399	32 Ch. 521	8, 100	11, 457	9, N.S., 240	108
Maddison v. Pye	32 Be. 658	...	...	...	...	158
Madras Irrigation Co., Re	16 C. D. 702	...	...	29, 520	...	84
Maltby v. Russell	2 S. & S. 227	3, O.S.Ch.85	...	...	...	58
Man v. Ricketts	7 Be. 93	13 Ch. 194	2, O.S., 456	...	8, 159	15
Manchester Paving Co. v. Slagg	} ...	...	47, 556	...	...	89
Manton v. Roe	14 Sim. 353	...	4, O.S., 190	...	...	140
March v. Russell	3 M. & Cr. 31	6 Ch. 303	...	...	...	182
Martin v. Bannister	4 Q. B. D. 491	48 Q.B. 677	...	28, 143	...	184
— v. Maugham	...	13 Ch. 392	3, O.S., 433	...	8, 609	140
Mason v. Bogg	2 M. & Cr. 443	...	...	...	1, 330	162, 170
— v. Wirral Highway Board	} 4 Q. B. D. 459	48 Q.B, 679	...	27, 676	...	189
Massey v. Massey	2 J. & H. 728	32 Ch. 13	7, 311	...	...	17
Matthews v. Matthews	...	45 Ch. 711	34, 718	...	...	75
— v. Palmer	...	...	...	11, 610	...	75
Mayd v. Field	...	...	34, 614	24, 660	...	158
Mayer v. Murray	8 C. D. 424	47 Ch. 605	...	26, 690	...	16, 17, 53
Meakin v. Sykes	...	...	...	24, 293	...	20
Mellor v. Sidebottom	5 C. D. 342	46 Ch. 398	37, 7	25, 401	...	19
— v. Swire	21 C. D. 647	...	46, 437	30, 525	...	72, 73, 75
Menzies v. Connor	3 Mac. & G. 648	...	18, O.S., 337	...	...	74
Merry v. Nickalls	8 Ch. 205	42 Ch. 479	28, 296	21, 305	...	183
Mersey Steel & Iron Co. v. Naylor	} 9 Q. B. D. 648	51 Q.B. 576	47, 369	31, 80	...	170, 173
Metcalfe v. Hutchinson	1 C. D. 591	45 Ch. 210	...	...	...	95, 164
Meyer v. Montriou	4 Be. 343	...	...	...	...	64
Micklethwait v. Winstanley	} ...	34 Ch. 281	11, 582	13, 210	...	93, 106
Middleton v. Reay	7 Ha. 106	18 Ch. 153	...	...	13, 116	54
Miles v. Harrison	9 Ch. 316	43 Ch. 585	30, 190	22, 441	...	159, 176
Miller v. Priddon	1 Mac. & G. 687	...	...	...	...	13
Mills v. Jennings	13 C. D. 639	49 Ch. 209	42, 169	28, 549	...	43
Minors v. Battison	1 App. Cas. 428	46 Ch. 2	35, 1	25, 27	...	55
Mirehouse v. Herbert	...	...	...	5, 583	3, N.S., 1238	52, 142
Mitchell, Re	...	33 Ch. 187	9, 282	12, 39	9, N.S., 1272	87
Mitchelson v. Piper	8 Sim. 64	5 Ch. 294	...	...	7, 3	55, 168
Mitford v. Reynolds	1 Ph. 706	...	...	...	...	101

NAMES OF CASES.	AUTHORISED REPORTS.	LAW JOURNAL. (New Series unless otherwise stated.)	LAW TIMES. (New Series unless otherwise stated.)	WEEKLY REPORTER.	JURIST. (Old Series unless otherwise stated.)	PAGE.
Montefiore v. Browne	7 H. L. C. 241	...	...	...	4, N.S., 1201	113
Moodie v. Bannister	4 Dr. 432	28 Ch. 881	32, O.S., 376	7, 278	5, N.S., 402	108, 109
Moore v. Frowd	3 M. & Cr. 45	6 Ch. 372	...	...	1, 653	147
— v. Moore	...	...	45, 466	...	...	121
— v. Morris	13 Eq. 139	41 Ch. 161	...	...	...	40
Moors v. Marriott	7 C. D. 543	47 Ch. 331	...	26, 626	...	163
Morewood v. Currey	...	...	...	28, 213	...	37
Morgan v. Davies	3 C. P. D. 260	...	39, 60	26, 816	...	189
— v. Elstob	4 Ha. 477	...	...	...	...	112
— v. Middlemiss	...	...	...	14, 414	...	139
— v. Morgan	13 Be. 441	...	...	...	15, 319	52
— v. Rees or Reiss	6 Q. B. D. 508	50 M. C. 27	43, 753	29, 213	...	190
Morley v. Finney	W. N. '70, 82	...	...	18, 490	...	106
— v. White	8 Ch. 731	42 Ch. 880	29, 282	21, 746	...	33
Morris v. Morris	10 Ch. 68	44 Ch. 178	31, 491	23, 120	...	166, 167
Morse v. Sadler	1 Cox, 352	...	...	...	...	42
Morshead v. Reynolds	21 Be. 638	...	...	...	...	112
Mortlock v. Leathes	2 Mer. 491	...	...	...	...	63
Morton v. Miller	3 C. D. 516	45 Ch. 613	...	24, 723	...	21
Mullins v. Smith	1 Dr. & S. 204	...	...	8, 739	...	119
Musbach v. Anderson	...	...	...	26, 100	...	84
Mutlow v. Mutlow	4 De G. & J. 539	...	...	...	...	160
Mutter v. Hudson	...	...	26, O.S., 116	...	2, N.S., 34	52, 53
Nash v. Dillon	1 Moll. 236	...	...	...	...	151
Nayler v. Blount	...	...	...	27, 865	...	9
Neal, Ex parte	14 C. D. 579	...	43, 264	28, 875	...	172, 173
Neeves v. Burrage	14 Q. B. 504	19 Q. B. 68	14, O.S., 394	...	14, 177	58
Nelson, Ex parte	14 C. D. 41	49 Bk. 44	42, 389	28, 554	...	170
— v. Booth	3 De G. & J. 119	27 Ch. 782	32, O.S., 45	6, 845	5, N.S., 28	52
Nesbitt v. Baldwin	7 C. D. (Ir.) 134	...	...	...	...	68
Neve v. Weston	3 Atk. 557	...	...	...	...	74
Newbegin v. Bell	23 Be. 386	...	...	...	...	156
Newbery, Re	...	...	...	10, 373	...	4, 6
Newell v. Nat. Prov. Bank	1 C. P. D. 496	45 C.P. 285	34, 533	24, 458	...	81
Newland v. Steer	...	...	13, 111	13, 1014	11, N.S., 596	108
Newmarch v. Storr	9 C. D. 12	48 Ch. 28	39, 146	27, 104	...	174
Newton v. M. R. Co.	1 Dr. & Sm. 583	...	5, 542	10, 102	...	27
— v. Sherry	1 C. P. D. 246	45 C.P. 257	34, 251	24, 371	...	4, 37
Nichols v. Nichols	...	...	...	10, 598	...	26
Nicholson v. Falkiner	1 Moll. 555	...	...	...	...	151
Noble v. Brett	24 Be. 499	27 Ch. 516	31, O.S., 228	6, 219	4, N.S., 623	116
Nokes v. Steppings	2 Ph. 19	...	...	...	...	64
Norton Ironworks Co., Re	...	47 Ch. 9	...	26, 53	...	172
Norvall, or Nowall, v. Pascoe	...	31 Ch. 456	10, 809	10, 338	...	72, 124
Norway v. Norway	2 M. & K. 278	{ 3 Ch.111, 163 }	...	...	...	152
Nunn v. Barlow	1 S. & S. 588	...	...	...	...	55
Obbard, Re	...	...	24, 145	19, 563	...	169
O'Conour v. Haslam	5 H. L. C. 170	...	25, O.S., 237	...	...	165

NAMES OF CASES.	AUTHORISED REPORTS.	LAW JOURNAL. (New Series unless otherwise stated.)	LAW TIMES. (New Series unless otherwise stated.)	WEEKLY REPORTER
Offley v. Jenny	3 Ch. Rep. 92	...	...	...
Ogden v. Lowry	...	25 Ch. 198	...	4, 156
Oldfield v. Cobbett	6 Be. 515	...	1, O.S., 455	...
Orr v. Newton	2 Cox, 274	...	...	...
Orr-Ewing v. Orr-Ewing.	22 C. D. 456	...	...	31, 464
Orrell v. Busch	5 Ch. 467	...	22, 461	18, 588
Osbaldiston v. Crowther	1 Sm. & G. App. 12	...	20, O.S., 322	1, 255
Ostell v. Le Page	2DeG. M.&G.892	21 Ch. 501	20, O.S., 204	1, 18
Ottley v. Gilbey	8 Be. 602	14 Ch. 177	4, O.S., 411	...
Overington v. Ward	34 Be. 175	...	...	...
Owen v. Delamere	15 Eq. 134	42 Ch. 232	27, 647	21, 218
Owens v. Dickenson	Cr. & Ph. 48	...	...	...
PACKWOOD v. Maddison	1 S. & S. 232	1, O.S., Ch. 107	...	...
Paddy, Ex parte	3 Madd. 241	...	...	...
Palmer v. Jones	W. N. '74, 17	43 Ch. 349	...	...
— v. Perry	W. N. '70, 58	...	...	...
Pannell, Ex parte	6 C. D. 335	47 Bk. 21	37, 450	26, 194
Parker v. Ringham	33 Be. 535	...	...	...
Parkin v. Proudfoot	(Seton, 974)	...	...	...
— v. Seddons	16 Eq.	42 Ch. 470	28, 353	21, 538
Parkinson v. Lucas	28 Be. 627	...	...	...
Parry v. Ashley	3 Sim. 97	...	...	...
Parsons v. Harris	6 C. D. 694	...	...	25, 410
Parsons v. Neville	3 Bro. C. C. 365	...	...	...
Partington v. Reynolds	4 Dr. 253	27 Ch. 505	31, O.S., 7	6, 388
Passingham v. Sherborn	9 Be. 424	...	...	...
Patching v. Barnett	(1909) 2 Ch. 151	51 Ch. 74	45, 292	...
Paterson v. Scott	1DeG.M.&G.537	21 Ch. 346	18, O.S., 343	...
Payne v. Collier	1 Ves. jun. 170	...	...	...
— v. Evens	18 Eq. 356	...	...	...
Paynter v. Houston	3 Mer. 297	...	...	...
Pearce v. Spickett	W. N. '76, 109	...	...	...
Peat v. Jones	8 Q. B. D. 147	51 Q.B. 128	...	30, 433
Pelham v. Hilder	1 Y. & C. C. 3	...	...	...
Pemberton v. Barnes	13 Eq. 349	41 Ch. 209	26, 389	...
— v. Topham	1 Be. 316	...	...	...
Penney v. Francis	...	30 Ch. 185	...	9, 8
Penny v. Penny	11 C. D. 440	48 Ch. 691	40, 393	...
— v. —	9 Ha. 39	20 Ch. 339	...	...
— v. Watts	2 Ph. 149	16 Ch. 146	...	...
Perpetual Insur. Co. v. Gillespie	W. N. '82, 4	...	...	...
Perry v. Meldowcroft	4 Be. 197	...	...	...
Peruvian Guano Co. v. Bockwoldt	W. N. '83, 26	...	48, 7	...
Peterson v. Peterson	...	...	16, 377	...
— v. —	3 Eq. 111	36 Ch. 101	...	15, 164
Petty v. Petty	12 Be. 170	...	...	...
Philanthropic Society v. Hobson	2 M. & K. 357	3 Ch. 97	...	...

TABLE OF CASES. xxxi

NAMES OF CASES.	AUTHORISED REPORTS.	LAW JOURNAL. (New Series unless otherwise stated.)	LAW TIMES. (New Series unless otherwise stated.)	WEEKLY REPORTER.	JURIST. (Old Series unless otherwise stated.)	PAGE.
Philippo v. Munnings	2 M. & Cr. 309	...	...	...	...	165
Phillips v. Beal	32 Be. 26	...	...	...	...	55, 109
— v. Parry	22 Be. 279	...	...	...	...	164
Phillipson v. Gatty	{ 6 Ha. 26 2 H. & Tw. 459 }	17Ch.241	11, O.S., 472	...	12, 430	42
Pickford v. Hunter	5 Sim. 122	...	...	...	...	74
Pierce v. Hammond	...	...	10, 261	12, 686	...	99
Pierpoint v. Cartwright	5 C. P. D. 139	...	42, 259	28, 583	...	189
Pigott v. Pigott	2 N. R. 14	...	8, 268	...	...	43
— v. Young	...	...	...	7, 235	...	7, 8
Pinchard v. Fellows	17 Eq. 421	43 Ch. 227	29, 882	22, 612	...	154
Pinney v. Pinney	8 B. & C. 335	...	...	...	...	14, 27
Player v. Foxhall	1 Russ. 538	...	...	...	...	55
Plunkett v. Lewis	11 Sim. 379	...	...	...	...	72
Pointon v. Pointon	12 Eq. 547	40 Ch. 609	25, 294	19, 1051	...	24
Polini v. Gray	W. N. '74, 3	...	...	22, 255	...	3
Pollard v. Doyle	1 Dr. & Sm. 319	...	3, 432	9, 28	6, N.S., 1139	148
Portarlington v. Damer	2 Ph. 262	16 Ch. 370	...	...	11, 443	69, 70
Postmaster-General, Ex parte	10 C. D. 595	48 Bk. 84	40, 16	27, 325	...	163
Pott v. Gallini	1 S. & S. 206	...	...	...	...	74
Pottinger, Ex parte	8 C. D. 621	47 Bk. 43	38, 432	26, 648	...	107, 173
Powell v. Wallworth	2 Madd. 183	...	...	...	...	122
Price v. North	2 Y. & C. Ex.620	...	...	...	...	122
— v. Price	15 Sim. 484	18 Ch. 232	...	...	...	167
Prince v. Nicholson	5 Taunt. 665	...	...	...	...	58
Prosser v. Mossop	W. N. '81, 38	...	...	29, 439	...	11
Proudfoot v. Hume	4 Be. 476	...	...	...	...	60
Prowse v. Spurgin	5 Eq. 99	37 Ch. 251	17, 590	...	...	121
Purcell v. Blennerhassett	3 Jo. & L. 24	...	...	...	...	119
— v. Manning	...	...	30, O.S., 50	...	3, N.S., 1070	99
RANKIN v. Harwood	2 Ph. 22	15 Ch. 446	7, O.S., 467	...	10, 794	83
Ratcliffe v. Winch	16 Be. 576	22 Ch. 915	21, O.S., 30	...	17, 586	80, 84
Rawlings v. Lambert	1 J. & H. 458	...	...	...	...	39
Raymond v. Tapson	22 C. D. 430	...	...	31, 394	...	91, 92
Rayner v. Green	2 Curt. 248	...	...	...	...	33
— v. Koehler	14 Eq. 262	41 Ch. 697	27, 506	20, 859	...	38
Rees v. George	15 C. D. 490	49 Ch. 568	...	...	...	130
Reeve's Trusts, Re	4 C. D. 841	46 Ch. 412	36, 906	25, 628	...	157
— v. Goodwin	...	...	8, O.S., 251	...	10, 1050	9, 61
Regent United Service Stores, Re	...	...	38, 130	26, 579	...	172
Rex v. Haines	Skinn. 583	...	...	...	...	13
Rhodes v. Barret	12 Eq. 479	41 Ch. 103	24, 654	19, 871	...	71, 72
— v. Rhodes	1 Ch. 483	35 Ch. 729	...	...	...	88
Riboldi v. Maireau	(Fry, J., 1883)	...	...	...	...	36
Rice v. Gordon	11 Be. 265	...	...	...	...	25
— v. Orgles	W. N. '71, 177	...	25, 263	...	...	151
Richards, Re	8 Eq. 119	...	...	...	...	119
Richardson v. Bank of England	4 M. & Cr. 165	8 Ch. 1	...	...	2, 911	63
— v. Horton	7 Be. 112	13 Ch. 186	...	...	...	166
— v. Richardson	14 C. D. 611	49 Ch. 612	43, 279	28, 942	...	153, 155

NAMES OF CASES.	AUTHORISED REPORTS.	LAW JOURNAL. (New Series unless otherwise stated.)	LAW TIMES. (New Series unless otherwise stated.)	WEEKLY REPORTER.
Richardson v. Ward	13 Be. 110	20 Ch. 227	...	...
Richmond v. White	12 C. D. 361	48 Ch. 798	41, 570	27, 878
Ridley v. Tiplady	20 Be. 44	24 Ch. 207	24, O.S., 296	3, 276
Ritchie v. Humberstone	...	22 Ch. 1006	...	...
Roberts v. Roberts	2 Ph. 534	17 Ch. 174	11, O.S., 285	...
Robertson v. Norris	1 Giff. 428	..	1, 123	...
Robinson v. Elliott	1 Russ. 599	...	...	...
— v. Geldard	3 Mac. & G. 735	18 Ch. 454	19, O.S., 365	...
Rocke, Ex parte..	6 Ch. 795	40 Bk. 70	25, 287	19, 1129
Rodney v. Rodney	16 Sim. 307	...	11, O.S., 532	...
Rogers v. James	7 Taunt. 147	...	...	...
— v. Powell	...	38 Ch. 648	...	18, 282
— v. Soutten	2 Ke. 598	7 Ch. 118	...	...
Roper v. Roper	3 C. D. 714	...	35, 155	24, 1013
Roper's Trusts, Re	11 C. D. 272	...	40, 97	27, 408
Ross v. Ross	12 Be. 89	...	...	...
— v. Tatham	W. N. '69, 183	38 Ch. 577	21, 351	17, 960
Rossiter v. Rossiter	13 C. D. 355	49 Ch. 36	42, 353	28, 238
Rothwell v. Rothwell	2 S. & S. 217	...	...	...
Roupell v. Parsons	W. N. '76, 61	...	34, 56	24, 269
Rowcliffe v. Leigh	3 C. D. 202	...	...	24, 782
Rowles v. Mayhew	5 C. D. 596	46 Ch. 552	37, 48	25, 521
Rowley v. Burgess	..	...	...	2, 652
Rowsell v. Morris	17 Eq. 20	43 Ch. 97	29, 446	22, 67
Roy v. Gibbon	4 Ha. 65	...	...	...
Rump v. Greenhill	20 Be. 512	24 Ch. 90	24, O.S., 124	3, 51
SALTER v. Tildesley	...	...	11, 759	13, 376
Sampson, Re	...	...	14, 97	14, 472
Samson v. Samson	...	39 Ch. 592	22, 457	18, 530
Samuel v. Jones	2 Ha. 246	12 Ch. 496	...	...
— v. Samuel	12 C. D. 152	47 Ch. 716	41, 462	26, 750
Sander v. Heathfield	19 Eq. 21	44 Ch. 113	31, 400	23, 331
Sanders v. Miller	25 Be. 154	...	...	...
Sanderson, Re	7 C. D. 176	...	38, 379	26, 309
— v. Stoddart	32 Be. 155	...	7, 662	11, 275
Sandilands v. Innes	3 Sim. 263	...	...	...
Sawyer v. Birchmore	1 Ke. 391, 825	6 Ch. 277	...	...
Say v. Creed	3 Ha. 455	...	...	...
Scaffold v. Hampton	W. N. '73, 218	43 Ch. 137	29, 575	22, 182
Scales v. Collins	9 Ha. 656	...	...	...
Schofield, Ex parte	12 C. D. 337	48 Bk. 122	40, 823	27, 925
Score v. Ford	7 Be. 333	...	...	...
Scott v. Bentley	1 K. & J. 281	24 Ch. 244	25, O.S., 114	3, 280
— v. Briant	6 N. & M. 381	...	...	...
— v. Cumberland	18 Eq. 578	44 Ch. 226	31, 26	22, 840
— v. Jones	4 Cl. & F. 382	...	...	...
— v. Spashett	3 Mac. & G. 599	21 Ch. 349	19, O.S., 37	...
Scurrah v. Scurrah	...	...	...	2, 53
Scurry v. Morse	9 Moo. 89	...	...	...
Sellon v. Watts	...	...	...	9, 847
Senior v. Hereford	4 C. D. 494	...	...	25, 223

TABLE OF CASES.   xxxiii

NAMES OF CASES.	AUTHORISED REPORTS.	LAW JOURNAL. (New Series unless otherwise stated.)	LAW TIMES. (New Series unless otherwise stated.)	WEEKLY REPORTER.	JURIST. (Old Series unless otherwise stated.)	PAGE.
well v. Ashley	10 Ha. App. 66 3DeG.M.&G.933	22Ch.659	21, O.S., 39	1, 260	17, 269	4, 6, 35
— v. Moxsy	2 Sim. N.S. 189	21 Ch. 824	18, O.S., 270	...	16, 608	31
xton v. Smith	3 DeG.&Sm.694	...	...	...	...	81
ymour v. Coulson	5 Q. B. D. 359	49 Q.B.604	...	28, 664	...	189
iarman v. Radd	...	27 Ch. 844	31, O.S., 325	...	4, N.S., 527	55
arp v. Lush	10 C. D. 468	48 Ch. 231	...	27, 528	...	93, 95, 159
aw v. Hardingham	...	...	...	2, 657	...	43
iearman v. Robinson	15 C. D. 548	49 Ch. 745	43, 372	29, 168	...	26
iepheard v. Beetham	6 C. D. 597	46 Ch. 763	36, 909	25, 764	...	159, 176
iepherd v. Towgood	T. & R. 379	...	...	...	...	74
ieppard v. Sheppard	33 Be. 129	...	...	...	...	159
ierwin v. Selkirk	12 C. D. 68	...	40, 701	27, 842	...	107, 162
iewen v. Vanderhorst..	2 R. & M. 75	1 Ch. 107	...	...	...	55, 108, 109
iirreff v. Hastings	6 C. D. 610	47 Ch. 137	...	25, 842	...	162
iortley v. Selby	5 Madd 447	...	...	...	...	154
iuttleworth v. Howarth	Cr. & Ph. 228	...	...	5, 499	...	157
ilibourne v. Newport..	1 K. & J. 602	...	...	3, 653	1, N.S., 608	56
lver v. Stein	1 Dr. 295	21 Ch. 312	...	...	...	34
mons v. McAdam	6 Eq. 324	37 Ch. 751	18, 678	16, 963	...	187
mpson v. Bathurst	5 Ch. 193	...	23, 29	18, 772	...	143
ms v. Ridge	3 Mer. 458	...	...	...	...	123
iey v. Bennett	2 Y. & C. C. 405	...	...	...	7, 571	196
inner v. Anglesey (M.)	(Kay, J., 1882)	...	...	...	...	166, 168
iottowe v. Young	11 Eq. 474	40 Ch. 366	24, 220	19, 583	...	181
eech v. Thorington	2 Ves. sen. 560	...	...	...	...	119
eight v. Lawson	3 K. & J. 292	26 Ch. 553	29, O.S., 379	5, 589	...	17, 75
nart v. Bradstock	7 Be. 500	...	...	4, 353	...	44
nith v. Andrews	...	...	...	...	...	43
— v. Armstrong	6DeG.M.&G.150	...	26, O.S., 251	...	2, N.S., 359	134
— v. Althus	11 Ves. 564	...	...	...	...	90
— v. Chambers	2 Ph. 221	...	...	...	11, 359	17
— v. Dale	18 C. D. 516	50 Ch. 352	44, 460	29, 330	...	147
— v. Guy	2 Ph. 159 2C. P. Coop. 289	...	...	...	...	125
— v. Morgan	5 C. P. D. 337	49 C.P. 410	...	...	...	163
— v. Poole	12 Sim. 17	10 Ch. 192	...	...	...	168
— v. Spilsbury	1 Dr. & Sm. 153	...	...	8, 596	...	5
— v. Watts	22 C. D. 5	52 Ch. 209	48, 167	31, 262	...	92
— v. Whichcord	...	...	...	24, 900	...	79
— v. White	1 Eq. 626	35 Ch. 454	14, 350	...	...	26
ackman v. Timbrell	8 Sim. 253	6 Ch. 147	...	...	...	166
iarling v. Parker	9 Be. 450	16 Ch. 57	7, O.S., 465	...	10, 448	176
iensley v. Harrison	15 Eq. 16	42 Ch. 21	...	21, 95	...	154
ierling v. Rochfort	16 C. D. 18	50 Ch. 1	44, 161	29, 84	...	165
iurway v. Glynn	9 Ves. 483	...	...	...	...	119
acey v. Elph	1 M. & K. 195	2 Ch. 50	...	...	...	33
afford v. Fiddon	23 Be. 386	...	...	...	...	133
ahlschmidt v. Lett	1 Sm. & G. 415	...	21, O.S., 208	...	...	108
ainton v. Carron Co.	21 Be. 500	...	...	...	...	79
ammers v. Elliott	3 Ch. 195	37 Ch. 353	18, 1	16, 489	...	146
— v. Halliley	12 Sim. 42	...	...	...	5, 817	177
amper v. Stamper	...	...	46, 372	...	...	31

c

TABLE OF CASES.

NAMES OF CASES.	AUTHORISED REPORTS.	LAW JOURNAL. (New Series unless otherwise stated.)	LAW TIMES. (New Series unless otherwise stated.)	WEEKLY REPORTER.	JURIST. (Old Series unless otherwise stated.)	PAGE.
Stanhope S. Collieries Co., Re	11 C. D. 160	48 Ch. 409	40, 204	27, 561	...	169
Stanton v. Hatfield	1 Ke. 358	...	...	...	...	153, 154
Starten v. Bartholomew	6 Be. 143	12 Ch. 179	...	...	...	31
Stead v. Hardaker	15 Eq. 175	42 Ch. 317	...	21, 258	...	157
— v. Stead	2 C. P. Coop. 311	...	...	...	...	70, 77
Stebbing v. Atlee	...	26 Ch. 265	28, O.S., 172	...	2, N.S., 1161	91, 92
Steele v. Cobham	1 Ch. 325	...	14, 242	14, 493	...	127
Stephens v. Pillen	...	17 Ch. 214	...	...	12, 282	146
Sterndale v. Hankinson	1 Sim. 393	...	...	...	...	{ 106, 109, 110, 140
Stevenson v. Abington	...	...	8, 719	11, 936	...	94
Stirling-Maxwell v. Cartwright	11 C. D. 522	48 Ch. 562	40, 669	27, 850	...	36, 73
Stone v. Van Heythuysen	Kay, 721	...	...	...	18, 344	126
Story v. Fry	1 Y. & C. C. 603	11 Ch. 373	...	...	6, 1029	164
Stott v. Meanock	...	31 Ch. 746	6, 592	10, 605	...	97
Strange v. Harris	3 Bro. C. C. 365	...	...	...	...	60
Strickland v. Strickland	12 Sim. 463	11 Ch. 198	...	...	...	26, 32
Strong v. Moore	...	22 Ch. 917	...	1, 509	...	41, 47, 49
Sullivan v. Beavan	20 Be. 299	...	...	...	...	141
Summer, Re	...	...	30, 377	22, 639	...	182
Sutton v. Mashiter	2 Sim. 513	...	...	...	...	106
— v. Sutton	22 C. D. 511	...	48, 95	31, 369	...	165
Swale v. Swale	22 Be. 401	...	...	...	...	77
Sykes v. Brook	W. N. '80, 187	50 Ch. 744	45, 172	29, 821	...	51
Symonds v. Jenkins	W. N. '76, 78	...	34, 277	24, 512	...	61
TABOR v. Brooks	10 C. D. 273	48 Ch. 130	39, 528	...	...	57
Tadman v. D'Epineuil	20 C. D. 217	51 Ch. 491	46, 409	30, 423	...	170
Talbot v. Frere	9 C. D. 568	...	...	27, 148	...	166, 168
— v. Marshfield	3 Ch. 622	37 Ch. 52	19, 223	...	...	143
— v. —	2 Dr. & Sm. 285	...	12, 761	...	...	62
Tann v. Tann	7 Eq. 436	38 Ch. 459	...	...	...	139
Tanqueray-Willaume and Landau, Re	20 C. D. 465	51 Ch. 434	46, 542	30, 801	...	164
Tardrew v. Howell	2 Giff. 530	30 Ch. 191	3, 661	9, 296	7, N.S., 937	152
Taylor v. Duckett	W. N. '75, 193	...	...	...	...	21
— v. Glanville	3 Madd. 176	...	...	...	...	142
— v. Linley	...	...	33, O.S., 232	...	5, N.S., 701	159
— v. Southgate	4 M. & Cr. 203	8 Ch. 137	...	...	3, 214	74
— v. Taylor	10 Eq. 477	39 Ch. 676	23, 134	18, 1102	...	117, 183
— v. —	17 Eq. 324	43 Ch. 314	30, 49	22, 349	...	178
Tebbs v. Carpenter	1 Madd. 290	...	...	...	...	142, 143
Teed v. Beere	...	28 Ch. 782	33, O.S., 26	7, 394	5, N.S., 381	117
Tempest v. Camoys (Lord)	35 Be. 201	...	14, 8	14, 326	12, N.S., 539	32
— v. —	21 C. D. 571	51 Ch. 785	48, 13	31, 326	...	57, 58
Tennant v. Rawlings	4 C. P. D. 133	...	...	27, 682	...	189
Therry v. Henderson	1 Y. & C. C. 481	...	...	...	6, 386	70
Thomas v. Elsom	6 C. D. 346	...	...	25, 871	...	89
— v. Griffith	2 De G. F. & J. 555	30 Ch. 465	3, 761	9, 293	7, N.S., 293	113, 116
— v. Jones	1 Dr. & Sm. 134	29 Ch. 570	2, 77	8, 328	6, N.S., 391	{ 153, 155, 156
— v. Montgomery	1 R. & M. 729	...	...	...	...	182

TABLE OF CASES.

NAMES OF CASES.	AUTHORISED REPORTS.	LAW JOURNAL. (New Series unless otherwise stated.)	LAW TIMES. (New Series unless otherwise stated.)	WEEKLY REPORTER.	JURIST. (Old Series unless otherwise stated.)	PAGE.
Thomas v. PatentLionite Co.	17 C. D. 250	50 Ch. 544	44, 392	29, 596	...	172
Thompson v. Bennett	6 C. D. 739	46 Ch. 803	37, 119	25, 862	...	167
— v. Cooper	1 Coll. 81	13 Ch. 416	2, O.S., 419	...	...	167
— v. —	2 Coll. 87	14 Ch. 318	5, O.S., 191	...	9, 768	154
— v. Dunn	5 Ch. 573	...	...	18, 854	...	60
— v. Harris	19 C. D. 552	51 Ch. 273	46, 359	30, 293	...	156, 158
— v. Hope	(Seton, 84)	...	...	...	...	60
— v. Reynolds	3 Car. & P. 123	...	...	...	...	27
— v. Thompson	...	...	8, 490	11, 797	...	6
— v. Trotter	3 M. & Cr. 193	...	...	...	...	22
Thomson v. Eastwood	2 App. Cas. 215	...	...	...	...	165
— v. Flinn	17 Eq. 415	43 Ch. 256	29, 829	22, 293	...	186
— v. Grant	1 Russ. 540 n.	...	...	...	...	164, 167
Thorne v. Kerr	2 K. & J. 54	25 Ch. 57	26, O.S., 233	...	...	9
Threlfell v. Harrison	W. N. '77, 192	...	...	...	...	155
Tickner v. Smith	3 Sm. & G. 42	...	25, O.S., 44	3, 224	...	143
Timms, Re	W. N. '78, 141	47 Ch. 831	38, 679	26, 692	...	85
Tipping v. Power	1 Ha. 405	11 Ch. 257	...	...	6, 434	151, 152
Todd v. Studholme	3 K. & J. 324	26 Ch. 271	29, O.S., 24	5, 277	...	116
Tolputt v. Wells	1 M. & S. 395	...	...	...	...	58
Tombs v. Roch	2 Coll. 490	15 Ch. 308	7, O.S., 428	...	10, 534	165
Tomkins v. Colthurst	1 C. D. 626	...	33, 591	24, 267	...	157, 165
Tomlin v. Tomlin	1 Ha. 236	...	...	...	...	15
Townsend v. Townsend	W. N. '83, 34	...	...	...	...	73
Towsey v. Groves	...	32 Ch. 225	7, 778	11, 252	9, N.S., 194	31
Travers v. Townsend	1 Moll. 496	...	...	...	...	142
Trestrail v. Mason	7 C. D. 655	47 Ch. 249	...	26, 260	...	174
Trethewy v. Helyar	4 C. D. 53	46 Ch. 125	...	...	...	157
Trick's Trusts, Re	5 Ch. 170	39 Ch. 201	21, 739	18, 123	...	138
Tubby v. Tubby	2 Coll. 136	...	...	...	9, 486	30
Tuckley v. Thompson	1 J. & H. 126	29 Ch. 548	2, 565	8, 302	...	154
Tulloch v. Tulloch	3 Eq. 574	...	...	...	...	95
Turner v. Bridgett	8 Q. B. D. 392	51 Q.B. 374	...	30, 586	...	170
— v. Buck	18 Eq. 301	43 Ch. 583	...	22, 748	...	119
— v. Hancock	20 C. D. 303	51 Ch. 517	46, 750	30, 480	...	141, 149
— v. Mullineux	...	...	3, 687	9, 252	...	145
— v. Reunoldson	16 Eq. 37	42 Ch. 510	28, 330	21, 558	...	2, 184
— v. Turner	1 J. & W. 39	...	...	...	...	58, 132
— v. —	30 Be. 414	...	...	...	...	59
— v. —	1 Sw. 154	...	...	...	...	99
Turquand v. Kirby	4 Eq. 123	36 Ch. 570	16, 260	{ 15, 633, 730 }	...	25
Tyler v. Bell	2 M. & Cr. 89	6 Ch. 169	...	...	...	35
Underwood v. Hatton	5 Be. 36	...	...	...	...	55
— v. Jee	{ 1 Mac. & G. 276 / 1 H. & Tw. 379 }	19Ch.171	14, O.S., 123	...	...	74
Upton v. Brown	20 C. D. 731	...	47, 289	30, 817	...	87, 88, 95
Van Ghelüve v. Nerinckx	21 C. D. 189	51 Ch. 929	47, 46	30, 759	...	161, 163
Van Kamp v. Bell	3 Madd. 430	...	...	...	...	129

c 2

NAMES OF CASES.	AUTHORISED REPORTS.	LAW JOURNAL. (New Series unless otherwise stated.)	LAW TIMES. (New Series unless otherwise stated.)	WEEKLY REPORTER.	JURIST. (Old Series unless otherwise stated.)	PAGE.
Vanderwell v. Vanderwell	...	...	1, 266	...	...	124
Vane (E.) v. Rigden	5 Ch. 663	39 Ch. 797	...	18, 1092	...	58
Vanreuen v. Piffard	...	...	...	13, 425	...	4, 75
Venables v. Schweitzer	16 Eq. 76	42 Ch. 389	28, 462	21, 505	...	92
Veret v. Duprez	6 Eq. 329	37 Ch. 552	18, 501	16, 750	...	34
Vickers v. Bell	4 DeG.J.&S. 274	...	10, 77	12, 589	10, N.S., 376	33
Vigrass v. Binfield	3 Madd. 62	...	...	...	...	63
Virtue v. Miller	...	...	..	19, 406	...	69, 71
Vyse v. Foster	10 Ch. 236	44 Ch. 344	...	23, 299	...	88, 89
WADDELL v. Toleman	9 C. D. 212	...	38, 910	26, 802	...	171
Wadham v. Rigg	2 Dr. & Sm. 78	...	6, 180	10, 365	8, N.S., 206	6, 88
Waite v. Bingley	21 C. D. 674	51 Ch. 651	...	30, 698	...	15
Walker v. Seligmann	12 Eq. 152	40 Ch. 601	25, 294	...	...	48
— v. Smalwood	Ambl. 676	...	...	...	...	59
— v. Woodward	1 Russ. 107	...	...	...	...	15
Waller v. Barrett	24 Be. 413	27 Ch. 214	30, O.S., 216	...	4, N.S., 128	142, 183
Walters v. Pfeil	Mo. & Ma. 362	...	...	...	...	14, 27
— v. Walters	18 C. D. 182	50 Ch. 819	44, 769	29, 888	...	167
— v. Woodbridge	7 C. D. 504	47 Ch. 516	38, 83	26, 469	...	142
Wankford v. Wankford	1 Salk. 299	...	...	...	...	27
Warburton v. Hill	Kay, 470	23 Ch. 633	23, O.S., 57	2, 365	...	81
Ward v. Mackinlay	2 DeG.J.&S.358	34 Ch. 52	11, 326	13, 65	10, N.S.,1063	154
— v. Raw	15 Eq. 83	...	27, 601	21, 116	...	188
— v. Wyld	5 C. D. 779	...	37, 68	25, 866	...	186
Ware v. Watson	7 DeG.M.&G.739	25 Ch. 199	26, O.S., 251	4, 223	2, N.S., 129	98
Waring v. Danvers	1 P. Wms. 295	...	...	...	...	58
Waterton v. Burt	W. N. '70, 106	39 Ch. 425	...	18, 683	...	97, 111
— v. Ennis	W. N. '80, 154	...	43, 748	28, 885	...	198
Watkins v. Brent	{ 7 Sim. 512 1 M. & Cr. 97 }	} 5 Ch. 49				26
Watson v. Birch	15 Sim. 523	16 Ch. 188	8, O.S., 531	...	11, 198	110
— v. Parker	6 Be. 283	12 Ch. 221	...	...	7, 143	25, 43
— v. Row	18 Eq. 680	43 Ch. 664	...	22, 793	...	147
Wearmouth Crown Glass Co., Re }	19 C. D. 640		45, 757	30, 316		172
Weaver, Re	21 C. D. 615	...	48, 93	31, 224	...	26, 57
Webb v. Adkins	14 C. B. 401	23 C. P. 96	22, O.S., 260	2, 225	...	28
— v. Shaftesbury (E.)	7 Ves. 480	...	...	...	...	54, 56
— v. Webb	16 Sim. 55	17 Ch. 13	10, O.S., 154	...	...	147
Webster v. Spencer	3 B. & Al. 360	...	...	...	...	26, 27
Wedgwood v. Adams	8 Be. 103	...	...	..	...	149
Wells v. Borwick	17 C. D. 798	50 Ch. 241	44, 49	29, 834	...	177
Werderman v. Soc. Gén. d'Electricité }	19 C. D. 246		45, 514	30, 33		40
West v. Laing	3 Dr. 331	...	26, O.S., 66	4, 1	...	6
— v. Swinburne	...	19 Ch. 81	15, O.S., 43	...	14, 360	76
Westbourne Grove Drapery Co., Re }	5 C. D. 248	46 Ch. 525	36, 439	25, 509		170, 172
Weston v. Clowes	15 Sim. 610	...	...	...	...	155
Wetenhall v. Dennis or Davis }	33 Be. 285		9, 361	12, 66	9, N.S., 1216	155, 156
Wheeler, Re	1 Sch. & Lef. 242	...	...	...	...	114
— v. Gill	19 Eq. 316	44 Ch. 181	31, 641	23, 227	...	110

TABLE OF CASES.

NAMES OF CASES.	AUTHORISED REPORTS.	LAW JOURNAL. (New Series unless otherwise stated.)	LAW TIMES. (New Series unless otherwise stated.)	WEEKLY REPORTER.	JURIST. (Old Series unless otherwise stated.)	PAGE.
Whitaker v. Robinson	W. N. '77, 201	...	...	...	...	84
— v. Wright	2 Ha. 310	12 Ch. 241	...	...	7, 320	{ 105, 106, 107
White v. Barton	18 Be. 192	...	...	...	...	33, 63
— v. Cordwell	20 Eq. 644	44 Ch. 746	...	23, 826	...	145
— v. Jackson	15 Be. 191	...	...	...	...	142
— v. Stewart	35 Be. 304	...	...	...	...	44
Whitmore v. Oxborrow	2 Y. & C. C. 13	12 Ch. 21	...	...	6, 985	25
— v. Turquand	1 J. & H. 296	...	...	...	...	61
Whitney v. Smith	4 Ch. 513	...	20, 468	17, 579	...	16, 48
Whittaker v. Whittaker	21 C. D. 657	51 Ch. 737	46, 802	30, 787	...	106
Whittington v. Edwards	3 De G. & J. 243	...	32, O.S., 187	7, 72	...	3, 69
Whittle v. Henning	2 Be. 396	...	...	...	...	50
Wickenden v. Rayson	6 DeG.M.&G.210	25 Ch. 162	26, O.S., 192	4, 39	...	196
Widdowson v. Duck	2 Mer. 494	...	...	...	...	54
Wiglesworth v. Wiglesworth	16 Be. 269	...	...	...	...	60, 64, 65
Wildes v. Dudlow	19 Eq. 198	44 Ch. 341	...	23, 435	...	166
Wiles v. Cooper	9 Be. 294	15 Ch. 129	...	...	...	147
Williams, Ex parte	7 Ch. 314	41 Bk. 38	26, 303	20, 430	...	163, 169
— , —	16 C. D. 590	50 Ch. 303	44, 336	29, 419	...	171
— v. Chard	5 De G. & Sm. 9	21 Ch. 9	18, O.S., 71	...	15, 1026	123
— v. Headland	4 Giff. 505	34 Ch. 20	9, 824	12, 367	10, N.S., 384	183
— v. Hopkins	18 C. D. 370	...	45, 117	29, 767	...	171
— v. — (No. 2)	...	...	44, 773	29, 752	...	171
— v. Kershaw	1 Ke. 274 n.	...	...	...	...	176
— v. Williams	W. N. '68, 241	37 Ch. 854	18, 785	...	...	188
— v. —	15 Eq. 270	42 Ch. 158	28, 17	21, 160	...	163
Williamson v. Jefferys	...	...	10, 330	12, 403	...	44
Wills v. Rich	2 Atk. 285	...	...	...	...	27
Wilson v. Henton	11 Be. 492	...	...	...	...	159
— v. Squire	13 Sim. 212	12 Ch. 139	...	...	...	137, 157
— v. Wilson	2 Moll. 328	...	...	...	...	98
Wiltshire's Estate, Re	...	...	...	8, 133	6, N.S., 190	5
Winchouse v. Winchouse	20 C. D. 545	51 Ch. 560	46, 362	30, 729	...	163
Winkworth v. Winkworth	32 Be. 233	32 Ch. 40	7, 303	11, 15	9, N.S., 61	181
Withernsea Brickworks, Re	16 C. D. 337	50 Ch. 185	43, 713	29, 178	...	170
Wollaston v. Wollaston	7 C. D. 58	47 Ch. 117	37, 631	26, 77	...	{ 24, 29, 138
Wood v. Ordish	3 Sm. & G. 125	...	25, O.S., 327	...	1, N.S., 584	157, 165
— v. Weightman	13 Eq. 434	...	26, 385	20, 459	...	103
Woodcock's Settled Estates, Re	13 Eq. 183	41 Ch. 22	25, 459	...	...	68
Woodgate v. Field	2 Ha. 211	11 Ch. 321	...	...	6, 871	{ 13, 50, 105
Woods v. Greenwell	W. N. '82, 10	...	45, 707	30, 283	...	169
— v. Sowerby	...	...	...	14, 9	...	29
Wooldridge v. Norris	6 Eq. 410	37 Ch. 640	19, 144	16, 965	...	25
Woolf v. Pemberton	6 C. D. 19	...	37, 328	25, 873	...	31
Wormald v. Muzeen	17 C. D. 167	{ 50 Ch. 482, 776	44, 409 45, 115	29, 753, 795	...	178
Wormsley v. Sturt	22 Be. 398	...	...	...	...	91
Worraker v. Pryer	2 C. D. 109	45 Ch. 273	...	24, 269	...	1, 9

NAMES OF CASES.	AUTHORISED REPORTS.	LAW JOURNAL. (New Series unless otherwise stated.)	LAW TIMES. (New Series unless otherwise stated.)
Worth, Re	18 C. D. 521	50 Ch. 262	44, 462
Wright v. Callander	2 De G. M. & G. 652	21 Ch. 787	19, O.S., 308
— v. Lukes	13 Be. 107	20 Ch. 32	16, O.S., 257
Wroughton v. Colquhoun	1 De G. & Sm. 357	...	...
Wyatt v. Sadler	5 Sim. 450	...	...
— v. Sharratt	3 Be. 498	...	...
Wycherley v. Barnard	Johns. 41	28 Ch. 562	32, O.S., 370
Wynne v. Hughes	26 Be. 377	28 Ch. 283, 485	32, O.S., 329
Wythe v. Henniker	2 M. & K. 635	3 Ch. 221	
Yare v. Harrison	2 Cox, 377	...	...
Yeomans v. Haynes	24 Be. 127	...	...
York and North Midland Ry. Co. v. Hudson	18 Be. 70	23 Ch. 695	22, O.S., 151
Youde v. Cloud	18 Eq. 634	44 Ch. 93	...
Young, Ex parte	21 C. D. 642	51 Ch. 940	47, 644
— v. Dolman	...	...	44, 499
— v. Everest	1 R. & M. 426	...	...
— v. Hodges	10 Ha. 158	...	...
— v. Martin	2 Y. & C. C. 582	...	2, O.S., 165
Zambaco v. Cassavetti	11 Eq. 439		24, 770

TABLE OF CASES.

	PAGE
ABINGTON, Stevenson v.	94
Abraham, Bethell v.	54, 56
Acland, Edmunds v.	123
Adams, Wedgwood v.	149
Adamson, Christian v.	142
Adkins, Webb v.	28
Agate, Jeudwine v.	125
Alcan, Cohen v.	6
Alexander, Bell v.	37
— Gillespie v.	113, 115, 116
Allen, Croggan v.	136
Allingham, Cox v.	14
Allsop, Inchley v.	125
Althus, Smith v.	90
Anderson, Acaster v.	5
— Musbach v.	82
Andrews, Smith v.	43
Angel, Davis v.	24, 25
Angell, Henshaw v.	99
Anglesey (M.), Skinner v.	166, 168
Archer, Kelk v.	71
Armstrong, Smith v.	134
Arnold, Butlin v.	125
Ashley, Parry v.	61, 65
— Sewell v.	4, 6, 35
Ashurst, Annesley v.	59
Aston, James v.	34
— Johnson v.	63
Atlee, Stebbing v.	91, 92
Austin, Curling v.	131
— Farrow v.	140, 149
— Hall v.	39
BACKHOUSE, Pickering v.	197
Badley, Brook v.	130
— Green v.	52
— Frowd v.	71, 76
Baldwin, Nesbitt v.	68
Ballard, Collinson v.	51
Bank of England, Richardson v.	63
Bannister, Martin v.	184
— Moodie v.	108, 109
Barlow, Nunn v.	55
Barnard, Wycherley v.	55
Barnes, Bond v.	77
— Pemberton v.	96
Barnett, Patching v.	158
Barret, Rhodes v.	71, 72

	PAGE
Barrett, Hawkes v.	71
— Waller v.	142, 183
Barry, Haly v.	81
Bartholomew, Starten v.	31
Barton, White v.	33, 63
Bartrum, Couldery v.	171
Basham, Hannay v.	145
Bather, Donald v.	36
Bathurst, Simpson v.	143
Battison, Minors v.	55
Batty, Day v.	93, 95
Baxter, Bennett v.	126
— Hunter v.	109
Beal, Phillips v.	55, 109
Beavan, Sullivan v.	141
Beaumont, Gardner v.	124
Beere, Teed v.	117
Beetham, Shepheard v.	159, 176
Bell, Bath v.	139
— Blann v.	157
— Newbegin v.	156
— Tyler v.	35
— Van Kamp v.	129
— Vickers v.	33
Bennett, Jesse v.	39
— Skey v.	196
— Thompson v.	167
Bent, Cafe v.	30, 56, 136
Bentley, Scott v.	30
Binfield, Vigrass v.	63
Bingley, Waite v.	15
Binney, Hill v.	13
Birch, Watson v.	110
Birchmore, Sawyer v.	114, 120
Birks, Hitchen v.	34
Blake, Hinde v.	64
Blennerhasset, Purcell v.	119
Blissett, Cooper v.	9
Blount, Nayler v.	9
Blundell, Bootle v.	164
Bockwoldt, Peruvian Guano Co. v.	79
Bogg, Mason v.	162, 170
Bogle, London & Provincial Bk. v.	166
Bolton, Cook v.	123
Booth, Nelson v.	52
Borwick, Wells v.	177
Bourne, Aspinall v.	134
Bowen, Bennett v.	22, 191
Bowle, Lawrence v.	147

TABLE OF CASES.

	PAGE
Bradley, Harvey v.	16
Bradstock, Smart v.	44
Brancker, Carne v.	131
Brazier, Lechmere v.	133, 153, 154
Brent, Watkins v.	26
Brett, Noble v.	116
Briant, Scott v.	14
Bridges, Hill v.	107, 173
Bridgett, Turner v.	170
Broadmead, Dilkes v.	166
Brodrick, Hollingsworth v.	79
Bromfield, Cummins v.	147
Brook, Sykes v.	51
Brooks, Tabor v.	57
Broughton, Gowan v.	156
Brown, Eltoft v.	22
— Upton v.	87, 88, 95
Browne, Montefiore v.	113
Brudenell, Lenton v.	108
Bryant, Ford v.	16
— King v.	22, 140
Buchanan, Fleming v.	165
Buck, Turner v.	119
Bullock, De Balinhard v.	44
Bult, Gough v.	119
Burgess, Rowley v.	182
Burnell, Foley v.	182
Burrage, Neeves v.	58
Burt, Birt v.	58
— Waterton v.	97, 111
Busch, Orrell v.	78, 79
Butler's Wharf Co., Anderson v.	89
CALLANDER, Wright v.	178
Camoys (Lord), Tempest v.	32, 57
Campbell, Hoskins v.	72
Capell. Creak v.	65
Carmichael, Brett v.	114
— Hudson v.	100
Carnegie, Hope v.	82
Carpenter, Tebbs v.	142, 143
Carron Co., Stainton v.	79
Carter, Chubb v.	52, 182
— Coope v.	17
— Low v.	142
Cartwright, Corser v.	166
— Pierpoint v.	189
— Stirling-Maxwell v.	36, 73
Cassavetti, Zambaco v.	70, 74, 77
Cely, Cowslad v.	32
Chaband, Catherwood v.	14
Chaffers, Howard v.	132
Chambers, Hunt v.	50
— Smith v.	17
Chard, Williams v.	123
Chennell, Jones v.	131, 149
Cheston, Holloway v.	89
Cheyne, Kidd v.	49

	PAGE
Childe, Delevante v.	5
Clark, A.-G. v.	57
Clagett, Fordham v.	88
Clark, Cumberland v.	76
Claxton, Adams v.	134
Clement, Freme v.	165
Cloud, Yonde v.	143
Clowes, Weston v.	155
Cobbett, Oldfield v.	126
Cobbold, Bruff v.	49
— Lewellin v.	61
Cobham, Steele v.	127
Coleby, Green v.	21
Collier, Payne v.	63
Collins, Browne v.	89
— Littlewood v.	72
— Scales v.	175
Colquhoun, Wroughton v.	156, 178
Colthurst, Tomkins v.	157, 165
Colvin, Hartwell v.	113
Concannon, Betagh v.	62
Coney, Burch v.	25, 106
Connor, Menzies v.	74
Cook, Boyes v.	21
Cooke, Barton v.	138
Cooper, Aldridge v.	175
— Thompson v.	154, 167
— Wiles v.	147
Cordwell, White v.	145
Cottee, Knott v.	124, 144, 158
Coulson, Seymour v.	189
Cox, Eyre v.	8, 9
— Freeman v.	68
Coxwell, Harvey v.	122
Creed, Say v.	130
Croall, McVeagh v.	108
Croft, Dymond v.	21
Crook, Cheetham v.	72
Croome, Duignan v.	167
Cross, Lloyd v.	47
— Lyttleton v.	55
Crowther, Osbaldiston v.	6
Cruise, Concannon v.	14
Cumberland, Scott v.	156
Currey, Morewood v.	137
Currie, Hagell v.	60
DALE, Smith v.	147
Dalton, David v.	21
Damer, Portarlington v.	69, 70
Daniell, Bland v.	157
Danvers, Waring v.	58
Darby, Harbin v.	148
Darling, Mackie v.	30, 62
— Morgan v.	189
Davis, Finlay v.	192
— Handley v.	157
— Knight v.	174

TABLE OF CASES.

	PAGE		PAGE
Dawes, De Feuchères v.	32, 33	Flagstaff Mining Co., Davis v.	187
Dawley, Gibbons v.	24	Flinn, Thomson v.	186
Dawson, Maclean v.	34	Flint, Fearnside v.	165
Delamere, Owen v.	26	Floyer, Farquharson v.	157, 165
Dennis, Wetenhall v.	155, 156	Ford, Score v.	62, 63
D'Epineuil, Tadman v.	170	Forrest, Douglas v.	32
De Tastet, Brown v.	66	Foster, Christian v.	158
Dewes, Chissum v.	156	— Dryden v.	74
De Zichy, Hertford (M.) v.	42	— Hewett v.	144
Dickenson, Owens v.	105, 109, 167	— Macdonald v.	192
Dillon (Lord), Fallows v.	131	— Vyse v.	88, 89
— Nash v.	151	Foulkes, Jones v.	35
Dixon, Clough v.	34	Foxhall, Player v.	55
Dodds, Henderson v.	152, 153, 154	Francis, Penney v.	71
Dolman, Young v.	159	Fraser, Lovat v.	164
Douthwaite, Spensley v.	66	Frere, Talbot v.	166, 168
Dowbiggin, Fraser v.	37	Frowd, Moore v.	147
Doyle, Pollard v.	148	— David v.	113, 120
Duck, Widdowson v.	54	Fry, Story v.	164
Duckett, Taylor v.	21	Fryer, Hensman v.	157, 165
Dudding, Dimsdale v.	137	Fulford, Hilliard v.	139
Dudgeon, McArthur v.	91	Fulton, Lowry v.	33
Dudlow, Wildes v.	166		
Dunn, Thompson v.	60	GALLINI, Pott v.	74
Duprez, Veret v.	34	Gandy, Harris v.	70
Dyson, Pickles v.	192	Garrett, Gardner v.	76, 84
		Gatty, Phillipson v.	42
EADES, Hughes v.	13	Gaukroger, Berry v.	99
East, Fleming v.	131, 132	Gee, Carmichael v.	178
— Jolliffe v.	136	— Laming v.	16
Easton, Howard v.	142	Geldard, Robinson v.	176
Eastwood, Thomson v.	165	George, Rees v.	48, 130
Eckford, Haldane v.	32, 46	Gibbon, Roy v.	64
Edwards, Whittington v.	3	Gibbons, Berry v.	56, 58, 96
Eley, Bates v.	91	Gibson, Ferguson v.	55, 152, 166
Elliott, Beaney v.	131	Gilbey, Ottley v.	139
— Robinson v.	140	Gill, Alcock v.	87
— Stammers v.	146	— Wheeler v.	110
Ellis, Down v.	105	Gillespie, Perpetual Insur. Co. v.	19
Ellison, Glover v.	91	Gittings, Cooke v.	39
Elph, Stacey v.	33	Glanville, Taylor v.	142
Elsom, Thomas v.	89	Glynn, Spurway v.	119
Elstob, Morgan v.	112	Goode, Joseph v.	93, 153
Elworthy, Densem v.	43	Goodwin, Reeve v.	9, 61
Ennis, Waterton v.	198	Gordon, Rice v.	25
Evens, Payne v.	143	Graham, Bond v.	35
Everard, Dove v.	33, 34	— Harrison v.	33
Everest, Young v.	130	Grant, Heighington v.	143
		— Thomson v.	164, 167
FAIRLIE, Freeman v.	64	Gray, Polini v.	3
Falconer, Hull v.	114	Green, Fuller v.	140
Falkiner, Nicholson v.	151	— Rayner v.	33
Farlie, Lowe v.	36	Greenhill, Rump v.	4, 5
Fellows, Pinchard v.	154	Greenhough, Barraclough v.	14
Fiddon, Stafford v.	133	Greenwell, Woods v.	169
Field, Mayd v.	158	Gregory, Beardmore v.	39
— Woodgate v.	13, 50, 105, 197	Gregson, Cook v.	167
Finney, Morley v.	106	Griffin, Bowyer v.	144, 145
Fisher, Longbourne v.	127	Griffith, Thomas v.	113, 116

	PAGE
Groves, Towsey v.	31
Gudgeon, Linford v.	185, 188
Gurney, Boswell v.	107, 111, 173
— Harrison v.	82
Guy, Smith v.	125
Gwynne, James v.	124
HACON, Eames v.	36
Haddon, Angell v.	114
Haines, Austen v.	46
— Rex v.	13
Hallet, Hall v.	142
Halliley, Stammers v.	177
Hamilton, Griffiths v.	13
— Johnstone v.	38, 48, 49
Hammersley, Johnson v.	125
Hammett, King v.	141
Hammond, Pierce v.	99
Hampton, Scaffold v.	19
Hancock, Turner v.	141, 149
Handley, Foster v.	167
Hankinson, Sterndale v.	106, 110, 140
Harben, Godfrey v.	165
Hardaker, Stead v.	157
Harding, Livesey v.	196
Hardingham, Shaw v.	43
Hardy, Lockhart v.	106
Harmby, Cuthbert v.	46, 102
Harris, Dickins v.	37
— Harmer v.	145
— Parsons v.	19, 20
— Strange v.	60
— Thompson v.	156, 158
Harrison, Dickson v.	90
— Miles v.	159, 176
— Spensley v.	154
— Threlfall v.	155
— Yare v.	62
Harwood, Rankin v.	83
Haslam, O'Connor v.	165
Hastings, Shirreff v.	162
Hatfield, Stanton v.	153, 154
Hatton, Underwood v.	55
Hawke, Cardell v.	107
Hawtin, Dowd v.	127
Haynes, Flintoff v.	111, 133
— Yeomans v.	112
Headlam, Chaffers v.	62
Headland, Williams v.	183
Heathfield, Sander v.	167
Heaton, Wilson v.	159
Hebblethwaite, Berry v.	154
Helyar, Trethewy v.	157
Henderson, Carr v.	154
— Halliley v.	87
— Therry v.	70
Hennet, Furze v.	19, 71
Henniker, Wythe v.	175
Henning, Whittle v.	50

	PAGE
Herbert, Mirehouse v.	142
Hereford, Senior v.	19
Heslop, Hepworth v.	154
Hicks, Graves v.	178
Higginbottom, Chatham v.	197
Higgins, Doody v.	42, 43, 47
Hilder, Pelham v.	17
Hildick, Hipkins v.	169
Hill, Warburton v.	81
Hilliard, Clowes v.	25
— Eiffe v.	127
Hills, Cary v.	32, 33
Hinxman, Bridges v.	13
Hitchcock, McIlardy v.	69
Hobson, Philanthropic Society v.	137
Hodges, Young v.	11
Hogg, Lashley v.	10, 113
Holmes, Gaskell v.	130
Hope, Thompson v.	60
Hopkins, Williams v.	171
Horton, Richardson v.	166
Houston, Paynter v.	106
How, Jones v.	43
Howarth, Shuttleworth v.	157
Howell, Tardrew v.	152
Huber, Crompton v.	100
Hudson, Mutter v.	52, 53
— York, &c. Ry. Co. v.	89
Hughes, Arthur v.	36
— Wynne v.	73
Humberstone, Ritchie v.	75
Hume, Proudfoot v.	60
Hunasgeria Coffee Co., Cocq v.	78
Hunter, Gledhill v.	29
— Law v.	15, 16
— Pickford v.	74
Huntley (M.), Beauchamp (E.) v.	82, 84
Hutchinson, Booth v.	173
— Metcalfe v.	95, 164
ICKERINGILL, Hinsley v.	165
Iggulden, Lancefield v.	112, 157, 165
Ingleby, Carr v.	178
Ingledon, Humphreys v.	27
Innes, Sandilands v.	36
Iremonger, Barnewell v.	158
JACKSON, White v.	142
James, Rogers v.	27
Jee, Underwood v.	74
Jefferys, Williamson v.	44
Jenkins, Howells v.	175
— Symonds v.	61
Jenny, Olley v.	32
Jessop, Bluett v.	140
Jones, Palmer v.	144
— Peat v.	173
— Samuel v.	145
— Scott v.	165

TABLE OF CASES.

	PAGE		PAGE
Jones, Thomas v.	. 153, 155, 156	Lush, Sharp v.	93, 95, 159
Jukes, Jones v.	. . . 55	Lynch, Keaton v.	. . . 13
KEARTON, Dawson v.	. . . 173	McADAM, Simons v.	. . . 187
Keble, Graham v.	. . . 34	McAulay, Elmslie v.	. . . 26
Kennington, Cross v.	. . . 156	Macguire, Ashburner v.	. . . 179
Kerr, Thorne v.	. . . 9	Mackinlay, Ward v.	. . . 154
Kershaw, Williams v.	. . . 176	Mackrell, Barber v.	. . . 52
Key, Hughes v.	. . . 147	Maclaren, Carron Iron Co. v.	. . 83
Kightley, Howell v.	. . . 99	Maddison, Packwood v.	. 77, 138
Kilburn, Hankin v.	. . . 178	Mahood, Gee v.	. 150, 178
King, Cox v.	. . . 106	Maireau, Riboldi v.	. . . 36
— Hill v.	. . . 97	Malcott, King v.	. . . 26
Kinnaird, Alvanley (Lord) v.	. 123	Maltby, Cross v.	. . . 99
Kinton, Guidici v.	. . 18, 36	Manning, Purcell v.	. . . 99
Kirby, Turquand v.	. . . 25	Margerison, Bateman v.	. 39, 131
Knight, Chapman v.	. . . 190	Marriott, Bunting v.	. . . 183
Koehler, Rayner v.	. . . 38	— Moors v.	. . . 163
		Marsden, Eyre v.	. . . 158
LAING, West v.	. . . 6	— Ballard v.	. . . 146
Lake, Brown v.	. . 114, 125	Marsh, Goodrich v.	. . . 43
Lambert, Rawlings v.	. . . 39	Marshfield, Talbot v.	. 62, 143
Lane, Groves v.	. . . 34	Martin, Baker v.	. 55, 106
Latham, Hubbard v.	93, 95, 119, 130	— Young v.	. . . 158
Laurie, Chalmers v.	. . 45, 47	Mashiter, Sutton v.	. . . 106
Lavender, Greedy v.	. . . 150	Mason, Berkeley v.	. 3, 6, 35, 41
Lawes, A.-G. v.	. . 137, 157	— Chapman v.	. . . 84
Lawson, Sleight v.	. . 17, 75	— Trestrail v.	. . . 174
Lea, Hares v.	. . . 186	Matthew, McMurray v.	. . . 70
Leaf, Jackson v.	. . . 76	Maudesley, Drever v.	. . . 113
Leake, Daubney v.	. . 95, 130	Maugham, Martin v.	. . . 140
Leathes, Mortlock v.	. . . 63	Maxwell, Graham v.	. 76, 82
Lee, Gilbert v.	. 142, 143, 144	May, Croxton v.	. . . 182
Legge, Bagot v.	. . . 158	— Halton v.	. . . 178
Leigh, Bedford v.	. . . 9	— Hicks v.	. . . 114
— Roweliffe v.	. . . 106	Mayer, Ancaster D. v.	164, 174
Le Page, Ostell v.	. . . 79	Mayhew, Rowles v.	. . . 151
Lett, Stahlschmidt v.	. . . 108	Meanock, Stott v.	. . . 97
Lewis, Donne v.	. . 164, 165	Measures, Green v.	. . . 47
— Evans v.	. . . 131	Meddowcroft, Perry v.	. . . 157
— Leeds v.	. . . 87	Meux, Dorrett v.	. . . 14
— McHenry v.	. . . 79	Mew, Doe d. Bassett v.	. . . 14
— Plunkett v.	. . . 72	Michael, Doe d. Ashburnham v.	. 15
Leycester, Booth v.	. . . 82	Micklethwait, Birks v.	. . . 144
Lightfoot, Harris v.	. . 70, 71	Middlemiss, Morgan v.	. . . 139
Lindsay, Ambler v.	. . . 38	Midland Ry. Co., Newton v.	. . 27
Linley, Taylor v.	. . . 159	Miller, Morton v.	. . . 21
Littlewood, Garland v.	. . . 52	— Sanders v.	. . . 158
Lloyd, Eustace v.	. . . 82	— Virtue v.	. 69, 71
Lombard Bank, Cousins v.	. 189	Mills, Joel v.	. . . 30
London (Corporation of), Chilton v.	19	Mockett, Breton v.	. . . 21
Longrigg, Hetherington v.	. 18, 68	Mole. Bourne v.	. 64, 66
Lord, London Syndicate v.	. 66, 67	Montgomery, Thomas v.	. . . 182
Lovell, Levy v.	. . . 170	Montriou, Meyer v.	. . . 64
Lowry, Ogden v.	. . . 7	Moorat, De la Salle v.	. . . 7
Lucas, Parkinson v.	. . . 124	Moore, Bennett v.	. 18, 68
Luke, Kitto v.	. . . 145	— Strong v.	41, 47, 49
Lukes, Wright v.	. . . 66	Morgan, Smith v.	. . . 163
Luntley, Gouldsmith v.	. . 181	Morrall, Jones v.	. 16, 52

TABLE OF CASES.

	PAGE
Morris, Dean v.	158
— Hales, v.	52
— Jenner v.	90
— Moore v.	40
— Rowsell v.	29, 38
Morse, Scurry v.	32
Mortan, Dawkins v.	88, 90
Mossop, Prosser v.	11
Motley, Bick v.	97
Moxsy, Sewell v.	31
Mullineux, Turner v.	145
Munnings, Philippo v.	165
Murray, Mayer v.	16, 17, 53
Musgrave, Clarkson v.	190
Muzeen, Wormald v.	178
NATIONAL Provcl. Bank, Newell v.	81
Naylor, Mersey Steel & Iron Co. v.	170, 173
Nelthorp or Nathorp, Hoe v.	13
Nerinckx, Van Ghelnive v.	161, 163
Nettleship, Bradford v.	181
Neville, Parsons v.	42
Newport, Sillibourne v.	56
Newton, Golden v.	22
— Heatley v.	90
— Orr v.	33
Nicholson, Prince v.	58
Nickalls, Merry v.	183
Noble, Garrett v.	18
Norris, Robertson v.	89
— Wooldridge v.	25
North, Price v.	122
Nuttall, Lee v.	55, 56, 163, 170
OGLANDER, Harmood v.	164, 165
Oliveira, Beaumont v.	176
Ordish, Wood v.	157, 165
Ogles, Rice v.	151
Orpen, Beswick v.	146
Orton, Lamble v.	134
Ottoman Bank, Bank of Turkey v.	60
Owen, Cradock v.	134
Oxborrow, Whitmore v.	25
Oxenham, Glass v.	38
PALMER, Johnson v.	9
— Matthews v.	75
Parker, Cash v.	32
— Cresswell v.	36
— Sparling v.	176
— Watson v.	25, 43
Parry, Phillips v.	164
Parsons, Roupell v.	20
Partridge, Ingle v.	65
Pascoe, Norvall v.	72, 124
Patent Lionite Co., Thomas v.	172
Paterson, Jennings v.	42
Patterson, Flood v.	35

	PAGE
Pease, Jackson v.	157
Pemberton, Woolf v.	31
Pennington, Freeman v.	30, 42
Penny, Greenwood v.	175
Perry, Palmer v.	131
Perssé, Hill v.	190
Peterson, Gwyer v.	75
Pfeil, Walters v.	14, 27
Phillips, Chester v.	43
— Clark v.	53
Piffard, Vaurenen v.	4, 75
Pillen, Stephens v.	146
Piper, Cradock v.	147
— Mitchelson v.	55, 168
Pittman, Brown v.	32
Plestow, Davey v.	76
Poole, Danby v.	15
— Smith v.	108
Powell, Bolton v.	26
— Rogers v.	106
Power, Tipping v.	151, 152
Powys-Keck, Lilford (Lord) v.	175
Poyser, Cast v.	92, 108
Prendergast, Johnson v.	133
Prescott, Forrest v.	164
Price, Gresham v.	144
— Hayward v.	92
Priddon, Miller v.	13
Pridham, Luckraft v.	157
Prior, Fleming v.	123
Pritchard, Lodge v.	151
Proudfoot, Parkin v.	181
Pryer, Worraker v.	1, 9
Pryke, Cobbold v.	80, 184
Pye, Maddison v.	158
Radcliffe, European Assurance Society v.	58
Raw, Ward v.	188
Rawlings, Tennant v.	189
Rayson, Wickenden v.	196
Redman, Fuller v.	109
Reay, Middleton v.	54
Rees, Morgan v.	190
Reilly, Lockhart v.	147
Remoldson, Turner v.	2, 184
Reynal, Fowler v.	132
Reynolds, Brooks v.	81
— Mitford v.	101
— Morshead v.	112
— Partington v.	5, 49, 52
— Thompson v.	27
Rich, Wills v.	27
Richards, Harrison v.	126
Ricketts, Man v.	15
Ridge, Sims v.	123
Rigden, Vane (E.) v.	58
Rigg, Wadham v.	6, 88
Ringham, Parker v.	163

TABLE OF CASES.

	PAGE
Robarts, Anon. v.	54
Roberts, Burton v.	81
— Fowler v.	81
Robins, Collis v.	152
Robinson, Creasor v.	39
— Hamp v.	37
— Shearman v.	26
— Whitaker v.	84
Roch, Tombs v.	165
Rochfort, Sperling v.	165
Roe, Manton v.	140
Rogers, Barker v.	43, 114, 117
Rolfe, Chester v.	26
Row, Watson v.	147
Rowland, Clegg v.	4, 37
Royle, Fryer v.	9
Rudd, Sharman v.	55
Rumney, Lewis v.	108
Rundell, Hume v.	14
Rusbridger, Governesses' Benevolent Institution v.	61, 157
Russell, Crowle v.	81
— Maltby v.	53
— Marsh v.	182
Rutland, Gage v.	144
Rye, Brown v.	187
Rylance, Jacubs v.	146
Sadler, Bain v.	168
— Morse v.	42
— Wyatt v.	126
Sage, Budgen v.	72
Sampson, Catley v.	30
Sanders, Carter v.	30
Sanderson, Eglin v.	142, 143
Scard, Heugh v.	142
Schweitzer, Venables v.	92
Scott, Paterson v.	175
Searles, Hatch v.	112
Seddons, Parkin v.	28
Selby, Shortley v.	154
Seligmann, Walker v.	48
Selkirk, Shirwin v.	107, 162
Serra, Basevi v.	150
Sewell, Ashley v.	4, 6, 35
Shaftesbury (E.), Webb v.	54, 56
Shakeshaft, Hollingsworth v.	16, 133
Sharp, Bentall v.	77
Sharratt, Wyatt v.	63
Shaw, Brown v.	189
Sherborn, Passingham v.	52
Sherry, Newton v.	4, 37
Sherson, Bothamley v.	174
Shirley, Fisher v.	163
Shore, Humble v.	12, 42
Sidebottom, Earle v.	122
— Mellor v.	19
Siggers, Lucas v.	78, 79
Silverwood, Birks v.	186

	PAGE
Simons, Cattell v.	114
Slagg, Manchester V. Paving Co. v.	89
Slater, Cumming v.	72
Sloane, Ladbroke v.	76
Smalwood, Walker v.	59
Smart, British Mutual Investment Co. v.	166
— Hooper v.	116
Smith, Bear v.	132
— Bridson v.	19
— Burrell v.	155, 167
— Farrell v.	37
— Gilbert v.	19
— Mullins v.	119
— Sexton v.	81
— Tickner v.	143
— Whitney v.	16, 48
Société Gén. d'Électricité, Werderman v.	40
Somerville, Greig v.	115
Southgate, Taylor v.	74
Sontten, Rogers v.	119
Sowerby, Woods v.	29
Spashett, Scott v.	181
Spencer, Webster v.	26, 27
Spensley, Douthwaite v.	66
Spickett, Pearce v.	20
Spilsbury, Smith v.	5
Spurgin, Prowse v.	121
Squire, Wilson v.	137, 157
Stafford, Davenport v.	51, 132
Stainton, Maclaren v.	79
Stannard, Bolton v.	43
Steer, Newland v.	108
Stein, Silver v.	34
Stelfox, Bradley v.	73, 74
Steppings, Nokes v.	64
Stevens, Hunt v.	13, 27
Steward, White v.	44
Stewart, Crowder v.	56, 163, 166
Stirling-Maxwell, Cartwright v.	36
Stoddart, Sanderson v.	151
Stone, Brown v.	117
Stonehewer, Goldsmid v.	42, 43
Storer, Armstrong v.	10, 154
Storie, Handford v.	10
Storr, Newmarch v.	174
Stotherd, Loomes v.	166, 167
Stratton, Cotterell v.	149
Stroud, Brookes v.	27
Strousberg, Costa Rica (Rep.) v.	92
Stubbs, Hanson v.	163
Studholme, Todd v.	116
Sturrock, Lee v.	47
Sturt, Wormsley v.	91
Swinburne, West v.	76
Swire, Mellor v.	72, 73, 75
Sykes, Meakin v.	20

TABLE OF CASES.

	PAGE
Tapson, Raymond v.	91, 92
Tatham, Ross v.	183
Taylor, Fenner v.	139
— Gaunt v.	147, 151
— Mackenzie v.	139
Teasdale, Dickenson v.	165
Terrett, Goodchild v.	13
Terrington, Grace v.	44
Thacker, Drewry v.	80
Thompson, Cockburn v.	44
— Egremont v.	46
— Tuckley v.	154
Thorington, Sleech v.	119
Tibbut, Briant v.	99
Tildesley, Salter v.	70
Timbrell, Spackman v.	166
Timms, re	85
Tiplady, Ridley v.	95, 124
Titmuss, Field v.	105
Tofield, Bray v.	9, 110
Toleman, Waddell v.	171
Tonkin, Luke v.	17, 53
Topham, Pemberton v.	140
Topp, Davies v.	168
Towgood, Anson v.	74
— Shepherd v.	74
Townsend, Travers v.	142
Trask, Lewis v.	144, 145
Trollope, Alston v.	109
Trotter, Dowbiggin v.	71, 122
— Thompson v.	22
Turner, Bell v.	129
— Colman v.	7
— Haukin v.	120
— Leigh v.	134
Turnley, Kennedy v.	54
Turquand, Whitmore v.	61
Vanderhorst, Shewen v.	55, 108, 109
Van Heythuysen, Stone v.	126
Wait, Baker v.	185
Walker, Hamond v.	60, 62
— Hill v.	55
Waller, Adams v.	109
Wallis, Braithwaite v.	61, 181
— Fordham v.	175
Wallworth, Powell v.	122
Walrond, Guthrie v.	32
Ward, Davey v.	57
— Frost v.	71
— Hutchinson v.	191, 192
— Overington v.	32, 33
— Richardson v.	134
Warth, Ibberson v.	181
Watkins, Bayliss v.	99
— Bush v.	132

	PAGE
Watson, Ware v.	98
Watts, Duncan v.	177
— Penny v.	38, 39
— Sellon v.	157, 165
— Smith v.	92
Weatherstone, Isaacs v.	68
Webster, Gatti v.	23
Weightman, Wood v.	103
Weldhen, Lyall v.	78
Wells, Tolputt v.	58
West, Bray v.	152
Westbrook, Aldridge v.	147, 154
Weston, Neve v.	74
Wharmley, Cuthbert v.	102
Whichcord, Smith v.	79
White, Hargraves v.	12
— Jervis v.	67
— Morley v.	33
— Richmond v.	56, 58, 156
— Smith v.	26
Whitear, Gunnell v.	138
Whittaker, Day v.	192
Whittington, Coote v.	38
Wieland, Barnard v.	19
Wilcock, Lee v.	97
Wilde, Harvey v.	164
Williams, Courtenay v.	146
— Davies v.	187
— Lucas v.	82
Wills, Fenton v.	157
Wilson, Briggs v.	109
— Dean v.	124
Winch, Ratcliffe v.	80, 84
Windsor, Lincoln v.	148
Winstanley, Mickelthwait v.	93, 106
Winterbotham, Aylmer v.	137
Wirral Highway Board, Mason v.	189
Withers, Buller v.	181
— Dighton v.	155
Wolferstan, Jervis v.	117
Wood, Ashton v.	99
— Bartlett v.	136
Woodbridge, Walters v.	142
Woodward, Walker v.	15
Woolwich Building Soc., Button v.	189
Wreford, Knapman v.	146
Wright, Dean v.	28
— Graves v.	28
— Whitaker v.	106, 107
Wyatt, Dixon v.	125
Wyld, Ward v.	186
Wynne, Hughes v.	165
Yates, Dicks v.	150
Yorke, Brewer v.	183
Young, Adair v.	183
— Hunter v.	37, 116
— Pigott v.	7, 8
— Skottowe v.	181

ABBREVIATIONS

USED IN REFERENCE TO

LAW REPORTS AND TEXT BOOKS.

ABBREVIATIONS.	NAME OF WORK, ETC.
Ad. & El.	Adolphus & Ellis' Reports.
Ambl.	Ambler's Reports.
App. Cas.	Law Reports, Appeal Cases.
Atk.	Atkyns' Reports.
B. & Al.	Barnewall & Alderson's Reports.
B. & B.	Ball & Beatty's Reports (Ireland).
B. & C.	Barnewall & Cresswell's Reports.
Beav. or Be.	Beavan's Reports.
Bing.	Bingham's Reports.
Bro. C. C.	Brown's Chancery Reports.
C. B.	Common Bench Reports, or Manning, Granger & Scott's Reports.
C. D.	Law Reports, Chancery Division.
C. P. D.	Law Reports, Common Pleas Division.
C. P. Coop.	C. P. Cooper's Cases, *temp.* Cottenham.
C. & L.	Connor & Lawson's Reports (Ireland).
Car. & P.	Carrington & Payne's Reports.
Ch.	Law Reports, Chancery Appeals.
Ch. Cas.	Cases in Chancery.
Ch. Rep.	Reports in Chancery.
Cl. & F.	Clarke & Finnelly's Reports.
Coll.	Collyer's Reports.
Comp. Exors.	Walker's Compendium of the Law of Executors.
Cons. Ord.	Consolidated Orders of the Court of Chancery.
Cr. & Ph.	Craig & Phillips' Reports.
Curt.	Curteis' Ecclesiastical Reports.
Dan. or Dan. Pr.	Daniell's Chancery Practice.
Dan. Forms	Daniell's Chancery Forms.
De G. F. & J.	De Gex, Fisher, & Jones' Reports.
De G. & J.	De Gex & Jones' Reports.
De G. J. & S.	De Gex, Jones, & Smith's Reports.
De G. M. & G.	De Gex, Macnaghten, & Gordon's Reports.
De G. & Sm.	De Gex & Smale's Reports.
Dick.	Dickens' Reports.
Dow	Dow's Reports.
Dr.	Drewry's Reports.
Dr. & Sm.	Drewry & Smale's Reports.
Dr. & War.	Drury & Warren's Reports (Ireland).

ABBREVIATIONS.	NAME OF WORK, ETC.
Eq.	Law Reports, Equity Cases.
Ex. D.	Law Reports, Exchequer Division.
Giff.	Giffard's Reports.
Gilb.	Gilbert's Cases in Law and in Equity.
H. L. C.	Clark's House of Lords Reports.
H. & M.	Hemming & Miller's Reports.
H. & N.	Hurlstone & Norman's Reports.
H. & Tw.	Hall & Twells' Reports.
Ha.	Hare's Reports.
Ir. Ch.	Irish Law and Equity Reports, New Series.
Ir. Eq.	Irish Law & Equity Reports.
J. & H.	Johnson & Hemming's Reports.
Jo. & L.	Jones & Latouche's Reports (Ireland).
J. & W.	Jacob & Walker's Reports.
Jac.	Jacob's Reports.
Johns.	Johnson's Reports.
Jur.	Jurist Reports.
Jur. N. S.	,, ,, New Series.
K. & J.	Kay & Johnson's Reports.
Kay	Kay's Reports.
Ke.	Keen's Reports.
L. J. O. S.	Law Journal, Old Series.
L. J.	,, ,, New Series.
L. R.	The Law Reports.
L. T.	Law Times Reports, Old Series; and New Series, from Vol. 35.
L. T. N. S.	,, ,, New Series.
Ld. Ray.	Lord Raymond's Reports.
M. & Cr.	Mylne & Craig's Reports.
M. & K.	Mylne & Keen's Reports.
M. & S.	Maule & Selwyn's Reports.
McCl. & Y.	McCleland & Young's Reports.
Mac. & G.	Macnaghten & Gordon's Reports.
Madd.	Maddock's Reports.
Mer.	Merivale's Reports.
Mo. & Ma.	Moody & Malkin's Reports.
Moll.	Molloy's Reports (Ireland).
Moo.	Moody's Chancery Cases.
N. R.	New Reports.
N. & M.	Nevill & Manning's Reports.
O.	Rules and Orders of the Supreme Court.
P. D.	Law Reports, Probate Division.
P. Wms.	Peere Williams' Reports.
Pemb.	Pemberton's Judgments & Orders.
Ph.	Phillips' Reports.
Prec. Ch.	Precedents in Chancery (Finch).
Q. B.	Adolphus & Ellis; Queen's Bench Reports, New Series.
Q. B. D.	Law Reports, Queen's Bench Division.
R. & M.	Russell & Mylne's Reports.
Russ.	Russell's Reports.
S. & S.	Simons and Stuart's Reports.
Salk.	Salkeld's Reports.
Sch. & Lef.	Schoales & Lefroy's Reports.
Set. or Seton	Seton's Decrees.
Sim.	Simons' Reports.
Sim. N. S.	,, ,, New Series.
Skinn.	Skinner's Reports.
Sm. & G.	Smale & Giffard's Reports.
Sw.	Swanston's Reports.
Sw. & Tr.	Swabey & Tristram's Reports.
T. & R.	Turner & Russell's Reports.

ABBREVIATIONS.	NAME OF WORK, ETC.
Taunt.	Taunton's Reports.
Ves. sen.	Vesey's, sen., Reports.
Ves.	Vesey's, jun., Reports.
W. N.	Law Reports, Weekly Notes.
W. R.	Weekly Reporter.
Wh. & Tud.	White & Tudor's Leading Cases.
Y. & C. C.	Younge & Collyer's Chancery Cases.
Y. & C. Ex.	Younge & Collyer's Exchequer Cases.
Younge	Younge's Reports.

ADDENDA AND CORRIGENDA.

Page 4, n. (r), *dele* "*Wood* v. *Wood*, 21 W. R. 135."

,, 23, *l.* 19, *for* "51," *read* "52."

,, 54, n. (c), *add* a reference to *Eastwood* v. *Clarke*, 31 W. R. 417; W. N. 1883, 44, where the Irish decision is followed.

,, 71, n. (o), *add* a reference to *Re Prime's Estate*, 48 L. T. 208.

,, 105, last *l.*, *add* "But the rule does not apply to trials by jury of claims against the estate; *Lawrence* v. *Rowley*, C. A. April 3, 1883."

,, ,, n. (s), *add* a reference to *Wynne-Finch* v. *Wynne-Finch*, 48 L. T. 129; W. N. 1883, 56.

,, 143, *l.* 22, *add* "A creditor, plaintiff in an administration action against an executor *de son tort* who declines to prove the will by which he is appointed executor, is entitled to have his costs of a motion for a receiver, pending a grant of probate, paid by the executor; *Foster* v. *Davis*, 31 W. R. 411."

,, 147, n. (e), *add* "See, however, *ante*, p. 145, (o) and (p)."

,, 171, *l.* 17, *add* "But when a secured creditor proves for his debt and values his security, and his proof is rejected on the ground that less is due to him than the amount of his valuation, he is remitted to all his former rights, and may retain out of his security more than the amount of his valuation; *Williams* v. *Hopkins*, (3), W. N. 1883, 53; 31 W. R. 495."

,, 173, n. (h), *add* a reference to *Green* v. *Smith*, 22 C. D. 586; 48 L. T. 254; 31 W. R. 413, where the proper course of proceeding with reference to the mutual-credit clause is pointed out.

,, 180, n. (d). It is hardly necessary to state that the reference is to Lord Romilly and Sir George Jessel (to whom allusion is also made, p. 143, l. 3), whose death the profession will not soon cease to lament.

ADMINISTRATION ACTIONS.

CHAPTER I.

INSTITUTION OF PROCEEDINGS FOR ADMINISTRATION.

A. *By Originating Summons.*

a. *As to Personal Estate.*

By the 45th section of the Chancery Procedure Act, 1852 (*a*), it is enacted that it shall be lawful for any person claiming to be a creditor (*b*), or a specific, pecuniary, or residuary legatee, or the next of kin, or some or one of the next of kin, of a deceased person, to apply for and obtain, *as of course*, without bill or claim filed (*i.e.*, when translated into the nomenclature of the present practice, without suing out a writ of summons), or any other preliminary proceeding, a summons (*c*) from the Master of the Rolls (*d*), or any of the Vice-Chancellors (*e*), requiring the executor or administrator, as the

A. Administration summons.
a. Personal estate.

(*a*) 15 & 16 Vict. c. 86.
(*b*) Under the old practice, the Court required all parties interested to be present; but, where the parties were too numerous, it allowed one member of the class to sue on behalf of the rest. That was the theory of creditors' suits (*per* Jessel, M. R., *Worraker* v. *Pryer*, 2 C. D. p. 110).
(*c*) For Form of Summons, see Appendix, *post*, p. 193.

(*d*) The Master of the Rolls, having been transferred to the Court of Appeal (44 & 45 Vict. c. 68, s. 2), and having thus lost his original jurisdiction, can no longer issue this summons.
(*e*) Whose jurisdiction is now by the Judicature Act, 1873, ss. 16 (1), 34 (3), transferred to and vested in the Chancery Division of the High Court of Justice.

case may be, of such deceased person to attend before him at chambers for the purpose of showing cause why an order for the administration of the personal estate of the deceased should not be granted; and, upon proof by affidavit of the due service of such summons, or on the appearance in person or by his solicitor or counsel of such executor or administrator, and upon proof by affidavit of such other matters, if any, as such judge shall require, it shall be lawful for such judge, if *in his discretion* he shall think fit so to do, to make the *usual* order for the administration of the estate of the deceased, with such variations, if any, as the circumstances of the case may require; and the order so made shall have the force and effect of a decree to the like effect made on the hearing of a cause or claim between the said parties, provided that such judge shall have full discretionary power to grant or refuse such order, or to give any special directions touching the carriage or execution of such order, and, in the case of applications for any such order by two or more different persons or classes of persons, to grant the same to such one or more of the claimants or of the classes of claimants as he may think fit; and, if the judge shall think proper, the carriage of the order may subsequently be given to such party interested, and upon such terms as the judge may direct; see *post*, Ch. X.

Assignees may obtain the summons.

The words of the section which define the persons who may initiate proceedings under it have received a liberal interpretation. They mean all those persons (including assignees) who represent the several interests there stated (*f*). Although not strictly within the words of sections 45, 47, it is the established practice to make administration orders on the application of persons claiming under persons therein mentioned, and against the repre-

---

(*f*) *Per* Malins, V.-C., *Turner* v. *Rennoldson*, 16 Eq. 40.

sentatives of deceased executors (*g*). The doubt on this point, which was raised, but not solved, in *Whittington* v. *Edwards* (*h*), is now therefore disposed of.

The summons must be served seven clear days before the return thereof upon the executor or administrator of the deceased, who is the only person to be served therewith (*i*). A duplicate or copy of the summons shall, previously to the service thereof, be filed in the Record and Writ Clerk's office ; and no service thereof upon any executor or administrator shall be of any validity, unless the copy so served shall be stamped with a stamp of such office indicating the filing thereof (*j*). Where, from any cause, the summons may not have been served seven clear days before the return thereof, an indorsement may be made upon it and upon a copy thereof stamped for service, appointing a new time for the party not before served to attend at the chambers of the Judge ; such indorsements shall be sealed at the Judge's chambers, and the service of the copy so indorsed and sealed shall have the same force and effect as the service of any original summons ; and where a party has been served before such indorsement, the hearing thereof may, upon the return of the summons, be adjourned to the new time so appointed (*k*). The party served shall, before he is heard in chambers, enter an appearance in the Record and Writ Clerk's office, and give notice thereof (*l*). If when summoned to attend the Judge in chambers he fail so to attend, whether upon the return of the summons or at any time appointed for the consideration or further con-

Representatives of the accounting representative may be defendants.

Upon whom it must be served.

Copy to be filed.

Extension of time for appearance.

Appearance to be entered.

Court may make order ex parte in default of appearance.

(*g*) Daniell, 1071, n. (*p*).
(*h*) 3 De G. & J. 245, 247.
(*i*) Cons. Ord. XXXV. r. 7 ; *Berkeley* v. *Mason*, 19 Eq. 467. There is no objection to proceedings against the Crown, where the Treasury solicitor has taken out administration to the deceased, being initiated by summons under the Chancery Procedure Act ; *Polini* v. *Gray*, 22 W. R. 255.
(*j*) Chancery Procedure Act, 1852, s. 46.
(*k*) Cons. Ord. XXXV. r. 8.
(*l*) Ibid. r. 9.

sideration of the matter, the Judge may proceed *ex parte*, if, considering the nature of the case, he think it expedient so to do (*m*).

Summons by executor against co-executor.

Although the 45th section, which requires the executors and administrators to be made defendants, gives legal personal representatives acting together no power of initiative, yet one of them, *if also a beneficiary*, may take out the summons against the other, as was done in *Vanrenen* v. *Piffard* (*n*), where the plaintiff who had not proved the will, sued as residuary legatee, and submitted to account as executor; see Daniell, 1076, note (*s*). Under Sir G. Turner's Act (*o*), as amended by 23 & 24 Vict. c. 38, s. 14, the Court may, at the instance of a personal representative, direct an account to be taken of the debts and liabilities affecting the *personal* estate of the deceased, if no other proceeding for administration be pending (*p*). As, however, an executor or administrator cannot be sued by a creditor, or even by the next of kin (*q*), after having issued advertisements under 22 & 23 Vict. c. 35, ss. 27—32, and distributed the assets amongst the persons claiming in answer to such advertisements, or of whose claims he may have had notice *aliunde* (*r*), these provisions are not now acted on.

Discretion of judge to refuse order for administration upon summons.

The Judge's complete discretion to refuse to exercise the jurisdiction conferred by the section has been fully recognised—*e.g.*, by Knight-Bruce, L. J. (*s*), Romilly, M. R. (*t*), and Kindersley V.-C. (*u*).

The jurisdiction only exercised in simple cases.

The Court only makes the common order on summons, and will not make it if there are complicated questions in

(*m*) Cons. Ord. XXXV., r. 10.
(*n*) 13 W. R. 425.
(*o*) 13 & 14 Vict. c. 35, s. 19.
(*p*) See Dan. 1076—1082, and Seton, 846, 847.
(*q*) *Clegg* v. *Rowland*, 3 Eq. 368; *Newton* v. *Sherry*, 1 C. P. D. 246.

(*r*) *Wood* v. *Wood*, 21 W. R. 135; *Re Land Credit Co. of Ireland*, W. N. 1872, 210.
(*s*) *Sewell* v. *Ashley*, 3 De G. M. & G. p. 936.
(*t*) *Rump* v. *Greenhill*, 20 Beav. p. 520.
(*u*) *Re Newbery*, 10 W. R. p. 379.

the case (v), or if a release be pleaded, there being no jurisdiction to set a release aside on summons (x), or if it is sought to make a defendant liable on a balance of account, or where there is a point of construction on the will to be decided (y), or where any person is *primâ facie* a necessary party in addition to the executor (z). The only order that can be made on summons under this section is the usual one — that the executor or administrator shall account for the personal estate which has been received by him — and it confers no jurisdiction to make on summons in chambers an order that he shall account for what, without his wilful neglect or default, he might have received, or to make him accountable for any misconduct. The words "with such variations, if any, as the circumstances of the case may require" are only intended to enable the Judge to adapt the precise terms of the usual order to the circumstances of the case, and not to enable him to pronounce any other than the usual administration judgment. If such a special judgment is desired, the party seeking it must proceed by writ (a). So, under an order made on summons, an executor or trustee cannot be charged with breach of trust, though the chief clerk's certificate has provided the materials for such a charge on further consideration (b), nor can he be surcharged on the ground of constructive receipt (c), nor charged upon an admission of assets (d). However, where a decree has been made, the Judge *may*, if he thinks fit, decide questions

<small>Only the usual order can be made;</small>

<small>e.g., no account for wilful default.</small>

<small>Questions arising out of usual order may be determined;</small>

(v) *Rump* v. *Greenhill*, 20 Beav. 519.
(x) *Acaster* v. *Anderson*, 19 Beav. 161.
(y) *Smith* v. *Spilsbury*, 1 Dr. & Sm. 153.
(z) *Re Sampson*, 14 W. R. 472.
(a) See *per* Kindersley, V.-C., *Partington* v. *Reynolds*, 4 Dr. p. 259;

Blakeley v. *Blakeley*, 1 Jur. N. S. 368; *re Fryer*, 3 K. & J. 317.
(b) *Deleraine* v. *Childe*, 6 Jur. N. S. 118; and see *post*, p. 52.
(c) *Peterson* v. *Peterson*, 16 L. T. 377.
(d) *Re Wiltshire's Estate*, 8 W. R. 133.

properly arising out of such decree (e); but even then, if the Judge sees that there are questions depending on controverted facts, or questions partly of fact and partly of law, he ought to say, in the exercise of his discretion, that the matter should be made the subject of an action (*f*).

but an administration action will generally be directed.

Administration of property appointed by will of feme covert.

An order may be made on summons for the administration of the property appointed by the will of a married woman under a power contained in a deed (*g*) or will (*h*).

Service of summons out of jurisdiction.

Appointment of guardian ad litem to lunatic defendant.

An administration summons, relating to stocks and shares in England, was allowed to be served out of the jurisdiction, as being a "suit" within 4 & 5 Will. 4, c. 82 (*i*), and a guardian *ad litem* may be appointed for a lunatic defendant to such a summons (*k*).

Where an administration summons has been refused on the merits, the plaintiff cannot, it has been held, institute an action for the same object in another branch of the Court; if dissatisfied he must, it is said, appeal from the order (*l*). It is respectfully submitted that this decision is not altogether sound. It is absolutely in the discretion of a judge to grant or refuse the common order on summons (*m*); but it is at least doubtful whether he is not *bound* to grant it in an action properly constituted, at the suit of a competent plaintiff (*n*). Moreover, the grant or refusal of the order on summons being discretionary, it is questionable whether an appeal against such a refusal would in any case lie.

(*e*) *West* v. *Laing*, 3 Dr. 331; *Wadham* v. *Rigg*, 2 Dr. & Sm. 78.
(*f*) *West* v. *Laing, ubi supra*.
(*g*) *Sewell* v. *Ashley*, 3 De G. M. & G. 933.
(*h*) *Berkeley* v. *Mason*, 19 Eq. 467; compare *re Newbery*, 10 W. R. 378.
(*i*) Since repealed: see now O. XI.; *Cohen* v. *Alean*, 1 De G. J. & S. 398.
(*k*) *Osbaldiston* v. *Crowther*, 1 Sm. & G. App. 12.
(*l*) *Thompson* v. *Thompson*, 11 W. R. 797.
(*m*) *Ante*, p. 4.
(*n*) *Post*, Ch. iii.

b. *As to Real Estate.*

By the 47th section of the Chancery Procedure Act, 1852, it was enacted that it should be lawful for any person claiming to be a creditor of any deceased person, or interested under his will, to apply for and obtain in a summary way, in the manner thereinbefore provided with respect to the personal estate of a deceased person, an order for the administration of the real estate of a deceased person, where the whole of such real estate was by devise vested in trustees, who were by the will empowered to sell such real estate, and authorised to give receipts for the rents and profits thereof, and for the produce of the sale of such real estate; and that all the provisions thereinbefore contained with respect to the application for such order in relation to the personal estate of a deceased person, and consequent thereon, should extend and be applicable to an application for such order as last thereinbefore mentioned with respect to real estate. The references are to the 45th section, *q. v. ante*, p. 1.

b. Real estate.

The Court has jurisdiction under the 47th section to make an order on summons for the administration and sale of a testator's real estate, where the will only gives the executors a power to sell such estate and to give receipts, without vesting it in them by devise (*o*), or where it contains a clause conditionally postponing the sale for a fixed period (*p*), or where the devise is made subject to the payment of debts, funeral and testamentary expenses (*q*).

Jurisdiction where executors have only power of sale,

or sale is conditionally directed to be postponed.

The section, it will be observed, makes no provision for administering the real estate of an *intestate*.

No jurisdiction in case of intestacy.

(*o*) *Colman* v. *Turner*, 10 Eq. 230.
(*p*) *De la Salle* v. *Moorat*, 11 Eq. 8.
(*q*) *Ogden* v. *Lowry*, 4 W. R. 156; *Pigott* v. *Young*, 7 W. R. 235.

B. *By Writ.*

B. Administration action.

It appears from what has gone before that procedure by originating summons is of limited operation. In all cases in which that procedure cannot properly be resorted to, proceedings for the administration of the estates of deceased persons must be initiated by writ, which is the first step in a formal action (*r*). Such a writ must be

Title of writ.

intituled "In the matter of the estate of A. B., deceased" (*s*), as well as between the parties. It should be issued for the Chancery Division of the High Court (*t*), and marked with the name of some one of the Judges of

Indorsements on writ;

that Division (*u*). It must be indorsed with a statement of the nature of the claim made, or of the relief or remedy required in the action (*x*); but such indorsement need not set forth the precise ground of complaint, or the precise remedy or relief to which the plaintiff considers himself

claiming that accounts be taken;

entitled (*y*). The writ may, if desired, be further indorsed with a claim that the executors' or trustees' accounts be taken (*z*): such an indorsement, though optional, is generally advisable, as giving the plaintiff the benefit of the summary procedure under O. XV., presently noticed (*a*).

for a receiver;

It has also been held that the claim for the appointment of a receiver should be indorsed, when that is a substan-

showing representative capacity of parties.

tial object of the action (*b*). And it should be borne in mind, as specially applicable to administration actions, that if the plaintiff sues or the defendant or any of the defendants is sued in a representative capacity, the indorsement must show in what capacity the plaintiff or defendant sues

---

(*r*) O. I. r. 1. An action commenced by writ may, in a fitting case, be adjourned to, and carried out in, chambers (*Pigott* v. *Young*, 7 W. R. 235).
(*s*) *Eyre* v. *Cox*, 24 W. R. 317.
(*t*) Jud. Act, 1873, s. 34 (3).

(*u*) O. V., rr. 4, 4*a*.
(*x*) O. II., r. 1.
(*y*) O. III., r. 2.
(*z*) O. III., r. 8.
(*a*) *Post*, p. 22.
(*b*) *Colebourne* v. *Colebourne*, 1 C. D. 690.

FOR ADMINISTRATION.

or is sued (c). Where the action is brought by a creditor, who seeks administration of both real and personal estates, Hall, V.-C., held that it was not necessary for him to indorse his writ as suing on behalf of himself *and all other the* *creditors* (d); but Jessel, M.R. (e), and Bacon, V.-C. (f), have declined to follow this decision, and it must now be taken as settled practice that, in such an action, the plaintiff's claim should be expressed to be on behalf of all the creditors, though, if the statement of claim states that he so sues, the writ, if it has omitted to state it, need not be amended (g); indeed, as a general rule, where a statement of claim has been delivered, it is unnecessary to amend the indorsement on the writ to correspond (h).

Special indorsement necessary in creditors' actions for administration of real and personal estate;

The Court never administers the real (i) assets of a testator on behalf of any one creditor (k).

Where, however, the action is for administration of the personal estate only, a creditor may sue on his own behalf alone, by analogy to the practice under an originating summons (l).

optional in case of personal estate only.

Although, however, the action be expressed to be instituted on behalf also of the other creditors, the plaintiff is *dominus litis* until judgment, and may dismiss the

---

(c) O. III., r. 4; and App. A., ii. s. 1.
(d) *Cooper* v. *Blissett*, 1 C. D. 691.
(e) *Worraker* v. *Pryer*, 2 C. D. 109.
(f) *Fryer* v. *Royle*, 5 C. D. 540.
(g) *Eyre* v. *Cox*, 24 W. R. 317.
(h) *Large* v. *Large*, W. N., 1877, 198; approved by Coleridge, L. C. J., in *Johnson* v. *Palmer*, 4 C. P. D. p. 262.
(i) One who has or claims a specific charge upon the real estate may maintain his action to have his charge satisfied thereout, but this is not administration. And, where a bond-creditor, claiming also as

equitable mortgagee, sued for foreclosure, and failed to establish his mortgage, it was held that he could not, on such a record, ask, as a specialty creditor, for administration of the real estate generally (*Chapman* v. *Chapman*, 13 Beav. 308).
(k) *Reeve* v. *Goodwin*, 10 Jur. 1050; *Bedford* v. *Leigh*, 2 Dick. 707; *Thorne* v. *Kerr*, 2 K. & J. p. 62.
(l) *Nayler* v. *Blount*, 27 W. R. 865; and see, *per* Jessel, M. R., *Bray* v. *Tofield*, 18 C. D. p. 554, "it is no longer the practice, so far as *personal* estate is concerned, to bring an action by one creditor on behalf of others."

action (*m*); after judgment, the other creditors can of course insist upon the action being prosecuted (*n*), and it will not be dismissed, even with the consent of all creditors who have come in, and though the time named has elapsed, for other creditors may still come in (*o*).

(*m*) *Handford* v. *Storie*, 2 S. & S. p. 198; *semble*, even after judgment in another action, *Armstrong* v. *Storer*, 9 Beav. 277.

(*n*) *Handford* v. *Storie*; see *post*, p. 125.

(*o*) *Lashley* v. *Hogg*, 11 Ves. 602; but it was there intimated that the fund in Court might be distributed by consent, upon further consideration.

CHAPTER II.

HOW JUDGMENT FOR ADMINISTRATION MAY BE OBTAINED.

JUDGMENT (*a*) for administration may be obtained in at least seven different ways, according to the circumstances of each case. It may be mentioned here that where the residuary estate of one testator has devolved upon another, and the relations between the two estates are complicated, both estates may be administered in one action (*b*). *Judgment for administration.*

I. *Where the Proceedings have been Originated by Summons.*

I. In proceedings by summons.

The practice in this case has been stated, *ante*, p. 3.

II. *Where the Proceedings have been Originated by Writ.*

II. In administration actions;

(1.) *At the trial*, in cases in which both plaintiff and defendant have pleaded, and issue has been joined. This will be the case with many, if not most, of the actions in which wilful default is charged, or in which the plaintiff asks for something more than the common order (*c*). But it not uncommonly happens that the plaintiff's demand for administration is actually or practically unopposed (*d*). (1.) At the trial.

(*a*) The Court may of course order administration before the expiration of one year from the testator's death (*Prosser* v. *Mossop*, 29 W. R. 439).

(*b*) *Young* v. *Hodges*, 10 Ha. 158.

(*c*) As to which, see *ante*, p. 5.

(*d*) There is no objection, on the ground of improper collusion, to a trustee procuring a plaintiff to obtain the common order against him

In such a case he will probably desire to avail himself of the opportunity so given of having the trial of the action advanced. When a cause involves no question of difficulty, and is not likely to take up much time in argument—not more than ten minutes as a rule (*e*)—or is such that the subject-matter of it would authorize the Court to make a decree as of course, it may be heard as a short cause amongst the short causes, for the hearing of which one day in each week is appointed. To obtain this privilege, there must be a certificate—which, however, in one case (*f*) was dispensed with—from the counsel of the plaintiff that the cause is fit to be heard as a short cause, but the consent of the solicitors for any of the defendants will not be required. Upon the production of such certificate to the Registrar's clerk at the order of course seat, he will mark the cause as "short" in the cause-book. Notice that the cause has been so marked must be given to the other solicitors in the cause by the solicitor of the plaintiff. The plaintiff, thus advancing a cause, proceeds at his peril; and if, on the cause coming on, it appears that it is not one which is entitled to be so advanced, the costs occasioned by the advancement will have to be paid by the plaintiff (*g*).

As to *evidence*, it must be proved, if not admitted, as a foundation for a common judgment (*h*), that the plaintiff is a person entitled to sue (*i*), and the defendant or the principal defendant a person liable to be sued (*k*), for administration. A beneficiary suing must show that he

Marginal notes: As a short cause, ; after notice. ; Evidence. ; Plaintiff's right to sue must be proved or admitted.

to account (*Humble* v. *Shore*, 3 Ha. 119). See, however, the practice with reference to concurrent actions, *post*, Ch. vii.
(*e*) *Anon.*, 17 Jur. 435.
(*f*) *Hargraves* v. *White*, 17 Jur. 436.

(*g*) Daniell (685), 836.
(*h*) For the distinction between this and a special judgment, see *ante*, p. 5.
(*i*) *Post*, Ch. iii.
(*k*) *Post*, Ch. iii.

fills the character he alleges (*l*). A creditor plaintiff's debt must be proved or admitted. Whether an admission by the legal personal representative that he believes the debt to be due is sufficient has been doubted (*m*), but in *Hughes* v. *Eades* (*n*), the decree was made against the real estate upon the admission of the executors and trustees, and some of the beneficiaries, others not being *sui juris*. It was said in *Keaton* v. *Lynch* (*o*), that the plaintiff did not sufficiently prove his debt by exhibiting to an affidavit a bill of exchange drawn by him upon, and accepted by, the testator—apparently on the ground that he had not proved any consideration for the bill—but this decision is open to grave doubt, for a consideration is presumed to have been given for every bill or note till the contrary is shown (*p*), and to found a judgment for administration, *primâ facie* evidence of the suing creditor's debt is in the first place sufficient (*q*); nor, since the 3 & 4 Will. 4, c. 104, is it necessary to establish the will against the heir, or to make the heir a party as well as the devisee (*r*).

Creditor plaintiff.

Holder of a bill of exchange.

The title of legal personal representatives is properly proved by the production of the probate or letters of administration (*s*), or of examined or office copies thereof respectively (*t*); but the Probate Act-book, and even an unstamped copy thereof, has been admitted as evidence of the appointment of executors, without the non-production

Title of legal personal representatives;

(*l*) See *Miller* v. *Priddon*, 1 Mac. & G. 687.

(*m*) *Hill* v. *Binney*, 6 Ves. 738.

(*n*) 1 Ha. 486.

(*o*) 1 Y. & C. C. 437.

(*p*) Byles on Bills, 12th ed. 119; *Woodgate* v. *Field*, 2 Ha. p. 217.

(*q*) *Per* Wigram, V.-C., *Hughes* v. *Eades*, 1 Ha. 486. He must prove his debt subsequently in chambers, like any other creditor; *post*, p. 105.

(*r*) *Goodchild* v. *Terrett*, 5 Beav. 398; *Bridges* v. *Hinxman*, 16 Sim. 71; see also Cons. Ord. VII., r. 1, Appendix, *post*, p. 194.

(*s*) *Griffiths* v. *Hamilton*, 12 Ves. 298; *Hunt* v. *Stevens*, 3 Taunt. 113.

(*t*) *R.* v. *Haines*, Skinn. p. 584, *per* Lord Holt: *Hoe* v. *Nelthorpe*, 3 Salk. 154; S. C. *sub nom. Hoe* v. *Nathorp*, 1 Ld. Ray. 154.

of the probate being accounted for (*u*). The title of several claiming as executors is well evidenced by the probate, granted to one only, of the will appointing them all (*x*). The title of an administrator *de bonis non* is sufficiently proved by the production of letters *de bonis non*, without producing the letters granted to the original

of devisees; administrator (*y*). The title of the devisees of the deceased's real estate must, however, as a rule, be otherwise established. Probate is not conclusive proof that instruments, so far as they affect real estates, are of a testamentary character (*z*), unless the will has been proved in solemn form (*a*). But, even where the will has been proved in common form, the probate or an office copy may be made evidence in actions concerning real estate by following the course pointed out by the 64th section of the same Act (*b*). In all cases of testacy in which the will has not been proved, or administration *cum testamento annexo* granted, in solemn form, or in which the notice prescribed by the 64th section has not been given, or in which, though such notice has been given, a counter-notice that the validity of the testamentary disposition is disputed has been received, the title of devisees must be proved by formally verifying the will in the usual way—viz., by the evidence of all the attesting witnesses, or proof of their deaths and handwritings (*c*)—subject to this, that a will thirty years old (*d*),

(*u*) *Cox* v. *Allingham*, Jac. 514; *Dorrett* v. *Meux*, 15 C. B. 142. The will itself is no evidence as to personal estate (*Pinney* v. *Pinney*, 8 B. & C. 335); except that where, as in the Bishop's Courts at Winchester and Wells, no Act-book was kept, production of the will, with an indorsement thereon by the Registrar that the probate had passed the seal, has been held sufficient (*Doe* d. *Bassett* v. *Mew*, 7 Ad. & El. 240).

(*x*) *Walters* v. *Pfeil*, Mo. & Ma.

362; *Scott* v. *Briant*, 6 N. & M. 381; see *post*, p. 26.

(*y*) *Catherwood* v. *Chabaud*, 1 B. & C. 150.

(*z*) *Hume* v. *Rundell*, 6 Madd. 331.

(*a*) Probate Act, 1857, s. 64.

(*b*) Appendix, p. 194; see *Barraclough* v. *Greenhough*, L. R. 2 Q. B. 612.

(*c*) *Concannon* v. *Cruise*, 2 Moll. 332.

(*d*) The time is to be computed from the date of the will (not from

produced from the proper custody, proves itself (*e*), attesting witnesses being presumed, after the lapse of that time, to be dead (*f*). For the purposes of the usual preliminary judgment in a partition action (and *semble*, for all purposes), letters testimonial of the Supreme Court of a colony having probate jurisdiction, setting out the will verbatim, are sufficient proof of a will made and proved in the colony of real estate in England (*g*). Where the deceased died *of heir of an intestate,* intestate, and the real estate descended to his heir, the heirship must be established by proving the pedigree of the heir.

Evidence of the kind specified above will usually be *Evidence required for* sufficient to entitle the plaintiff to the *common* judg- *common judgment;* ment for administration, which is generally regarded as of course on the mere proof that the plaintiff is entitled to have, and the defendant liable to render, a general account; the only question at the original hearing, said Lord Gifford, M.R., is whether the defendant is an accounting party (*h*). The same learned judge laid it down strongly, after an elaborate discussion, that the Court will not at the hearing go into, or enter as read, evidence as to the items of the defendant's accounts, that being matter for Chambers (*i*), and this rule—though Wigram, V.-C., as strongly dissented from it, at all events in cases where the defendant did not in terms concede the plaintiff's right to an account (*k*)—is still, it is submitted, the practice of the Court (*l*).

If, however, the plaintiff asks for a *special* judgment— *for special judgment;* *e.g.*, one founded on wilful default or breach of trust— *e.g.*, wilful default,

the death of the testator) to the time of its production (*Man* v. *Ricketts*).
(*e*) *Man* v. *Ricketts*, 7 Beav. 93.
(*f*) Per Lord Campbell, *Doe* d. *Ashburnham* v. *Michael*, 15 Jur. 679.
(*g*) *Waite* v. *Bingley*, 21 C. D. 674; and see *Danby* v. *Poole*, 10

W. R. 515.
(*h*) *Walker* v. *Woodward*, 1 Russ. p. 110.
(*i*) *Law* v. *Hunter*, 1 Russ. p. 101; *Walker* v. *Woodward*.
(*k*) *Tomlin* v. *Tomlin*, 1 Ha. p. 245.
(*l*) See Daniell (582) 753.

something further in the way of both allegation and evidence is required from him. You cannot charge an executor or administrator with wilful default without making out a case (*m*), and charging him in the pleadings (*n*); and an application for leave to interrogate an executor, the object being to charge him with a breach of trust not raised by the pleadings, has been refused with costs (*o*). So, too, the Court refused to order at the original hearing any inquiries as to income, the tenant for life not being a party (*p*), and as to an executor's balances, with a view of charging him with interest upon them, unless on a special case made by the plaintiff or admissions by the defendant (*q*); but it must be added that such special inquiries are not necessarily a condition precedent to the establishment of such a charge at a later stage of the action, for executors may, on further consideration, if the certificate supplies the necessary materials, be charged with interest on their balances, though only the common judgment for administration has been taken, and the point has not been raised on the pleadings (*r*); and in *Laming* v. *Gee* (*s*) leave was given by the Court to bring a fresh action against a defendant against whom the plaintiff had previously obtained a common administration judgment, for the purpose of charging him with wilful default in the administration of the same estate, upon evidence showing that when the first judgment was obtained he was not aware of the circumstances on which the second action was founded ; and where, in an action by a residuary legatee against the executors, wilful default was charged by the

(*m*) Per Jessel, M. R., *Job* v. *Job*, 6 C. D. p. 564.
(*n*) Per eundem, *Mayer* v. *Murray*, 8 C. D. p. 427.
(*o*) *Ford* v. *Bryant*, 9 Beav. 410.
(*p*) *Whitney* v. *Smith*, 4 Ch. 513.

(*q*) *Law* v. *Hunter*, 1 Russ. 101.
(*r*) *Jones* v. *Morrall*, 2 Sim. N. S. 241 ; *Hollingsworth* v. *Shakeshoft*, 14 Beav. 492 ; and see *post*, p. 52.
(*s*) 10 C. D. 715 ; see also *Harvey* v. *Bradley*, 4 Eq. 13.

plaintiff but denied by the defendants, and only the common administration judgment was obtained (the claim to relief on the footing of wilful default not being dismissed), it was held, on further consideration, that the plaintiff was then entitled to relief on that footing (*t*). The charge of wilful default, unless originally pleaded, must be introduced by amendment, that is, of course, by amendment at any stage of the action at which amendments may be made, namely, before judgment (*u*). It was Lord Eldon's rule, that, in order to obtain an inquiry as to wilful neglect or default, the plaintiff must allege and prove at least one act of wilful neglect or default, and it is still the rule of the Court (*v*). True, it was said by Knight Bruce, L. J., in *Coope* v. *Carter* (*x*), that a case of wilful default might be alleged, and a prayer might be founded on it, but the circumstances appearing by admission or proof might only raise a case of suspicion in the mind of the Court, on the question whether an act of wilful default has been committed, and that in such a case he could conceive that the Court, if it were likely that further evidence might be obtained, ought to direct an inquiry (*y*) short of directing wilful default, in order to ground upon that a new order, and to direct an inquiry as to wilful default at a future stage; but these observations were not meant to let in general allegations of default, but to meet the case of specific allegations imperfectly proved at the hearing (*z*). Reference may

generally before judgment, after amendment of the pleadings, if necessary. Lord Eldon's rule that one act of wilful default must be proved, before inquiry directed, still the rule of the Court.

(*t*) *Luke* v. *Tonkin*, 21 C. D. 757.
(*u*) Per Jessel, M. R., *Mayer* v. *Murray*, *ubi supra*.
(*v*) *Sleight* v. *Lawson*, 3 K. & J. 292; *Massey* v. *Massey*, 2 J. & H. 728.
(*x*) 2 De G. M. & G. 298.
(*y*) See *Smith* v. *Chambers*, 2 Phill. p. 226, *per* Lord Cottenham, "the pleadings afforded quite sufficient foundation for an inquiry whether the expenses, the incurring of which was charged as wilful default, were properly incurred, without going into any such evidence at the hearing."
(*z*) Per Wood, V.-C., *Sleight* v. *Lawson*, *Massey* v. *Massey*; cf. *Pelham* v. *Hilder*, 1 Y. & C. C. C. 3.

c

here be made to *Guidici* v. *Kinton* (a). There, under a decree in a legatee's suit to take the usual accounts, A. B. went in and claimed the residue, which the Master found him entitled to, but the residue was not then ascertained, and no order was made in respect of it, and it was held that he was not precluded from afterwards asking relief against the executor, in respect of an alleged breach of trust, in a suit of his own, he not having been, in the first suit, in a situation to investigate the accounts of the executor, or to ask the relief which he claimed in the second. In *Garrett* v. *Noble* (b) it was laid down that, if a plaintiff sues for an account against executors, and does not seek to charge them with wilful default, his personal representatives cannot, on his death, so charge them, if the acts complained of were known to the deceased plaintiff.

(2.) Upon motion for judgment:

(2.) *On Motion for Judgment*, in four ways, as follows:—

(a) upon admissions in the pleadings;

(a) *On admissions in the defendant's pleadings*, under O. XL. r. 11, which provides that any party to an action may at any stage thereof apply to the Court or a judge for such order as he may, upon any admissions of fact in the pleadings, be entitled to, without waiting for the determination of any other question between the parties; that any such application may be made by motion, so soon as the right of the party applying to the relief claimed has appeared from the pleadings, and that the Court or a judge may, on any such application, give such relief, subject to such terms, if any, as such Court or judge may think fit (c).

As to what admissions will be sufficient to enable a plaintiff to move under this rule, see *ante*, p. 12.

(a) 6 Beav. 517.
(b) 6 Sim. 504.
(c) *Bennett* v. *Moore*, 1 C. D. 692; *Hetherington* v. *Longrigg*, 10 C. D. 162.

In any case, however, the admissions must be such *but only in simple cases,* as would show that the plaintiff is clearly entitled to the order asked for; the rule was not meant to apply when there is any serious question of law to be argued (*d*): in such a case a judge would have a discretion whether or not to make an order on motion, and with the exercise of that discretion the Court of Appeal ought not to interfere (*e*).

A motion under this rule is made on motion-day. The *and subject to the discretion of the Court to order the action to go into the general paper.* action need not be set down, but, if, on the motion being made, it appears that there must be a discussion or argument, it will (or, at least, may) be ordered to go into the general paper, subject to an order for its being advanced (*f*). Two clear days' notice of the motion must be given unless the Court or a judge give special leave to the contrary (*g*).

If the circumstances warrant it, a plaintiff may combine a motion against one defendant on admissions with a motion against another defendant on default of pleading (*h*). *Motion on admissions combined with motion in default of pleading.*

(*b*) *In default of defendant pleading*, under O. XXIX. r. 10, by which it is provided that, if the defendant makes default in delivering a defence or demurrer, the plaintiff may set down the action on motion for judgment, and such judgment shall be given as upon the statement of claim (*i*) the Court shall consider the plaintiff to be entitled to. As to what allegations will entitle him to *(b) In default of defendant pleading;*

(*d*) Per Mellish, L. J., *Gilbert* v. *Smith*, 2 C. D. 689; *Chilton* v. *Corporation of London*, 7 C. D. 735.

(*e*) *Mellor* v. *Sidebottom*, 5 C. D. 342.

(*f*) Registrars' Notice, W. N. 1877, 58, Miscellaneous.

(*g*) O. LIII. r. 4.

(*h*) *Bridson* v. *Smith*, 24 W. R. 392; *Parsons* v. *Harris*, 6 C. D. 694. Under the old practice, too, an administration order could by consent be obtained on motion; see *Furze* v. *Hennet*, 2 De G. & J. 125; *Scaffold* v. *Hampton*, W. N., 1873, 218.

(*i*) It has been thought, that, on motion under this order, the statement of claim should be concisely verified by affidavit, *Senior* v. *Hereford*, 4 C. D. 494; but there the defendant was an infant; see also *Barnard* v. *Wieland*, 30 W. R. 917, and *Perpetual Insurance Co.* v. *Gillespie*, W. N., 1882, 4.

an order for administration, see *ante*, p. 12 : r. 11 of the same Order provides that, where there are several defendants, then, if one of such defendants make such default as aforesaid, the plaintiff may either set down the action at once on motion for judgment against the defendant so making default, or may set it down against him at the time when it is entered for trial, or set it down on motion for judgment against the other defendants.

<small>either as short causes, or in their regular turn in the general paper.</small>

Motions for judgment under these rules are not to be brought on as ordinary motions—though, if all parties appear and consent this may be done (*k*)—but to be set down in the cause-book. They can be marked "short" on production of the usual certificate of counsel (*l*), and will then be placed in the paper on the first short-cause day after the day for which notice is given (*m*). If not marked "short" they will come into the general paper in their regular turn. It is advisable that the notices of motion for judgment should, if it is intended to mark them "short," contain a statement to that effect, and also a statement that no further notice will be given of their having been so marked : such statement will dispense with the necessity for giving defendants further notice that motions for judgment have been marked "short." (*n*).

<small>Notice of motion.</small>

Two clear days' notice of motion must be given, unless short notice be specially allowed (*o*). As against a defen-

---

(*k*) *Bowen* v. *Bowen*, 24 W. R. 246 ; *Pearce* v. *Spickett*, W. N., 1876, 109, in which a motion for judgment in default of a defence was allowed to be brought on on a motion-day, though the defendant did not appear on the motion, was anterior to the Registrars' Notice referred to in the text, and would not now be followed. The motion should have been brought on among the short causes.

(*l*) *Ante*, p. 12.

(*m*) Where, on such a short cause being called on, the defaulting defendant appeared and opposed, the M. R. made no order then, but fixed an early day for the hearing (*Meakin* v. *Sykes*, 24 W. R. 293).

(*n*) Registrars' Notice, W. N., 1877, 58, Miscellaneous.

(*o*) O. LIII. r. 4 ; *Roupell* v. *Parsons*, 24 W. R. 269 ; *Parsons* v. *Harris*, 6 C. D. 694.

dant who has not appeared, the notice of motion must be filed (p).

As to combining a motion on default of pleading with one on admissions, see *ante*, p. 19.

(c) *Where there are no pleadings at all.*—As notice of trial can only be given after issue joined, the proper course, where there are no pleadings, is to set the action down on motion for judgment under O. XL. r. 1, which provides that, except where by the Judicature Act or the rules made under it, it is provided that judgment may be obtained in any other manner—and neither Act nor Rules contain any express provision for the decision of a case in which no statement of claim has been delivered—the judgment of the Court shall be obtained by motion for judgment (q). As to marking such a motion "short," see *ante*, p. 20. As to evidence, see *ante*, p. 12.

(c) Where there are no pleadings.

There has been a conflict of opinion as to the proper course to be pursued, with reference to the delivery of a statement of claim, where the defendant consents at the outset to a judgment for administration. In the case of a creditors' action, Jessel, M. R., has said that the defendant ought to require the plaintiff not to deliver one (r), and Hall, V.-C., has in a beneficiaries' action also pronounced the delivery unnecessary (s); but Malins, V.-C. (t), who draws a distinction between these two classes of actions, and Bacon, V.-C. (u), have in beneficiaries' actions ordered a statement of claim to be delivered. Unless the distinction drawn by Malins, V.-C., be taken as a guide, it is submitted that the propriety of delivering a statement of claim, where the action is intended to be heard "short," must

In what cases statement of claim should be delivered.

(p) *Dymond* v. *Croft*, 3 C. D. 512; *Morton* v. *Miller*, ibid. 516.
(q) Registrars' Notice, W. N., 1877, 58, Miscellaneous.
(r) *Taylor* v. *Duckett*, W. N., 1875, 193.

(s) *Green* v. *Coleby*, 1 C. D. 693.
(t) *Breton* v. *Mockett*, 33 L. T. 684; and see *Boyes* v. *Cook*, ibid. 778.
(u) *David* v. *Dalton*, W. N., 1879, 86.

depend upon the terms of each will and the complexity of the case.

Another mode of taking the common judgment for administration without pleadings is pointed out below (3).

(d) In default of appearance.

(*d*) *In default of appearance.*—By O. XIII. r. 9, it is provided that in actions by the 34th section of the Judicature Act, 1875, assigned to the Chancery Division (including administration actions) in case the party served with the writ does not appear within the time limited for appearance, upon the filing by the plaintiff of a proper affidavit of service, the action may proceed as if such party had appeared (*x*).

(3.) Upon summons for accounts and inquiries;

(3.) *By Summons*, under O. XV., which provides (*y*) that in default of appearance to a writ of summons indorsed under O. III., r. 8 (*z*), and after appearance, unless the defendant, by affidavit or otherwise, satisfy the Court or a judge that there is some preliminary question to be tried, an order for the account claimed (*a*), with all directions usual in the Chancery Division in similar cases, shall be forthwith made; that an application for such an order may be made at any time after the time for entering an appearance has expired, and that it shall be made by summons, and be supported by an affidavit filed on behalf of the plaintiff, stating concisely the grounds of his claim to an account (*b*). Under these rules the *common* (*c*) judg-

---

(*x*) Where an order to account has been made upon a defendant in default of appearance, the account may be taken *ex parte* (*Thompson* v. *Trotter*, cited 3 M. & Cr. 193; *Elliot* v. *Brown*, 2 Ha. 621; but see *Golden* v. *Newton*, Johns. 720); but where the order has been made in default of pleading, the defendant is entitled to attend the taking of the accounts (*King* v. *Bryant*, 3 M. & Cr. 191; compare *Hayn* v. *Hayn*, Jac. 49).

(*y*) R. 1.

(*z*) As to which, see *ante*, p. 8.

(*a*) *i.e.*, an "ordinary account," see O. III. r. 8, and note (*c*) below.

(*b*) R. 2.

(*c*) An order for an account on the footing of wilful default is not an "ordinary account," and cannot be made under this Order (*Bennett* v. *Bowen*, 20 C. D. 538).

ment for administration may be obtained, as it may be to a considerable extent under O. XXXIII., which enables the Court or a judge, at any stage of the proceedings in a cause or matter, to direct any necessary inquiries or accounts to be made or taken, notwithstanding that it may appear that there is some special or further relief sought for or some special issue to be tried, as to which it may be proper that the cause or matter should proceed in the ordinary manner. Application under the last-mentioned order may be made by summons.

Though the common administration order under O. XV. is usually obtained in cases where a statement of claim has not been, and is not intended to be, delivered, yet there is no objection to the order being made after delivery of the claim, and, *e converso*, a claim may be delivered after the order has been made (*d*), but it would be improper then to deliver one, unless for the purpose of raising issues not covered by the order, and of obtaining an addition to the order in respect of those issues. As to adding to the order, see *post*, p. 51. either after statement of claim, or where none intended to be delivered.

After an order for preliminary accounts and inquiries, the hearing should not be brought on until the Chief Clerk has made his certificate, and a postponement will be ordered at the costs of the party bringing on the hearing (*e*).

It may be mentioned that the common order for administration is often made, by consent, at the hearing of some preliminary motion, *e.g.*, for a receiver, it being unnecessary to set the action down formally.

(*d*) See *Gatti* v. *Webster*, 12 C. D. 771.   (*e*) *Bath* v. *Bell*, 30 L. T. 422.

CHAPTER III.

OF THE PARTIES TO ADMINISTRATION ACTIONS.

I. *Who may maintain Actions as Plaintiffs.*

A. *As to Personal Estate.*

I. PLAINTIFFS.
A. Personal estate.
(1 & 2.) Beneficiaries,

(1.) ANY *legatee*, or an *annuitant*, whose annuity is charged upon the residuary personalty (*a*).

(2.) Any *residuary legatee*, or *next of kin* (*b*), though the testator may have directed that the quantity of the residue should be as the executor voluntarily, and without being thereto compelled by law, should declare (*c*). It is not necessary that the plaintiff's interest should be a

although their interest contingent, if present or existing;

vested, provided it be a present one. An existing interest, said Lord Westbury, whether it be vested or contingent, however future or remote, may, if it be a present interest, form the foundation of a right in the party representing it to come here with a bill to have the share secured (*d*). But an action for administration cannot be maintained by one who has only an expectation, and not an interest. On

seems, if an expectancy only.

this principle it was decided, where there was a gift to the testator's nephew for life, with remainder to his eldest or only child, subject to a condition precedent that the nephew should marry a specified niece of the testator, and the nephew, in the testator's lifetime, married someone

(*a*) *Wollaston* v. *Wollaston*, 7 C. D. 58.

(*b*) Chancery Procedure Act, 1852, s. 42, r. 1; *Painton* v. *Painton*, 12 Eq. 547, 550.

(*c*) *Gibbons* v. *Dawley*, 2 Ch. Cas. 198.

(*d*) *Davis* v. *Angel*, 4 De G. F. & J. p. 529.

else, and he, his wife, and a son were living at the testator's death, that the possibility of the nephew's wife predeceasing him and his marrying the niece did not confer upon the nephew's son an interest sufficient to enable him to maintain a bill (e) : and that, where there was a bequest, on the death of the testator's daughters without issue, to the persons who would be entitled under the Statute if the testator had then died intestate, an administration action brought in the lifetime of the daughters, and before they had had any issue, by persons who would then be next of kin, *if* the daughters were dead without issue, did not lie (f).

(3.) Any *creditor* of the deceased (g), or of the firm in which the deceased was a partner (h), whether suing singly or on behalf of himself and all other the creditors. The liquidator of a company, of which the legal personal representative of the deceased has, as such, been made a contributory, provided such representative has made default in paying any sum ordered in the winding up to be paid by him (i) ; a creditor having *debitum in præsenti solvendum in futuro* (k) ; a voluntary covenantee (l) ; one whose claim is for unliquidated damages recoverable for breach of covenant (m) ; a surety on a bond secured by a bond of indemnity given by the testator who had devised certain property specifically upon trust to pay the debt (n): all these can, as creditors of the deceased, maintain an action for the administration of his estate. Again, where a man has been found lunatic, and has died, the solicitor to the inquisition may, if the inquisition was for the

(3.) Creditors,

including voluntary covenantees.

(e) *Davis* v. *Angel.*
(f) *Clowes* v. *Hilliard*, 4 C. D. 413, in which *Roberts* v. *Roberts*, 2 Ph. 534, is considered.
(g) See *ante*, p. 9.
(h) *Rice* v. *Gordon*, 11 Beav. 265.
(i) 25 & 26 Vict. c. 89, s. 105 ;

see *Turquand* v. *Kirby*, 4 Eq. 123.
(k) *Whitmore* v. *Oxborrow*, 2 Y. & C. C. C. 13.
(l) *Watson* v. *Parker*, 6 Beav. 283.
(m) *Burch* v. *Coney*, 14 Jur. 1009.
(n) *Wooldridge* v. *Norris*, 6 Eq. 410.

lunatic's benefit, institute a creditors' action for administration in respect of his costs (*o*). But such an action is not maintainable by a lessor of the deceased to whom nothing is due, in respect of possible future breaches of covenant (*p*), nor by a person claiming to be a creditor of the testator's business carried on under the will by the executors, and suing for administration of the estate so employed (*q*), nor by a creditor of a residuary legatee (*r*), nor, *semble*, by a creditor in respect of an illegal debt (*s*). As to whether and under what circumstances a person claiming under an administration-bond (*t*) can sue upon such bond for administration of the estate of the obligor, see *Bolton* v. *Powell* (*u*). A creditor who sues for administration of the estate, and afterwards himself takes out representation, is still to be regarded as plaintiff in a creditors' action (*v*). As to the practice where it is found that a plaintiff, suing as a creditor, is in fact not a creditor, see *post*, p. 125.

But the debt must be debitum in præsenti.

(4.) Legal personal representatives or one of them; sufficient if one at least has proved the will.

(4.) An *executor* or *administrator* (*x*), or one of two or more executors or administrators (*y*).

Probate granted to one of several executors enures for the benefit of all, and, upon the death of the executor to whom probate has been granted, the other executors may accept the office, and, upon doing so, fully represent the testator without further probate (*z*), so that executors who

---

(*o*) *Chester* v. *Rolfe*, 4 De G. M. & G. 798. The costs may be treated as incurred for the lunatic's benefit notwithstanding the pendency of a traverse of the inquisition (*Re Cumming*, 5 De G. M. & G. 30); but see *Re Weaver*, 21 C. D. 615.

(*p*) *King* v. *Malcott*, 9 Ha. 692; but see *post*, p. 183.

(*q*) *Owen* v. *Delamere*, 15 Eq. 134; and see *Shearman* v. *Robinson*, 15 C. D. 548.

(*r*) *Elmslie* v. *McAulay*, 3 Bro. C. C. 624, 626.

(*s*) *Smith* v. *White*, 1 Eq. 626.

(*t*) This is now given under 20 & 21 Vict. c. 77, ss. 81, 82, 83, not to the Ordinary, but to the Judge.

(*u*) 14 Beav. p. 290; 2 De G. M. & G. 1. See further as to the bond, Comp. Exors., Chap. XV.

(*v*) See *Nichols* v. *Nichols*, 10 W. R. 598.

(*x*) Chancery Procedure Act, 1852, s. 42, r. 6.

(*y*) *Latch* v. *Latch*, 10 Ch. 464.

(*z*) *Cummins* v. *Cummins*, 3 Jo. & L. 64; per Bayley, J., *Webster* v. *Spencer*, 3 B. & Ald. 363; *Watkins*

have not proved may join in bringing actions with one who has (a).

An executor may commence an action for administration before probate, but he cannot go on with it beyond the stage at which he has to prove his title: at which stage the executor suing must prove that he is executor, and that he can only do by producing the probate (b). He need not have obtained probate at the time he delivers his pleadings; it is sufficient if he have it, when it is wanted in evidence (c). Where the probate was necessary to prove the title of an executor moving, it was held sufficient to produce it when the motion was actually heard, though the will had not been proved at the time for which notice of motion was given (d). It must be borne in mind that not proving the will is only an impediment to the action: the right of action is the same before probate as after (e). In like manner, under the fiction of relation (f), one may sue before the grant to him of letters of administration, but he meets with the same impediment that confronts an executor suing before probate: he cannot proceed beyond the point where proof of his title becomes necessary, without producing the letters of administration (g), though it is sufficient to produce them then (h). A receiver of the personal estate and of the rents of the real estate,

Executor may even commence action before probate,

and deliver pleadings,

but must produce probate before motion made,

for right of action is not dependent on probate.

So also in the case of plaintiff taking out administration after action brought.

v. *Brent*, 7 Sim. 512; *Strickland* v. *Strickland*, 12 Sim. 463.

(a) *Brookes* v. *Stroud*, 1 Salk. 3; *Webster* v. *Spencer*; *Walters* v. *Ifeil*, Mo. & Ma. 362. See further, as to the nature and effect of probate and administration, Comp. Exors., Chap. XVI.

(b) *Wankford* v. *Wankford*, 1 Salk. p. 303; *Wills* v. *Rich*, 2 Atk. 285; *Pinney* v. *Pinney*, 8 B. & C. 335; compare *Rogers* v. *James*, 7 Taunt. 147, *Ex parte Paddy*, 3 Madd. 241.

(c) *Thompson* v. *Reynolds*, 3 Car. & P. 123. It would be prudent, however, for the pleader to aver probate, to avoid difficulties on demurrer: see *Humphreys* v. *Ingledon*, 1 P. Wms. 752.

(d) *Newton* v. *M. R. Co.*, 1 Dr. & Sm. 583.

(e) *Wankford* v. *Wankford*, 1 Salk. 303.

(f) See Comp. Exors., Chap. XIX.

(g) *Hunt* v. *Stevens*, 3 Taunt. 113.

(h) *Horner* v. *Horner*, 23 L. J. Ch. 10.

has been appointed, pending the grant of probate, which was delayed on account of a *caveat* being entered (no probate action having been actually commenced), upon the application of the plaintiff, named sole executor and residuary legatee and devisee, the defendant alleging himself to be heir-at-law and one of the next of kin (*i*).

This right not to be used oppressively. It would appear, however, that an executor's or administrator's right to sue before taking out representation is not quite absolute. It has been held that, where it appears that a plaintiff, by suing as executor when he had not proved the will, is abusing the process of the Court, the Court has a common-law jurisdiction, under its general superintending power to prevent its process from being used for the purpose of oppression and injustice, to stay the proceedings until probate shall be taken out; but some good ground must be shown by a defendant making such an application (*k*).

Proceedings when plaintiff's title as legal personal representative lost after judgment. Where a decree for administration was obtained by an administrator, but his letters of administration were afterwards revoked, the suit was stayed, and the plaintiff was deprived of his costs, his right being in dispute when the bill was filed (*l*); but where judgment had been obtained at the suit of residuary legatees for the administration of the real and personal estate of a testator, and after this, a subsequent will having been discovered by which the estate was disposed of in a different way, probate of the old will had been recalled, and letters of administration with the later will annexed had been granted to one of the beneficiaries, the Court of Appeal made an order dismissing the action, the administratrix, with the new will annexed, undertaking to pay the costs, charges, and expenses of the defendants out of the assets (*m*).

(*i*) *Parkin* v. *Seddons*, 16 Eq. 34.
(*k*) *Webb* v. *Adkins*, 14 C. B. 401.
(*l*) *Houseman* v. *Houseman*, 1 C.
D. 535; compare *Graves* v. *Wright*, cited *post*, p. 125.
(*m*) *Dean* v. *Wright*, 21 C. D. 581.

B. *As to Real and Personal* (n) *Estate.*

(1.) Any *legatee* interested in a legacy charged upon real estate (o), or an *annuitant* whose annuity is charged upon the residuary realty (p).

(2.) Any *person interested in the proceeds* of real estate directed to be sold (q).

(3.) Any *residuary devisee* (r), or *heir* (s).

(4.) Any *creditor* of the deceased, as interpreted above (t), provided he sue on behalf of all the creditors (u), and not singly (v). A testator empowered and directed the trustees of his real estate to raise by mortgage thereof any sum not exceeding £20,000, and to apply the same in paying such of the creditors of M. as they should think fit. The trustees raised £6,000, and in their answer to a bill by a judgment-creditor of M. to enforce his lien, they stated that they had raised this sum, but had not further exercised their power, and refused to do so, except under the direction of the Court. They then filed a bill to have the trusts carried into execution by the Court, and to this bill they made the judgment-creditor a party, and stated in it that they intended to raise the

B. *Real and personal estate.*
(1.) Legatee, when legacy charged on land.
(2.) Persons interested in proceeds of sale of realty.
(3.) Residuary devisee or heir.
(4.) Creditor.

(n) The Court will not administer the real estate alone (*Rowsell* v. *Morris*, 17 Eq. p. 21).
(o) Chancery Procedure Act, s. 42, r. 2.
(p) *Wollaston* v. *Wollaston*, 7 C. D. 58.
(q) Chancery Procedure Act, s. 42, r. 2.
(r) An action to "establish title" to real estate, not claiming possession, is not an action "for the recovery of land," so as to require the leave of the Court under Ord. XVII., r. 2, for its joinder with another cause of action (*Gledhill* v. *Hunter*, 14 C. D. 492); *secus*, as to a claim by heir-at-law, one of the next of kin, to recover real estate in the hands of an administratrix, and to administer the personalty (*Kitching* v. *Kitching*, 24 W. R. 901).
(s) Chancery Procedure Act, 1852, r. 3.
(t) A. (3), *ante*, p. 25.
(u) In *Woods* v. *Sowerby*, 14 W. R. 9, the Court, at the hearing, directed the bill of a single creditor to be taken as a bill on behalf of all the creditors, and ordered the real estate to be sold, if necessary.
(v) *Ante*, p. 9.

whole £20,000. It was held that the judgment-creditor had an equity to sue to have the fund raised secured, if not to have the whole £20,000 raised and distributed; and that the trustees were bound, if not by the will, by their answer and the statement in their bill, to raise the whole £20,000 (*x*).

(5.) Trustee, but not executor or administrator as such.

(5.) Any *trustee* (*y*), but not an executor or administrators as such (*z*).

Assignees of persons who might have been plaintiffs may sue, both as to real and personal estate,

It may be laid down as a rule, to which there is probably no exception, that in all cases, in which, but for an assignment or devolution of his interest, any particular person might have maintained an action for administration, such action may be maintained by the person or persons who have taken an assignment of that interest or upon whom it has devolved by act of law. In accordance with this principle, actions to administer the estate of a deceased person may be brought by assignees (*a*), mortgagees (*b*), Scotch *curatores bonis* (*c*), and legal personal representatives (*d*), of persons beneficially interested in the estate. The list, of course, might easily be extended; trustees, *e.g.*, in the bankruptcy or liquidation, and committees of the estate in the lunacy, of persons who, but for such bankruptcy, liquidation, or lunacy, might have sued, may themselves sue, for administration. It was formerly held that a voluntary assignee of a debt due from a testator could not sue for administration of his estate, on the ground that as the law then stood, he could not have enforced his assignment (which operated merely as an agreement) against his assignor, and therefore could not be treated as

including mortgagees, legal personal representatives, trustees in bankruptcy,

and, semble, since the Judicature Act, voluntary assignees of a debt due from a testator.

(*x*) *Joel* v. *Mills*, 3 K. & J. 458.
(*y*) Chancery Procedure Act, s. 42, r. 6.
(*z*) *Tubby* v. *Tubby*, 2 Coll. 136; compare *Cutley* v. *Sampson*, 33 Beav. 551; *Carter* v. *Sanders*, 23 L. J. Ch. 679.

(*a*) *Cafe* v. *Dent*, 5 Ha. 24.
(*b*) *Freeman* v. *Pennington*, 3 De G. F. & J. 295.
(*c*) See *Scott* v. *Bentley*, 1 K. & J. 281; and compare *Mackie* v. *Darling*, 12 Eq. 319.
(*d*) See *ante*, p. 2.

a creditor of the deceased (e) : but the law as to the
assignment of debts and choses in action has recently
been altered, and now a voluntary assignee in writing
of a debt due from the deceased is competent to sue for
administration of the debtor's estate, provided express
notice in writing of the assignment shall have been given
to the debtor, trustee, or other person from whom the
assignor would have been entitled to receive or claim the
debt.

When any person entitled to sue for administration is *Infant or lunatic plaintiff, and feme covert.*
an infant, or otherwise not *sui juris*, the action may be
brought by him or her by his or her next friend (f) or
committee (g) as the case may be (h); but by sec. 12 of
the Married Women's Property Act, 1882 (i) it is enacted
that every married woman shall have *in her own name*
the same civil remedies for the protection and security of
her own separate property as if such property belonged to
her as a *feme sole*, and by secs. 2 and 5 all property of
women married after the commencement of the Act (1st
January, 1883), and all property of women married before
that date the title to which shall accrue after that date,
shall be held and disposed of as their separate property.

II. *Who are necessary or proper Defendants.*

To actions for administration of personal estate instituted *II. DEFENDANTS.*
by beneficiaries or creditors *all* the legal personal repre- *A. In administration of personal estate*

(e) *Sewell* v. *Moxsy*, 2 Sim. N. S. 189; see now Judicature Act, 1873, s. 25, sub-s. 6.

(f) The principles on which the Court acts in the case of suits instituted on behalf of infants are well stated by Lord Langdale in *Starten* v. *Bartholomew*, 6 Beav. 143; and see *Towsey* v. *Groves*, 9 Jur. N. S. 194. In *Woolf* v. *Pemberton*, 6 C. D. 19, the infant's father successfully applied to be substituted for a self-constituted next friend.

(g) For a recent and instructive case of administration at suit of lunatic by his committee, see *Stamper* v. *Stamper*, 46 L. T. 372.

(h) See Daniell (104—153) 65—119.

(i) 45 & 46 Vict. c. 75.

сentatives must be defendants (*k*), if they have respectively elected to act (*l*), and (as it would seem) have signified that election by proving the will. It is not sufficient to omit some of them from the record, and serve them subsequently with notice of the judgment (*m*), for, as hereafter appears (*n*), a party so served cannot be made to account. And, where one of several persons named executors has not proved or acted at the time of the action being commenced, but afterwards proves or acts, he must be added to the record as a defendant (*o*).

At suit of beneficiaries or creditors, all executors proving or acting must be defendants.

Any proving or acting afterwards must be added as defendants.

A bill for administration was allowed against an executor before probate by Lord Lyndhurst (*p*); but such bills have, on the other hand, not infrequently been disallowed, it being held in such cases that the Court is limited to granting protection to the estate (*q*), even though the defendant had possessed himself of part of the personal estate (*r*). If (said Lord Romilly, in the case last cited) the defendant had possessed himself of every penny of the personal estate, that would not entitle the plaintiff to the relief he asks: if a person has taken possession of the

Relief in actions against executors before probate generally confined to appointment of receiver.

(*k*) *Offley* v. *Jenny*, 3 Ch. Rep. 92; *Scurry* v. *Morse*, 9 Mod. 89; *Latch* v. *Latch*, 10 Ch. 464. But proceedings have been allowed against one only of co-executors for an account of his own payments and receipts alone (*Cowslad* v. *Cely*, Prec. Ch. 83).

(*l*) *Brown* v. *Pitman*, Gilb. 75; *Strickland* v. *Strickland*, 12 Sim. 463. It would be injustice to allow actions to be brought against one appointed executor, who never meant to act as such, before he had an opportunity of renouncing. If he be liable to actions before he has acted as executor or proved the will, his liability must arise on the instant of the death of the testator, and many actions might be brought against him before he could renounce, and from these actions he could not be relieved without expense and trouble (*per* Best, C. J., *Douglas* v. *Forrest*, 4 Bing. 704).

(*m*) *Latch* v. *Latch*.

(*n*) *Post*, p. 48.

(*o*) See *Haldane* v. *Eckford*, 14 W. R. 300; *Guthrie* v. *Walrond*, 22 W. R. 723.

(*p*) *Blewitt* v. *Blewitt*, Younge, 541.

(*q*) *Baron de Feuchères* v. *Dawes*, 5 Beav. 110; *Overington* v. *Ward*, 34 Beav. 175; compare *Tempest* v. *Lord Camoys*, 35 Beav. 201; and see *Cash* v. *Parker*, 12 C. D. 293.

(*r*) *Cary* v. *Hills*, 15 Eq. 79.

estate, you may file a bill for a receiver to take care of the property until a legal personal representative is appointed, and the Court will appoint a receiver (s) for that purpose, but that is a totally different thing from making a decree for general administration. It will thus be seen that the practice in this respect can hardly be called settled. Since one who has been named an executor, if he has elected to act, is veritably an executor before probate, deriving, as he does, his authority not from the probate, but from the will (t), the reason of the thing would seem to be with Lord Lyndhurst's decision in *Blewitt* v. *Blewitt;* but the authorities are principally the other way. It was decided in *Vickers* v. *Bell* (u) that an executor, who had acted, but had not proved, might be joined as co-defendant in an administration suit with the executors who had proved ; but this is not necessarily inconsistent with *Baron de Feuchères* v. *Dawes*, *Overington* v. *Ward*, and *Cary* v. *Hills*, above referred to, for probate by one of co-executors enures for the benefit of them all (v). In *Morley* v. *White* (x), the executor who had not proved or acted seems to have been made a defendant *quâ* debtor to the estate, not in any alleged representative capacity.

One named executor may excuse himself from accountability by showing that he has acted merely as agent or attorney of those who were named co-executors with him (y), even where he has not formally renounced (z), and *Person named executor, but not proving or acting except as agent of other executors.*

(s) In *Blackett* v. *Blackett*, 19 W. R. 559, a receiver and manager was appointed, on an *ex parte* motion, before administration, all the parties to the suit being infant children of the intestate.

(t) See Comp. Exors. Chap. XIX.

(u) 4 De G. J. & S. 274.

(v) *Ante*, p. 26.

(x) 8 Ch. 731.

(y) *Rayner* v. *Green*, 2 Curt. 248;
per Lord Hardwicke, *Harrison* v. *Graham*, cited 1 P. Wms. ed. 6, 241 (7); *Dove* v. *Everard*, 1 R. & M. 231; *Lowry* v. *Fulton*, 9 Sim. 115; but see *White* v. *Barton*, 18 Beav. 192, where the defence of agency was disallowed, apparently, however, on the ground that it had not been properly pleaded ; and consider *Orr* v. *Newton*, 2 Cox. 274.

(z) *Stacey* v. *Elph*, 1 M. & K. 195.

such an agent ought not to be made a party to an action for administration of the estate (a). But an executor can only thus excuse himself, where he has not proved the will. An executor who has proved cannot act in any other character: he cannot renounce his executorship, and act only under power of attorney from his co-executors (b).

Appointment of administrator ad litem by Chancery Division insufficient to enable administration judgment to be obtained.
An administrator *ad litem* appointed under the 44th section of the Chancery Procedure Act, 1852, does not, in an action for administration, sufficiently represent the deceased's estate (c), for the section does not apply where the estate, to which it is desired to appoint a representative, is the estate to be administered by the Court (d).

Full personal representative necessary.
To administer you must have a full personal representative constituted. So said Kindersley, V.-C. (e), who on another occasion declared that, until it was decided by a higher Court to be proper, he would never make a decree to distribute an estate without a proper representative (f): and the Court of Appeal has recently decided that such a course would be improper (g). Nor is the section applicable to an action which, though not in terms asking administration, prays relief which, if granted, would involve or lead up to it (h).

So, as to administrator ad litem appointed by Probate Division.
Equally insufficient as a representative of an estate to be administered is an administrator *ad litem* (i) appointed by the Probate Division under its ordinary jurisdiction (k); and the fact of that Division appointing a person administrator for the purpose of taking, or being a

---

(a) *Dove* v. *Everard*, 1 R. & M. 231.
(b) *Graham* v. *Keble*, 2 Dow. 17.
(c) *Groves* v. *Lane*, 16 Jur. 1061.
(d) *Silver* v. *Stein*, 1 Dr. 295; *Maclean* v. *Dawson*, 1 Sw. & Tr. 425.
(e) *Groves* v. *Lane*.
(f) *James* v. *Aston*, 2 Jur. N. S. 224.
(g) *Dowdeswell* v. *Dowdeswell*, 9 C. D. 294.
(h) *Maclean* v. *Dawson* (No. 1), 27 Beav. 21, 23; *Dowdeswell* v. *Dowdeswell*, 9 C. D., p. 304.
(i) But after such an appointment the Court will not appoint a receiver of the personal estate, considering that such an administrator has the same power of protecting the property (*Veret* v. *Duprez*, 6 Eq. 329; *Hitchen* v. *Birks*, 10 ib. 471.
(k) See *Dowdeswell* v. *Dowdeswell*; *Clough* v. *Dixon*, 10 Sim. 564.

party to, proceedings in the Chancery Division, does not estop the latter Division from saying the appointment is insufficient for the purpose (*l*). There is nothing in the Judicature Act which enables the Court in this respect to depart from the ordinary course. It is still necessary, as it was before, that in an action involving administration there should be, not a limited administrator, but a general administrator, in order to enable the Court to make a decree (*m*). But an executor or administrator *cum testamento annexo* of a married woman's testamentary appointment, though the grant to him be limited to such property as she had power to dispose of by will, is not such a limited personal representative that judgment for administration cannot be had against him (*n*).

To an action which seeks an account of the assets of one who died out of the jurisdiction, possessed by a personal representative there, a personal representative constituted in England is a necessary party, although it does not appear that the deceased at the time of his death had any assets in England (*o*); it is not sufficient to make the representative out of the jurisdiction a party, and pray process against him when within the jurisdiction (*p*), and to an action in respect of assets remitted from India, in the hands of an executor residing in England, but who was only constituted executor in India (*q*), a personal representative constituted in England is a necessary party. *A fortiori*, the same rule applies, where the assets are in the hands of a mere agent, to whom they have been

<small>Where testator died out of the jurisdiction.</small>

(*l*) *Dowdeswell* v. *Dowdeswell*, esp. *per* Cotton, L. J., p. 305.
(*m*) *Per* Cotton, L. J., S. C. 306. It has been thought (*Jones* v. *Foulkes*, 10 W. R. 55) that the strictness of the rule may be relaxed by the consent of the parties; *sed quære*.

(*n*) *Sewell* v. *Ashley*, 3 De G. M. & G. 933; *Berkeley* v. *Mason*, 19 Eq. 467.
(*o*) *Tyler* v. *Bell*, 2 M. & Cr. 89; *Flood* v. *Patterson*, 29 Beav. 295.
(*p*) *Tyler* v. *Bell*.
(*q*) *Bond* v. *Graham*, 1 Ha. 482.

remitted by the executors resident abroad (*r*). But, where a man died intestate in India, and representation was taken out both there and here, his legal personal representative constituted in this country was held entitled as such to sue the Indian administrator for an account of assets possessed in India as well as here (*s*), and, conversely the foreign personal representative may maintain an action against the English one for an account of the English assets (*t*).

Where the will of a domiciled Scotchman having at his death personal estate both in England and Scotland, is proved in both countries, judgment for administration of the whole of his personal estate wheresoever situated, will be made in an action instituted by a minority of the executors in the High Court—if a person is found here who is accountable, or who is within the jurisdiction of the Court (*u*), even though the English assets have been removed to Scotland for administration there since the testator's death (*x*). The only bar to the action would, it seems, be a decree for the administration of the estate by the Scotch Courts (*z*). *Semble*, any executor residing out of the jurisdiction, and made a defendant, might in such a case, before the hearing, successfully apply (*a*) to have the order for service on him out of the jurisdiction, obtained under O. XI., discharged, but if this be not done, there is no defence to the action (*b*).

(*r*) *Lowe* v. *Farlie*, 2 Madd. 101. See and distinguish *Arthur* v. *Hughes*, 4 Beav. 506, where the fund was clear and ascertained.

(*s*) *Sandilands* v. *Innes*, 3 Sim. 263, and compare *Eames* v. *Hacon*, 16 C. D. 407, 18 *ib*. 347.

(*t*) *Guidici* v. *Kinton*, 6 Beav. 517.

(*u*) *Stirling-Maxwell* v. *Cartwright*, 11 C. D. 522; O. XI. rr. 1, 1a.

(*x*) *Orr-Ewing* v. *Orr-Ewing*, 22

C. D. 456.

(*z*) *Stirling-Maxwell* v. *Cartwright*; *Orr-Ewing* v. *Orr-Ewing*; *Riboldi* v. *Maireau*, Fry, J., Feb. 1, 1883.

(*a*) As in *Cresswell* v. *Parker*, 11 C. D. 601.

(*b*) *Orr-Ewing* v. *Orr-Ewing*. Judgment for administration could not formerly have been obtained against a personal representative out of the jurisdiction (*Donald* v.

The Attorney-General does not, as a party to the cause, sufficiently represent the estate of an illegitimate person who has died intestate (c).

The mere fact of one executor having paid over the personal estate to the other is no discharge of the executor who has paid the money. He remains liable to account (d), but no action, either by creditors (e) or by the next of kin (f), can be brought against him, after distributing the assets amongst persons coming in under advertisements issued in accordance with 22 & 23 Vict. c. 35, ss. 27—32 (g) and à fortiori after distribution by the Court the executors cannot be sued (h).

In an action brought against a married woman who was an executrix (or administratrix), it was formerly necessary that her husband also should be a party, unless he had abjured the realm, or she had obtained a protection order, or was judicially separated (i); but under the recent Act (j), she may sue or be sued as if she were a *feme sole*.

Married woman defendant.

The cases do not seem to afford a very clear answer to the question, under what circumstances, in an action to administer the assets of a testator or intestate, the plaintiff ought to join, with the existing personal representatives, such parties as fill the position of administrators or executors of a former representative of the original

Representatives of deceased executors.

Bather, 16 Beav. 26); *semble*, an administrator must have been first appointed under 38 Geo. 3, c. 87, ss. 1, 2, 3 ; and 20 & 21 Vict. c. 77, s. 74, as to which statutes and grants of administration thereunder, see Comp. Exors., Chap. XII. ; but in *Dickins* v. *Harris*, 14 L. T. N. S. 98, a receiver was appointed, the sole executor being abroad, and the beneficiaries being unable to obtain an account from the persons left in control of the property, which was in England ; see also *Fraser* v.

Dowhiggin, V.-C. B., Dec., 1882.
(c) *Bell* v. *Alexander*, 6 Ha. 543.
(d) *Per* Turner, L. J., *Hamp* v. *Robinson*, 3 De G. J. & S. p. 109.
(e) *Clegg* v. *Rowland*, 3 Eq. 368.
(f) *Newton* v. *Sherry*, 1 C. P. D. 246.
(g) See *ante*, p. 4, and *Hunter* v. *Young*, 4 Ex. D. 256.
(h) *Farrell* v. *Smith*, 2 B. & B. 337.
(i) Mitford, 5th ed, 32 ; 20 & 21 Vict. c. 85, ss. 21, 25, 26.
(j) 45 & 46 Vict. c. 75, s. 18.

estate. It is conceived, however, that the practice in this respect is now settled, viz., to make the personal representatives of a deceased executor parties, where he has received assets of the testator for which he has not accounted with the surviving executor, and in respect of which it is sought to charge his estate; but where this is not the case, to introduce into the statement of claim an allegation that the deceased executor fully accounted with the survivor, and that nothing is due from his estate to the testator, and not to make his representative a party to the action. The fact of such deceased executor having died insolvent, or without having received assets, would in all cases probably prevent his executors being proper parties (*k*).

When administrator durante minore ætate a necessary party.

Unless an administrator *durante minore ætate* has fully accounted with the infant, when of age, he remains a necessary party to an action relating to the estate (*l*).

Where it is necessary to bring the Attorney-General before the Court, he should be made a defendant. He cannot be bound by service of the judgment on him under the practice hereafter referred to (*m*), so as to preclude the institution on behalf of the Crown of further inquiries (*n*).

Executor de son tort cannot be sued for administration;

An executor *de son tort* cannot be sued for the administration of the estate of the deceased, even though it be alleged by the plaintiff that the defendant, being the person entitled to take out representation, refuses to apply for it, and impedes the plaintiff in procuring a grant to any other person (*o*), an executor *de son tort* being only treated as executor for the purpose of being charged, not

---

(*k*) Daniell, (241) 222.
(*l*) *Glass* v. *Oxenham*, 2 Atk. 121.
(*m*) *Post*, p. 40.
(*n*) *Johnstone* v. *Hamilton*, 11 Jur. N. S. 777.
(*o*) *Penny* v. *Watts*, 2 Ph. 149:

Rowsell v. *Morris*, 17 Eq. 20 (M. R.), dissenting from *Rayner* v. *Koehler*, 14 Eq. 262, and *Coote* v. *Whittington*, 16 Eq. 534 (Malins, V.-C.); see *Ambler* v. *Lindsay*, 3 C. D. 198.

for any other purpose (*p*). So he cannot be sued for an account unless the legal personal representative be before the Court (*q*), though he be himself the proper person to take out administration (*r*). When, however, it is said that such actions will not lie against an executor *de son tort*, apparently no more is meant than that, if the defendant can by any means bring the action to a hearing while the record is imperfect as regards parties, the plaintiff must fail; for the plaintiff's action is good, if he can at the hearing produce the letters of administration, it being immaterial that the action was commenced before the grant (*s*). If one of several executors sues for administration, he must make all the other executors defendants (*t*).

<small>nor for an account, unless legal personal representative be before the Court;

at least before the hearing.</small>

In actions for administration of real estate *all* the trustees are necessary defendants (*u*), and if, in addition to seeking administration, it is sought to make the trustees liable for breaches of trust, in which *cestuis que trustent* have participated, the latter should also be made defendants (*v*). But the heir-at-law need not also be joined (*x*).

<small>B. In administration of real estate, *all* the trustees must be parties.</small>

Where one of two trustees of an estate which was being administered in Court died intestate, and, as was alleged, insolvent, after a decree for an account against himself and his co-trustee, and after the certificate made in pursuance thereof had been settled by the Chief Clerk, except in some formal particulars, it was held that the proceedings ought to be carried on in the absence of a representative of his estate, although considerable balances were proved to be due from the trustees, and although one of

<small>Practice where one of two trustees dies insolvent after judgment.</small>

(*p*) Per Lord Cottenham, *Penny* v. *Watts*, 2 Ph. p. 152.

(*q*) *Humphreys* v. *Humphreys*, 3 P. Wms. 349; *Beardmore* v. *Gregory*, 2 H. & M. p. 496; *Rawlings* v. *Lambert*, 1 J. & H. 458; *Creasor* v. *Robinson*, 14 Beav. 589; and see *Cooke* v. *Gittings*, 21 Beav. 497. But it is sufficient if such representative be added by amendment (*Beardmore* v. *Gregory*).

(*r*) *Creasor* v. *Robinson*.

(*s*) *Horner* v. *Horner*, 23 L. J. Ch. 10; *Bateman* v. *Margerison*, 6 Ha. 496; and see *ante*, p. 27.

(*t*) *Latch* v. *Latch*, 10 Ch. 464.

(*u*) *Hall* v. *Austin*, 2 Coll. 570; *Penny* v. *Penny*, 9 Ha. 39.

(*v*) *Jesse* v. *Bennett*, 6 De G. M. & G. 609.

(*x*) *Ante*, p. 13.

the parties having the conduct of the cause was entitled to take out representation to the deceased trustee (y).

It may be added that under the Judicature Acts, a demurrer for want of parties will not lie (z).

III. *Who ought to be Served with Notice of the Judgment.—The Practice as to Service.—The Effect of Service on the Status of Parties served.*

(III.) PERSONS SERVED WITH NOTICE OF THE JUDGMENT. After providing in effect, as before mentioned, that any residuary legatee or next of kin, as regards personal estate, and as regards real estate, any legatee interested in a legacy charged upon real estate, any person interested in the proceeds of real estate directed to be sold, and any residuary devisee or heir, might have a decree for administration against the executor, administrator, or trustee, without serving any person beneficially entitled, and that any executor, administrator, or trustee might obtain a decree against any one legatee, next of kin, or *cestui que trust*,

All who would formerly have been necessary parties. the Chancery Procedure Act, 1852, enacts that in all the above cases the persons who, according to the then practice of the Court, would be necessary parties to the suit, shall be served with notice of the decree (a);

Trustees represent their *cestuis que trustent*. and (b) that in all suits concerning real or personal estate vested in trustees under a will or otherwise, such trustees shall represent the persons beneficially entitled under the trust, in the same manner and to the same extent as the executors or administrators in suits concerning personal estate represent the persons beneficially interested in such personal estate, and that in such cases it shall not be necessary to make the persons beneficially entitled under the trusts parties to the suit; but the Court might, upon consideration of the matter, at the

(y) *Moore* v. *Morris*, 13 Eq. 139.
(z) *Werderman* v. *Soc. Gén. d Electricité*, 19 C. D. 246.

(a) S. 42, r. 8. See *post*, p. 47 (f).
(b) R. 9; and see *post*, p. 43.

hearing, if it should so think fit, order such persons, or any of them, to be made parties. These provisions are by O. XVI. r. 12 confirmed, and directed to be in force as to actions in the High Court.

The result of the practice established by the Chancery Procedure Act, and continued under the Judicature Act, is to make it unnecessary, in a case where only the common judgment for administration is required, to name as defendants on the record any persons other than the executors, administrators, or trustees, but to make it incumbent on the plaintiff, when he has obtained his judgment, to serve notice of it on all those persons, if any, who, but for the practice so introduced, must have been parties to the record. It is obvious, therefore, that the old cases as to who were necessary parties in the first instance survive as authorities upon the question what persons ought to be served with notice of the judgment.

Formerly it was necessary that a party coming to a Court of Equity for relief should bring regularly before the Court, either as co-plaintiffs with himself or as defendants, all persons so circumstanced that, unless their rights were bound by the decree of the Court, they might cause future molestation or inconvenience to the party against whom the relief was sought; but now a plaintiff is enabled, in many cases, to avoid the expense of making such persons active parties to the cause by serving them with notice of the judgment (c).

Reason for bringing all interested parties before the Court.

We proceed to consider upon whom such notice ought to be served, premising that the Court has power to direct service of an order made on an originating summons (d) with the like effect as service of a judgment pronounced in an action commenced by writ (e).

(c) Daniell (194, 275) 172, 358. 467; *Strong* v. *Moore*, 22 L. J. Ch.
(d) As to which, see *ante*, p. 1.   917.
(e) *Berkeley* v. *Mason*, 19 Eq.

OF THE PARTIES TO ADMINISTRATION ACTIONS.

All interested in personalty alone represented by the executor.
An executor represents sufficiently all who are interested in the personalty (*f*), and accordingly legatees out of personal estate only need not, while those whose legacies are charged on the realty must be served with notice of the judgment (*g*). It is perfectly settled, as a general rule, that a pecuniary legatee need not be served in an action for an account of personal estate, it being the duty of the executors to protect the estate from improper demands (*h*), nor need legatees and annuitants who have no charge on the real estate, in a suit for administration of real and personal estate, although they may collaterally or incidentally be interested in the real estate (*i*).

In general, all residuary devisees and legatees must be before the Court.
Subject to the rule above mentioned as to trustees representing beneficiaries (read by the light of the cases presently cited), and to the rule referred to below as to one member of a class being taken to represent the whole class, and to the decision that it is not necessary to serve persons who, on a disputed construction of a will, have no reasonable ground of claim (*k*), and to the power vested in the Court by the Cons. Ord. referred to below to dispense with service, all residuary devisees (*l*), though but contingently entitled (*m*), or their assignees or mortgagees *pendente lite* (*n*), and residuary legatees (*o*), must be served with notice of the judgment. It is a general rule (with a possible exception in some cases of extreme difficulty) that, where an estate is to be sold under the directions of the Court, all the persons interested in the proceeds

(*f*) *Goldsmid* v. *Stonehewer*, 9 Ha. App. 38.
(*g*) *Morse* v. *Sadler*, 1 Cox, 352.
(*h*) Per Lord Langdale, *Marquis of Hertford* v. *Count de Zichy*, 9 Beav. 15; and see *post*, p. 93 (*y*).
(*i*) Per Romilly, M. R., *Jennings* v. *Paterson*, 15 Beav. p. 30.
(*k*) *Doody* v. *Higgins*, 9 Ha. App. 32.

(*l*) *Parsons* v. *Neville*, 3 Bro. C. C. 365; *Doody* v. *Higgins*.
(*m*) *Phillipson* v. *Gatty*, 6 Ha. 26.
(*n*) *Humble* v. *Shore*, 3 Ha. 119; *Freeman* v. *Pennington*, 3 De G. F. & J. 295; *Brandon* v. *Brandon*, 3 N. R. 287.
(*o*) Daniell, (223) 198.

OF THE PARTIES TO ADMINISTRATION ACTIONS. 43

must, if not already parties, be so served (*p*). Where a testator has directed the produce of real estate to be held in strict settlement, all persons entitled under the directed settlement down to and including the first vested estate of inheritance must be served (*q*). It is not necessary to serve notice of the judgment on persons claiming specific portions of property in the possession of the deceased at his death (*r*).

Executors with a power of sale are trustees within the meaning of the 9th rule (*s*) of the 42nd section of the Chancery Procedure Act (*t*), but, notwithstanding the rule, it was formerly held that trustees of the real estate only represent infant, not adult *cestuis que trustent* (*u*); if, however, an adult has settled his share, the trustees of such settlement must be served, and then represent, under the rule, the beneficiaries under their settlement (*x*). But having regard to the express words of O. XVI. r. 7, and to the observations thereon in *Mills* v. *Jennings* (*y*), it is submitted that in the absence of any direction of the Court to the contrary, trustees do now represent all their *cestuis que trustent* for the purposes of an administration action, unless any questions arise between the various *cestuis que trustent* (*z*). Where A. has covenanted with B. to transfer stock into the names of trustees upon trust for B., it is not necessary, in an action by B. as creditor for the administration of A.'s estate, to serve notice of the judgment on those trustees (*a*).

How far trustees represent their *cestuis que trustent*.

(*p*) *Doody* v. *Higgins*.
(*q*) *Pigott* v. *Pigott*, 2 N. R. 14.
(*r*) *Barker* v. *Rogers*, 7 Ha. 19.
(*s*) *Ante*, p. 40.
(*t*) *Shaw* v. *Hardingham*, 2 W. R. 657; and see *Smith* v. *Andrews*, 4 W. R. 353; *Bolton* v. *Stannard*, 4 Jur. N. S. 576.
(*u*) *Goldsmid* v. *Stonehewer*, 9 Ha.

App. 38; and see *Jones* v. *How*, 7 Ha. 267, 270.
(*x*) *Densem* v. *Elworthy*, 9 Ha. App. 42.
(*y*) 13 C. D. 639.
(*z*) See also *Goodrich* v. *Marsh*, W. N., 1878, 186.
(*a*) *Watson* v. *Parker*, 6 Beav. 283.

Where a person who has been served with notice of the judgment effects a settlement of his share, the trustees thereof must be served (*b*). But it has been said that trustees of the deceased's estate appointed after judgment cannot properly be brought before the Court by service of the judgment, not being within the words of r. 8 of 42nd section of the Chancery Procedure Act (*c*).

Where the suit was by appointees, and there was a question as to the validity of the appointment, it was held that the party entitled in default of appointment ought to be brought before the Court (*d*).

One or more of a class in same interest allowed or appointed to sue or be sued on behalf of or for all.

Where there are numerous parties having the same interest in one action, one or more of such parties may sue or be sued, or may be authorised by the Court to defend in such action, on behalf or for the benefit of all parties so interested (*e*). See also r. 9a, under which the Court is empowered to appoint any person or persons to represent any heir-at-law, next of kin, or class, before such heir, next of kin, or class shall have been ascertained (*f*). So, under the old practice, where the residuary legatees were very numerous, some of them sufficiently represented the rest (*g*).

The Judge in Chambers will not, in general, in the first instance direct upon whom the notice of the judgment is to be served (*h*).

Service upon infants, &c.

Until recently, where any person required to be served with notice of a judgment was an infant or a person of unsound mind not so found by inquisition, the notice was to be served upon such person or persons, and in such

---

(*b*) *White* v. *Stewart*, 35 Beav. 304.
(*c*) *Colyer* v. *Colyer*, 11 W. R. 355; see *Williamson* v. *Jefferys*, 12 W. R. 403.
(*d*) *Grace* v. *Terrington*, 1 Coll. 3.
(*e*) O. XVI. r. 9. This may be done at the hearing.
(*f*) See *Chester* v. *Phillips*, 4 C. D. 230.
(*g*) *Cockburn* v. *Thompson*, 16 Ves. 328; *Harvey* v. *Harvey*, 4 Beav. 215; and see *Smart* v. *Bradstock*, 7 Beav. 500.
(*h*) Daniell (277) 396; but see *De Balinhard* v. *Bullock*, 9 Ha. App. 13.

OF THE PARTIES TO ADMINISTRATION ACTIONS. 45

manner as the Judge to whose court the cause was attached might direct (*i*), and for the purpose of procuring this direction the plaintiff was by the 7th of the "Regulations" of August 8, 1857 (*j*), directed to make an *ex parte* application by summons, and thereupon to show by affidavit certain particulars relating to the infant or person of unsound mind as therein mentioned. As a rule an infant might be served personally (*k*), but now notice of a judgment or order on an infant or person of unsound mind not so found by inquisition is to be served in the same manner as a writ of summons in an action (*l*), *i.e.*, in the case of an infant, unless otherwise ordered (*m*), on the infant's father or guardian, or, if there be no father or guardian, on the person under whose care the infant is, or with whom the infant resides (*n*), and, in the case of a person of unsound mind not so found (unless otherwise ordered), on the person under whose charge such person is, or with whom he or she resides (*o*). Where a husband and wife have to be served, the notice must be served on each personally, notwithstanding that they are residing together (*p*). Where, upon the hearing of the summons to proceed (*q*), it appears to the Judge that by reason of absence, or for any other sufficient cause, the service of notice upon any party cannot be made, or ought to be dispensed with, the Judge may, if he shall think fit, wholly dispense with such service, or may, at his discretion, order any substituted service or notice by advertisement or otherwise in lieu of service (*r*). An application

Service dispensed with,

or substituted service allowed.

(*i*) Cons. Ord. VII. r. 5.
(*j*) Morgan, 5th ed. 166.
(*k*) *Clarke* v. *Clarke*, 1 W. R. 48; *Chalmers* v. *Laurie*, 10 Ha. App. 27.
(*l*) O. XVI. r. 12a.
(*m*) But the Court or a Judge may order that service made or to be made on the infant shall be deemed good service (*ibid.*, and see Seton, 1624, No. 7; Pemb. 10).
(*n*) O. IX. r. 4.
(*o*) O. IX. r. 5.
(*p*) Braith. 520; and see 45 & 46 Vict. c. 75, s. 1 (2).
(*q*) See *post*, p. 86.
(*r*) Cons. Ord. XXXV., r. 18.

under this order is usually required to be made by *ex parte* summons, supported by evidence of the facts on which it is founded; and, where a special mode of service is directed, an order is ordinarily drawn up by the Registrar, which will contain a direction that a copy of it shall be served with the notice. Where service is dispensed with, an order to that effect is not usually drawn up, but the fact is stated in the Chief Clerk's certificate of the result of the proceedings (*s*).

<small>Birth of infant beneficiary after action brought.</small> If during the progress of an administration suit a child was born who took an interest in the property, and it was desired that he should be bound by the proceedings, there was jurisdiction to make an order under 15 and 16 Vict., c. 86, s. 52, bringing the child before the Court, and directing that he should be so bound (*t*) if no proceedings had been taken in the action after his birth (*u*); otherwise a supplemental suit was necessary (*x*); and in a subsequent case, a Chief Clerk's certificate, which had been filed after the infant's birth, was allowed to be taken off the file and the usual supplemental order was then made (*y*); and though, by Order L. r. 4, it is expressly provided that in such a case an order may be obtained that the proceedings may be carried on between the continuing parties and the infant, upon an allegation of the child's birth, it has been held that this is subject to the same proviso—that no proceedings have been taken since the birth (*z*).

<small>Entry of memorandum of service.</small> A memorandum of the service upon any person of notice of the judgment shall be entered in the office of the Clerks of Records and Writs upon due proof by affidavit of such service (*a*).

(*s*) Daniell, (277) 361.
(*t*) *Egremont* v. *Thompson*, 4 Ch. 448.
(*u*) *Capps* v. *Capps*, 4 *ibid.* 1; *Austen* v. *Haines*, 4 *ibid.* 445.
(*x*) *Ibid.*

(*y*) *Cuthbert* v. *Harmby*, 13 Eq. 202.
(*z*) *Haldane* v. *Eckford*, W. N., 1879, 80.
(*a*) Cons. Ord. XXIII. r. 19.

Notice of a judgment shall be intituled in the cause, and there shall be indorsed thereon a memorandum in the prescribed form or to that effect (*b*). Title and endorsement of notice.

Notice of a judgment may be served out of the jurisdiction, whether pronounced on an originating summons or in an action instituted by writ (*c*), but an order is necessary for leave to do so (*d*). Service out of the jurisdiction.

Service of a copy of the judgment is regarded as service of notice of the judgment, but the copy must be indorsed in like manner as a notice (*e*). Service of a copy.

Persons who are not made parties, and have not yet been served with notice of the judgment, have no *locus standi*, though interested in the subject matter of the action (*f*).

Persons served with notice of the judgment are after such notice bound by the proceedings in the same manner as if they had been originally made parties to the action (*g*). Notice of the judgment is notice of the subsequent proceedings, and persons once served with notice of the judgment, though they have not attended the proceedings, need not, as a rule, be served with any further notice (*h*), nor, before the certificate be signed, with a summons to proceed (*i*), but where it was desired on further consideration to obtain a *personal* order for payment of money against parties who had been served with notice of the judgment, but who had not obtained an order to attend the proceedings, Jessel, M. R., considered that they ought to be served with notice of the Persons served bound by the proceedings,

---

(*b*) Cons. Ord. XXIII. r. 20; for the form, see Appendix, p. 195.
(*c*) *Strong* v. *Moore*, 22 L. J. Ch. 917; *Chalmers* v. *Laurie*, 10 Ha. App. 27.
(*d*) Daniell, (277) 360.
(*e*) Braith. 519.
(*f*) *Lloyd* v. *Cross*, W. N., 1871, 101.
(*g*) Chancery Procedure Act, 1852, s. 42, r. 8; and see *Doody* v. *Higgins*, 9 Ha. App. 32.
(*h*) *Lee* v. *Sturrock*, W. N., 1876, 226.
(*i*) *Green* v. *Measures*, W. N., 1866, 122.

action having been set down on further consideration, and directed that the further consideration should stand over for that purpose (*k*).

<small>but cannot be made to account till made parties.</small>

Though bound by the proceedings, a person served is under no liability to account: a plaintiff must make a person against whom he seeks an account a party to the action, and pray specific relief against him, or else some independent proceeding must be taken to enforce the liability (*l*).

<small>Nor can they be treated as co-plaintiffs, and obtain inquiries as such.</small>

On the other hand, persons served cannot be treated as co-plaintiffs, and no inquiries can be obtained in the action for their benefit that could not be obtained between co-defendants (*m*), unless, as it would seem, the party served be the Attorney-General (*n*). Where, however, the plaintiff in an action for administration was, after judgment, found to have no title, the action was stayed on the application of a party served with a notice of the judgment (*o*).

<small>Parties served may obtain order of course to attend the proceedings.</small>

Parties served may by an order of course have liberty to attend the proceedings under the judgment (*p*), but not necessarily at the expense of the estate (*q*). A copy of every such order should be served on the solicitors of all parties in the cause, and of all persons who have leave to attend the proceedings, and a copy, certified by the solicitor to be a true copy, should be left at the Judge's Chambers (*r*).

<small>Infants.</small>

Infants and persons of unsound mind not so found by inquisition, attend the proceedings by their guardians *ad litem*, who are appointed in the same manner as guardians *ad litem* to defend actions (*s*), and the Judge may, at any time during

---

(*k*) *Rees* v. *George*, 15 C. D. 490.
(*l*) *Walker* v. *Seligmann*, 12 Eq. 152; cf. *Rees* v. *George, ubi supra*.
(*m*) *Whitney* v. *Smith*, 4 Ch. 513.
(*n*) See *Johnstone* v. *Hamilton*, cited, *post*, (*z*).

(*o*) *Houseman* v. *Houseman*, 1 C. D. 535.
(*p*) Chancery Procedure Act, 1852, s. 42, r. 8.
(*q*) See *post*, p. 93.
(*r*) Daniell, (279) 363.
(*s*) Daniell, (280) 363.

proceedings in Chambers under any judgment require a guardian *ad litem* to be appointed for any infant or person of unsound mind not so found, who has been served with notice of such judgment (*t*).

A party served may, within one lunar month after service, apply to the Court to add to, or appeal from (*u*) the judgment (*x*); but, *semble*, the time may be extended in the case of a person out of the jurisdiction (*y*), and the limit does not apply to the Crown (*z*). Such application is usually made on summons (*a*); but where a party served, who is aggrieved by the decree, is unable to raise his case (*e.g.* a charge of wilful default or breach of trust) under the pleadings, he should move on notice for leave to institute an action in the nature of review (*b*).

Persons served may apply to add to the judgment.

(*t*) Cons. Ord. VII. rr. 6, 7.
(*u*) *Bruff* v. *Cobbold*, 7 Ch. 217.
(*x*) Chancery Procedure Act, 1852, s. 42. r. 8; Cons. Ord. XXIII. r. 18; XXXVII. r. 10; see *post*, Ch. iv.
(*y*) See *Strong* v. *Moore*, 22 L. J. Ch. 917.
(*z*) *Johnstone* v. *Hamilton*, 11 Jur. N. S. 777.
(*a*) Daniell (279) 363.
(*b*) *Kidd* v. *Cheyne*, 18 Jur. 348; *Partington* v. *Reynolds*, 4 Dr. 253.

CHAPTER IV.

THE JUDGMENT AND ADDITIONS MADE TO IT.

Administration judgment moulded to enable the Court to deal with the whole action on further consideration.

It does not fall within the scope of this treatise to deal with the various forms which, according to the circumstances of each case, a judgment for administration assumes. A few of the more ordinary Forms are, by the kind permission of Mr. Pemberton, printed in the Appendix, *post*, p. 195 (*a*); and it is sufficient here to say that except where the executor or administrator admits assets, and, in a creditors' action, the debt of the plaintiff is proved or admitted, or, in a legatee's action, the legacy is assented to (*b*), such accounts and inquiries will be directed, and such declarations made, as are required in each case to enable the Court, when the action shall come on for further consideration, to deal effectively with the estate. Where, however, the debt is so proved or admitted, or the executor or administrator has assented to the legacy, and assets are admitted, the plaintiff, whether creditor or legatee (*c*), is entitled at the hearing to an immediate judgment for payment, with costs, and not merely to a judgment for an account, for, the legal personal representative making himself liable, the other creditors cannot be prejudiced (*d*);

(*a*) This subject is amply discussed and illustrated in Seton, 801—827, 848—855, and Pemberton, Ch. vi., to which the reader is referred.

(*b*) Where assets are admitted (as to which, see Comp. Exors., 223—225), but the debt is disputed, and the defendant desires a trial by jury, the proper course is to transfer the action to the Queen's Bench Division, unless the Judge sees reasons for trying the question without a jury (*Hunt* v. *Chambers*, 20 C. D. 365); and see *Beynon* v. *Beynon*, W. N. 1873, 186. As to what acts amount to assent to a legacy, see Comp. Exors. 120—123, and Seton, 860, 861, where the cases are collected.

(*c*) *Woodgate* v. *Field*, 2 Ha. 211; *Whittle* v. *Henning*, 2 Beav. 396.

(*d*) *Woodgate* v. *Field*, 2 Ha., p. 213.

and, by admitting assets, the executor of an executor renders himself liable to the same judgment as the executor himself, if living, would have been liable to in respect of the *personal* estate of the original testator (*e*).

It will be seen on reference to the forms given in the works above mentioned, that, although the purview of the judgment, when pronounced at the instance of a creditor, is more limited than when it is obtained by a beneficiary, executor, administrator, or trustee, yet in each, accounts are directed to be taken of the deceased's debts, funeral expenses, and personal, or real and personal estate, including (*f*) an inquiry what parts, if any, of his personal estate are outstanding or undisposed of. In the former case, however, the payment of debts is the object principally aimed at, the plaintiff's interest in the estate ceasing with the satisfaction of his claim (*g*) ; while, in the latter, the Court goes further, providing for the payment not only of the creditors, but also of the legatees, and, in short, supervises the complete administration of the estate. As to the distinction between common judgments and judgments charging the trustees on the footing of wilful neglect or default, see *ante*, p. 15.

<small>Less extensive in creditors' actions.</small>

The accounts and inquiries directed by the judgment are usually taken and made in chambers, but they may be referred to an official referee (*h*).

(*e*) *Davenport* v. *Stafford*, 2 De G. M. & G. 901.

(*f*) Under Cons. Ord. XXIII. r. 14.

(*g*) Accordingly, in a creditors' action, no inquiries will be ordered as to the propriety of proceedings proposed to be taken for the beneficial management and realisation of the estate (*Collinson* v. *Ballard*, 2 Ha. 119) ; but after providing for payment of costs and of the debts, the residue of the estate (if any) will, on further consideration, be carried over to a separate account, with liberty (for beneficiaries) to apply ; see the Form of Order, Seton, 837. It may be mentioned that in taking the accounts of the personal estate, property specifically bequeathed is not excepted in a creditors' action, as in a legatee's ; Seton, 955 ; Pemb. 178 ; Appendix, *post*, pp. 195, 199.

(*h*) *Sykes* v. *Brook*, 50 L. J. Ch. 744 ; but in a partnership action

THE JUDGMENT AND ADDITIONS MADE TO IT.

Further accounts or inquiries may be ordered;

It was provided by Cons. Ord. XXXV. r. 19, that, where, in the prosecution of the decree or order, it appeared to the Judge that it would be expedient that further accounts should be taken or further inquiries made, he might order the same to be taken or made accordingly. In pursuance of this rule, a further inquiry was directed as to leases granted by a trustee, and his expenditure in repairs (*i*). But it was considered that a decree for administration in the common form could not be so added to as to charge the defendants on the footing of wilful default (*k*), though Stuart, V.-C., was of a different opinion (*l*); nor, after the common decree, could the defendants be so charged on further consideration, or an inquiry be then directed on the subject, though the chief clerk's certificate had laid the foundation for such a charge or inquiry, and wilful default had been sufficiently alleged on the pleadings (*m*), on the principle that matters in issue at the first hearing, which were neither decided, put into a train of investigation, nor reserved, must, on further consideration, be regarded either as abandoned or as points on which the plaintiff was entitled to no order (*n*). But now, by O. XXXIII., the Court or a Judge may, *at any stage* of the proceedings in a cause or matter, direct any necessary inquiries or accounts to be made or taken (*o*); and, if wilful default is properly charged in the statement of claim, it would appear that, under the new practice, a

but formerly, not so as to charge defendants with wilful default;

otherwise, under the new practice.

(*Hales* v. *Morris*, 1882) Kay, J. said that though there was an advantage that the proceedings continued *de die in diem*, yet the expense was so much greater that this course should never be directed unless both parties desired it.

(*i*) *Mutter* v. *Hudson*, 2 Jur. N. S. 34.

(*k*) See *Partington* v. *Reynolds*, 4 Dr. 261, and compare *Nelson* v. *Booth*, 3 De G. & J. 119.

(*l*) *Mirehouse* v. *Herbert*, 5 W. R. 584.

(*m*) *Garland* v. *Littlewood*, 1 Beav. 527; *Green* v. *Badley*, 7 Beav. 274; *Coope* v. *Carter*, 2 De G. M. & G. 292; *Jones* v. *Morrall*, 2 Sim. N. S. 241; compare *Morgan* v. *Morgan*, 13 Beav. 441.

(*n*) *Passingham* v. *Sherborn*, 9 Beav. 424.

(*o*) *Barber* v. *Mackrell*, 12 C. D. 534.

judgment on that footing may be pronounced, or inquiries directed, at any time during the progress of an action (*p*), provided, of course, the plaintiff establish his case by sufficient evidence (*q*). Stuart, V.-C., said that a Judge may direct any further account or inquiry that may seem to him necessary, without evidence, on the suggestion of a suitor (*r*); but it is submitted that the practice is not so, except in quite simple and ordinary cases, certainly not where it is sought to charge for wilful default.

An application for further accounts or inquiries may be made on summons or motion. If, however, it should be made on motion, when the cheaper procedure would be equally available, the applicant might be ordered to pay the extra costs occasioned thereby. How application made to add to judgment.

If desired by any party, the Judge may direct the further accounts or inquiries to be considered in open Court (*s*).

(*p*) *Job* v. *Job*, 6 C. D. 562; *Mayer* v. *Murray*, 8 C. D. 424; *Luke* v. *Tonkin*, 21 C. D. 757; and see *ante*, p. 16.
(*q*) See *ante*, p. 17.

(*r*) *Mutter* v. *Hudson*, 2 Jur. N. S. 35.
(*s*) Cons. Ord. XXXV. 19; see *Clark* v. *Phillips*, 2 W. R. 331.

CHAPTER V.

THE EFFECT OF JUDGMENT FOR ADMINISTRATION ON POWERS AND DISCRETION OF TRUSTEES AND EXECUTORS.

WE have to consider in this chapter what effect the mere institution of an action for administration, and what effect judgment for administration has upon the powers and discretion of trustees and executors. These questions have several times arisen for decision, but the cases on the subject are not always to be easily reconciled one with another.

After judgment, new trustee cannot be appointed without approval of the Court; nor investments made, nor powers of management exercised.

After judgment the Court will restrain a trustee from appointing new trustees, except under its direction. It does not, said Lord Eldon, prevent the exercise of his discretion, but takes care that it shall be duly exercised (*a*). So, after judgment, trustees and executors cannot exercise powers of investment, except under direction of the Court (*b*); for then all powers of management (*e.g.*, a discretionary power of investment), which may be vested in them are subject to the control of the Court, and the Judge who exercises such control must be personally satisfied of the propriety of the course proposed to be adopted by the trustee (*c*). An estate was administered under the

---

(*a*) *Webb* v. *Earl of Shaftesbury*, 7 Ves. 480, 487; and see *Anon.* v. *Roberts*, 1 J. & W. 251; *Middleton* v. *Reay*, 7 Ha. 106. But the Court is bound to adopt the nominee of the person to whom the power of appointment is given, unless he refuses to nominate any but a person who is unfit (*Kennedy* v. *Turnley*, 6 Ir. Eq. R. 399).

(*b*) *Widdowson* v. *Duck*, 2 Mer. 494.

(*c*) *Bethell* v. *Abraham*, 17 Eq. p. 27; *Eadwwyn Clarke, 23 C.D. 134; allen v Norris, 27 ib. 333.*

EFFECT OF JUDGMENT ON POWERS OF TRUSTEES.

Court, and all claims being provided for, the devisee was let into possession; a further claim being afterwards made against the estate, it was held that the trustees were not justified of their own authority in taking possession to provide for it (*d*). And, in general, after having invoked the aid of the Court in administering an estate, and after judgment for administration has been obtained, they cannot act (*e*) in the matter of the administration except under the sanction of the Court (*f*).

Although up to judgment for administration an executor may prefer any creditor over others of equal degree, and pay his debt in full (*g*), after judgment he is not at liberty to prefer one to another, or do any act which affects their relative rights (*h*), and therefore has no power to give a creditor a valid acknowledgment of his debt, so as to take it out of the Statute of Limitations (*i*); nor will he be allowed payments made to creditors after judgment, though he will be permitted to stand in their place (*k*). But unless he has waived his right by his form of pleading (*l*), he may exercise his right of retainer, notwithstanding judgment for administration has been given in an action by the other creditors, and the assets out of which he seeks to retain have come to his hands after judgment (*m*); and

Nor may one creditor be preferred to another.

But an executor may exercise his right of retainer.

(*d*) *Underwood* v. *Hatton*, 5 Beav. 36.

(*e*) Shadwell, V.-C., refused to hold that an annuity given to an executor "for his trouble" ceased upon the institution of a suit, unless it could be shown that the trouble of the executorship had ceased; *Baker* v. *Martin*, 8 Sim. 25.

(*f*) *Minors* v. *Battison*, 1 App. Cas. p. 453.

(*g*) *Lyttleton* v. *Cross*, 3 B. & C. p. 322, and see *post*, p. 58.

(*h*) *Shewen* v. *Vanderhorst*, 2 R. & M. 75; *per* James, L. J., *Lee* v.

Nuttall, 12 C. D. p. 64.

(*i*) *Phillips* v. *Beal* (No. 2), 32 Beav. 26. But he may retain for his own debt, statute-barred before the death of the testator; *Hill* v. *Walker*, 4 K. & J. 169;

(*k*) *Jones* v. *Jukes*, 2 Ves. 518; *Mitchelson* v. *Piper*, 8 Sim. 64; *Irby* v. *Irby*, 24 Beav. 525.

(*l*) *Player* v. *Foxhall*, 1 Russ. 538; and see *Ferguson* v. *Gibson*, 14 Eq. 379.

(*m*) *Nunn* v. *Barlow*, 1 S. & S. 588; *Sharman* v. *Rudd*, 27 L. J. Ch. 844.

this right is not affected by the statute 32 & 33 Vict. c. 46 (*n*), or by sect. 10 of the Judicature Act, 1875 (*o*), or by the fact that he is himself suing *as creditor* on behalf of himself and all other creditors (*p*), even though the fund out of which he claims to retain his debt has been paid into Court (*q*).

Executor may mortgage assets after judgment.

An executor can mortgage the assets after judgment, if no receiver has been appointed, and no injunction been granted restraining him from dealing with them (*r*). So, trustees can, after judgment, exercise discretionary powers of maintenance, education, &c. (*s*), for the doctrine of *Webb* v. *Earl of Shaftesbury* (*t*) applies only to cases of management (*u*).

Before judgment, trustees may exercise discretion.

In *Cafe* v. *Bent* (*x*) the question was as to an appointment of new trustees by a surviving trustee, after a bill for accounts had been filed against him, but *before decree*, and the Vice-Chancellor's judgment in that case is often cited on this subject. "There is no authority," he said, "for the proposition that the mere filing of a bill has the effect of suspending the power given by the will to the surviving or remaining trustee. There is no reason why the mere institution of a suit, which may never be prosecuted, should have the effect of preventing trustees from exercising their discretion. Where, indeed, the Court has assumed the execution of the trusts, it would be highly inconvenient, if not impracticable, that the trustees should afterwards act independently of the Court. The Court does not, however, in the absence of any misconduct

---

(*n*) *Crowder* v. *Stewart*, 16 C. D. 368; and see *post*, p. 164.
(*o*) *Lee* v. *Nuttall*, 12 C. D. 61; and see *post*, p. 164.
(*p*) *Campbell* v. *Campbell*, 16 C. D. 198.
(*q*) *Richmond* v. *White*, 12 *ibid*. 361; and see *post*, p. 58.

(*r*) *Berry* v. *Gibbons*, 8 Ch. 747.
(*s*) *Sillibourne* v. *Newport*, 1 K. & J. 602, approved by Jessel, M. R., *Bethell* v. *Abraham*, 17 Eq. p. 26.
(*t*) *Ubi supra*.
(*u*) *Per* Jessel, M.R., 17 Eq. 26.
(*x*) 3 Ha. 245.

of the trustees, deprive them of the exercise of their discretion, but only requires them to act under the control of the Court. That is all that the case of *Webb* v. *Earl of Shaftesbury* decided upon this point. If the trustees, by acting independently after the suit has been instituted, should occasion expense which might have been avoided if they had acted under the direction of the Court, they may be made to pay the expense occasioned by such conduct. The decision in *Attorney-General* v. *Cluck* (*y*) is to that effect. But the mere filing of a bill cannot have the effect of preventing trustees from doing acts which are necessary to the due execution of the trust which is imposed upon them. Such a rule might, in many cases, operate to destroy the trusts altogether" (*z*). So it has been held that where a discretionary trust (*e.g.*, for distribution of a fund) is vested in trustees, the Court will not interfere with the exercise of the discretion, if it be not capricious or improper, though a suit be instituted for the administration of the trust funds (*a*). It would seem, however, that unless there is an "absolute" or "uncontrolled" or "irresponsible" discretion given to the trustees, the Court will in a proper case interfere with their exercise of discretionary powers (*b*). The old distinction between what may be termed restrictive and mandatory interference, has recently been clearly pointed out by Jessel, M.R., in the following words: "It is settled law that where a testator has given a pure discretion to trustees as to the exercise of a power, the Court does not enforce the exercise of it against the wish of the trustees, but it does prevent them from exercising it improperly. The Court

And the Court will not interfere with "absolute" or "uncontrolled" discretion of trustee.

(*y*) 1 Beav. 467.
(*z*) *Per* Wigram, V.-C., 3 Ha., p. 249.
(*a*) *Gray* v. *Gray*, 13 Ir. Ch. R. 404.
(*b*) See and compare *Gisborne* v. *Gisborne*, L. R. 2 App. Cas. 300, *Tabor* v. *Brooks*, 10 Ch. D. 273, and *Tempest* v. *Lord Camoys*, 21 *ibid.* 571, with *Darcy* v. *Ward*, 7 *ibid.* 754, *Re Roper's Trusts*, 11 *ibid.* 272, and *Re Wearer*, 21 *ibid.* 615.

says that the power, if exercised at all, is to be exercised properly" (c). But, if trustees commence an action for administration, their discretion as to investments is, according to a decision of Romilly, M.R., taken away, and they must only act as the Court shall direct (d).

Payment of debts.

An executor may, however, after action brought against him by a creditor, but before judgment, confess a judgment in favour of another creditor of equal degree, and thus give the latter a preference (e), though he cannot so confess to a stranger, a mere trustee for creditors (f). So, after the commencement of a creditors' action and before judgment, an executor or administrator may voluntarily pay any (g) creditor in full, though he may have had notice of the action, and he will be allowed such payment in his accounts (h). The only way to prevent such preferential payments being made is for the plaintiff, upon issuing the writ, to immediately apply for and obtain a receiver (i). Such an appointment will also deprive (k) the executor of his right of retainer out of assets got in by the receiver (l). An executor can sell and make a good title to leaseholds at any time before judgment (m); but devisees of real estate could not, it was

Sale of real and leasehold estate.

(c) *Tempest* v. *Lord Camoys.*
(d) *Consterdine* v. *Consterdine*, 31 Beav. 333.
(e) *Prince* v. *Nicholson*, 5 Taunt. 665; *Waring* v. *Danvers*, 1 P. Wms. 295.
(f) *Tolputt* v. *Wells*, 1 M. & S. p. 403.
(g) A legatee cannot complain of the order in which an executor pays debts, even though he indirectly suffer loss (*Turner* v. *Turner*, 1 J. & W. 39).
(h) *European Assurance Society* v. *Radcliffe*, 7 C. D. 733. See further, *Maltby* v. *Russell*, 2 S. & S. 277; *Earl Vane* v. *Rigden*, 5 Ch. 663.
(i) Per Jessel, M. R., *European Assurance Society* v. *Radcliffe.*

(k) A receiver is never appointed except for misconduct or by the consent of the executor (Comp. Exors. 237—242; *Richmond* v. *White*, 12 C. D., p. 362). The Court more readily appoints a receiver where there is an administrator only; *e.g.*, on the ground of poverty; and absolute insolvency makes it "just and expedient" to appoint a receiver against an executor; *Gawthorpe* v. *Gawthorpe*, W. N. 1878, 91.
(l) See *Richmond* v. *White*, and *Birt* v. *Burt*, 31 W. R. 334.
(m) *Neeves* v. *Burrage*, 14 Q. B. 504; and see *Berry* v. *Gibbons*, cited *ante*, p. 56.

held, sell, except under the Court, after answer, though before decree (n), it being proper that trustees should obtain the sanction of the Court to their exercise of powers of sale and leasing (o).

This being the state of the authorities, a trustee or executor, who has instituted or has had instituted against him an action for administration, should be very cautious in committing himself, without the sanction of the Court, to any but formal acts in connection with the estate, even if judgment has not been pronounced in the action; for, though an act on his part may be valid and effectual as between himself and strangers to the trust, it by no means follows that it is justifiable as between himself and his *cestuis que trustent*.

(n) *Walker* v. *Smalwood*, Ambl. 676; *Annesley* v. *Ashurst*, 3 P. Wms. 282.

(o) *Turner* v. *Turner*, 30 Beav. 414.

CHAPTER VI.

AS TO SECURING TRUST FUNDS BY ORDERING THEM INTO COURT.

Funds admitted to be in hand ordered to be paid into Court upon interlocutory motion;

As soon as an executor, administrator, or trustee admits (*a*) a trust fund in hand, it is a matter of course, on an interlocutory motion, or where the application is unopposed, upon a summons (*b*), by a party sufficiently interested, to order it into Court (*c*), irrespective of danger to the assets or of misconduct by the trustee (*d*); and, where the admissions show the defendant to be a trustee of money, a mere formal denial of the fact will not prevent him from being ordered to bring in the money (*e*). But it has been said that the plaintiff's right must proceed upon admissions made in reference to an equity raised by him, not upon admissions in reference to an independent equity stated only in the admissions (*f*).

even though applicants may show only a prima facie title.

In order to entitle a plaintiff to have the fund secured in Court, it is not necessary that he should show an

---

(*a*) "The Court has always," said Lord Hatherley, "thought it desirable that an executor should, by his answer, make a full discovery of the assets, so that the plaintiff may be in a position to move to have the balance brought into Court" (*Thompson* v. *Dunn*, 5 Ch., p. 576); and see *Alison* v. *Alison*, 50 L. J. Ch. 574.

(*b*) See Daniell, 1629; *Thompson* v. *Hope*, cited Seton, 84.

(*c*) *Per* Romilly, M. R., *Danby* v. *Danby*, 5 Jur. N. S. 54; *Rothwell* v. *Rothwell*, 2 S. & S. 217.

(*d*) *Strange* v. *Harris*, 3 Bro. C. C. 365; *Blake* v. *Blake*, 2 Sch. & Lef. 26; *Hamond* v. *Walker*, 3 Jur. N. S. 686; but see *per* Lord Langdale, *Ross* v. *Ross*, 12 Beav. p. 90.

(*e*) *Hayell* v. *Currie*, **2** Ch. 449; and see *Bank of Turkey* v. *Ottoman Bank*, 2 Eq. 366.

(*f*) *Proudfoot* v. *Hume*, 4 Beav. 476; see *per* Romilly, M. R., *Wiglesworth* v. *Wiglesworth*, 16 Beav. 269.

absolute title to maintain an action for administration; for this purpose a *primâ facie* title, affording a reasonable expectation of success at the hearing, is sufficient (*g*). Nor need the applicant necessarily show an absolute or vested interest in the fund; for money has been ordered into Court on the application of a party entitled merely to a contingent interest, notwithstanding the opposition of all the other interested parties (*h*), though in one case such a motion was refused on the ground that there was no allegation of danger and that the fund might be sufficiently protected by *distringas*(*i*), and in another because all the persons interested in the fund had not been served with notice of the motion (*k*). In *Braithwaite* v. *Wallis* (*l*), Hall, V.-C., said that the rule was not absolute, though the fund would no doubt be brought into Court in any case where there was reasonable ground for the application.

In what cases the application refused.

The order for payment will go, where the trustee does not deny title in the applicant, but only does not admit that the title is as alleged (*m*). But the order has been refused to the plaintiff in a single creditor's suit, and to the next-of-kin of a deceased person, when they asked for it against the executor of an alleged will of the deceased, the validity of which was denied by them and was still *sub judice* (*n*); and a *curator bonis* and *factor loco tutoris* of Scotch infants was held not bound to pay into Court assets belonging to the infants receivable under an English will, of which the *curator* was administrator,

(*g*) *Danby* v. *Danby*, 5 Jur. N. S. 54; *Whitmore* v. *Turquand*, 1 J. & H. 296; *Parry* v. *Ashley*, 3 Sim. 100.

(*h*) *Bartlett* v. *Bartlett*, 4 Ha. 631; *Governesses' Benevolent Institution* v. *Rushbridger*, 18 Beav. 467.

(*i*) *Ross* v. *Ross*, 12 Beav. 89.

(*k*) *Lewellin* v. *Cobbold*, 1 Sm. & G. 572.

(*l*) 21 C. D. 121.

(*m*) *Symonds* v. *Jenkins*, 24 W. R. 512.

(*n*) *Reeve* v. *Goodwin*, 10 Jur. 1050; *Edwards* v. *Edwards*, 10 Ha. App. 63.

and which was in course of administration in England (o).

The conduct of a trustee being proper, the Court will not, in general, on the application of one of several *cestuis que trustent*—though it has power to do so—order payment into Court of the whole fund, but only of the applicant's aliquot share (p).

<small>The Court will exercise discretion to prevent needless payment in and out.</small>

The mere existence of a discretionary power in trustees over a trust fund would afford no reason why the ordinary right to have it paid into Court should not prevail, for bringing it into Court would not prevent the discretion being exercised. Where, however, in such a case, the trustees were about to exercise their discretion in a proper manner, the exigency contemplated by the power having already arisen, the Court, to prevent useless expense, refused to order the fund to be paid in (q).

An executor, having admitted a large balance to be in his hands, was ordered to pay the whole into Court, although he stated that an action at law was pending against him for a debt to a considerable amount due from the testator, but liberty was given him, in case the plaintiff in the action should recover, to apply to have a sufficient sum paid out again (r). However, in a like case in Ireland, the Court allowed the executor to retain sufficient not only for costs already incurred in connection with suits he was carrying on as executor, but also for probable growing costs (s).

<small>Debts admitted to be due from</small>

Where an executor admits himself to have been a debtor

(o) *Mackie* v. *Darling*, 12 Eq. 319.

(p) *Hamond* v. *Walker*, 3 Jur. N. S., 686; and see *Score* v. *Ford*, 7 Beav. 333; *Chaffers* v. *Headlam*, 17 Jur. 754.

(q) *Talbot* v. *Marshfield*, 2 Dr. & Sm. 285.

(r) *Yare* v. *Harrison*, 2 Cox, 377. The plaintiff in the action did recover, and the Court ordered the amount to be paid out to him, not to the executor (*ibid.*).

(s) *Betagh* v. *Concannon*, 2 Moll. 559.

to the testator at the time of his death, this has always *executor to the testator regarded as in his hands.* been held a clear admission of assets in his hands to the amount of the debt, and he is compelled to pay it into Court accordingly (*t*), even, in one case, where there were debts of the testator outstanding, the testator having died three years before (*u*). In these cases, the person to pay and the person to receive being the same, the Court assumes that what ought to have been done has been done, and orders the payment not as of a debt by a debtor, but as of moneys realised in the hands of the executor or trustee (*x*).

Moneys in the hands of his partner are moneys in an *So, as to moneys in the hands of executor's partner.* executor's own hands for the purpose of being ordered into Court, though the partner be not before the Court (*y*).

Where an executor admits that he has received a certain *What moneys may be deducted by executor.* sum, but adds that he has made payments, the amount of which he does not specify, the Court will allow him to verify the amount of his payments by affidavit, and order him to pay the balance into Court (*z*); but he cannot make any deductions in respect of moneys which he has improperly applied, as will appear from several of the cases presently cited. Thus, where money appears to have been invested on an improper security, *e.g.*, note of hand or bond (*a*), it will be ordered to be brought into Court within a given time; but in a proper case, the period will be extended from time to time to enable the defendant to realise the securities (*b*). And an administrator was ordered to transfer a sum of consols into Court upon an admission that he possessed it, and sold it out after the

(*t*) *Per* Leach, V.-C. E., *Rothwell* v. *Rothwell*, 2 S. & S., p. 218.

(*u*) *Mortlock* v. *Leathes*, 2 Mer. 491.

(*x*) *Per* Lord Cottenham, *Richardson* v. *Bank of England*, 4 M. & Cr. p. 174.

(*y*) *Johnson* v. *Aston*, 1 S. & S. 73; *White* v. *Barton*, 18 Beav.

192.

(*z*) *Anon.*, 4 Sim. 359.

(*a*) *Vigrass* v. *Binfield*, 3 Madd. 62; *Collis* v. *Collis*, 2 Sim. 365; and see *Payne* v. *Collier*, 1 Ves. jr. 170.

(*b*) *Score* v. *Ford*, 7 Beav. 333; *Wyatt* v. *Sharratt*, 3 Beav. 498.

bill was filed, and invested it in other securities which he did not specify (*c*); but, in a similar case, where a trustee had a power to vary investments, some admission of misapplication was required (*d*). Again, a trustee was directed to bring into Court the amount of the loss sustained on an improper investment (*e*), and, *à fortiori*, the amount appearing by the answer to be due, after deducting items for which the trustee had taken credit in a debtor and creditor account set out in the answer, by which, however, he also admitted that he had applied them to purposes not warranted by the trusts (*f*).

What amounts to an admission by executor.

In *Freeman* v. *Fairlie* (*g*), where an executor admitted that the whole amount of the property was near £40,000, and that the whole was invested in India on public securities, either in his name or in the name of the house in which he was a partner, but subject to his disposal, unless some part was in the hands of the said house at interest, which he believed might be the case, Lord Eldon held that there was not a sufficient admission of money in his hands to order the payment into Court of any part of it. But in *Roy* v. *Gibbon* (*h*), where the executor, who had proved the will in India, admitted that after payment of all the known debts, a certain balance of the estate remained in his hands, subject to other charges and expenses, the amount of which he had not ascertained, and that he had invested such balance on personal security in India, Wigram, V.-C., after remarking that the rule (as to precision of admission) was perhaps less strict at the present day than it was stated in *Freeman* v. *Fairlie*, ordered payment of the balance into Court, after retention

(*c*) *Hinde* v. *Blake*, 4 Beav. 597; *Wiglesworth* v. *Wiglesworth*, 16 Beav. 269.
(*d*) *Meyer* v. *Montriou*, 4 Beav. 343.
(*e*) *Bourne* v. *Mole*, 8 Beav. 177.
(*f*) *Nokes* v. *Steppings*, 2 Ph. 19.
(*g*) 3 Mer. 39.
(*h*) 4 Ha. 65.

of a reasonable sum in respect of the suggested charges and expenses, by a day which would afford time for the remittance of the fund from India.

Trustees sold out trust funds, and the produce was received by one alone, who misapplied it. The others were ordered to bring in the amount (*i*).

A testator charged his real estate, which consisted of a single house, with an annuity to his widow, and, subject thereto, devised it in fee to his executrix. The testator had insured the house, but the policy expired a few months after his death, and was then renewed by the executrix. Soon afterwards the house was burnt down. The insurance money was ordered into Court on the application of the annuitant, in a suit, to which the insurance company was a party, instituted by her for the administration of the testator's estate (*k*).

As to the stages at which a plaintiff may apply for an order on a defendant to pay trust money in his hands into Court, the rule seems now to be that he may obtain such an order, whenever and by what ever means the defendant has, by himself or his agent, admitted, or must be taken to have admitted, that he has such a fund in his hands, or under his control, and that the plaintiff has a sufficient interest therein to entitle him to apply for the order in question. In support of this proposition only a few cases, in addition to those already referred to, need be cited. According to the practice of the Court of Chancery, when it was sufficiently ascertained after decree, as Sir John Leach said in *Creak* v. *Capell* (*l*), that a sum of money would be due on taking the accounts, the Court had power —a discretionary power, undoubtedly—to order that sum to be brought into Court as security. That was the

At what stage in the action money will be ordered to be paid into Court.

(*i*) *Wiglesworth* v. *Wiglesworth*, 16 Beav. 269; *Ingle* v. *Partridge*, 32 Beav. 661.

(*k*) *Parry* v. *Ashley*, 3 Sim. 97.
(*l*) 6 Madd. 114.

general rule. Then how was it to be sufficiently ascertained? Sir John Leach gave three instances in that case, but there may be many others. Sufficiency of ascertainment cannot be positively defined *à priori*, nor can it be limited *à priori* to any number of particular modes of proceeding, and we have a very strong instance of that in the case of *Brown* v. *De Tastet* (m). That case is a very high authority to establish that without a confirmed report, but after accounts have been taken, the Court may look at the result of the accounts, and, upon being satisfied that there is a probability amounting to reasonable certainty that not less than a certain amount will be due from the defendants, may in its discretion direct the amount to be brought into Court. If the Judge finds that, by reason of unavoidable delay in ascertaining how much will be due, no certificate can be made, and no final decision as to the ultimate balance of the account arrived at, he has power to say, "I am satisfied now that this amount, at all events, has been sufficiently ascertained, and I will order the defendant to pay it into Court as security." This point is of general, if not of universal application, as regards the taking of accounts under judgments or decrees (n).

(m) 4 Russ. 126.

(n) Per Jessel, M. R., *London Syndicate* v. *Lord*, 8 C. D. 88, 89, 90. This case seems to over-rule the decision in *Douthwaite* v. *Spensley*, 18 Beav. 74, that money found due by a chief clerk's certificate will not be ordered into Court until the expiration of eight days, unless an objection to the report by the party charged thereby, has been sooner over-ruled. An order for payment into Court is not necessarily a final decision on the merits (see *per* Jessel, M. R., *London Syndicate* v. *Lord*, 8 C. D. 91), and, if thought expedient, the order may be expressed to be made without prejudice (*Bourne* v. *Mole*, 8 Beav. 177). Under the old practice a plaintiff could not after decree obtain an order for payment into Court on admissions in the answer, but must have proceeded on the examination or report (*Wright* v. *Lukes*, 13 Beav. 107); but this canon cannot be applied to the modern statement of defence, for by O. XL. r. 11 (*ante*, p. 18), motions founded on admissions in the pleadings may be made at any stage of the action.

There is not any virtue in one mode of admission rather than in another. What the Court has to be satisfied of is that the defendant has admitted the amount to be due. At one time it was supposed that the admission must be in an answer, and no doubt that was the practice of the Court of Chancery before decree. It was next settled that it need not be in the answer, but that it might be in an affidavit brought in by the defendant, or in an answer to a question which he could not help answering on an examination taken by direction of the Master. Whether it was a compulsory statement on oath or a voluntary statement on oath was immaterial, because it need not be upon oath at all. A man may admit by his agent or solicitor that the sum is due; he may put in a formal admission to that effect without any oath whatever, or he may act in such a manner as to authorize a third person to admit for him. There is no difficulty in doing that, and, if the Court ascertains he has done it, the Court will act upon the admission (o). Accordingly, where the Court had referred it to accountants to report on the accounts, and they verified by affidavit their report showing that £541 was due from defendant to plaintiff on the undisputed items, and that the disputed items were items of charge against the defendant, so that, however they were decided, the £541 would not be reduced, the Court ordered that amount into Court (p). Like orders have been made upon the joint result of an affidavit of a plaintiff charging the defendant with having a sum of money in his hands and an affidavit by the defendant before answer (q), and also in a case where the plaintiff, immediately after the issue of the writ, moved for payment into Court by the defendant of a trust fund which it was shown by affidavit he had received, and the defendant did not appear on the motion, the defendant

Immaterial in what manner the money is admitted to be in his hands.

(o) *Per* Jessel, M. R., *London Syndicate* v. *Lord*, 8 C. D. p. 90.

(p) *London Syndicate* v. *Lord*.

(q) *Jervis* v. *White*, 6 Ves. 738.

in these circumstances being treated as admitting that the money was in his hands for the purpose of the application (r).

<small>Motions under Order XL. r. 11.</small> Motions for payment into Court of funds admitted to be in a defendant's hands are constantly made under O. XL., r. 11 (s). The Order is stated *ante*, p. 18.

Money may be ordered into Court at the trial of an action without a notice of motion for that purpose (t).

In the Chancery Funds Consolidated Rules, 1874, are contained directions with respect to the payment of money and transfer of stock into Court.

<small>Investment of money in Court.</small> When paid into Court, money will either be placed on deposit at £2 per cent. per annum, or invested. Except however, in the case of legacies paid into Court under the Legacy Duty Acts (u), and money paid in under the Trustee Relief Acts, 1850 and 1852, no money in Court (whether cash, interest, or dividends) will be invested without an order (x), and notwithstanding an order for that purpose, a request must also be made to the Chancery Paymaster by the party interested or his solicitor (y). If there be no order for investment, money in Court will be placed on deposit (z).

(r) *Freeman* v. *Cox*, 8 C. D. 148 — a case, however, which the Court in Ireland has declined to follow, *Nesbitt* v. *Baldwin*, L. R. (Ir.) 7 C. D. 134.

(s) *Bennett* v. *Moore*, 1 C. D. 692; *Hetherington* v. *Longrigg*, 10 C. D. 162.

(t) *Isaacs* v. *Weatherstone*, 10 Ha. App. 30.

(u) 36 Geo. III. c. 52; 37 Geo. III. c. 135.

(x) Chancery Funds Rules, 1874, r. 36, and see rr. 61—67.

(y) *Re Woodcock's Settled Estates*, 13 Eq. 183.

(z) Chancery Funds Act, 1872, ss. 14, 15; Rules, 1874, rr. 68—80.

CHAPTER VII.

CONCURRENT ACTIONS FOR ADMINISTRATION—STAY—TRANSFER—CONSOLIDATION.

THE Court will not permit the assets of a deceased person to be wasted by suffering concurrent and competitive actions to be prosecuted for the ordinary administration of his estate. A common course is to direct a stay of all the actions except one; but cases of this kind being matters of discretion (*a*), the Courts, as will be seen from the authorities cited in this chapter, have not dealt with them according to any rigid rule, but have in each particular case aimed at making such an order as would secure justice to all parties, and discourage the practice of racing for judgments. Nevertheless, certain general principles are to be elicited from the decisions. _{One of two concurrent administration actions will be stayed.}

A stay of proceedings (*b*) will not be ordered, unless and until judgment for administration has been obtained in one of the actions, if there be no misconduct or other special circumstances to induce the Court to interfere (*c*). _{when judgment obtained in the other.}

The application to stay ought to be made by the defendant to the actions, but it may also be obtained by the plaintiff in the action in which judgment has been pronounced, although not a party to the other action, if he have an interest in staying the proceedings (*d*). The order _{Upon whose application.}

(*a*) *Per* Lord Cottenham, *M'Hardy* v. *Hitchcock*, 12 Jur. 781.

(*b*) Of course, proceedings may be stayed where an order has been obtained on originating summons in chambers (*Whittington* v. *Ed-*

wards, 3 De G. & J. 243), as wel as where judgment has been pronounced in Court.

(*c*) *M'Hardy* v. *Hitchcock*; compare *Virtue* v. *Miller*, 19 W. R. 106.

(*d*) *Portarlington* v. *Damer*, 2

70 CONCURRENT ACTIONS FOR ADMINISTRATION.

Mode of applying for stay. to stay may be obtained on special motion, or, where the judgment is in prosecution at Chambers, on special summons; and notice of the motion, or the summons, must be served on all parties to each action (*e*).

Principles on which order will be made. As to the propriety of staying the proceedings, the only question is whether the judgment which has been obtained will give the plaintiff in the other action all that he asks. It is no objection that the judgment embraces something more, and that its complexity may create delay (*f*), for the chief clerk may, in a proper case, make separate certificates, *e.g.* of debts, so that creditors whose action has been stayed shall not be delayed by proceedings with which they have nothing to do (*g*).

When relief claimed is co-extensive, which action will be stayed. Where the relief asked by the competitive actions is co-extensive, the rule is that that action shall be prosecuted in which the earlier judgment has been obtained (*h*). But the rule does not apply where the judgment has been snatched or unfairly or improperly obtained (*i*), and in this connection it may be noticed that, where a second administration action is instituted, and it is proposed to take a judgment by consent, the fact of there being already another action having the same object should be stated to the Court, upon the general principle that in all unopposed matters it is proper that everything should be mentioned (*k*). The Court may allow the action, in which judgment has been first but improperly obtained, to proceed, giving the conduct of it to the plaintiff in the other action (*l*). But in one case, on the consent of the admi-

Ph. 262; *Therry* v. *Henderson*, 1 Y. & C. C. C. 481; *Stead* v. *Stead*, 2 C. P. Coop. 311; *Zambaco* v. *Cassavetti*, 11 Eq. 444.

(*e*) Daniell, 700; and see 1438, and *post*, p. 77.

(*f*) Per Lord Cottenham, *Portarlington* v. *Damer*, 2 Ph. p. 265.

(*g*) *Golder* v. *Golder*, 9 Ha. 276,

and see *post*, p. 98.

(*h*) *Harris* v. *Gandy*, 1 De G. F. & J. 13; *McMurray* v. *Matthew*, 33 L. T. 804.

(*i*) *Harris* v. *Gandy*; *Salter* v. *Tildesley*, 13 W. R. 376; *Harris* v. *Lightfoot*, 10 W. R. 31.

(*k*) *Harris* v. *Lightfoot*.

(*l*) *Harris* v. *Lightfoot*; *Hawkes*

nistrator and heir-at-law, the Court gave immediate judgment on motion for the administration of the real and personal estate of an intestate at the suit of a creditor after a summons had been taken out by another creditor for the administration of the personal estate, which summons was returnable before the first day on which the suit, in which the motion was made, could be heard as a short cause (*m*). In determining which of two or more competitive actions for administration shall be stayed, and which prosecuted, the Court is also influenced by general considerations. Thus, residuary legatees being interested in reducing the expenses as much as possible, actions by them are preferred to actions by creditors (*n*), or by executors (*o*). A tenant for life, being more interested in effecting a speedy conversion, was preferred to the remainderman (*p*). Again, if two actions are instituted on behalf of an infant, one by a relative, the other by a stranger, as next friend, the former will be preferred (*q*); or an inquiry may be directed which action will be more beneficial to the infant (*r*). Two suits had been instituted on behalf of infants for the same purpose, and, the second being a friendly one, a decree had first been obtained in it; upon motion to stay the first suit, the Court ordered it to be stayed, giving liberty to the next friend in that

Action of residuary legatee preferred to that of a creditor;

tenant for life to remainderman.

Two actions by same infant.

v. *Barrett*, 5 Madd. 17 ; *Belcher* v. *Belcher*, 2 Dr. & Sm. 444 ; *Frost* v. *Ward*, 2 De G. J. & S. 70 ; *Rhodes* v. *Barret*, 12 Eq. 479 ; see also *Frowd* v. *Baker*, 4 Beav. 76.

(*m*) *Furze* v. *Hennet*, 2 De G. & J. 125. The circumstances of this case, one would have thought, laid it open to the suspicion of racing, but the Court was probably influenced by the fact that, while the summons only sought administration of the personal estate, the other suit asked for administration of the realty as well, and was therefore

(according to the rule presently stated in the text) to be preferred, as being more extensive in scope.

(*n*) *Penney* v. *Francis*, 9 W. N. 8.

(*o*) *Kelk* v. *Archer*, 16 Jur. 605.

(*p*) *Dowbiggin* v. *Trotter*, W. N., 1872, 150.

(*q*) *Frost* v. *Ward*, 2 De G. J. & S. 70 ; *Harris* v. *Lightfoot*, 10 W. R. 31.

(*r*) See *Virtue* v. *Miller*, 19 W. R. 406.

suit to apply in Chambers for the conduct of the second (*s*).

The Court may interfere ex mero motu. Where no application is made to stay proceedings, the Court may, of its own motion, instead of giving judgment in a second action, direct it to stand over, and come on with the action in which judgment has already been obtained, when that action is heard on further consideration (*t*).

Consolidation of concurrent administration actions. Instead of staying proceedings in either action, the Court may consolidate the actions, after pronouncing separate judgments in each (*u*), or one judgment in the two, and leaving the question of the conduct of the various inquiries directed to be decided in Chambers, the general rule, however, being that the plaintiff in the earlier action has the conduct of the proceedings (*v*). But, where two judgments have been obtained in different branches of the Court, and the actions are consolidated, the administration will be ordered to proceed in that branch in which the order is in the most perfect state, though posterior in date (*w*).

Palatine Court. The Palatine Court of Lancaster has only a concurrent jurisdiction with the High Court, even though the parties and the subject matter of the action be both within the local limits (*x*), and cannot restrain an action in the High Courts (*y*). There can be no question but that, if the two Courts have co-extensive jurisdiction and the two suits

---

(*s*) *Kenyon* v. *Kenyon*, 35 Beav. 300.

(*t*) *Cumming* v. *Slater*, 1 Y. & C. C. C. 484; and see *post* (*e*).

(*u*) *Budgen* v. *Sage*, 3 M. & Cr. 683; *Hoskins* v. *Campbell*, 2 H. & M. 43. It was held in *Plunkett* v. *Lewis*, 11 Sim. 379, that where decrees had been made in two suits, one a creditor's, the other a legatee's, the creditor had no right to a stay of proceedings in the legatee's suit, there being no suggestion of a deficiency of assets.

(*v*) *Norrall* v. *Pascoe*, 10 W. R. 338; *Rhodes* v. *Barret*, 12 Eq. 481; *Mellor* v. *Swire*, 21 C. D. 647.

(*w*) *Littlewood* v. *Collins*, 11 W. R. 387.

(*x*) *Cheetham* v. *Crook*, M'Cl. & Y. 30.

(*y*) *Re Alison's Trusts*, 8 C. D. 1.

STAY—TRANSFER—CONSOLIDATION. 73

are so constituted that all that is required in one may be obtained under the decree in the other, the High Court will stay the proceedings in the suit in which no decree has been made, and will allow the other to proceed (z), and even if the actions are not so constituted, the rule will prevail, special inquiries being by consent added to the judgment already obtained (a); so in *Jones* v. *Jones* (b), the action in the High Court was stayed, a judgment for administration having been already given in an action in the Palatine Court, the plaintiffs in the action stayed having liberty to apply in the Palatine Court for the conduct of the action in that Court. An action in the Palatine Court ought not to be stayed on the mere ground that the property concerned is without the local limits, if the parties are within the limits, the jurisdiction being *in personam* (c).

A person who has obtained a creditors' order for administration in the Palatine Court, and who neither is a party to an action in the High Court for the same purpose, nor has proved his debt under an administration order made subsequently to the order in the Palatine Court, is a mere stranger to the action in the High Court, and cannot be heard to ask in such action that the proceedings therein may be stayed (d).

So far we have been considering the practice applicable to concurrent actions claiming co-extensive relief; and we may add that, where, after notice of a judgment for administration, another action is instituted and brought to a hearing, asking no relief which could

Where relief claimed is not co-extensive.

(z) *Per* Romilly, M. R., *Wynne* v. *Hughes*, 26 Beav. 377. The order on appeal of this case (28 L. J. Ch. 485) was taken by arrangement between the parties; see 3 De G. J. & S. 406.

(a) *Mellor* v. *Swire*, 21 C. D. 647; and see *post*, p. 75.

(b) W. N. 1882, 6.

(c) *Re Longendale Cotton Spinning Co.*, 8 C. D. 150; and see *Stirling-Maxwell* v. *Cartwright*, and *Orr-Ewing* v. *Orr-Ewing*, cited *ante*, p. 36.

(d) *Bradley* v. *Stelfox*, 3 De G. J. & S. 402; but see *Townsend* v. *Townsend*, W. N. 1883, 34.

not be obtained in the former one, the later ought to be dismissed with costs (e), the earlier judgment being a bar (f). But, where a second action has a further object than the action in which judgment has been obtained, asks additional accounts not covered by the judgment, or seeks to charge the defendants upon a more stringent footing, it may be prosecuted, subject to risk of payment of costs by the plaintiff, if it shall turn out that he has come to the Court unnecessarily (g). But here again the practice is not uniform. Proceedings may be partially stayed, *i.e.*, so far only as the objects of the action are provided for by the judgment already obtained. Thus, where a creditors' bill was filed, which also prayed other relief, and soon after a simple creditor's bill was instituted by another party, and a decree obtained, the Court stayed the first suit so far only as it prayed administration, giving the plaintiff therein liberty to prove in the second suit for what he might eventually establish in his own (h). Or a second judgment may be pronounced, directing the usual accounts and giving the further relief asked, with liberty to the chief clerk to use the accounts taken under the former judgment (i), and *semble*, the Court here may adopt the result of proceedings in the Palatine Court (k), and accounts recorded in the Court of Chancery in Jamaica in a suit instituted against executors who had proved their testator's will in that island, were, in a suit against them in England, ordered to be taken, under 15 & 16 Vict. c. 86,

One action may be partially stayed;

or accounts in one ordered to be used in the other;

(e) *Menzies* v. *Connor*, 3 Mac. & G. 648.

(f) *Pott* v. *Gallini*, 1 S. & S. 206.

(g) *Anson* v. *Towgood*, 6 Madd. 374; *Shepherd* v. *Towgood*, T. & R. 379; *Pickford* v. *Hunter*, 5 Sim. 122; *Underwood* v. *Jee*, 1 Mac. & G. 276; *Taylor* v. *Southgate*, 4 M. & Cr. 203; *Zambaco* v. *Cassavetti*,

11 Eq. 439; see *Neve* v. *Weston*, 3 Atk. 557.

(h) *Dryden* v. *Foster*, 6 Beav. 146.

(i) *Pott* v. *Gallini*, 1 S. & S. 206.

(k) See *per* Lord Westbury, *Bradley* v. *Stelfox*, 3 De G. J. & S. 409.

s. 54, as *primâ facie* evidence of the truth of the matters therein contained, with liberty to the plaintiff to surcharge and falsify (*l*). Or proceedings in the second action may be entirely stayed, if the defendant in the first action undertake not to object to any additions to the decree already obtained which the Judge in Chambers may think reasonable (*m*). Similarly, where an action was commenced by a creditor, whose claim was disputed, to establish his claim, and also seeking general administration, and the common judgment for administration was subsequently obtained on a summons taken out by another creditor, the Court stayed the first action, added an inquiry as to incumbrances to the judgment in the second action, and gave the conduct of it to the plaintiff in the first action (*n*). The plaintiff in the wider action, while yet without a judgment, has no right to a stay of the more limited one. Whilst an administration suit was pending, but before a decree had been made, the defendant in the suit obtained the common order in Chambers upon a summons, and a motion to discharge such order was refused, although there were questions in the suit which could not be decided under the common order (*o*); so in *Ritchie* v. *Humberstone* (*p*) under almost similar circumstances, the action was stayed, directions being added to the decree made upon the summons sufficient to let the plaintiff charge the trustee for wilful default, the taxed costs of the plaintiff in the action stayed to be paid by the plaintiff in the other action, he to have them out of the estate.
<small>or one stayed, the judgment in the other being added to.</small>

As to the costs of applications for a stay of proceedings, the practice for some time varied, but is now fairly settled. <small>Costs of application to stay proceedings.</small>

(*l*) *Sleight* v. *Lawson*, 3 K. & J. 292.
(*m*) *Gwyer* v. *Petersen*, 26 Beav. 83; *Matthews* v. *Palmer*, 11 W. R. 610; *Mellor* v. *Swire*, 21 C. D. 647.
(*n*) *Matthews* v. *Matthews*, 34 L. T. 718.
(*o*) *Vanrenen* v. *Piffard*, 13 W. R. 425.
(*p*) 17 Jur. 756.

Where a stay is directed, the costs of the plaintiff in the action stayed up to the time of his having notice of the judgment in the second action, and also his costs of the motion to stay, are taxed. If the defendant, the executor, admits the debt and admits assets, then he should at once pay such costs; if the debt is disputed, or, the debt being admitted, upon affidavit being made that the executor has no assets, then the plaintiff in the action stayed is to be at liberty to add his costs to his claim and prove (*q*) for them under the judgment in the second action, the debt and costs to stand or fall together. The defendant's costs, and what, if anything, he shall pay to such plaintiff for his costs will be added to his costs in the second action, or allowed him in his accounts therein (*r*).

So also if a legatee's suit be stayed after a judgment for administration, he will be entitled to his costs up to notice of the judgment and the costs of the application, subject to the claims of creditors (*s*). But the costs of the plaintiff in the action stayed are only payable in a due course of administration, and have no priority over the costs of the plaintiff in the action which is allowed to go on, still less over those of the personal representative (*t*). A party prosecuting an action after notice of a judgment in another action, in which he may obtain all the relief which he seeks in his own, will be ordered to pay the costs of an application to stay proceedings (*u*). And if a trustee who is made defendant to two actions for administration

(*q*) If, however, assets are admitted, but the debt is disputed, the debt and costs must be paid so soon as the debt is proved; *King* v. *King*, 34 Beav. 10.

(*r*) The practice was so certified by the Registrars in *West* v. *Swinburne*, 19 L. J. Ch. 81, as explained in *Darcy* v. *Plestow*, ibid. 491; see also *Ladbroke* v. *Sloane*, 3 De G. & Sm. 291; *Golder* v. *Golder*, 9 Ha.

276; *Froud* v. *Baker*, 4 Beav. 76.

(*s*) *Jackson* v. *Leaf*, 1 J. & W. 229.

(*t*) *Cumberland* v. *Clark*, 4 Ch. 412.

(*u*) *Graham* v. *Maxwell*, 1 Mac. & G. 71; and see *Gardner* v. *Garrett*, 20 Beav. 469, where such costs were set off against the costs of the action stayed, prior to the notice.

refrains from moving to stay proceedings, where a sufficient judgment has been obtained in one of them, he may lose his costs (*x*).

Where actions for the administration of the same estate have been instituted in different branches of the Chancery Division, and a stay of proceedings in one of them is desired, it will be necessary, or at least expedient, first to procure a transfer of one of them to that branch of the Court in which the other has been instituted. *Transfer of one of two concurrent actions from one branch of Chancery Division to another.* Indeed, even where no stay of proceedings is in immediate contemplation, the parties ought to apply for a transfer; if they do not, it has been said the Court itself will make the application (*y*). Any action or actions may be transferred from one judge to another of the Chancery Division by the order of the Lord Chancellor (*z*), the Court of Appeal having no jurisdiction (*a*). Such an order will be made by his lordship on a written application to his secretary, accompanied by the written consent of all parties; where all parties do not consent, the application must be made to the Lord Chancellor himself (*b*), on motion (*c*), or petition (*d*), which must be served on all the parties who do not consent (*e*). On such an application, the Lord Chancellor has no jurisdiction to stay the action (*f*): for that purpose a subsequent application must be made to the

---

(*x*) *Stead* v. *Stead* 2 C. P. Coop. 311; *Puckwood* v. *Maddison*, 1 S. & S. 232.

(*y*) *Swale* v. *Swale*, 22 Beav. 401; and see *per* Lord Romilly, *Zambaco* v. *Cassavetti*, 11 Eq. p. 444; *ante*, p. 70 (*c*).

(*z*) O. LI. r. 1; and see r. 3.

(*a*) *Re Hutley*, 1 C. D. 11.

(*b*) Memorandum, 1 C. D. 41. The memorandum says "to the Lord Chancellor in Court," but as a matter of fact, he seldom sits in Court, and, in default of his so sitting, it is the practice to make the application to him at his private room at Westminster (as was done in *Davis* v. *Davis*) or at his residence, or wherever he may be found.

(*c*) As in *Davis* v. *Davis*, 48 L. J. Ch. 40.

(*d*) See the Forms in Seton, 318; Pemb. 96; Daniell's Forms, 1853.

(*e*) *Bond* v. *Barnes*, 2 De G. F. & J. 387.

(*f*) *Bentall* v. *Sharp*, cited Seton, 320; and see *Davis* v. *Davis*.

judge to whose Court the action shall have been transferred. As a general rule an action instituted in one branch of the Chancery Division when an action as to the same matter is pending in another branch of the same Division will be transferred to the latter branch (*g*), notwithstanding that in the first action judgment has not (*h*), but in the second has (*i*), been obtained. And the same rule applies where the actions, though not identical, are cognate in kind. Thus, where an action was brought, and judgment obtained, in the Chancery Division for administration of the personal estate of a deceased person, and for an inquiry whether his moiety of certain real estate had become assets of his partnership business carried on with B., and B. brought an action in another branch of the same Division for winding up the partnership, the Lord Chancellor, considering the two actions to be cognate, transferred B.'s action to the judge before whom the administration action was pending (*k*). The proper course is for the party who desires to transfer to apply to the party who has commenced the second action, and ask for his consent to the transfer (*l*); if such consent be refused on insufficient grounds, the party refusing will be ordered to pay costs, if the notice of motion or petition for transfer asks for them (*m*). On the other hand, where the plaintiff in the second action offered to consent to a transfer, if the costs of the application were made costs in the cause, and such offer was unreasonably refused by the plaintiff in the first action, the last-mentioned plaintiff had to pay the costs subsequent to the offer (*n*). Subject as above, the Court has generally acted on the principle that, if a suitor insists on proceeding in another Court, when a suit rela-

Which action will be transferred.

As to consent of plaintiff in second action.

(*g*) *Lyall* v. *Weldhen*, 9 Ch. 287.
(*h*) *Orrell* v. *Busch*, 5 Ch. 467.
(*i*) *Lucas* v. *Siggers*, 7 Ch. 517.
(*k*) *Davis* v. *Davis*, 48 L. J. Ch. 40.

(*l*) Per Lord Selborne, *Lyall* v. *Weldhen*, 9 Ch. p. 289.
(*m*) *Cocq* v. *Hunasgeria Coffee Co.*, 4 Ch. 415.
(*n*) *Lyall* v. *Weldhen*.

ting to the same matter is already in existence, he must expect to have to pay the costs of the transfer, if a transfer is ordered against his will (*o*).

Consolidation has been mentioned before in this chapter. By O. LI. r. 4, actions in any Division or Divisions may be consolidated by order of the Court or a Judge in the manner theretofore in use in the Superior Courts of common law. A consolidation order may be obtained at any time after service of the writ (*p*). Where actions are consolidated, leave will be given for evidence taken in any one of them to be used in them all (*q*). *Consolidation.*

The Court has also jurisdiction to stay proceedings in an action in this country by reason of a judgment in a foreign country. Such jurisdiction was fully recognised by Lord Cranworth in *Ostell* v. *Le Page* (*r*). But, before the Court will so interpose on an interlocutory application, it must be satisfied that such judgment does justice, and covers the whole subject of the action (*s*), and it has recently been held that although there is no doubt of the jurisdiction to stay an action here on the mere ground of an action having been brought between the same parties and for the same object in a foreign country, yet it would require very special grounds to obtain the injunction (*t*). *Staying proceedings after foreign judgment has been obtained.*

We have now discussed the practice of the Court where the executors or trustees are harassed, or the estate is likely to be impoverished, by a multiplicity of actions for its administration. But the protection of trustees from

(*o*) *Per* Lord Selborne, *ibid.* p. 289; *Orrell* v. *Busch*, 5 Ch. 467; *Lucas* v. *Siggers*, 7 Ch. 517.
(*p*) *Hollingsworth* v. *Brodrick*, 4 A. & E. 646.
(*q*) *Smith* v. *Whichcord*, 24 W. R. 900.
(*r*) 2 De G. M. & G. 892.

(*s*) *Ibid.*; and see *Stainton* v. *Carron Co.* (No. 3), 21 Beav. 500; *Maclaren* v. *Stainton*, 2 Jur. N. S. 49.
(*t*) *McHenry* v. *Lewis*, 22 C. D. 397; and see *Peruvian Guano Co.* v. *Bockwoldt*, 48 L. T. 7.

litigation after judgment for administration, does not stop there. They are equally entitled, as a rule, to be relieved against any other proceedings taken against them in the Queen's Bench Division or in the Chancery Division. This further protection we proceed to consider.

Staying creditors' actions in Queen's Bench Division after judgment for administration in Chancery Division.

Before the Judicature Act, the Court of Chancery used constantly to restrain creditors, after decree for administration, from proceeding at law against the executors, on the application of the latter (*u*), whether administration had been ordered in Chambers on an originating summons (*x*), or in Court on a bill filed. But by that Act (*y*), the power of restraining proceedings in the High Court or Court of Appeal by injunction was taken away (*z*). At the same time it was provided that nothing therein contained should disable either of those Courts from directing a stay of proceedings in any cause or matter pending before it, and that any person, whether a party thereto or not, who would formerly have been entitled to apply to any Court to restrain the prosecution thereof, should be at liberty to apply to the said Courts respectively, by motion in a summary way, for a stay of proceedings in such cause or matter, either generally, or so far as might be necessary for the purpose of justice. Since the Act, then, the course for the executor to pursue is to apply by motion to the Court, in which the proceedings are pending, for an order to stay them. The right of the executors to the protection of the Court arises directly judgment for administration has been pronounced, and accordingly, after judgment, creditors will not be

---

(*u*) *E.g.*, *Drewry* v. *Thacker*, 3 Sw. 544.

(*x*) *Ratcliffe* v. *Winch*, 16 Beav. 576.

(*y*) 36 & 37 Vict. c. 66, s. 24, sub-s. 5.

(*z*) For this reason, a County Court, before which an administration action is pending, cannot now restrain creditors' actions (*Cobbold* v. *Pryke*, 4 Ex. D. 315), these Courts having by 28 & 29 Vict. c. 99, s. 1 (see *post* p. 184), only "the power and authority of the High Court."

allowed to sue (*a*) executors, though the creditors have not yet been ascertained under the judgment (*b*); see, however, *Sexton* v. *Smith* (*c*), where, under special circumstances, persons whose claim under the decree had been rejected, were not restrained from suing the executrix at law for the same demand. But proceedings by a mortgagee to realise his security will not be stayed (*d*).

A creditor recovered judgment against his debtor, and issued a *fi. fa.* Shortly afterwards the debtor died. The creditor entered a suggestion on the record, entitling him to have execution against the executors, and obtained a charging order *nisi* upon shares belonging to the debtor. After the order *nisi* had been obtained, but on the same day, a decree was made for administration of the debtor's estate. The order *nisi* not having been made absolute the plaintiff in the administration suit applied for an injunction to restrain further proceedings by the judgment creditor. The Court of Appeal held (under the old practice) that an injunction ought not to be granted, a charging order, when made absolute, operating from the making of the order *nisi* (*e*). And where a creditor, before decree for administration, obtained judgment against an executor, the Court refused to enjoin him from enforcing his judgment against a debtor to the estate (*f*); and in such cases proceedings would not now be stayed. Nor will an action by a creditor be stayed, where an executor has rendered himself liable *de bonis propriis*,

---

(*a*) Nor can they, if also debtors to the estate, counter-claim against the executors suing for the debt (except by way of set-off or in the case of mutual credits and an insolvent estate, as to which see *post*, p. 173), *Newell* v. *National Provincial Bank*, 1 C. P. D. 496.

(*b*) *Brooks* v. *Reynolds*, 1 Bro. C. C. 183.

(*c*) 3 De G. & Sm. 694.

(*d*) *Crowle* v. *Russell*, 4 C. P. D. 186.

(*e*) *Haly* v. *Barry*, 3 Ch. 452, explaining *Warburton* v. *Hill*, Kay, 470.

(*f*) *Fowler* v. *Roberts*, 2 Giff. 226; *Burton* v. *Roberts*, 29 L. J. Ex. 484.

e.g., where, in carrying on his testator's business, he has given bills or notes (*g*).

Actions not in the High Court may still be restrained by Chancery Division.
It will be observed that the enactment above referred to abolishes the restraint of actions by injunction so far only as relates to actions in the High Court or the Court of Appeal. As regards, then, actions brought against him in the inferior Courts, or Courts of a foreign country (*h*), the executor's remedy is still to obtain (if he can make a case for it) an injunction from the Court, in which judgment for administration has been pronounced, restraining the other action (*i*).

After judgment in England for administration of a testator's estate in England and abroad, an incumbrancer upon the foreign estate, having come in and *proved* his debt (*k*), was restrained from proceeding in a creditors' action instituted by him abroad, receiving his costs up to the time of his having notice of the judgment and paying the costs of the application (*l*); and, generally, after judgment for administration, parties (*e.g.*, the trustees) will be restrained from proceeding abroad with an action having the like objects (*m*). In *Baillie* v. *Baillie* (*n*), creditors who had obtained judgment in Scotland against a beneficiary were restrained from suing the executors there to arrest the amount in their hands belonging to the beneficiary, the executors undertaking forthwith to obtain an administration decree here. The persons restrained not being creditors of the deceased, this case is not inconsistent with

---

(*g*) *Lucas* v. *Williams*, 10 W. R. 606.

(*h*) *E.g.*, in Ireland, as in *Beauchamp* v. *Huntley*, Jac. 546.

(*i*) *Eustace* v. *Lloyd*, 25 W. R. 211.

(*k*) As distinguished from carrying in a claim, and afterwards, before allowance, abandoning it (*Crofton* v. *Crofton*, 15 C. D. 591).

(*l*) *Beauchamp* v. *Huntley*; *Graham* v. *Maxwell*, 1 Mac. & G. 71.

(*m*) *Harrison* v. *Gurney*, 2 J. & W. 563; and see *Booth* v. *Leycester*, 3 M. & Cr. 459.

(*n*) 5 Eq. 175; and see *Hope* v. *Carnegie*, 1 Ch. 320.

Rankin v. *Harwood* (o), where it was held that the Court will not restrain a creditor from prosecuting his legal remedy against the personal representatives of his debtor, unless there is a decree under which he has a present right to go in and prove his debt.

The leading case on this branch of the subject is *Carron Iron Co.* v. *Maclaren* (p), in which the authorities were exhaustively discussed. The following was Lord Cranworth's statement of the law. " There is no doubt as to the power of the Court to restrain persons *within its jurisdiction* from instituting or prosecuting suits in foreign Courts, wherever the circumstances of the case make such an interposition necessary or expedient. The Court acts *in personam*, and will not suffer anyone within its reach to do what is contrary to its notions of equity, merely because the act to be done may be, in point of locality, beyond its jurisdiction. Where, therefore, pending a litigation here, in which complete relief may be had, a party to the suit institutes proceedings abroad, the Court in general considers that act as a vexatious harassing of the opposite party, and restrains the foreign proceedings. But is there any rule or principle of the Court, which, after a decree for administering a testator's assets, would induce it to interfere with a foreign creditor *resident abroad*, suing for his debts in the Courts of his own country? Certainly not. Over such a creditor the Court here can exercise no jurisdiction whatever. He is altogether beyond their reach, and must be left to deal as he may with his own *forum*, and to obtain such relief as the Courts of his own country may afford (q). If, however, the party sought to be re-

(o) 2 Ph. 22.
(p) 5 H. L. C. 416.
(q) To the foreign action so brought the legal personal representatives, if well advised, will not appear; judgment against them by default can only be treated here as *primâ facie* evidence of the debt (*per* Malins, V.-C., *Crofton* v. *Crofton*, 15 C. D. 591, 592).

strained had come in under the decree, so as to obtain payment partially from the English assets, a very different question would arise, according to the doctrine in *Beauchamp* v. *Marquis of Huntley*," cited *supra* (*r*).

As a rule, creditors whose actions were restrained were entitled to the costs of their proceedings down to the time of their being served with notice of the order for administration (*s*). But where a creditor continued his proceedings after such notice, he was ordered to pay the costs of a motion to restrain him, but allowed to set off against such costs his costs of the action at law down to the date of the notice (*t*). It is apprehended that like rules prevail now, under the new practice of staying proceedings.

Transfer to Chancery Division, after judgment for administration, of actions against executors or administrators. It is further provided by order of Court that when an order has been made by any judge of the Chancery Division for the administration of the assets of any testator or intestate, the judge in whose Court such administration shall be pending shall have power, without any further consent, to order the transfer to such judge of any action pending *in any other Division* (*u*), brought or continued by or against the executors or administrators of the testator or intestate whose assets are being so administered (*x*). But a transfer will not be ordered under this rule except of an action brought against the executors or administrators as such (*y*); nor, on a transfer being made, will an executor or administrator escape his liability, if any, by reason of judgment for administration having been pronounced, but the plaintiff will be entitled to

---

(*r*) 5 H. L. C. 436, 441, 442.

(*s*) *Ratcliffe* v. *Winch*, 16 Beav. 576.

(*t*) *Gardner* v. *Garrett*, 20 Beav. 469.

(*u*) See *Re Madras Irrigation Co.*, 16 C. D. 702.

(*x*) Ord. LI. r. 2a. The application may be made *ex parte*; *Whitaker* v. *Robinson*, W. N. 1877, 201; *Musbach* v. *Anderson*, 26 W. R. 100.

(*y*) *Chapman* v. *Mason*, 40 L. T. 678.

pursue his remedies in the Chancery Division just as he might have done in the other Divisions (z), unless a stay of proceedings, or a consolidation of the actions, be applied for and obtained.

(z) *Re Timms*, 38 L. T. 679.

CHAPTER VIII.

PROCEEDINGS IN CHAMBERS.

Prosecution of judgment.
IN all cases of proceedings in chambers under any judgment or order, the party prosecuting the same shall leave a copy of such judgment or order at the judge's Chambers, and shall certify the same to be a true copy of the judgment or order as passed and entered (*a*). Every judgment or order directing accounts or inquiries to be taken or made shall be brought into the judge's Chambers by the party entitled to prosecute the same within ten days after the same shall have been passed and entered; and in default thereof, any other party to the cause or matter shall be at liberty to bring in the same, and such party shall have the prosecution of such judgment or order, unless the judge shall otherwise direct (*b*). At the same time that any judgment or order made in a suit instituted by writ is left in Chambers, a print of the statement of claim, if any, is to be left (*c*); and a note stating the names of the solicitors for all the parties, and showing for which of the parties such solicitors are concerned, is to be left at Chambers with every judgment or order (*d*).

Directions by the judge.
Upon a copy of the judgment or order being left, a summons shall be issued to proceed with the accounts or inquiries directed; and, upon the return of such summons, the judge (by his deputy, the chief clerk), if satisfied by

---

(*a*) Cons. Ord. XXXV. r. 15. Ch. x.
(*b*) Cons. Ord. XXXV. r. 22. As to conduct of proceedings, see *post*,
(*c*) Reg., 8 Aug., 1857, r. 5.
(*d*) R. 6.

proper evidence that all necessary parties have been served with notice of the judgment or order (e), shall thereupon give directions as to the manner in which each of the accounts and inquiries is to be prosecuted, the evidence to be adduced in support thereof, the parties who are to attend on the several accounts and inquiries, and the time within which each proceeding is to be taken; and a day or days may be appointed for the further attendance of the parties, and all such directions may afterwards be varied or added to as may be found necessary (f).

A chief clerk should not adjourn a summons into Court, but to the judge in Chambers (g); but it is in the discretion of the judge to hear matters in Chambers or to adjourn them into Court (h). An adjournment [before the judge in Chambers personally or] into Court is merely a continuance of the hearing begun before the chief clerk, and the costs of such adjournment go with the costs in Chambers; the party at whose instance the adjournment is made will not have to pay the costs thereof, even if the question then appears unarguable, unless in the opinion of the judge there has been misconduct in bringing the matter before him in person (i). *Adjournment to the judge.*

Generally, when a summons is refused, the respondent should be allowed all the costs, not only of the adjournment, but in Chambers (k).

Before the Judicature Acts, where a judge had decided on an adjourned summons a question which had arisen in the proceedings in his Chambers, there could be no appeal, unless the judge thought fit to direct an order to be drawn up; the course was to wait for the certificate, *Appeal from judge.*

(e) As to this, see *ante*, p. 40.
(f) Cons. Ord. XXXV. r. 16.
(g) *Halliley* v. *Henderson*, 4 Jur. N. S. 202.
(h) *Re Agriculturist, &c., Co.*, 11 W. R. 330.
(i) *Leeds* v. *Lewis*, 3 Jur. N. S. 1290; *Re Mitchell*, 9 Jur. N. S. 1272; and see *Upton* v. *Brown*, cited *post*, p. 88.
(k) Per James, V.-C., *Alcock* v. *Gill*, W. N., 1869, 270.

and then apply to vary it (*l*); but in a recent case (*m*) it was held by the Court of Appeal that the disallowance by the judge of a creditor's claim made in answer to advertisements issued under a judgment for administration was a "refusal" within the meaning of O. LVIII., r. 15, from which an appeal could be brought, and that no order need be drawn up.

Suitor's right to be heard by judge himself. In proceedings in Chambers every party has the unqualified right to have his case, or the minutest point arising in Chambers, heard personally (in the first instance and not by way of appeal) by the judge, though there be no controversy between the parties, and the chief clerk cannot refuse an application to have it so heard (*n*). Again, any party shall, either during the proceedings before the chief clerk, or within four clear days after such proceedings shall have been concluded, and before the certificate or report shall have been signed and adopted [by the judge], be at liberty to take the opinion of the judge upon any particular point or matter arising in the course of the proceedings or upon the result of the whole proceeding, when it is brought by the chief clerk to a conclusion (*o*). Such opinion shall be taken by summons, to

How qualified. be obtained within the four clear days (*p*). "Under the Chancery Amendment Act, 1852," said Jessel, M.R. (*q*), "it is the right of the suitor to have the matter at once ad-

---

(*l*) *Rhodes* v. *Rhodes*, 1 Ch. 483; *Vyse* v. *Foster*, 10 Ch. 236. As to the application to vary the certificate, see *post*, p. 98.

(*m*) *Fordham* v. *Clagett*, 20 C. D. 734.

(*n*) *Re Agriculturist, &c., Co.*, 3 De G. F. & J. 194; *per* Kindersley, V.-C., *Wadham* v. *Rigg*, 2 Dr. & Sm. 80; *Re London and County Assurance Co.*, 5 W. R. 794; *Re Home Counties, &c., Co.*, 10 W. R. 457; *per* Wood, V.-C., *Dawkins* v. *Morton*, 10 W. R. 339; *Hayward* v. *Hayward*, Kay, App. 31.

(*o*) 15 & 16 Vict. c. 80, s. 33; Cons. Ord. XXXV. r. 49.

(*p*) Cons. Ord. XXXV. r. 50. Rules 49 & 50 of Cons. Ord. XXXV. do not, however, apply to certificates upon which the Paymaster-General is to act without further order, or to certificates on passing receivers' accounts, as to which, see *post*, p. 100.

(*q*) In *Upton* v. *Brown*, 20 Ch. D. 732.

journed before the judge without taking out any summons. Of course if a solicitor took an adjournment before the judge of every item in an account, no business could be transacted. In theory there is a right to do this, but in practice it is found impossible that it should be done. The practice is to wait until the taking of the account is completed, and then to take an adjournment once for all to the judge. When, however, a question of principle is involved in an item which decides the mode in which the account is to be taken, it is, of course, impossible to wait until the account is completed, and then it is quite right to adjourn (*r*) the item at once before the judge. If a solicitor were so unreasonable as to insist on the adjournment of every item in an account to which he might object, that would be an abuse of the process of the Court, and I have no doubt the judge would have jurisdiction to punish the solicitor by making him pay the costs personally." It has been laid down that where objections to the certificate are heard and disposed of by the judge himself in Chambers, they will not be reheard by the same judge in Court, the party's course being to proceed to the Court of Appeal (*s*); but this would seem not to be the present practice (*t*).

Rehearing by judge in Court.

Application should be made to a judge in Court to discharge an order made by him in Chambers within twenty-one days from the drawing up of the order, unless the

Time limited for re-hearing.

(*r*) A motion to obtain the opinion of the Court as to the principle on which an account ought to be taken, for the guidance of the chief clerk, has been held not irregular (*Robertson* v. *Norris*, 1 Giff. 428; and see *Vyse* v. *Foster*, 10 Ch. 238), and a petition for the like object has not been objected to (*Browne* v. *Collins*, 12 Eq. 586).

(*s*) *York & North Midland Railway Co.* v. *Hudson*, 18 Beav. 70; but a certificate should be obtained from the judge that he does not desire to hear any further argument in Court, *Thomas* v. *Elsom*, 6 C. D. 346, where the proper course is pointed out, if the judge declines to give such a certificate.

(*t*) See *Holloway* v. *Chester*, 19 C. D. 516, which, however, was not followed to its full extent by Hall, V.-C., in *Anderson* v. *Butler's Wharf Co.*, 21 C. D. 131; see also *Manchester, &c., Paving Co.* v. *Slagg*, 17 L. T. 556.

order is simply a refusal of an application, in which case the twenty-one days must be reckoned from the refusal (*u*).

Evidence.

The course of proceeding in Chambers shall ordinarily be the same as the course of proceeding in Court upon motions (*x*); but the party intending to use an affidavit shall give notice to the other parties concerned of his

Affidavits.

intention in that behalf (*y*). All affidavits which have been previously made and read in Court, upon any proceeding in a cause or matter, may be used before the judge in Chambers (*z*), subject of course to the general rules as to the admissibility of evidence (*a*). Where any account is directed to be taken, the accounting party, unless the judge shall otherwise direct, shall make out his account and verify the same by affidavit. The items on each side of the account shall be numbered consecutively, and the account shall be referred to by the affidavit as an exhibit, and be left in the judge's Chambers (*b*). Affidavits used in Chambers are, of course, subject to cross-examination, but not after the chief clerk's certificate has been signed and approved by the judge (*c*).

Notice of amount and particulars of charge beyond amount admitted.

Any party seeking to charge any accounting party beyond what he has by his account admitted to have received, shall give notice thereof to the accounting party, stating, as far as he is able, the amount sought to be charged, and the particulars thereof, in a short and succinct manner (*d*).

Cross-examination.

An affidavit filed by an accounting party in an administration action is subject to cross-examination (*e*); but he is entitled to notice of the points on

---

(*u*) See *Dickson* v. *Harrison*, 9 C. D. 243; *Heatley* v. *Newton*, 19 *ibid.*, 326.
(*x*) Cons. Ord. XXXV. r. 26.
(*y*) R. 27.
(*z*) R. 28.
(*a*) See *Handford* v. *Handford*, 5 Ha. 212; *Smith* v. *Althus*, 11 Ves. 564; and an undertaking not to use

an affidavit at the hearing does not preclude its use in Chambers (*Jenner* v. *Morris*, 10 W. R. 640).
(*b*) Cons. Ord. XXXV. r. 33.
(*c*) *Dawkins* v. *Morton*, 10 W. R. 339.
(*d*) Cons. Ord. XXXV. r. 34.
(*e*) It may be mentioned that when a person, though not a party

which he is to be cross-examined, in default of which, it would seem, he may decline to be sworn (*f*), and it is not sufficient to inform him that all the items but one are objected to (*g*) ; or the objecting party may examine the accounting party *vivâ voce* as his own witness, but in this case also he must give notice of the points as to which he wishes to examine (*h*). The rule as to notice applies to the case of a party seeking to charge by his account, as well as to the case of a merely accounting party (*i*). Each chief clerk has full power to summon witnesses, administer oaths, take affidavits, receive affirmations, and, when so directed by the judge to whose Court he is attached, to examine parties and witnesses either upon interrogatories or *vivâ voce*, as such judge shall direct (*k*), and a witness cannot refuse to be sworn in Chambers, on the ground that he desires to be examined before the examiner, where he would have the assistance of counsel, it being in the discretion of the judge whether the examination shall be before the examiner or in Chambers (*l*). If an examination is to be taken before an examiner, a *subpoena* should be issued for the attendance of the witness (*m*). Such *subpoena* was formerly issued upon a note from the judge (*n*), but now, any party may take it out (*o*) ; and subject to the power of the Court to prevent this right from being oppressively used, any person able to give information relating to the assets may be summoned, and is bound to attend before an examiner, and to answer all questions pro-

Powers of chief clerk.

Examiner.

to the proceedings, has made and filed an affidavit to be used in a pending matter, he cannot be exempted from cross-examination by the withdrawal of the affidavit (*Ex parte Young*, 21 C. D. 642).

(*f*) *Lord* v. *Lord*, 2 Eq. 605 ; and see *Glover* v. *Ellison*, 20 W. R. 408.

(*g*) *McArthur* v. *Dudgeon*, 15 Eq. 102.

(*h*) *Wormsley* v. *Sturt*, 22 Beav. 398.

(*i*) *Bates* v. *Eley*, 1 C. D. 473.

(*k*) 15 & 16 Vict. c. 80, s. 30.

(*l*) *Re Electric Telegraph Co. of Ireland*, 24 Beav. 137, 139.

(*m*) See *Stebbing* v. *Atlee*, 26 L. J. Ch. 265.

(*n*) Cons. Ord. XXXV. r. 29.

(*o*) *Raymond* v. *Tapson*, 22 C. D. 430.

perly put to him by the party having the conduct of the proceedings (*p*). Where a chief clerk is directed by the judge to examine any witness, the practice and mode of proceeding shall be the same as in the case of the examination of witnesses before an examiner, subject to any special directions which may be given in any particular case (*q*). The examiner is the proper person to take evidence in all cases, in the absence of any special directions for the examination of witnesses in Chambers or in Court; therefore no special order is necessary for transferring the cross-examination of a witness from the judge in Chambers to the examiner (*r*), and the leave of the judge is not necessary to give the examiner jurisdiction to take the cross-examination (*s*); but if the examination be in Chambers, the witness has the right to require that all or any part of it be adjourned before the judge personally (*t*); and if a person under examination in Chambers refuse to give a sufficient answer, the proper course is to apply to the judge to examine him personally, and then, if he refuse to answer, he may at once be committed (*u*). In a recent case (*v*) a person who refused to answer questions before a special examiner was (upon motion) ordered again to attend before him, and there and then to answer certain questions, which he had previously refused to do.

Mode of examining witness before chief clerk.

Practice where witness refuses to answer.

Persons having liberty to attend the proceedings.
In any cause for the administration of the estate of a deceased person, no party to the cause, other than the executor or administrator, shall, unless by leave of the judge, be entitled (*x*) to appear either in Court or in Chambers, on

(*p*) *Venables* v. *Schweitzer*, 16 Eq. 76; *Raymond* v. *Tapson*, 22 C. D. 430.
(*q*) Cons. Ord. XXXV. r. 30.
(*r*) *Stebbing* v. *Atlee*, 26 L. J. Ch. 265.
(*s*) *Cust* v. *Poyser*, 26 L. J. Ch. 93, 353.
(*t*) *Re London & County Assurance Co.*, 5 W. R. 794, and see *ante*, p. 88.

(*u*) *Hayward* v. *Hayward*, Kay, App. 31; and see *Re Esgair, &c., Co.*, 8 W. R. 660.
(*v*) *Republic of Costa Rica* v. *Strousberg*, 16 C. D. 8.
(*x*) In *Smith* v. *Watts*, 22 C. D. 5, Jessel, M. R., called attention to this rule, and stated that although in that case (where the defendant, the administrator, had taken out a summons against a creditor and

the claim of any person not a party to the cause against the estate of the deceased, in respect of any debt or liability; but the judge may (*y*) direct any other party to the cause to appear, either in addition to or in the place of the executor or administrator, upon such terms as to costs or otherwise as he shall think fit (*z*). Subject as above, any persons interested who ought to be served can, under the general practice, and as of course, attend the proceedings; but that does not entitle them to the costs of attending (*a*). Their right to costs is determined by the judge in Chambers, who, under a general order (*b*), decides what parties interested in the estate shall attend the taking of the accounts at the costs of the estate; that is the subject of a special application (*c*), and it has been recently decided (*d*) that mere liberty to attend the pro-

Their right to costs determined by the judge.

mortgagee) the Court had, in the absence of any opposition, heard counsel for the plaintiff, yet in future no costs would be allowed to persons appearing unnecessarily, within the meaning of the rule.

(*y*) As to the principle upon which this discretion will be exercised, see *Samuel* v. *Samuel*, 12 C. D., p. 160; "where in an administration suit there is reason to believe that the legal personal representative will not perform his duty and defend the estate, the right course to take is for somebody to appear in his name. A person who accepts a duty is not entitled to say he will not fulfil the duty because he has an adverse interest." See *ante*, p. 42.

(*z*) O. XVI. r. 12b.

(*a*) In *Joseph* v. *Goode*, 23 W. R. 225 (following *Armstrong* v. *Armstrong*, 12 Eq. 614), a plaintiff who had been deprived of the conduct of the proceedings was allowed his costs only up to the time at which he was so deprived, costs of subsequent attendances in chambers being disallowed, but obtained the costs of appearing at the further consideration to ask for such costs.

(*b*) Cons. Ord. XXXV. r. 16, cited *ante*, p. 87.

(*c*) Per Jessel, M. R., *Sharp* v. *Lush*, 10 C. D. 473. Where, on an administration action being stayed, the plaintiff's costs are provided for to date, and leave is given him to attend the proceedings in another administration action which is allowed to be prosecuted, such leave is not *per se* special leave entitling him to his costs of attending such proceedings (*Hubbard* v. *Latham*, 14 W. R. 553). So also, liberty given in one action to prove in another for an amount appearing due in the former does not confer an absolute right of proof in the latter, in which the Court must inquire whether the claim is valid and subsisting (*Micklethwait* v. *Winstanley*, 34 L. J. Ch. 281).

(*d*) *Day* v. *Batty*, 21 C. D. 830.

ceedings under the judgment (which was in the usual form) does not entitle the parties having the liberty to the costs of their attendance in Chambers; and that, in order to entitle them thereto, the order giving the liberty to attend should have expressly provided that they were to be entitled to their costs of such attendance. Where upon the hearing of the summons to proceed, or at any time during the prosecution of the decree or order, it appears to the judge, with respect to the whole or any portion of the proceedings, that the interests of the parties can be classified, he may require the parties constituting each or any class to be represented by the same solicitor; and, where the parties constituting such class cannot agree upon the solicitor to represent them, the judge may nominate such solicitor for the purpose of the proceedings before him; and, where any one of the parties constituting such class declines to authorise the solicitor so nominated to act for him, and insists upon being represented by a different solicitor, such party shall personally pay the costs of his own solicitor of and relating to the proceedings before the judge, with respect to which such nomination shall have been made, and all such further costs as shall be occasioned to any of the parties by his being represented by a different solicitor from the solicitor so to be nominated (*e*). And, even though no solicitor has been so nominated by the judge, yet, where a number of persons in the same interest, having liberty to attend the proceedings, appear separately on an adjourned summons, they may be allowed only one set of costs between them (*f*); and only one set of costs of taking the accounts will be allowed to parties appearing under leave to attend, if the interests of such parties are the same as those represented

---

(*e*) Cons. Ord. XXXV. r. 20. R. 936; see the *errata* to 11 W.
(*f*) *Stevenson* v. *Abington*, 11 W. R.

by the plaintiff, and *semble*, even such costs will only be allowed, where the plaintiff and defendant appear by the same solicitor, and it is necessary for the protection of the residuary legatees that they should be separately represented (*g*). Where any party appears upon any application or proceeding in Court or at Chambers in which he is not interested, or upon which, according to the practice of the Court, he ought not to attend, he is not to be allowed any costs of such appearance unless the Court or a judge shall expressly direct such costs to be allowed (*h*); to entitle a person interested in an administration action to the costs of attending proceedings in Chambers, he must attend by special leave of the judge, and, if he attends under the common order of course and without special leave, he may, in addition to paying his own costs, be ordered to pay the extra costs occasioned by his attendance (*i*).

Where a judgment or order is made (*k*), whether in Sale under judgment or order.

(*g*) *Daubney* v. *Leake*, 1 Eq. 495, approved in *Hubbard* v. *Latham*, 14 W. R. 553; but see *Sharp* v. *Lush*, 10 C. D., p. 474, cited *infra*, note (*i*).

(*h*) Rules of the Supreme Court, Costs, r. 21 (Spec. All.).

(*i*) *Sharp* v. *Lush*, 10 C. D. 468. "As a rule," said the M. R., "I give leave to one solicitor to attend on one side, and one solicitor on the other; when the residuary legatees come in, I let one solicitor take the accounts for the residuary legatee on the one side, and one solicitor take the accounts for the executors on the other"(*ibid.*, 474; and see *Day* v. *Batty*, 21 C. D. 830). Where a solicitor for a party attending the taking of accounts causes by his neglect unnecessary costs, he may be ordered to pay them personally, on the client undertaking not to bring an action against him in respect of his conduct of the proceedings (*Ridley* v. *Tiplady*, 20 Beav. 44; and see *Upton* v. *Brown*, cited, *ante*, p. 88).

(*k*) The Court has power, under the 15 & 16 Vict. c. 86, s. 55, at any time (even before the hearing *Tulloch* v. *Tulloch*, 3 Eq. 574), to direct real estate to be sold; but it is now the practice in a creditors' action, at the hearing, to direct the real estate, or a sufficient part thereof, to be sold, in case the personal estate proves insufficient to satisfy the debts and funeral expenses; Appendix, *post*, p. 196. But the beneficiaries may, upon payment of their proper proportion of the debt and costs, &c., prevent the sale being made (*Cooper* v. *Cooper*, L. R. 7 H. L., p. 72; *Lees* v. *Lees*, 15 Eq. 151; and see *Metcalfe* v. *Hutchinson*, 1 C. D. 591).

PROCEEDINGS IN CHAMBERS.

Court or in Chambers, directing any property to be sold, unless otherwise ordered, the same shall be sold with the approbation of the judge to whose Court the cause is attached, to the best purchaser that can be got for the same, to be allowed by the judge, and all proper parties shall join in the sale and conveyance as the judge shall direct (*l*). As to the conduct of sales, see *post*, p. 124. A sale under the Court is usually by auction (*m*). The judge in Chambers may fix reserved biddings upon a sale, direct deposits to be made, and appoint persons to receive the same, and receive proposals for private contract (*n*). Affidavits for the purpose of enabling the judge to fix reserved bids are to state the value of the property by reference to an exhibit containing such value, so that the value may not be disclosed by the affidavit when filed (*o*). As soon as particulars and conditions of sale, &c., settled at Chambers have been printed, two prints thereof, certified by the solicitor to be correct prints of the particulars and conditions settled at the judge's Chambers, are to be left at Chambers (*p*). Where, in pursuance of an order of the Court directing a sale by public auction, an attempt so to sell has been made and failed, the property cannot be sold otherwise than by public auction until a proper order for the purpose has been obtained (*q*).

The chief clerk's certificate.
The result of the proceedings before the chief clerk shall be stated in the shape of a short certificate, and shall not be embodied in a formal report, unless in any case the judge shall see fit so to direct (*r*). Where an account is directed, the certificate shall state the result of such account, and not set the same out by way of sche-

(*l*) Cons. Ord. XXXV. r. 13.
(*m*) *Pemberton* v. *Barnes*, 13 Eq. 349 ; for the practice before and at the auction, see Daniell, 1153, 1161.
(*n*) Morgan, 141.
(*o*) Reg., Aug. 8, 1857, r. 13.
(*p*) R. 14.
(*q*) *Berry* v. *Gibbons*, 15 Eq. 150.
(*r*) 15 & 16 Vict. c. 80, s. 32.

dule, but shall refer to the account verified by the affidavit filed, and shall specify (*s*) by the numbers attached to the items in the account, which, if any, of such items have been disallowed or varied, and shall state what additions, if any, have been made by way of surcharge. And where the account verified by the affidavit has been so altered that it is necessary to have a fair transcript of the account as altered, such transcript may be required to be made by the party prosecuting the judgment or order, and shall then be referred to by the certificate. The account, and the transcript (if any) referred to by the certificates, shall be filed therewith (*t*), but no copies thereof shall be required to be taken by any party (*u*). Where the chief clerk, by consent of all claimants, waives a question of title as to some of them, the certificate should be expressed to be without prejudice (*w*). When prepared and settled, it shall be transcribed by the solicitor prosecuting the proceedings, in such form and within such time as the chief clerk shall require, and shall then be signed by the chief clerk at an adjournment to be made for that purpose; but, where from the nature of the case the certificate can be drawn and copied in Chambers whilst the parties are present before the chief clerk, the same shall be then completed and signed by him without any adjournment (*x*).

(*s*) The chief clerk may not refer the whole of the accounts to an accountant, and then adopt his report as his own certificate (*Hill* v. *King*, 9 Jur. N. S. 527).

(*t*) See note (*b*), *infra*.

(*u*) Cons. Ord. XXXV. r. 46.

(*w*) *Waterton* v. *Burt*, 39 L. J. Ch. 425. It has been held that the certificate should state not facts merely, but conclusions drawn from the facts (*Lee* v. *Willock*, 6 Ves. 605; *Dixon* v. *Dixon*, 3 Bro. C. C. 509), though it would be sufficient if it stated a fact involving, according to the practice of the Court, a particular consequence (*Bick* v. *Motly*, 2 M. & K. 312). At the present time, however, it is considered that, if the circumstances warrant it, a certificate may state facts, and reserve for the consideration of the Court the legal questions arising out of them (*Stott* v. *Meanock*, 10 W. R. 605).

(*x*) Cons. Ord. XXXV. r. 48.

Certificates either general or separate.

Chief clerk's certificates are either general or separate. General certificates embrace the results of all the proceedings taken at Chambers under the judgment or order. A separate certificate comprises the result of only some one or more of them. Separate certificates are made in cases where it is not desirable to wait till the whole proceedings are completed. They will be prepared at the request of any of the parties interested, if the judge or his chief clerk is satisfied there is a sufficient reason for so doing (y).

Time for signature of certificate by judge.

At the expiration of four clear days after the certificate shall have been signed by the chief clerk, if no party has in the meantime obtained a summons to take the opinion of the judge thereon (z), the chief clerk shall submit the certificate to the judge for his approval, and the judge may thereupon, if he approve the same, sign such certificate in testimony of his adoption thereof, as follows:—
"Approved, this   day of   " (a).

Certificate, &c., signed and adopted by judge, to be filed, and be binding on all parties, unless discharged or varied within eight clear days.

When any certificate or report of the chief clerk shall have been signed and adopted by the judge, the same shall be filed (b), and shall thenceforth be binding on all the parties to the proceedings, unless discharged or varied, either at Chambers or in open Court, according to the nature of the case, upon application by summons or motion within eight clear days after the filing of such certificate (c). The eight days run during vacations (d).

A creditor who has proved in the action has a right to apply to vary the certificate (e).

Applications to discharge or vary certificate.

It is sufficient if a summons to vary be taken out within the eight days, although not returnable within that

---

(y) Daniell, 1215.
(z) As to which, see *ante*, p. 88.
(a) Cons. Ord. XXXV. r. 51.
(b) The certificate when signed by the judge, with the accounts (if any) to be filed therewith, shall be transmitted by the chief clerk to the Report Office, to be there filed (r. 55).
(c) 15 & 16 Vict. c. 80, s. 34; Cons. Ord. XXXV. r. 52.
(d) *Ware* v. *Watson*, 7 De G. M. & G. 739.
(e) *Wilson* v. *Wilson*, 2 Moll. 328.

period (*f*). But the practice has been otherwise laid down, where the application is by motion; in that case, it is not enough that notice of motion was served within the eight days, if the motion be not made until after their expiration (*g*); where, however, it is necessary or advisable to proceed by motion, and it is impossible to move on any motion day within the eight days, the Court will give special leave to serve notice of motion for some day within the eight days not a motion day (*h*).

Leave was given to move to vary the certificate, though application was not made until after the expiration of the eight days, where the omission to apply arose from pressure of business and mistake on the part of the solicitor, and where there was error apparent on the certificate (*i*); and in *Berry* v. *Gaukroger* (*j*), the Court of Appeal, notwithstanding lapse of time, varied the certificate (in which was a manifest error), and the order on further consideration, so far as it proceeded on the erroneous finding, the fund not having been distributed. So leave may be given after the eight days to take out a summons to vary; but after the eight days have elapsed, the certificate will not be discharged or varied, except on special grounds (*k*), nor while a judgment containing consequential directions founded on it stands (*l*).

An affidavit which was not used before the chief clerk cannot generally be used on an application to vary his certificate (*m*).

(*f*) *Wycherley* v. *Barnard*, Johns. 41.

(*g*) *Henshaw* v. *Angell*, 9 Eq. 451.

(*h*) *Cross* v. *Maltby*, 8 W. R. 646.

(*i*) *Briant* v. *Tibbut*, 17 W. R. 274; *Ashton* v. *Wood*, 8 De G. M. & G. 698; *Purcell* v. *Manning*, 3

Jur. N. S. 1070; see *post*, p. 134.

(*j*) W. N. 1882, 64.

(*k*) *Howell* v. *Kightley*, 8 De G. M. & G. 325.

(*l*) *Turner* v. *Turner*, 1 Sw. 154.

(*m*) *Davis* v. *Davis*, 2 Atk. 21; *Pierce* v. *Hammond*, 10 L. T. 261; *Bayliss* v. *Watkins*, 9 Jur. N. S. 570.

Applications to vary certificates are almost always adjourned so as to come on with the further consideration of the action (*n*).

Exceptions as regards certificates to be acted upon by Paymaster-General without further order, and certificates on passing receivers' accounts.

The rules above stated concerning certificates are subject to the following exceptions;—Where the Court directs any computation of interest or the apportionment of any fund which is to be acted on by the Paymaster-General or other person without any further order from the Court, the judgment or order made by the Court may direct such computation or apportionment to be made by one of the chief clerks attached to the Court of the judge, and may direct the certificate thereof, signed by such chief clerk, to be acted upon accordingly, without the same being signed and adopted by the judge (*o*). Such certificates shall be transmitted and filed in the same manner as those signed and adopted by the judge (*p*). Rules 49, 50 (*q*), 51, and 52 of Cons. Ord. XXXV. shall not apply to certificates which are to be acted upon by the Paymaster-General without any further order. Such certificates may be signed and adopted by the judge on the day after the same shall have been signed by the chief clerk, unless any party desiring to take the opinion of the judge thereon, obtains a summons for that purpose before twelve o'clock on that day. The time for applying to discharge or vary such certificates, when signed and adopted by the judge, shall be two clear days after the filing thereof (*r*). Neither shall Rules 49, 50, 51, and 52 apply to certificates on passing receivers' accounts. Such certificates may be approved and signed by the judge without delay, and, upon being so signed, shall be filed and forthwith acted upon (*s*).

(*n*) See *Crompton* v. *Huber*, 3 W. R. 347 ; *Hudson* v. *Carmichael*, 18 Jur. 851 ; *post*, p. 133.
(*o*) Cons. Ord. XXXV. r. 45.
(*p*) R. 56.
(*q*) *Ante*, p. 88.
(*r*) R. 53.
(*s*) R. 54.

If it should appear that the chief clerk has entirely overlooked a material element of the inquiry, the Court, without either allowing or disallowing an application to vary the certificate, may refer it back to him for review (*t*). <small>Certificate may be referred back.</small>

(*t*) *Mitford* v. *Reynolds*, 1 Ph. 706.

CHAPTER IX.

PROOF OF CLAIMS IN CHAMBERS.

A. Advertisements for creditors.

IN order to be in a position to answer the inquiry as to the debts of the deceased (*a*), it is usual for the judge in Chambers to order an advertisement to be issued for creditors affecting the deceased's estate, unless the executor or administrator has already issued advertisements under 22 & 23 Vict. c. 35, in which case it is unnecessary to issue fresh ones, and the chief clerk will take notice of those already issued without any special directions to that effect in the judgment (*b*). Every such advertisement issued pursuant to a judgment or order shall direct every creditor, by a time to be thereby limited, to send to the executor or administrator of the deceased, or to such other party as the judge shall direct, or to his solicitor, to be named and described in such advertisement, the name and address of such creditor, and the full particulars of his claim, and a statement of his account, and the nature of the security (if any) held by him; and such advertisement shall be in the prescribed form (*c*) with such variations as the circumstances of the case may require; and at the time of directing such advertisement a time shall be fixed for adjudicating on the claims (*d*). The advertisement shall be a peremptory and only one, unless for any special reason it may be thought necessary to issue a second

Peremptory.

(*a*) See *ante*, p. 51.
(*b*) *Cuthbert* v. *Wharmby*, W. N. 1869, 12.
(*c*) See Appendix, p. 200.
(*d*) Order 27th May, 1865, r. 1.

advertisement or further advertisements; and any adver- *In what papers inserted.*
tisement may be repeated as many times and in such
papers as may be directed (*e*), the common practice being
to direct its insertion in the *London Gazette*, and generally
in *The Times* as well, and also, if the deceased resided in
the country, in some local paper (*f*).

Where, many years after the division amongst creditors
of all the assets then available, further funds come in
belonging to the estate, fresh advertisements will be issued,
but if some only of the creditors or their representatives
then appear, they are only entitled to that proportion of
the fund which their debts bear to the entire liabilities of
the estate, and the residue will be retained to answer any
claims of the others in the future (*g*).

The advertisement shall be prepared by the party prose- *By whom prepared.*
cuting the judgment or order, and submitted to the chief
clerk for approval, and, when approved, shall be signed by
him, and such signature shall be sufficient authority to
the printer of the *Gazette* to insert the same (*h*).

No creditor need make any affidavit nor attend in *Creditor need not make affidavit or attend, unless required;*
support of his claim (except to produce his security), unless
he is served with a notice (*i*), requiring him to do so (*j*).
And the claimants filing affidavits shall not be required to *but party prosecuting cause to take office copies of affidavits, if any.*
take office copies, but the party prosecuting the cause
shall take office copies and produce the same at the hear-
ing, unless the judge shall otherwise direct (*k*). Every *Notice to creditor to produce security or other evidence.*
creditor shall produce the security (if any) held by him
before the judge at such time as shall be specified in the
advertisement for that purpose, being the time appointed
for adjudicating on the claims; and every creditor shall,

(*e*) Cons. Ord. XXXV. r. 35.
(*f*) See *per* Lord Romilly, M.R. *Wood* v. *Weightman*, 13 Eq. 436.
(*g*) *Ashley* v. *Ashley*, 4 C. D. 757.

(*h*) Cons. Ord. XXXV. r. 36.
(*i*) See Appendix, p. 200.
(*j*) Order, 27th May, 1865, r. 2.
(*k*) Cons. Ord. XXXV. r. 39.

if required, by notice in writing (*l*) to be given by the executor or administrator of the deceased, or by such other party as the judge shall direct, produce all other deeds and documents necessary to substantiate his claim before the Judge at his Chambers at such time as shall be specified in such notice (*m*).

Notice by post sufficient.

Every notice by the Order of 27th May, 1865, required to be given shall, unless the judge shall otherwise direct, be deemed sufficiently given and served if transmitted by the post, prepaid, to the creditor to be served, according to the address given by such creditor in the claim sent in by him pursuant to the advertisement, or, in case such creditor shall have employed a solicitor, to such solicitor, according to the address given by him (*n*).

Claims to be examined and result verified by affidavit of executor or other person appointed by judge.

The executor or administrator of the deceased, or such other party as the judge shall direct, shall examine the claims sent in pursuant to the advertisement, and shall ascertain, so far as he is able, to which of such claims the estate of the deceased is justly liable; and he shall, at least seven clear days prior to the time appointed for adjudication, file an affidavit, to be made by such executor or administrator, or one of the executors or administrators, or such other party, either alone or jointly with his solicitor, or other competent person, or otherwise as the judge shall direct, verifying a list of the claims the particulars of which have been sent in pursuant to the advertisement, and stating to which of such claims, or parts thereof, respectively, the estate of the deceased is, in the opinion of the deponent, justly liable, and his belief that such claims, or parts thereof respectively, are justly due and proper to be allowed, and the reasons for such belief. But in case the judge shall think fit so to direct, the making of the affidavit referred to in the preceding Rule numbered (5),

Such affidavit may be postponed,

(*l*) See Appendix, p. 201.   (*n*) R. 13.
(*m*) Order 27th May, 1865, r. 3.

shall be postponed till after the day appointed for adjudication, and shall then be subject to such directions as the judge may give. At the time appointed for adjudicating upon the claims, or at any adjournment thereof, the judge may, in his discretion, allow any of the claims, or any part thereof respectively, without proof by the creditors, and direct such investigation of all or any of the claims not allowed, and require such further particulars, information, or evidence, relating thereto, as he may think fit, and may, if he so think fit, require any creditor to attend and prove his claim, or any part thereof; and the adjudication on such claims as are not then allowed shall be adjourned to a time to be then fixed (o). Adjudication on the claims.

A creditor suing as plaintiff on behalf of himself and the other creditors, must prove his debt over again in Chambers, if there be no admission of assets (p), the Court not treating the judgment as conclusive evidence of the debt (q), even where it has been proved at the hearing after being put in issue on the pleadings; and accordingly the judgment will not, even in such a case, be prefaced with a declaration that the plaintiff is a creditor (r). Plaintiff must prove his debt in chambers, unless assets admitted.

It has been frequently laid down that the unsupported testimony of any person on his own behalf cannot, in adjudicating upon claims of creditors and others, be acted on in a Court of Equity. "Though in many cases," said Lord Romilly, M.R., "it may prevent a person from receiving what he is justly entitled to, still the Court cannot act on the mere unsupported testimony of any claimant (s). Evidence.

(o) Order 27th May, 1865, rr. 5, 6, 7; and see Cons. Ord. XXXV. r. 40, cited *post*, p. 118.

(p) As to the right of a creditor-plaintiff, when not only is his debt proved or admitted, but the executor or administrator admits assets, see *ante*, p. 50.

(q) See *ante*, p. 13; *Owens* v. *Dickenson*, Cr. & P. 48, 50; *per* Wigram, V.-C., *Woodgate* v. *Field*, 2 Ha. 213; *Whitaker* v. *Wright*, ibid. 310.

(r) *Field* v. *Titmuss*, 1 Sim. N. S. 218.

(s) *Grant* v. *Grant*, 34 Beav. 623; see also *Down* v. *Ellis*, 35 ib.

Claims for unliquidated damages.

A claim for unliquidated damages may be brought into Chambers as a debt (*t*), it being competent to the Judge in Chambers to take an account of a claim of unascertained amount (*u*), though the Court may, if it thinks right, direct an action, or such other proceeding as the exigency of the case may require (*x*). But, where a debt is due from the estate of a testator, one of whose executors is dead, and the estate of such deceased executor is being administered in an action, and the creditor of the original testator has sued for his debt and compelled the surviving executor to pay the whole amount into Court, such creditor cannot, for the purpose of enforcing contribution between the two executors, prove his debt against the estate of the deceased executor (*y*). A., the widow and administratrix of B., continued B.'s trade after his death. B., at his death was indebted to C. on balance of account. A. continued to receive goods from and to make payments to C., as B. had done, and she was charged in account by C. with the debt. The payments made by her to C. exceeded the debt, but a balance was ultimately due to C. Held that B.'s debt was discharged by A.'s payments, and that the ultimate balance could not be proved against B.'s estate (*z*).

In the proof of a bond debt in Chambers it is not the practice to require an affidavit of the consideration, unless a case of suspicion against the bond be raised (*a*), although,

---

578 ; *Rogers* v. *Powell*, 38 L. J. Ch. 648 ; *Morley* v. *Finney*, 18 W. R. 490 ; *Whittaker* v. *Whittaker*, 21 C. D. 657.

(*t*) *Sutton* v. *Mashiter*, 2 Sim. 513 ; *Burch* v. *Conry*, 14 Jur. 1009 ; *contra*, *Cox* v. *King*, 9 Beav. 530.

(*u*) *Sutton* v *Mashiter*, *Baker* v. *Martin*, 5 Sim. 380 ; *Paynter* v. *Houston*, 3 Mer. 297.

(*x*) *Lockhart* v. *Hardy*, 5 Beav.

305 ; *e.g.* a reference to an official referee, as in the case of a creditor's claim which was disputed ; *Rowcliffe* v. *Leigh*, 3 C. D. 292.

(*y*) *Mickelthwait* v. *Winstanley*, 13 W. R. 210.

(*z*) *Sternulale* v. *Hankinson*, 1 Sim. 393.

(*a*) *Whittaker* v. *Wright*, 2 Ha. 310.

as will be seen hereafter (*b*), creditors under voluntary bonds, though preferred to legatees, are only paid after all the other creditors are satisfied (*c*).

Under a judgment in an action by a creditor on behalf of himself and the other creditors, the executor may in Chambers impeach the validity of a bond on which the plaintiff sues, upon grounds which were not in issue at the hearing (*d*), and may even go into fresh evidence for the purpose of establishing a case of release, although there are allegations in the statement of claim upon which the defence of release might have been sufficiently raised at the hearing (*e*).

By sect. 10 of the Judicature Act, 1875, it is provided that, in the administration by the Court of the assets of any person dying insolvent on and after the 1st Nov., 1875 (*f*), the same rules shall prevail and be observed as to (*inter alia*) the valuation of annuities, and future and contingent liabilities respectively as may be in force for the time being under the Law of Bankruptcy with respect to the estates of bankrupts. Accordingly, a creditor in respect of an annuity payable until, and a debt payable upon the death of a person living at the date of the judgment for administration, was upon the death of that person before the certificate, held entitled to prove for the actual amount of the debt, and for the annuity upon the same principle, less a rebate of interest from the date of the administration judgment (*g*).

Contingent liabilities, &c.

(*b*) *Post*, pp. 161 (*h*), 173.

(*c*) The rule in bankruptcy is different; all debts, including those on voluntary bonds, are payable *pari passu* (*Ex parte Pottinger*, 8 C. D. 621). It is doubtful whether the alteration in the law made by the Judicature Act, 1875, sec. 10 (see *post*, p. 173) will affect this case.

(*d*) *Whitaker* v. *Wright*, 2 Ha. 310.

(*e*) *Cardell* v. *Hawke*, 6 Eq. 464.

(*f*) See *Sherwin* v. *Selkirk*, 12 C. D. 68.

(*g*) *Hill* v. *Bridges*, 17 C. D. 342; see also *Boswell* v. *Gurney*, 13 C. D. 136, where, the estate being insolvent, it was decided that interest on debts ought only to be allowed up to the date of the judgment.

PROOF OF CLAIMS IN CHAMBERS.

Cross-examination of creditor.

A creditor may be cross-examined on his affidavit in support of his claim (*h*); and a judgment creditor, bringing in his claim, may be cross-examined as to the validity of his judgment (*i*). If the documents by which a creditor supports his claim are believed to be forged, the party resisting the claim may have them deposited with the chief clerk, with liberty to have them produced for examination by experts, the creditor's solicitor being allowed to be present at such examination (*j*). On the other hand a creditor, who has come in under the judgment and produced *prima facie* evidence in support of his claim, may obtain an order directing the executors to file an affidavit as to their possession of documents relating to the claim or to any item of it (*k*).

Right of creditor to affidavit of documents by executors.

The Statute of Limitations.

The legal personal representative need not set up the Statute of Limitations (*l*) as a defence to a creditor's claim, and may *before judgment* pay (*m*) or retain a debt barred by the statute (*n*), or take it out of the statute by admissions in his answer (*o*), or by entering it as a debt in the residuary account (*p*), but *after judgment* (*q*) an executor cannot do any act which affects the relative rights of creditors (*r*), and as every creditor has a right to ques-

---

(*h*) *Cust* v. *Poyser*, 3 Sm. & G. 369; 26 L. J. Ch. 93; affirmed, *ibid.* 353; and see *ante*, p. 90.

(*i*) *Lenton* v. *Brudenell*, 12 W. R. 1127.

(*j*) *Groves* v. *Groves*, Kay, Ap. 19.

(*k*) *McVeagh* v. *Croall*, 1 De G. J. & S. 399; see *Newland* v. *Steer*, 11 Jur. N. S. 596.

(*l*) The statute runs during such time as the will is not proved. The creditor should either compel the executor to prove or take out administration; see *Boatwright* v. *Boatwright*, 17 Eq. 71; and Comp. Exors. 243.

(*m*) Even though the result of so doing be to throw other debts upon the real estate; *Lowis* v. *Rumney*, 4 Eq. 451.

(*n*) *Stahlschmidt* v. *Lett*, 1 Sm. & G. 415.

(*o*) *Moodie* v. *Bannister*, 4 Dr. 432.

(*p*) *Smith* v. *Poole*, 12 Sim. 17.

(*q*) A creditor whose debt is not statute-barred at the date of the judgment cannot of course be barred by lapse of time afterwards; *Re General Rolling Stock Company*, 7 Ch. p. 649.

(*r*) *Shewen* v. *Vanderhorst*, 2 R.

tion the claim of every other, because it may interfere
with his own (s), where the legal personal representative
refuses to set up the Statute of Limitations against a
claim brought into Chambers by a creditor coming in
under the judgment, any other creditor (t), or a residuary
legatee (u), may do so, unless judgment has, notwithstanding the statute, been recovered in respect of the debt
against the executors (w). The statute cannot, however,
be set up, as regards the *personal* estate of the deceased
against the plaintiff's claim, which is the foundation of
the judgment (x), though *cestuis que trustent* of devised
estates may set it up against a creditor on the *real*
estate, where the devisee in trust has not done so, for, but
for the Chancery Amendment Act, they would have been
necessary defendants (y). *Quære*, whether the Judge in
Chambers is himself *entitled* to set up the statute, where
it is not set up by any party or quasi-party (z). He was
clearly not *bound* to do so before the passing of the
Judicature Act, 1875, though there was a beneficiary not
before the Court (a), but it may be doubted whether this
rule is not altered in the case of insolvent estates by this
10th section of that Act (b), such a debt not being
proveable in bankruptcy (c).

As to the effect of the recent Statute of Limitations (d),
even where real estate is devised upon trust for payment
of debts, see *post*, p. 165 (u).

It was held in *Sterndale* v. *Hankinson* (e) that a The rule in

& M. 75, affd. 1 *ibid.* 347 ; *Phillips*
v. *Beal*, 32 Beav. 26 ; *ante*, pp.
55, 58.

(s) Per Lord Cottenham, *Owens*
v. *Dickenson*, Cr. & P. 56.

(t) *Shewen* v. *Vanderhorst* ; *Fuller* v. *Redman*, 26 Beav. 614.

(u) *Moodie* v. *Bannister*, 4 Dr.
432.

(w) *Hunter* v. *Baxter*, 3 Gif. 214.

(x) *Briggs* v. *Wilson*, 5 De G.

M. & G. 12 ; *Fuller* v. *Redman*, 26
Beav. 614 ; *Adams* v. *Waller*, 14
W. R. 789.

(y) *Briggs* v. *Wilson; ante*, p. 43.

(z) *Shewen* v. *Vanderhorst*.

(a) *Alston* v. *Trollope*, 2 Eq. 205.

(b) See *post*, p. 162.

(c) *Ex parte Dewdney*, 15 Ves
479.

(d) 37 & 38 Vict. c. 57.

(e) 1 Sim. 393.

decree on a bill for administration filed by one creditor on behalf (*f*) of himself and others would prevent the Statute of Limitations from running against any of the creditors who should come in under the decree; but this rule cannot be extended to the case of an action brought by an executor, who happens also to be a creditor (*g*), and Jessel, M. R., has said that creditors had better not rely upon the rule at all for the future, the decision in *Sterndale* v. *Hankinson* having depended upon a variety of circumstances of which, under the modern practice, none exist (*h*).

Sterndale v. *Hankinson*, *semble*, no longer prevails.

Interest on debts.

Where a judgment or order is made directing an account of the debts of a deceased person, unless otherwise ordered, interest shall be computed on such debts, as to such of them as carry interest, after the rate they respectively carry, and, as to all others, after the rate of 4 per cent. per annum, from the date (*i*) of the judgment or order (*j*). A creditor, whose debt does not carry interest, who comes in and establishes the same before a Judge in Chambers, under a judgment or order of the Court, or of a Judge in Chambers, shall be entitled to interest upon his debt at the rate of 4 per cent. per annum from the date of the judgment or order, out of any assets which may remain after satisfying the costs of the action, the debts established, and the interest of such debts as by law carry interest (*k*).

But when the estate is insolvent, interest will be allowed only up to the date of the administration judg-

---

(*f*) A *single* creditor's bill was held insufficient to stay the statute; *Watson* v. *Birch*, 15 Sim. 523.

(*g*) *Bray* v. *Tofield*, 18 C. D. 551.

(*h*) *Ibid.* 553, 554.

(*i*) Or, when the debt accrues due after judgment, from the time of its being proved; *Lainson* v.

Lainson, 18 Beav. 7.

(*j*) Cons. Ord. XLII. r. 9.

(*k*) R. 10. As to the application of these rules to suits pending in 1841, see *Wheeler* v. *Gill*, 19 Eq. 316, and cases there cited; and as to interest generally, see Dan. 1103—1107.

ment, which by virtue of sect. 10 of the Judicature Act, 1875, is equivalent to an adjudication in bankruptcy (*l*) As to subsequent interest, see *post*, p. 133.

A creditor who has come in and established his debt in the Judge's Chambers under a judgment or order in an action shall be entitled to the costs of so establishing his debt; and the sum to be allowed for such costs shall be fixed by the judge, unless he shall think fit to direct a taxation thereof; and the amount of such costs, or the sum allowed in respect thereof, shall be added to the debt so established. Where an account consists in part of any bill of costs, or where the judge is authorised to fix the amount of costs under r. 24, the judge may direct the taxing-master to assist him in settling such costs, not being the ordinary costs of passing the account of a receiver; and the taxing-master, on receiving such direction, shall proceed to tax such costs, and shall have the same powers, and the same fees shall be payable in respect thereof, as if the same had been referred to the taxing-master by an order, and he shall return the same with his opinion thereon to the judge by whose direction the same were taxed (*m*). These rules do not apply to the case of a creditor-plaintiff (*n*). In general a fixed sum of £1 13s. 4d. is allowed in respect of a debt under £5, and £2 2s. if it exceed that amount; but creditors attending by their solicitors to produce their securities under r. 3 of the Order of 27th May, 1865 (*ante*, p. 104), are allowed their proper costs of such attendance; Daniell, 1108. In *Waterton* v. *Burt* (*o*), three guineas each were allowed for the costs of copyholders successfully claiming a share of a fund paid into Court

Costs of creditors establishing claims;

(*l*) *Boswell* v. *Gurney*, 13 C. D. 136.
(*m*) Cons. Ord. XL. rr. 24, 25.
(*n*) *Flintoff* v. *Haynes*, 4 Ha. 309.
(*o*) 39 L. J. Ch. 425.

as compensation for rights of common. Where there is a deficiency of assets the costs of creditors proving their debts are not payable in full in the first instance, but are added to their debts, and if necessary apportioned with them (*p*). Where an alleged creditor carries in a claim which is disallowed, he may be ordered to pay the costs of the proceeding (*q*), and of an adjournment into Court (*r*), and may be refused the cost of an action which the Court gave him liberty to bring for the purpose of establishing his claim to damages, where the damages recovered by him were only nominal (*s*). In *Lancefield* v. *Iggulden* (*t*), the plaintiff, a devisee, unsuccessfully set up a claim as creditor, and was ordered to pay the costs of the proceedings occasioned by that claim.

and failing to establish them.

Notice shall be given by the executor or administrator, or such other party as the judge shall direct, to every creditor whose claim, or any part thereof, has been allowed, without proof by the creditor, of such allowance; and to every such creditor as the judge shall direct, to attend and prove his claim, or such part thereof as is not allowed, by a time to be named in such notice, not being less than seven days after such notice, and to attend at a time to be therein named, being the time to which the adjudication thereon shall have been adjourned; and in case any creditor shall not comply with such notice, his claim, or such part thereof as aforesaid, shall be disallowed (*u*). Any creditor who has not before sent in the particulars of his claim pursuant to the advertisement, may do so four clear days previous to any day

Notice to creditors of claims allowed or disallowed.

New claims before adjourned adjudication.

(*p*) *Morshead* v. *Reynolds*, 21 Beav. 638.
(*q*) *Hatch* v. *Searles*, 2 Sm. & G. 147; *Yeomans* v. *Haynes*, 24 Beav. 127.
(*r*) *Bentley* v. *Bentley*, 1 N. R. 390.
(*s*) *Morgan* v. *Elstob*, 4 Ha. 477.
(*t*) 10 Ch. 136.
(*u*) Order 27th May, 1865, r. 8.

to which the adjudication is adjourned (v). This is as of right. *Special leave to make claims* But after the time fixed by the advertisement, no claim shall be received (except as before provided in case of an adjournment), unless the judge shall think fit to give special leave upon application made by summons, and then upon such terms and conditions as to costs and otherwise as the judge shall direct (w). *after time fixed by advertisement;* This is by favour of the Court. The practice is to admit all (x) creditors whose debts have become due before the date of the certificate (y), and the indulgence of the Court goes yet further: letting in a creditor after certificate, where he has not been guilty of wilful default, is "every day's practice" (z). *even after certificate.* "Although the language of the decree, where an account of debts is directed, is that those who do not come in shall be excluded from the benefit of that decree, yet the course is to permit a creditor, he paying the costs of the proceedings, to prove his debt, so long as there happens to be a residuary fund in Court or in the hands of the executor, and to pay him out of that residue" (a).

The Court may, by additional orders, deal with a fund which is still in Court; but, where the party requiring the Court to deal with the fund might have appeared at an earlier stage of the action, he will be required to pay all the additional costs which have been occasioned by the imperfect manner in which his claim was brought forward (b). And, the fund being still in Court, a creditor has been let in upon terms as to costs, though he knew of the suit, and omitted to prove within the time limited

---

(v) *Ibid.*, r. 9.
(w) R. 10.
(x) A foreign creditor, as a condition of being let in after certificate, has been ordered to give security for costs; *Drever* v. *Maudesley*, 5 Russ. 11.
(y) *Per* Turner, L. J., *Thomas* v. *Griffith*, 2 De G. F. & J. p. 564.

(z) *Per* Leach, M. R., *David* v. *Frowd*, 1 M. & K. p. 209.
(a) *Per* Lord Eldon, *Gillespie* v. *Alexander*, 3 Russ. p. 136; *Lashley* v. *Hogg*, 11 Ves. 602; *Hartwell* v. *Colrin*, 16 Beav. 140.
(b) *Montefiore* v. *Browne*, 7 H. L. C. 241.

I

by the advertisements (b). So in *Hicks* v. *May* (c), a creditor, after the order on further consideration had been made, was allowed to have an additional sum due to him raised by sale or mortgage out of the testator's real estate, although in making his claim under the decree he had used a book wherein he subsequently found evidence to support his additional claim, but the circumstances of the case were such as to negative any imputation of laches.

As to claims after apportionment. But, after apportionment, the Court has declined to let in a creditor who had been guilty of laches and delay, where to do so would deprive another creditor of a debt which he had established (d); and, after an order had been made for payment of a dividend to the creditors who had proved, Kindersley, V.-C., refused to allow a creditor who had not proved to stay the payment of the dividend in order to have an opportunity of establishing his claim (e), though a stay had been directed by Plumer, V.-C., in a like case, on the creditor paying the costs of the application and the expenses incident to a re-casting of the apportionment (f); and, after distribution amongst the beneficiaries had been ordered, a stay was directed on the application of the executors, who were being sued in France by creditors who had not come in under the decree (g).

Creditor may obtain proportion only of his claim; Where a creditor is let in late, he will be put on an equality with the other creditors before any further dividend is paid to them (h), but it does not follow that he will be able to get the whole of his debt paid, unless he takes proceedings to make legatees refund. Thus, where a creditor did not establish his debt until the fund had been

(b) *Brown* v. *Lake*, 1 De G. & Sm. 144, affirmed by Lord Cottenham; and see *Sawyer* v. *Birchmore*, cited *post*, p. 120.
(c) 13 C. D. 237.
(d) *Cattell* v. *Simons*, 8 Beav. 243.
(e) *Hull* v. *Falconer*, 11 Jur. N. S. 151.

(f) *Angell* v. *Haddon*, 1 Madd. 529; and see *Barker* v. *Rogers*, cited *post*, p. 117.
(g) *Brett* v. *Carmichael*, 35 Beav. 340.
(h) As in Bankruptcy, *Re Wheeler*, 1 Sch. & Lef. 242.

apportioned and part of it paid over, while the remainder had been carried to the account of particular legatees, it was held that he was entitled to receive out of the funds of the legatees so remaining in Court, not the whole of the debt, but only a part of it, bearing the same proportion to the whole as the legacies given to those legatees bore to the whole amount of legacies given by the will (*i*). In a suit instituted in 1814 to administer the personal estate of an intestate who died in 1807, the Master reported that no debts had been proved, and by the decree on further directions in 1817 the whole of the residue was apportioned and distributed; but, as the plaintiff was then an infant, his share, amounting to four-ninths of the fund, was retained and carried to his separate account. In 1825 a foreign prince, claiming to be a creditor of the intestate, applied for leave to prove his debt against the sum remaining in Court, and the plaintiff coming of age soon after applied to have that sum paid out. It was held that the creditor was not precluded by the previous proceedings or the lapse of time, from tendering such proof before the Master, but that every defence should be allowed there which would have been competent upon a new bill; that the debt, if established, must be restricted, as against the fund in Court, to that proportion which the plaintiff's share bore to the whole amount distributed; and, therefore, that after reserving a sum equal to four-ninths of the claim, the residue of the fund ought to be paid to the plaintiff (*k*). So, where a fund paid into Court has been distributed by mistake among specialty and simple contract creditors to the exclusion of a mortgagee, the Court holds such creditors liable to repay *pro ratâ;* but no creditor will be fixed with liability in respect of the rateable part

---

(*i*) *Gillespie* v. *Alexander*, 3 Russ. 130.

(*k*) *Greig* v. *Somerville*, 1 R. & M. 338.

which the mortgagee may fail to recover from another creditor (*l*). Where, however, all the certified debts had been paid, and the residuary legatees, having been declared entitled to the estate, subject to an annuity, to provide for which a fund was retained in Court, had assigned their shares for value, and stop orders had been obtained, other creditors establishing their claims in another suit to which the executor and residuary legatees were parties, were held entitled to payment out of the fund in Court in priority to the assignees of the residuary legatees (*m*); but it would seem that if, under similar circumstances, an assignee for value of part of a residue had been actually paid, he would not be liable to refund, and that the person entitled to the remainder of the residue would be ordered to refund *pro ratâ* only (*n*).

and may be obliged to sue legatees.
If a creditor does not come in till after the residue has been paid away, he is not without remedy, though he is barred the benefit of the decree. If he has a mind to sue the legatees and bring back the fund, he may do so, but he cannot affect them except by suit, and he cannot affect the executor (*o*) at all (*p*). Where, however, a debt has been claimed to be due from the estate, and the claim has been fully investigated and disallowed, the alleged creditor cannot afterwards maintain a suit to enforce the claim against the residuary devisees or legatees; in such cases the rule of *res judicata* must apply (*q*).

In a suit for administering the estate of one who had

(*l*) *Todd* v. *Studholme*, 3 K. & J. 324.
(*m*) *Hooper* v. *Smart*, 1 C. D. 90.
(*n*) *Noble* v. *Brett*, 24 Beav. 499.
(*o*) In *Hunter* v. *Young*, 4 Ex. D. 256, where a creditor brought an action against persons to whom the residuary estate of his debtor had been assigned, without making the surviving executor of the testator a party, it was held by the Court of Appeal that even if the executor was a necessary party, the defendants could bring him before the Court under Order XVI. r. 17, and the action was not demurrable.
(*p*) *Per* Lord Eldon, *Gillespie* v. *Alexander*, 3 Russ. p. 136.
(*q*) *Per* Turner, L. J., *Thomas* v. *Griffith*, 2 De G. F. & J. p. 562.

been the legal personal representative of another, the party entitled to a share of the residuary estate of such other person carried in a claim for such share as a debt, but the claim was disallowed. It was held that the claimant ought forthwith to have applied to the Court for a direction that the claim be received, or to be examined *pro interesse suo*, or for leave to file a bill for administration of the estate in question, and to stay the distribution of the estate of the representative in the meantime, and that he ought not to have delayed his claim until after the certificate and the order on further consideration ; and where, after such delay the claimant filed his bill against the parties in the administration suit, the Court, though it stayed the general distribution of the fund, would not stay the payment of the costs under the order on further consideration (*r*).

An executor who distributes the assets with notice of a debt must of course satisfy the debt himself, and cannot recover over from the legatee (*s*), but notice of a remote contingent liability is not enough to prevent an executor from recovering from the residuary legatee (*t*).

Where an account is ordered to be taken of the legacies or annuities given by a will, no advertisement for such legatees and annuitants to come in need be issued where their names appear by the will. If, however, legacies are given to a class (*u*), and its members cannot be conclusively shown by evidence, or where it is unknown whether a legatee is still living, or, though he be proved to be dead, who is his personal representative, or where an inquiry is directed as to incumbrances created by legatees or next of kin upon their legacies or shares of residue, advertisements

B. Advertisements for claimants *not named* in will.

(*r*) *Barker* v. *Rogers*, 7 Hn. 19 ; cf. *Teed* v. *Beere*, 5 Jur. N. S. 381.
(*s*) See *Taylor* v. *Taylor*, 10 Eq. 477; *Jervis* v. *Wolferstan*, 18 Eq. 18.
(*t*) *Jervis* v. *Wolferstan*.
(*u*) As to the form of the inquiry, see *Brown* v. *Stone*, 30 W. R. 923.

calling upon such legatees or next of kin, or the persons claiming under them, to come in and prove their claims, are often directed to be issued (*x*).

Advertisements for claimants other than creditors (*y*) shall fix a time for them to come in and prove their claims, and shall appoint a day for the hearing and adjudicating thereon, and may be in a form similar to the form hereinafter set forth (*z*), with such variations as the circumstances of the case may require (*a*). Claimants coming in pursuant to advertisement shall enter their claims at the chambers of the judge in the "Claims Book" for the day appointed for hearing by the advertisement, and shall give notice thereof and of the affidavit filed to the solicitors in the cause, within the time specified in the advertisement for bringing in claims (*b*). Where, on the day appointed for hearing the claims, any of them remain undisposed of, an adjournment day for hearing such claims shall be fixed; and, where further evidence is to be adduced, a time may be named within which the evidence on both sides is to be closed; and directions may be given as to the mode in which such evidence is to be adduced (*c*). Any claimant who has not before entered his claim, may be heard on such adjournment day, provided he has entered his claim and filed his affidavit four clear days prior to such day, and no certificate of claims has been made in the meantime (*d*). After the time fixed by the advertisement no claim shall be received (except, as before mentioned, in case of an adjournment), unless the judge at chambers shall think

Claims book.

Adjournment; closing further evidence.

Claims heard on adjournment day.

Admitting further claims.

(*x*) Daniell, 1109.
(*y*) The actual words of r. 37 are "creditors or other claimants," but the Rules numbered 37, 38, 41, 42, and 43, of the 35th Consolidated General Order are abrogated so far as the same relate to *creditors;*

(Order 27th May, 1865, r. 11).
(*z*) See Appendix, p. 201.
(*a*) Cons. Ord. XXXV. r. 37.
(*b*) R. 38.
(*c*) R. 40.
(*d*) R. 41.

fit to give special leave upon application made by summons, and then upon such terms and conditions as to costs or otherwise as the judge shall think fit (e). A list of all claims allowed shall, when required by the judge, be made out and left in the judge's chambers by the party prosecuting the judgment or order (f). List of claims allowed.

Where a judgment or order is made directing an account of legacies, interest shall be computed on such legacies after the rate of four per cent. per annum from the end of one year after the testator's death, unless otherwise ordered, or unless any other time of payment or rate of interest is directed (g) by the will, and in that case according to the will (h). The legatee may, through laches, be deprived of interest except from the time of bringing his action (i); and by 3 & 4 Will. IV. c. 27, s. 42, no more than six years' interest on legacies can be obtained, except (k) when charged on real estates (l). There are, however, cases in which interest is payable from the death of the testator, although there be no such direction in the will, e.g., where he is the parent or grandparent of the legatee or puts himself *in loco parentis* (m), where the legacy is specific (n), or payable out of land (o), but not when payable out of proceeds of sale of land (p). Interest on legacies.

Next of kin are entitled to the costs of proving their title (q). Costs of next of kin.

Where an intestate's estate has been distributed under Refunding.

(e) R. 43.
(f) R. 44.
(g) As by empowering executors to apply the income of the legacy for maintenance of infant legatee, *Re Richards*, 8 Eq. 119.
(h) Cons. Ord. XLII. r. 11.
(i) *Purcell* v. *Blennerhasset*, 3 J. & Lat. 24.
(k) *Gough* v. *Bull*, 16 Sim. 323.
(l) See also 37 & 38 Vict. c. 57,

ss. 8, 10, cited *post*, p. 165.
(m) *Ellis* v. *Ellis*, 1 Sch. & Lef.
p. 5; *Rogers* v. *Soutten*, 2 Ke. 598.
(n) *Sleech* v. *Thorington*, 2 Ves.
Sen. 560; *Mullins* v. *Smith*, 1 Dr. & S. 204.
(o) *Spurway* v. *Glynn*, 9 Ves. 483.
(p) *Turner* v. *Buck*, 18 Eq. 301.
(q) *Hubbard* v. *Lathem*, 14 W. R. 553.

a judgment in an administration action among persons found by the certificate to be his next of kin, a person claiming to be the sole next of kin is not precluded from suing the persons alleged to have been erroneously found the next of kin for the purpose of obtaining restitution of the fund so distributed, and, if the right of the plaintiff so claiming shall be established, the persons among whom the fund has been so distributed will be compelled to repay it to the plaintiff, but the plaintiff will be bound by the accounts taken in the administration action (*r*). And the Court will not refuse its assistance, though the plaintiff had full notice of the proceedings in the suit in which the fund was distributed (*s*). But where the Probate Division has granted letters of administration to a person as one of the next of kin of the intestate, it is not open to a person claiming to be sole next of kin to sue the administrator for administration in the Chancery Division; he must first apply to the Probate Division to have the letters of administration recalled (*t*).

A legatee paid voluntarily by an executor is not bound to refund to him, nor to the other legatees, unless the executor proves insolvent (*u*); and where one of several residuary legatees or next of kin has received his share of the estate of a testator or an intestate, the others cannot call upon him to refund, if the estate is subsequently wasted; *secus*, if they can prove that the wasting took place before such share was received (*x*). Where, however, a residuary legatee is the plaintiff in an administration action, he can, under an undertaking implied by the fact of bringing the action, be compelled to refund for the purpose of paying legacies of legatees not parties to

(*r*) *David* v. *Frowd*, 1 M. & K. 200.
(*s*) *Sawyer* v. *Birchmore*, 1 Keen, 391, 825.
(*t*) *Hankin* v. *Turner*, 10 C. D.
(*u*) Comp. Exors. 177, 183.
(*x*) *Peterson* v. *Peterson*, 3 Eq. 111.

the action, assets paid him by the executor before action (y).

Executors paying a legacy not charged on the real estate to a legatee who was also legatee of the proceeds of sale of realty, he covenanting to refund if the principal estate should prove insufficient, were allowed to retain as against subsequent mortgagees of the interest of the legatee in the proceeds of sale (z).

(y) *Prowse* v. *Spurgin*, 5 Eq. 99.   (z) *Moore* v. *Moore*, 45 L. T. 466.

CHAPTER X.

THE CONDUCT OF ADMINISTRATION ACTIONS AND OF PROCEEDINGS ARISING THEREOUT.

Plaintiff has prima facie right to conduct of proceedings.

WE have already (*a*) had occasion to consider the subject of the conduct of proceedings, where two distinct and independent actions have been brought for the administration of the same estate, and an application has been made for the stay of one, or the consolidation of both, of them. But the question who ought to have the conduct of the proceedings also arises in many cases, where only one administration action is pending. It is a matter entirely in the discretion of the Judge in Chambers, whether the proceedings have been commenced by originating summons (*b*), or by writ (*c*), and the Court of Appeal will not interfere (*d*). The general rule, however, is that the plaintiff has the conduct, though, as will be seen, he may, for sufficient reason, be deprived of it.

Practice when plaintiff guilty of delay.

If there has been unreasonable delay on the part of the plaintiff in an administration action in prosecuting the judgment, or mismanagement or misconduct on his or his solicitor's part (*e*), the conduct of the action may be given to a creditor who has come in under the judgment, whether the action has been instituted by a creditor (*f*),

---

(*a*) *Ante.* pp. 70—72, 75.
(*b*) See *ante*, p. 1.
(*c*) *Harvey* v. *Coxwell*, 32 L. T., N. S. 52.
(*d*) *Dowbiggin* v. *Trotter*, 20 W. R. 1024.

(*e*) *Price* v. *North*, 2 Y. & C. Ex. 628 ; and see *Earle* v. *Sidebottom*, 37 L. J. Ch. 503.
(*f*) *Powell* v. *Wallworth*, 2 Madd. 183.

a *cestui que trust* (g), a next of kin (h), or a legal personal representative (i), and though it had become abated by the death of the defendant (k); or the conduct may be given to one who has been found a legatee under the will of the deceased (l). In connection with the subject of delay in the prosecution of proceedings in Chambers it will be convenient here to state the provisions of two rules of Court relating thereto. If the party having the prosecution of the judgment does not bring the same into Chambers within the time limited, any other party may do so, and such party shall have the prosecution unless otherwise directed (m). Again, in case any proceeding at Chambers is not prosecuted with due diligence, the parties, or any of them, may be required to attend at Chambers at a time to be appointed for that purpose, to show cause why such proceeding has not been prosecuted : and thereupon such directions may be given at Chambers, or by adjournment in open Court as shall be proper to ensure the prosecution thereof by some person interested therein ; or a certificate by the chief clerk of such neglect as aforesaid, or of any abandonment or abatement of the proceedings, or otherwise according to the facts, may be made and filed, without any fee being payable thereon ; and after such certificate shall have been so made, unless the same shall be discharged, none of the parties shall be at liberty to further prosecute the proceedings at Chambers, unless or until the Court or Judge shall upon application make an order directing the same to be prosecuted ; and upon such certificate becoming binding, any party may apply to the Court, and the Court may make such order relative to

(g) *Edmunds* v. *Aeland,* 5 Madd. 31 ; *Lord Alvanley* v. *Kinnaird,* 8 Jur. 114.
(h) *Sims* v. *Ridge,* 3 Mer. 458.
(i) *Fleming* v. *Prior,* 5 Madd. 423.

(k) *Cook* v. *Bolton,* 5 Russ. 282 ; and see *Lord Alvanley* v. *Kinnaird.*
(l) See *Williams* v. *Chard,* 5 De G. & Sm. 9.
(m) Cons. Ord. XXXV. r. 22, fully cited, *ante,* p. 86.

costs, and to relieve any party from the effect of any judgment or order before made, or proceeding taken which shall not have been duly prosecuted, or otherwise, as may be thought proper (*n*).

Conduct of different inquiries given to different persons; e.g., conduct of sale given to trustees.

If the Court thinks fit, the conduct of the different inquiries in Chambers may be given to different persons (*o*), or the conduct of a particular order (*e.g.*, to pay money into Court) may be taken from a plaintiff, while he is allowed to retain the general conduct of the action (*p*). In accordance with the principle of the case last cited is the recent rule (*q*), that where in actions for administration, or for the execution of the trusts of a settlement, a sale of property vested in trustees upon trust for, or with a power of sale, is ordered, the trustees shall have the conduct of the sale, unless otherwise ordered (*r*); and no other person has the right to interfere without the leave of the Court (*s*). Where one of four trustees, being also tenant for life, was plaintiff, and the remaining three trustees were defendants in an administration action, the conduct of a sale which was ordered, of property vested in the trustees with power of sale, was, under this rule, committed to the defendants (*t*).

When one of two co-plaintiffs refuses to concur in the appointment of a solicitor, there being no solicitor on the record, the proper course is for the other plaintiff to apply in Chambers for the sole conduct of the cause, on a summons assumed to be taken out in person against the

---

(*n*) Cons. Ord. XXXV. r. 23; see *James* v. *Gwynne*, 2 Jur. N. S. 436; *Ridley* v. *Tiplady*, 20 Beav. 44; *Parkinson* v. *Lucas*, 28 Beav. 627.

(*o*) See *Norvall* v. *Pascoe*, cited, ante, p. 72.

(*p*) *Vanderwell* v. *Vanderwell*, 1 L. T., N. S., 266.

(*q*) Ord. LII. r. 6a.

(*r*) This rule was promulgated because the practice which formerly prevailed of giving the conduct of sales to plaintiffs, *quâ* plaintiffs, (*Knott* v. *Cottee*, 27 Be. 33), so frequently frustrated the intentions of testators and settlors.

(*s*) *Dean* v. *Wilson*, 10 C. D. 136.

(*t*) *Gardner* v. *Beaumont*, 48 L. J. Ch. 644.

refusing plaintiff only: a motion to strike out the name of the refusing party as plaintiff, and make him a defendant, will be dismissed (*u*).

Where a creditors' suit was brought by one, who on the accounts being taken, was found to be a debtor to the estate, the Court ordered him to bring in the amount due from him, and to pay the costs occasioned by his alleging he was a creditor, and retained the suit for the benefit of the other creditors (*x*): but a plaintiff, who sues as creditor, will not be deprived of the conduct of the cause, because it has been certified that he is not a creditor, if exceptions to that finding are pending, and there is no reason to suppose that the exceptions will not be prosecuted actively (*y*). Plaintiff in creditors' action found to be a debtor to estate.

The Court will not, on the mere ground of irregularity in a creditor's judgment, take the conduct from the plaintiff, and give it to another creditor, though collusion be suggested (*z*).

If a creditor plaintiff dies, leaving a legal personal representative, the latter has the first right to an order for carrying on the proceedings (*a*); but, if the deceased plaintiff left no such representative an order that another creditor do carry on the proceedings may be obtained on a creditor's application (*b*), though not on the application of the accounting parties (*c*). Death of creditor plaintiff.

It is enough if one applying as a creditor for the conduct of proceedings has been allowed as a creditor, though the certificate has not been signed (*d*): indeed, if the account

---

(*u*) *Butlin* v. *Arnold*, 1 H. & M. 715.

(*x*) *Graves* v. *Wright*, 1 C. & L. 267. Compare *Houseman* v. *Houseman*, cited *ante*, p. 28, and see *post*, p. 149.

(*y*) *Jeudwine* v. *Agate*, 5 Russ. 283.

(*z*) *Smith* v. *Guy*, 2 Ph. 159.

(*a*) *Dixon* v. *Wyatt*, 4 Madd. 392.

(*b*) *Brown* v. *Lake*, 2 Coll. 620; *Lowes* v. *Lowes*, 2 De G. M. & G. 784; *Johnson* v. *Hammersley*, 24 Beav. 498.

(*c*) *Johnson* v. *Hammersley*.

(*d*) *Inchley* v. *Allsop*, 9 W. R. 649.

of debts has not yet been taken, it would presumably be enough if the applicant *claim* to be a creditor (*e*), though in this case it is submitted that he should at least adduce *primâ facie* evidence in support of his claim.

Application for conduct to be made in chambers.

Applications as to conduct of proceedings should be made in Chambers (*f*), as well where they are in two actions as in one (*g*). Though the chief clerk has refused an application to take the conduct from the plaintiff, the Court may grant it, on the application being renewed, the the chief clerk's judgment not being final (*h*).

Where the prosecution of a judgment has been taken from A., and given to B., A.'s solicitor must allow B.'s to inspect and take copies of all the papers in the cause in his possession (*i*).

Conduct of proceedings arising out of the administration action.

We have thus far been considering to whom the conduct of an administration action and the prosecution of the judgment will be committed. But this does not conclude the subject. In the course of the administration it may become necessary to take proceedings (*e.g.*, for the recovering of outstanding estate of the deceased) external to the administration action (*k*). The rule as to the conduct of such external proceedings is clear. If an executor refuses to take proceedings which ought to be taken, the Court will give the plaintiff power to take them in his name; but, where there is no case of misconduct made out against the executor, and he is willing to conduct the proceedings, the Court will not take them out of his hands (*l*).

The cases where a legatee may himself sue for recovery

(*e*) See *Bell* v. *Bell*, 12 W. R. 231.
(*f*) 15 & 16 Vict. c. 80, s. 26.
(*g*) *Stone* v. *Van Heythuysen*, 18 Jur. 344.
(*h*) *Wyatt* v. *Sadler*, 5 Sim. 450.
(*i*) *Bennett* v. *Baxter*, 10 Sim. 417.
(*k*) After an estate has been fully administered by the Court, an executor cannot without leave sue any party to the action to recover assets ; *Oldfield* v. *Cobbett*, 6 Beav. 515.
(*l*) *Per* Turner, L. J., *Harrison* v. *Richards*, 1 Ch. 475 ; and see *Samuel* v. *Samuel*, 12 C. D. 152, cited *ante*, p. 93.

of assets are collected and discussed in the judgment of the Vice-Chancellor of Ireland in *Eiffe* v. *Hilliard* (*m*). The principle upon which alone the Court takes from an executor the legal power which he possesses is well understood and established. It is in cases of misconduct, cases when justice may be thwarted or impeded by permitting the individual who is named to carry on the suit, notwithstanding his legal right to do so. But no such order has ever been made, according to the practice of the Court, unless there was a clear case of misconduct made out (*n*). Therefore, where in an administration action it was found necessary to take proceedings to recover misappropriated funds due to the testator's estate, and an action was begun by the executor against his father and half-uncle, who were the accounting parties, the Court held that the executor was entitled to commence the action, notwithstanding an allegation by the beneficiaries, who applied to have the conduct of the litigation given to them, that the executor's object was, by obtaining the conduct of the action, to be in a position to shield his father (*o*). But, where the administrator is bankrupt, the plaintiff was allowed to conduct the litigation in the administrator's name (*p*). In such a case, it is of course that a receiver should be appointed (*q*), but the *conduct* is now never given to the receiver (*r*). An application for the conduct of proceedings arising out of an administration action is properly made in the Court to which the administration is attached, though the proceedings for the conduct of which such application is made have been taken in another Court (*s*).

(*m*) L. R. 7 H. L. p. 43.
(*n*) Per Bacon, V. C., *Longbourne* v. *Fisher*, 27 W. R. 406.
(*o*) *Longbourne* v. *Fisher*.
(*p*) *Dowd* v. *Hawtin*, 19 C. D. 61.
(*q*) Ibid.; *Steele* v. *Cobham*, 1 Ch. 325.
(*r*) *Dowd* v. *Hawtin*.
(*s*) Ibid.

CHAPTER XI.

FURTHER CONSIDERATION.

When and how actions set down on further consideration.

WHERE accounts or inquiries have been directed (*a*), the judgment at the original hearing adjourns the further consideration of the action; and, in order to obtain a final judgment, the action must be set down to be heard on further consideration. This cannot, however, be done until the accounts or inquiries directed by the judgment, have been taken or made, and the chief clerk's certificate of their result has been filed; or a special certificate obtained, showing why the accounts or inquiries, or any of them, have not been proceeded with (*b*).

When any cause shall, at the original or any subsequent hearing thereof, have been adjourned for further consideration, such cause may, after the expiration of eight days and within fourteen days from the filing of the certificate of the chief clerk of the judge to whose court the cause is attached, be set down by the registrar in the cause-book for further consideration, on the written request of the solicitor for the plaintiff or party having the conduct of the cause; and after the expiration of such fourteen days the cause may be set down by the registrar on the written request of the solicitor for the plaintiff or for any other party (*c*), [and in either case upon production of the judgment or order adjourning further consideration or an office

---

(*a*) After a judgment merely directing accounts and inquiries, an action may be dismissed on further consideration; *Barton* v. *Barton*, 3

K. & J. 512.
(*b*) Daniell, 1228.
(*c*) Cons. Ord. XXI. r. 10.

copy thereof, and an office copy of the chief clerk's certificate, or a memorandum of the date when such certificate was filed indorsed on the request by the Clerk of Reports (*d*)]; but the cause, when so set down, shall not be put into the paper for further consideration until after the expiration of ten days from the day on which the same was so set down, and shall be marked in the cause-book accordingly. And notice thereof shall be given to the other parties in the cause at least six days before the day for which the same may be so marked for further consideration (*e*).

A cause may be marked for hearing on further consideration as a short cause, upon production of the certificate of the plaintiff's counsel that the cause is fit to be so heard, without the consent of the solicitors for any of the defendants; but it will not be so marked for any day, until after the expiration of the ten days above mentioned; unless by consent of all parties (*f*), and notice that it has been so marked should be given by the plaintiff's solicitor to the solicitors of other parties (*g*).

Short cause.

The certificate above referred to, is the chief clerk's general certificate. An action cannot be set down on further consideration on a separate certificate (*h*): an order on such a certificate must be sought on petition (*i*) or summons (*j*).

Notice that an action has been set down on further consideration, or the summons for the further consideration thereof, must be served on any person who has been served with notice of the judgment, and has obtained an order for leave to attend the proceedings (*k*), as well as on the

Notice of setting down, and appearances, and costs of persons unnecessarily appearing.

(*d*) Registrars' Regulations, March 15, 1860, r. 9.
(*e*) Cons. Ord. XXI. r. 10.
(*f*) Ibid., r. 10.
(*g*) Daniell, 1234.
(*h*) For the distinction between general and separate certificates, see *ante*, p. 98.

(*i*) *Van Kamp* v. *Bell*, 3 Madd. 430.
(*j*) Daniell, 1216; and see *Bell* v. *Turner*, 2 C. D. 409.
(*k*) Where no such order has been obtained, if it is desired to obtain against any such person an order for payment of money personally,

parties named on the record. If any person has obtained a stop order, he must be served with notice, where it is intended to deal in any manner with the fund to which the stop order applies (*l*). Even though not served with notice, a person interested may appear on further consideration, if the case which he has to make depends only upon what appears in the certificate (*m*). The principle of *Daubney* v. *Leake*, as to the costs of persons appearing unnecessarily (*n*), applies also to further considerations (*o*).

Declaration of title, and distribution of fund.

In general, if the case is such as will admit of it, the Court will, upon the first hearing on further consideration, deliver a final judgment; and, when preliminary accounts and inquiries have been directed (*p*), it will, when the case comes before it on the chief clerk's certificate, declare the rights of the parties in the matters in question, and, if possible, distribute the funds which are the subject matter of the action (*q*).

Questions arising under the Mortmain Acts have, of course, frequently to be determined on further consideration (*r*).

If the declaration of the Court, or the result of the former inquiries, renders any further inquiries necessary, the Court will take this occasion to direct such further inquiries, adjourning again the further consideration of the cause; and this it will repeat as often as may be neces-

he should be served with the notice (*Rees* v. *George*, 15 C. D. 490).

(*l*) Daniell, 1235.

(*m*) See *Young* v. *Everest*, 1 R. & M. 426.

(*n*) See *ante*, p. 94.

(*o*) *Hubbard* v. *Latham*, 14 W. R. 553.

(*p*) It is not the practice of the Court, except under special circumstances, to decide on the construc-

tion of a will, until the accounts have been taken (*Gaskell* v. *Holmes*, 3 Ha. 438); and when, as in *Say* v. *Creed*, 3 *ibid.* 455, the estate has been finally disposed of at the hearing, the executors admitting assets for all purposes, the rights of creditors have been expressly saved.

(*q*) See *post*, p. 180.

(*r*) As in *Brook* v. *Badley*, 4 Eq. 106.

sary (*s*), but as a rule, the creditors will be paid at once (*t*).

Where in an administration action a party was accepted as lessee, and afterwards broke his contract, the Court on further consideration granted an inquiry as to damages caused by the breach (*u*). Inquiry as to damages.

The Court usually, at the hearing on further consideration, disposes of the costs of the action (*x*) so far as they have not been already disposed of (*y*). Costs of action dealt with.

The Court will not, upon the question of costs or interest, look at any evidence but that in the cause, and will not look at the proceedings and evidence in Chambers, or on interlocutory motion (*z*); and, generally, evidence used in Chambers cannot be read on further consideration, unless notice of an intention to read it has been given (*a*), though a technical objection of this kind to the reception of evidence ought to be removed, by the Court, whether so requested or not, granting an adjournment upon proper terms as to costs and otherwise (*b*), and, even though the evidence be rejected, an inquiry may, if necessary, be directed upon the suggestion of counsel (*c*). But matters material on costs may be brought before the Court by any party on affidavit (*d*). Evidence.

It shall be lawful for the Court, at the hearing of any cause or of any further directions therein, to receive proof by affidavit of all proper parties being before the Court, and of all such matters as are necessary to be proved for

---

(*s*) Daniell, 1230.
(*t*) See *post*, p. 133.
(*u*) *Carne* v. *Brancker*, 17 W. R. 342; see however *ibid.*, 837.
(*x*) See *post*, p. 135.
(*y*) Daniell, 1230.
(*z*) *Curling* v. *Austin*, 2 Dr. & Sm. 129.
(*a*) *Jones* v. *Chennell*, 8 C. D. 492, 504.

(*b*) *Ibid.*, 506.
(*c*) *Fleming* v. *East*, Kay, App. 52; *Howard* v. *Chaffers*, 9 Jur. N. S. 634.
(*d*) *Fallows* v. *Lord Dillon*, 2 W. R. 507; *Palmer* v. *Perry*, W. N., 1870, 58; *Beavey* v. *Elliott*, W. N., 1880, 99; *contra*, *Bateman* v. *Margerison*, 2 W. R. 607; *Evans* v. *Lewis*, 2 L. T. N. S. 559.

enabling the Court to order payment of any monies belonging to any married woman, and of all such other matters not directly in issue in the cause as, in the opinion of the Court, may safely and properly be so proved (*e*). Under this enactment, an affidavit by the parents as to the members constituting a class of children has been admitted on further consideration, instead of an inquiry being directed (*f*), and also an affidavit as to the apportionment of a fund amongst creditors (*g*). But evidence discovered after the original hearing, and raising a new issue and a new defence, cannot be admitted under this section upon further consideration; though, if justice cannot be otherwise done, the Court will direct an inquiry (*h*).

Questions cannot generally be raised on further consideration which have not been pleaded.

The decision last cited leads up to the proposition that, where a question is not raised on the pleadings, and there is no direction or inquiry concerning it in the judgment, it cannot be raised on further consideration (*i*). At least, this is the general rule; but an executor has been held liable on further consideration for a breach of trust, though the particular matter was not charged in the bill, where the certificate afforded the necessary materials (*k*). If the matter which is first insisted on in argument on further consideration has already been raised on the pleadings the case is different, see *ante*, p. 16; and it is well settled that an executor may, on further consideration, be charged with interest (*l*) on balances, though it was neither asked for by the statement of claim, nor adverted to in the judgment (*m*); so a reference to compute interest on

Interest on balances,

or debts.

(*e*) 13 & 14 Vict. c. 35. s. 28.
(*f*) *Bush* v. *Watkins*, 14 Beav. 33; and see *Fowler* v. *Reynal*, 3 Mac. & G. 500.
(*g*) *Bear* v. *Smith*, 5 De G. & Sm. 92.
(*h*) *Howard* v. *Chaffers*, 9 Jur. N. S. 634; *Fleming* v. *East*, Kay, App. 52.

(*i*) *Morgan* v. *Morgan*, 13 Beav. 441; and see *ante*, p. 17.
(*k*) *Davenport* v. *Stafford*, 14 Beav. 319; affirmed, 2 De G. M. & G. 901.
(*l*) As to the rate at which interest will be charged, see Set. 478, 479, Pemb. 151; a special case is required to charge more than 4 per cent.
(*m*) *Turner* v. *Turner*, 1 J. & W.

debts may be ordered on further consideration, although not directed at the hearing (*n*). Subsequent interest will (*o*) be ordered to be computed and certified (*p*) or verified by affidavit (*q*), and, subject to the payment of costs (*r*), the total amount of their debts, or, in case of an insolvent estate, a rateable proportion, will at once be paid to the creditors. Sums under £10 may be ordered to be paid to the solicitor of the plaintiff upon his undertaking to apply them properly. By rule 12 of the Order of May 27, 1865, where any decree or order is made for payments by the Accountant-General to creditors, the party whose duty it is to prosecute such decree or order is required to send to each such creditor, or his solicitor (if any), a notice that the cheques may be received from the Accountant-General; and when required, to produce (*s*) such decree or order, and any papers necessary to enable such creditors to receive their cheques and get them passed. By rule 13 of the same Order, every such notice shall, unless the judge shall otherwise direct, be deemed sufficiently given and served if transmitted by the post, prepaid, to the creditor to be served, according to the address given by such creditor in the claim sent in by him pursuant to the advertisement, or in case such creditor shall have employed a solicitor, to such solicitor, according to the address given by him.

It has been already stated that where a summons has been taken out to discharge or vary the chief clerk's certificate, such summons is generally directed to

Certificate cannot be varied, unless on regular application,

39; *Hollingsworth* v. *Shakeshaft*, 14 Beav. 492; *Stafford* v. *Fiddon*, 23 Beav. 386; *Johnson* v. *Prendergast*, 28 Beav. 480.
(*n*) *Flintoff* v. *Haynes*, 4 Ha. 309.
(*o*) Except in the case of an insolvent estate, as mentioned, *ante*,

p. 110.
(*p*) See also Chancery Funds Rules, 1874, r. 10.
(*q*) See Forms 1 & 2, Set. 836, 837.
(*r*) See *post*, p. 135.
(*s*) See also *Lechmere* v. *Brazier*, 1 Rus. 72.

come on together with the further consideration of the action (*t*). If no summons has been taken out either to refer the certificate to the judge (*u*) or to vary it, the certificate cannot be objected to on further consideration (*x*). Where, however, there is error *apparent* in a judgment or certificate, the Court, of its own motion may, and indeed is bound, to set it right (*y*).

except where error apparent.

(*t*) Ante, p. 100.
(*u*) As to which, see *ante*, p. 98.
(*x*) *Lambe* v. *Orton*, 8 W. R. 111; *Smith* v. *Armstrong*, 6 De G. M. & G. 150; *Aspinall* v. *Bourne*, 29 Beav. 462; and see *Leigh* v. *Turner*, 14 W. R. 361. See further *ante*, p. 99.
(*y*) *Cradock* v. *Owen*, 2 Sm. & G. 241, 247; *Adams* v. *Claxton*, 6 Ves. 226; *Richardson* v. *Ward*, 13 Beav. 111.

CHAPTER XII.

COSTS OF ADMINISTRATION ACTIONS.

BY the order on the further consideration of an administration action, after providing for the payment first of costs and secondly of debts, the residue of the estate (if any) is, in a *creditors'* action, ordered to be carried to a separate account, to be intituled "Residue of the estate of A., deceased, subject to legacy duty," liberty being reserved to beneficiaries to apply as to the distribution thereof (*a*), whereas the order in an action by a legatee or personal representative goes on to direct distribution of the residue amongst the beneficiaries (*b*). The costs (*c*), and debts must in each case be first provided for. *Costs and debts first provided for on further consideration.*

We now proceed to consider the principles upon which the Court deals with the costs of the action, and in the next chapter shall discuss the order in which resort is had to the several classes of assets for the payment of debts, and, as subsidiary thereto, the rights of certain of the creditors or beneficiaries to have the assets marshalled in their favour. *Costs.*

It will be convenient to consider, *first*, what parties are entitled to their costs out of the estate, and under what circumstances ; *secondly* (where the assets are insufficient

(*a*) See Seton, 837.
(*b*) See Seton, 863.
(*c*) The higher scale of Costs (see Ord. VI. r. 1 of Additional Rules of Court, August, 1875) applies where the gross value of the estate actually amounts to £1000 at the institution of the action, and for this purpose where part of the estate consists of an equity of redemption, the value of the equity of redemption only is to be calculated (*Re Sanderson*, 7 C. D. 176.

to pay all costs properly payable thereout), which of these parties have priority; and, *thirdly*, out of what funds the costs are payable.

<small>Principles on which costs are allowed out of the estate.</small>

It has long been the rule that "wherever a testator has expressed himself so ambiguously as to make it necessary to come to the Court, his general assets must pay the costs" (*d*); and although it has also been laid down that "no costs ought to be given out of an estate, except for those proceedings only which are in their origin directed with some show of reason, and a proper foundation for the benefit of the estate, or which have in their result conduced to that benefit" (*e*), yet to the detriment of residuary legatees, very slight reasons have frequently been allowed to justify an administration action, and throw the costs of it upon the estate. But in a recent case (*f*), the principle of *Bartlett* v. *Wood* was approved and followed, and the costs of the plaintiff, a tenant for life whose income had been regularly paid, were disallowed, with almost an expression of regret that the practice of the Court did not permit the judge (*g*) to require her to pay the whole costs of the action; and as some of the accounts insisted upon were idle and unnecessary, she was ordered to pay the costs relating thereto.

<small>Costs of plaintiffs.</small>

It has been stated (*h*) that an action for the administration of the personal estate of a testator may be brought by any legatee, or annuitant whose annuity is charged upon the residuary personalty, or any residuary legatee or next of kin, creditor, executor, or administrator, and for the administration also of the real estate by any legatee whose legacy is charged on the real estate, any person interested in the sale of the realty, any residuary devisee

---

(*d*) Per Lord Thurlow, *Jolliffe* v. *East*, 3 Bro. C. C. 25.
(*e*) Per Lord Westbury, *Bartlett* v. *Wood*, 30 L. J. Ch. 614; see also *Cafe* v. *Bent*, 5 Ha. p. 38.

(*f*) *Croggan* v. *Allen*, 22 C. D. 101.
(*g*) Fry, J.
(*h*) *Ante*, Ch. III.

COSTS OF ADMINISTRATION ACTIONS.   137

or heir, creditor, or trustee, but it is not a matter of
course for all those persons to be allowed their costs out
of the estate.

In a suit by a mere pecuniary legatee, he will not be *Mere pecuniary*
allowed his costs, unless he has exhausted every other *legatee.*
means of obtaining his legacy (*i*), but in a proper case,
where assets are admitted and the executor has assented
to the legacy, the judgment for payment of the legacy (*k*)
will be made with costs, as "admission of assets for payment of the legacy is admission (*l*) of assets for the purposes
of the suit, and prevents all accounts being taken. It
extends, therefore, to an admission of assets for the payment of costs" (*m*). Where, however, judgment for administration is obtained by a legatee, a question frequently
arises whether the general estate or the legacy should bear
the costs of the action. The rule upon this point has *Rule in*
been thus stated: "If a fund is separated from the bulk *Wilson* v.
of the testator's estate, and then a question arises about *Squire.*
it, the fund pays the costs. But if the question is who
is entitled to the fund in the first instance, that question
is raised by the testator himself, and his estate must bear
the costs; for a testator's estate bears the costs of all the
questions that arise, on his will, respecting it" (*n*); and
the meaning of the rule was in *A.-G.* v. *Lawes* (*o*) thus
explained by Wigram, V.-C.: "I take the meaning of the
rule to be this: that if the executors, admitting the legacy
to be payable, sever it from the estate (*p*) and a dispute

(*i*) *Aylmer* v. *Winterbotham*, 4 Jur. N. S. 19.

(*k*) See *ante*, p. 50.

(*l*) But payment of one legacy is not an absolute admission of assets for the payment of all other legacies; each case will be determined with regard to its own circumstances; *Morewood* v. *Currey*, 28 W. R. 213; and see *ante*, p. 50 (*b*).

(*m*) *Philanthropic Society* v. *Hobson*, 2 My. & K. 357, *per* Leach, M. R.; and see *Dinsdale* v. *Dudding*, 1 Y. & C. C. 265, 270.

(*n*) *Per* Shadwell, V.-C., *Wilson* v. *Squire*, 13 Sim. 212.

(*o*) 8 Ha. p. 43.

(*p*) Where a particular fund is paid into Court under the Trustee Relief Act by an executor who has the

afterwards arises between the persons to whom or some of whom the legacy belongs, and the Court has to decide to whom it belongs, there the particular fund bears the costs: but if the dispute arises between the persons claiming the legacy and those claiming the estate or the residue, *whether the legacy is payable or not*, that cannot be the case of a severance in the sense in which the rule applies, because there, until the Court makes its decree that the legacy is payable, the legacy is not severed from the estate; the executors have kept it under their control for the purpose of having the point decided."

<small>Legatee plaintiff generally allowed his costs.</small>

Subject to this rule, it requires a strong case to induce the Court to order the costs to be borne by the legacy, and so to throw upon the legatee the costs of the action (*q*); but where a legatee's suit was brought to a hearing, although the plaintiff might have obtained payment of his legacy by petition in another administration action, neither the legatee nor the executor was allowed any costs (*r*).

<small>Concurrent actions.</small>

As to the costs of concurrent actions by legatees, see *ante*, p. 76.

<small>Annuitant.</small>

The costs of an administration action instituted by an annuitant whose annuity is charged on the residuary personalty would seem, from the judgment of Fry, J., in *Wollaston* v. *Wollaston* (*s*) to be payable as a general rule out of the estate.

general residue in his hands, the Court has jurisdiction to order the costs of a petition relating to that fund to be paid out of the general residue (*Re Trick's Trust*, 5 Ch. 170); and *semble*, when it is doubtful to whom a legacy is payable, the better course is not to pay it into Court under that Act, but to take out an administration summons, waiving accounts, simply for the purpose of obtaining the decision of the judge, or after taking out such summons, where the parties agree, to submit a statement of facts in the nature of a special case for the opinion of the judge; and if the executor does so pay it in, he will be left to take his costs out of the residuary estate, and will not have them out of the legacy (*Re Birkett*, 9 C. D. 576; but see *Gunnell* v *Whitear*, 10 Eq. 664).

(*q*) See *Burton* v. *Cooke*, 5 Ves. 464.
(*r*) *Packwood* v. *Maddison*, 1 S. & S. 232; and see *ante*, p. 77.
(*s*) 7 C. D. 58; see especially the report in 26 W. R. 77.

COSTS OF ADMINISTRATION ACTIONS.

With regard to the costs of an action instituted by a residuary legatee or one of the next of kin, the costs are *primâ facie* (*t*) payable out of the residue in which he is himself interested, unless through the executor's misconduct (*u*) he should be ordered to pay the whole or part; but where executors have made a proper distribution *pro tanto*, and have been ready to produce proper accounts to the unpaid residuary legatees, who then institute an administration action, if it turns out that the accounts are substantially correct, the costs of the action must be borne by the residuary legatees only who take the benefit of it. Where, however, in such an action it turns out that the executors have made serious mistakes whereby they have overpaid some of the residuary legatees, they cannot call upon them to refund, but must stand in the same position as if no distribution had taken place, and the costs will be paid as out of the entire estate, so as to charge the executors with the share of costs (*x*) attributable to each of the distributed shares, and they must pay the balance necessary to make up to each of the unpaid legatees his proper share of the residue (*y*).

Residuary legatees or next of kin.

Where executors have overpaid some of the residuary legatees, and the others obtain administration judgment.

Although, however, the costs of a residuary legatee are ordered to be paid out of the residue in which he is himself interested, they will not be so paid as between solicitor and client, without the consent of all parties interested (*z*),

Costs of residuary legatee not allowed as between solicitor and client, except

---

(*t*) The Court will not encourage useless litigation, and will deprive a residuary legatee of his costs in a proper case (*Ottley* v. *Gilbey*, 8 Beav. 602); but where the estate is considerable, and it is doubtful whether there will be a residue, it is his clear right to bring an action (*Morgan* v. *Middlemiss*, 14 W. R. 414; and see *post*, p. 155.

(*u*) See *post*, p. 143.

(*x*) In *Bath* v. *Bell*, 30 L. T. 422, all the costs of the accounts and inquiries were thrown on the undistributed assets, though the action by the persons entitled thereto was rendered necessary by the conduct of the executors, who were ordered to pay such proportion of the rest of the costs as the distributed bore to the undistributed assets.

(*y*) *Hilliard* v. *Fulford*, 4 C. D. 389, following the principle of *Mackenzie* v. *Taylor*, 7 Beav. 467, and *Tann* v. *Tann*, 7 Eq. 436.

(*z*) *Fenner* v. *Taylor*, 6 Madd.

140   COSTS OF ADMINISTRATION ACTIONS.

By consent, and should never be allowed where infants interested.

for of course the costs of the various parties interested may not be in proportion to their shares, and in no case, it is believed, did the present Master of the Rolls, when a judge of first instance, allow such costs where infants were interested.

Appeal for costs.

Notwithstanding the Judicature Act, 1873, s. 49, if the costs of a residuary legatee are disallowed, he is entitled to appeal, as such costs are not costs in the discretion of the Court (a).

Creditor generally allowed his costs.

The costs of a creditor plaintiff have already been in some measure considered (b). As a general rule a creditor of a deceased person bringing himself within any of the descriptions mentioned in Chapter III. is entitled to his costs of an action for administration, if instituted to obtain payment of his debt.

It has been stated (c), that he is entitled to immediate payment with costs, if his debt and assets be admitted, and upon payment by the executor, at any time before judgment, of the debt (with interest at 4 per cent.) and costs as between party and party, including the costs of any other defendants, the action will be dismissed (d), for until judgment, the other creditors have only an inchoate interest in the action (e).

When ordered to pay the costs,

If, however, a creditor commences, or, after commencing, prosecutes an action, in the face of information that the assets are insufficient for the payment of any part of his debt, and this turns out to be correct, he must pay the costs (f); but in *Robinson* v. *Elliott* (g), the bill was dismissed without costs, where in the answer the accounts

or deprived of his costs.

3; *Martin* v. *Maugham*, 8 Jur. 609.
(a) *Farrow* v. *Austin*, 18 C. D. 58.
(b) *Ante*, pp. 76, 84.
(c) *Ante*, p. 50; and see p. 137.
(d) *Pemberton* v. *Topham*, 1 Beav. 316; *Manton* v. *Roe*, 14 Sim.

353.
(e) *Sterndale* v. *Hankinson*, 1 Sim. 393.
(f) *Bluett* v. *Jessop*, Jac. 240; *King* v. *Bryant*, 4 Beav. 460; *Fuller* v. *Green*, 24 ibid. 217.
(g) 1 Russ. 599.

were not very satisfactory, and the Master had charged
the executrix with more than she had admitted, though
there were even then no assets for payment of the plaintiff's debt; and if the action is *properly* instituted by a
simple contract creditor, and the assets are found insufficient for payment of specialty debts, and consequently the
plaintiff receives nothing, he may still be allowed his
costs (*h*). This case will, since the 32 & 33 Vict. c. 46 (*i*),
be of rare occurrence.

As to the costs of creditors coming in under the judg- Costs in chambers.
ment and proving their debts in Chambers, see *ante*, p. 111.

The costs of an executor or administrator, whether plain- Executor or administrator.
tiff or defendant, are subject to the same rules as those of
trustees, which have been recently referred to by Jessel,
M.R., in the following terms :—" It is not the course of the General rule as to costs of trustees and executors.
Court in modern times to discourage persons from becoming
trustees by inflicting costs upon them if they have done
their duty, or even if they have committed an innocent
breach of trust. The earlier cases had the effect of
frightening wise and honest people from undertaking
trusts, and there was a danger of trusts falling into the
hands of unscrupulous persons who might undertake them
for the sake of getting something by them " (*k*). Where a
suit was instituted for the administration of the estate of
a supposed intestate, which, after the decree had been made
and the accounts taken, was rendered useless by the revocation of the former letters of administration, and by

---

(*h*) *King* v. *Hammett*, 11 L. J. N. S. Ch., p. 15. In *Sullivan* v. *Bearan*, 20 Beav. 399, the suit was properly instituted, but improperly prosecuted after notice of a similar deficiency of assets, and the plain-tiff was allowed his costs only up to the time of receiving such notice.

(*i*) See *post*, p. 161.

(*k*) *Turner* v. *Hancock*, 20 C. D. p. 305. In this case a trustee who had alleged that he had expended more than he had received, but was eventually charged on taking the accounts with £62, was allowed his full costs, as between solicitor and client.

probate being granted of a will made in favour of one of the next of kin, a defendant in the suit, in whose possession the will had been retained, the costs incurred in the suit were ordered to be borne by the party entitled under the will, who by delaying the probate had occasioned the litigation (*l*). And, as executors can only be fully protected from future claims by an administration action (*n*), the Court will require a strong case to induce it to deprive (*o*) them of the costs of one (*p*), still more so, to make them pay them (*q*). In accordance with this principle, it has been held that the mere fact of executors neglecting to render accounts when asked (*r*) or being charged with interest on balances in their hands (*s*), is not of itself sufficient to make them liable for the costs of an administration action (*t*); the true rule being, as laid down by Plumer, V.-C. (*u*), that "if the misconduct of the executor was the *sole* occasion of the suit, he ought then to pay the costs." And where a trustee defends an action for the benefit of his testator's estate, he will be allowed his costs of it out of the estate, though he may have also defended his own character from a charge of fraud (*x*).

_{Strong case required to deprive them of costs; still stronger to make them pay them.}

(*l*) *Mirehouse* v. *Herbert*, 5 W. R. 583; but see *Houseman* v. *Houseman*, 1 C. D. 535, cited *ante*, p. 28.

(*n*) See *Low* v. *Carter*, 1 Beav. 426; *Waller* v. *Barrett*, 24 *ibid.* 413.

(*o*) But where the executor was guilty of gross misconduct and delay, though he could not be altogether deprived of the costs of an action instituted by himself, as the estate consisted to an appreciable extent of leaseholds, he was allowed only such costs as would have been incurred if judgment had been obtained upon an administration summons (*Howard* v. *Easton*, 29 W. R. 885).

(*p*) See *Hall* v. *Hallet*, 1 Cox, p. 141; *Taylor* v. *Glanville*, 3 Madd. 176.

(*q*) *Gilbert* v. *Lee*, 34 Beav. 574.

(*r*) *White* v. *Jackson*, 15 Beav. 191; *Heugh* v. *Scard*, 24 W. R. 51.

(*s*) See the observations of Stuart, V.-C., in *Eglin* v. *Sanderson*, 3 Giff. pp. 441, 442.

(*t*) *White* v. *Jackson*, 15 Beav. 191; and see *Travers* v. *Townsend*, 1 Moll. 496.

(*u*) *Tebbs* v. *Carpenter*, 1 Madd. 290, 308.

(*x*) *Walters* v. *Woodbridge*, 7 C. D. 504; but see *Christian* v. *Adamson*, W. N., 1869, 208.

Executors will, however, be deprived (*y*) of their costs (*z*), or ordered to pay the costs (*a*) of such inquiries as are rendered necessary by their own misconduct; and they were ordered to pay the costs of the administration of the *personal* estate, when they had disproved charges relating to the *real* estate, the costs of which the plaintiff was ordered to pay (*b*). In *Payne* v. *Evens* (*c*), a bill for administration was dismissed *without costs*, on the ground that, though the estate, had been, in fact, fully administered many years before, yet owing to the negligence of the trustees in not preserving accounts and vouchers, there was some colour for the institution of the suit (*d*); and where a trustee took upon himself to be a partisan of one of the parties to the action, and threw impediments in the way of the other, though, in the absence of any improper motive, he was not ordered to pay any costs, he was not allowed his costs out of the estate (*e*); but where trustees had refused information and an account, and other proceedings had subsequently been taken, whereby the costs were greatly increased, they were ordered to pay the costs of the suit up to the hearing, and as to the rest of the costs, each party had to bear his own (*f*).

Executors however have frequently been ordered to pay all the costs of the action (*g*), *i.e., up to the hearing*; for the costs of taking the accounts must in general be borne by the estate (*h*); and on this principle they have been

(*y*) Executors may be deprived of their costs when the estate is administered upon summons, as well as in an action, *Gilbert* v. *Lee*, 34 Beav. 574.
(*z*) *Colyer* v. *Colyer*, 32 L. J. Ch. 101.
(*a*) *Tebbs* v. *Carpenter*, 1 Madd. 290; *Heighington* v. *Grant*, 1 Ph. 600.
(*b*) *Eylin* v. *Sanderson*, 3 Giff. 434.
(*c*) 18 Eq. 356.
(*d*) See also *Youde* v. *Cloud*, 18 Eq. 634.
(*e*) *Simpson* v. *Bathurst*, 5 Ch. 193.
(*f*) *Talbot* v. *Marshfield*, 3 Ch. 622.
(*g*) *Tickner* v. *Smith*, 3 Sm. & G. 42.
(*h*) See *Tebbs* v. *Carpenter;*

allowed their costs, upon making good the breach of trust and otherwise complying with the order of the Court (*i*); but in *Birks* v. *Micklethwait* (*j*), Westbury, C., said, "I cannot understand how the principles of this Court can be abided by as to the mode of dealing with executors and trustees, if I am to give a man all his costs of coming here to account for property which he has withheld, to make good sums of money which he has fraudulently omitted to carry to an account upon a former occasion, and also to make good the loss incurred by his neglect and delay. If to a trustee standing in this predicament I am to give the costs occasioned by the necessity of bringing him here, then it would be a premium to defaults and misconduct of this kind, instead of being the exercise of that wholesome control over the conduct of trustees which it is abundantly necessary that this Court should at all times carefully preserve;" and it is submitted that the Court would hesitate to extend the doctrine in the slightest degree (*k*).

Executors improperly bringing an action for administration which is dismissed will be ordered to pay the costs (*l*), for "the Court," said Bacon, V.-C., "will not allow itself to be made the instrument of mere litigation, when the only result would be to despoil infant children and a widow of the little property they possess. The will involved no question of any difficulty, and the action, which has been improperly instituted, must be dismissed with costs to be paid by the plaintiff."

In *Bowyer* v. *Griffin* (*m*), a suit for the execution of certain trusts, a defaulting trustee who had lost part of the trust funds by his own default was held to be entitled to

Knott v. *Cotlee*, 16 Beav. 77; *Gilbert* v. *Lee*, 34 Beav. 594; *Gresham* v. *Price*, 35 ibid. 47.
(*i*) *Hewett* v. *Foster*, 7 Beav. 348; and see *Lewis* v. *Trask*, 21 C. D. 862, and *post*, (*o*) and (*p*).
(*j*) 34 L. J. Ch. 362.
(*k*) See *Palmer* v. *Jones*, 43 L. J. Ch. 349.
(*l*) *Gaye* v. *Rutland*, W. N., 1882, 92.
(*m*) 9 Eq. 340.

his costs incurred after his bankruptcy, or after the registration of a creditor's deed executed by him under the Bankruptcy Act, 1861 : and though in an earlier case (*n*), where an executor becoming bankrupt in the course of the suit was allowed to set off his costs *before* bankruptcy against the balance due from him to the estate, and held entitled to his costs incurred subsequently to the bankruptcy, the reasons given for the order were that it would be harsh to deprive of his costs an executor who had become bankrupt, but by whose exertions the estate had been got in, until he had repaid the debt due at his bankruptcy, and that the *bankruptcy is the statutory mode by which in such a case the debt is discharged*, yet it would seem that neither of these circumstances is necessary to induce the Court to make the order (*o*). It has, however been still more recently held (*p*), that a defaulting executor is only entitled to costs incurred after his bankruptcy upon making good his default, unless by express request of the beneficiaries he has been kept before the Court to assist in getting in the estate.

It may here be remarked that a debtor to the estate who is entitled to costs out of the fund, will not be allowed to receive payment of them, while his debt continues unsatisfied; but the costs due to him will be set off *pro tanto* against the debt due from him (*q*); indeed, whenever a person beneficially interested in the estate either as legatee or one of the next of kin (*r*) is also a debtor thereto, his beneficial interest may be set off against the

<small>Costs set off against debt to estate;</small>

<small>so as to legacy or share of residue,</small>

<small>(*n*) *Samuel* v. *Jones*, 2 Ha. 246.
(*o*) *Turner* v. *Mullineux*, 9 W. R. 252 ; *Bowyer* v. *Griffin ; Clare* v. *Clare*, 21 C. D. 865 ; but see *Lewis* v *Trask*, 21 C. D. 862, where the bankrupt, though held entitled to his costs, was not to receive them until he should have made good his default.
(*p*) *Hannay* v. *Basham*, ~~W. N.~~ 23 C.D. 195; ~~1882, 7~~; and see *Kitto* v. *Luke*, 28 W. R. 411.
(*q*) *Harmer* v. *Harris*, 1 Russ. 155.
(*r*) *White* v. *Cordwell*, 20 Eq. 644.</small>

L

amount due from him (s), though statute-barred (t), except where the debtor became bankrupt in the lifetime of the creditor, in which case only the dividend received by the other creditors may be retained (u), or where, the bankruptcy having occurred after the death of the creditor, the executor (v) or (even without the leave of the Court) a receiver (x), has proved for the debt therein (y). So also, a trustee who is himself a beneficiary and indebted to the estate, cannot claim any part of it until the debt is made good (z); although he may have become entitled derivatively, *e.g.*, as being one of the next of kin of an intestate *cestui que trust* (a); but if the debt be not presently payable, he will have his costs at once, unless there is reason to fear he may become insolvent before the debt is actually due (b).

except where debtor bankrupt before death of creditor.

Bankruptcy of one of two co-executors.

If one of two co-executors represented by the same solicitor upon a joint retainer, becomes bankrupt, and is a debtor to the estate, the costs incurred by them prior to the bankruptcy will be distinguished, and the solvent executor will be allowed only his own proportion out of the fund, the defaulter's proportion being set off against the debt due from him, the solvent executor being regarded, by reason of the joint retainer, as a surety only in respect of the bankrupt's costs; but the costs incurred

---

(s) So, in *Knapman* v. *Wreford*, 18 C. D. 300, where legatees had been ordered to pay the executor's costs of probate litigation, the executor was allowed to set off their legacies against his costs, both as against the legatees and their assignees.

(t) *Courtenay* v. *Williams*, 3 Ha. 539; S. C. 13 L. J. Ch. 461, affirmed, 15 *ibid.* 204.

(u) *Beswick* v. *Orpen*, 16 C. D. 202.

(v) *Stammers* v. *Elliott*, 3 Ch. 195.

(x) *Armstrong* v. *Armstrong*, 12 Eq. 614.

(y) But where an executor has set apart and appropriated assets to meet a legacy, he cannot retain or impound them to meet a debt from the legatee to the estate (*Ballard* v. *Marsden*, 14 C. D. 374).

(z) *Irby* v. *Irby*, 25 Beav. 632.

(a) *Jacubs* v. *Rylance*, 17 Eq. 341.

(b) *Stephens* v. *Pillen*, 17 L. J. Ch. 214.

by both subsequently to the bankruptcy will be allowed in full (c).

Although the Court will not, in ordering executors to pay costs, distinguish, as between them and the persons beneficially entitled to the estate, the amount of culpability of the several executors, but will make the order upon them jointly (d), yet as between the executors themselves one may be primarily and the other secondarily liable (e); and the fact of one only being guilty of a breach of trust will justify him in severing in his defence, in which case he may be awarded the whole of the single set of costs allowed (f). *Where innocent executor ordered to pay costs jointly with guilty executor.*

In general, trustees should not sever in their defence, and, if they do so improperly, only one set of costs will be allowed (g). On the other hand, an executor refusing in a proper case to join his co-executor as plaintiff, and in consequence made a defendant, would not be allowed his costs (h). *Trustees should not generally sever in their defence.*

Although an executor who is a solicitor will as a general rule be allowed merely his costs out of pocket (i), unless the will directs that he shall be allowed his usual professional charges, yet in *Cradock* v. *Piper* (k) it was held that the circumstance of a solicitor being a trustee would not prevent him from receiving his usual costs where he acted as solicitor in a suit *for himself and his co-trustees*, and entered a joint appearance for himself and them, provided *Costs of an executor who is a solicitor.*

(c) *Smith* v. *Dale*, 18 C. D. 516; *Watson* v. *Row*, 18 Eq. 680, not followed.
(d) *Lawrence* v. *Bowle*, 2 Ph. 140.
(e) *Lockhart* v. *Reilly*, 1 De G. & J., p. 477; [illegible]
(f) *Webb* v. *Webb*, 16 Sim. 55.
(g) *Gaunt* v. *Taylor*, 2 Beav. 346; and compare *Cummins* v. *Blomfield*, 3 Jur. N. S. 657; *Aldridge* v. *West-*

brook, 4 Beav. 212; and *Wiles* v. *Cooper*, 9 Beav. p. 298.
(h) *Hughes* v. *Key*, 20 Beav. p. 397.
(i) *Moore* v. *Froud*, 3 M. & Cr. 46; *Broughton* v. *Broughton*, 5 De G. M. & G. 160.
(k) 1 Mac. & G. 664; see the observations on this case in Lewin on Trusts, 7 Ed. p. 259, and *Broughton* v. *Broughton*.

the costs were not increased by his being one of the parties for whom such joint appearance was made. "There is, however," said Turner, V.-C., in *Lincoln* v. *Windsor* (*l*), "a marked difference between the cases of costs incurred in a suit, and of costs incurred in the administration of an estate without the intervention of the Court. The general principle of the rule disallowing professional charges by a trustee is this—that a trustee cannot be permitted to profit or to place himself in a situation to profit by his trust. Now, where a trustee is brought into Court in a suit, he can have no opportunity of placing himself in a situation to profit by his trust. Therefore, if a trustee be necessarily made a party to a suit, and the costs be not increased by any conduct of his, there appears to be no reason why he should not be allowed his costs. The reason of the general rule appears to be inapplicable to the case of a suit under such circumstances; but this does not extend to the case of the costs of administration out of Court;" and even when there is a special direction in the will, an executor who acts as solicitor to the trust is not entitled to employ another solicitor to transact all the ordinary affairs which he may have to perform, such as personal attendances, correspondence, &c.; *e.g.*, though it is absolutely necessary to attend personally at the Bank of England to transfer stock, unless a power of attorney be obtained, the expense of such a power will not be allowed to an executor, unless it was really necessary, and the right to profit costs where a solicitor is entitled to them by the will, will be examined upon this principle (*m*). In *Pollard* v. *Doyle* (*n*), it was held that a solicitor administrator who instituted and conducted proceedings to recover property which

---

(*l*) 9 Ha. 158, approved in *Broughton* v. *Broughton*, 5 De G. M. & G. 160.

(*m*) *Harbin* v. *Darby*, 28 Beav. 325.

(*n*) 1 Dr. & Sm. 319.

belonged to the estate, and made a judgment creditor party to the suit, was, upon objection by the judgment creditor, only allowed his costs out of pocket, the estate, including the amount recovered in the suit, being insufficient to pay the judgment creditor.

The right of an executor to appeal for costs has been upheld in a recent case (o), where it was held that sec. 49 of the Judicature Act, 1873, has not taken away the right which was recognized in *Cotterell* v. *Stratton* (p). Executors or trustees may appeal for costs.

The costs of executors and trustees are always taxed and paid "as between solicitor and client," and on the suggestion of counsel, they will be also allowed any charges and expenses properly incurred in the administration. Their costs are payable as between solicitor and client.

Where the real estate is also administered, the costs of the plaintiff and the costs of trustees will be dealt with upon the same principles; but, as will be seen hereafter, they will be apportioned between the real and personal estate. Real estate.

The costs of persons attending the proceedings have been already considered (q). Costs of persons attending the proceedings.

Although in any of the cases mentioned above the plaintiff may fail to substantiate his claim, it is possible that he may be allowed the whole or part of his costs. "If," said Lord Langdale, M. R., in *Wedgwood* v. *Adams* (r), "through the exertions of a plaintiff, the Court is enabled to distribute a fund, or if it makes a declaration of rights necessary for its administration, there, although the plaintiff may fail in his claim, the Court will not permit the other parties to carry off the fruit of his exertions without defraying his costs out of the fund;" but see *Houseman* v. *Houseman* (s). It will, however, be Plaintiff not succeeding may be allowed his costs;

(o) *Farrow* v. *Austin*, 18 C. D. 58, overruling *Re Hoskins' Trusts*, 6 *ibid.* 281; and see *Turner* v. *Hancock*, 20 *ibid.* 303, cited *ante*, p. 141; and *Jones* v. *Chennell*, 8 *ibid.* 492.

(p) 8 Ch. 295.
(q) *Ante*, pp. 93—95.
(r) 8 Beav. 103; see the cases on this point collected at p. 164.
(s) 1 C. D. 535, cited *ante*, p. 28; and see *ante*, p. 125.

observed that in no case has a defendant been ordered *personally* to pay such costs, and in *Dicks* v. *Yates* (t), it was said by Jessel, M. R., that although "the Court has a discretion to deprive a defendant of his costs though he succeeds in the action, and it has a discretion to make him pay perhaps the greater part of the costs by giving against him the costs of issues on which he fails, or costs in respect of misconduct by him in the course of the action, a judgment ordering the defendant to pay the whole costs of the action cannot be supported unless the plaintiff was entitled to bring the action."

but not from the defendants personally.

The principle that persons having the same interest ought to appear by the same solicitor is carried out in the case where persons interested in the estate have assigned or mortgaged their shares. The practice was first settled in *Greedy* v. *Lavender* (u), where it was determined that only one set of costs, namely the costs to which the assignor or mortgagor would have been entitled if he had not dealt with his share, ought to be allowed to each legatee out of the estate, and that as between him and his assignee or mortgagee they should be paid to the latter, so far as required to satisfy his costs, the assignor or mortgagor receiving the balance (if any) towards his own costs and the deficiency (if any) of the mortgagee's costs being paid out of his assignor's share (v). It will be seen that unless assignor and assignee appear separately, they do not suffer any loss under this rule.

Costs of assignees or mortgagees of beneficiaries.

So, where long inquiries were necessary by reason of the bankruptcy of a person entitled to a share in the residue, the costs were apportioned (w), but if a mortgagee, who has taken a mortgage from an executor *quâ* beneficiary not

---

(t) 18 C. D., p. 85.
(u) 11 Beav. 417 ; see also *Coates* v. *Coates*, 3 N. R. 355.
(v. See also Seton, 879.

(w) *Basevi* v. *Serra*, 14 Ves. 313 ; but see *Gee* v. *Mahood*, W. N., 1874, 207.

quâ executor, is made a party to an action for administration, his costs cannot come out of the estate; they must be added to his security (*x*).

We have hitherto assumed that the assets are sufficient for the payment of all the costs properly payable thereout: we now proceed to consider the practice where this is not the case.

<small>Rules where fund deficient.</small>

The first and most important rule is that the costs, charges, and expenses of the executor or administrator (*y*), have priority over all other liabilities of the testator's estate, including (*z*) his debts and the costs of all other parties, and that as between solicitor and client. "That general rule," said Stuart, V.-C., in *Lodge* v. *Pritchard* (*u*), "proceeds on a very plain principle, that before what has been entrusted to them and is in their hands is taken out of their hands they shall be indemnified against all expenses incurred in the discharge of their duty" (*b*), but in that case, where it would seem from the headnote that the executors had denied assets, an apparent exception to the rule was laid down, and the creditor's debt and costs were ordered to be paid first. This may, however, be regarded rather as a deprivation of part of an executor's costs than a departure from the rule. Executors are not deprived of the benefit of the rule even where they have exhausted the assets by confessing judgments (*c*).

<small>Costs of executor paid in priority.</small>

When the *whole* of the real estate is found to belong to the creditors, the heir-at-law, seised of the legal estate, is

<small>When heir regarded as trustee for creditors.</small>

(*x*) *Scurrah* v. *Scurrah*, 2 W. R. 53.

(*y*) As to costs of an administrator *ad litem*, see *Nash* v. *Dillon*, 1 Moll. 236; *Nicholson* v. *Falkiner*, *ibid.* 555.

(*z*) Including also costs incurred in Probate litigation, and by an order of the Probate Division directed to be paid "out of the estate, and to have priority over other claims on the estate" (*Rowles* v. *Mayhew*, C. D. 596); and costs of an executrix of a deceased administratrix; *Rice* v. *Orgles*, W. N. 1877, 177.

(*a*) 4 Giff. p. 298.

(*b*) See also *Tipping* v. *Power*, 1 Ha. 405, and *Gaunt* v. *Taylor*, 2 *ibid.* 413.

(*c*) *Sanderson* v. *Stoddart*, 32 Beav. 155.

regarded as a trustee, and is allowed his costs out of the proceeds of sale thereof as between solicitor and client; where *part* only is required for debts, as between party and party (*d*). In *Tipping* v. *Power* (*e*), devisees received their costs next after those of the executors and the plaintiff, an equitable mortgagee of the estate devised to them (they having disclaimed by their answer), and in priority to the debts of the testator; and on the like principle, in a suit by creditors to administer the realty, there being no personalty, and the realty proving deficient, the Court ordered the costs of the plaintiffs and of the defendants, who were beneficial devisees, to be taxed as between party and party, and paid *pari passu* out of the fund, and the balance (if any) of the fund then remaining to be applied in payment of plaintiff's extra costs between solicitor and client, and then towards payment of debts (*f*).

Costs of disclaiming trustees as between party and party only.

Persons named as trustees will, on disclaiming, be entitled to costs as between party and party only, as they thereby divest themselves of the character of trustees (*g*).

Executors, as such, not entitled to costs out of real estate.

We have already seen that executors are entitled to their costs, charges, and expenses in priority to other parties, but, *quâ* their costs as *executors*, only out of the personal estate, unless the realty be charged therewith. Thus executors cannot have judgment for administration of the realty in order to obtain payment of costs incurred in probate litigation (*h*), and even where trustees' "costs, charges, and expenses" are charged upon the realty, *semble*, funeral expenses and costs of probate are not included (*i*).

(*d*) *Tardrew* v. *Howell*, 2 Giff. 530.
(*e*) 1 Ha. 405.
(*f*) *Henderson* v. *Dodds*, 2 Eq. 532; *Ferguson* v. *Gibson*, 14 Eq. 379.
(*g*) *Bray* v. *West*, 9 Sim. 429;

Norway v. *Norway*, 2 M. & K. 278.
(*h*) *Charter* v. *Charter*, 3 C. D. 218.
(*i*) *Collis* v. *Robins*, 1 De G. & Sm., p. 135.

The rule as to the costs of creditors, plaintiffs in administration actions, where the assets are deficient, is well stated in *Thomas* v. *Jones* (*j*), where Kindersley, V.-C., says, " If a creditor files a bill on behalf of himself and all other creditors, and the fund applicable to the payment of the debts turns out to be insufficient for the purpose, that fund, to use the language in one of the cases, belongs exclusively to the creditors. When, therefore, one creditor institutes a suit for the benefit of himself and all other creditors, such creditors being represented only by him, and if in that suit he recovers payment of the debts due to the creditors generally, then he is recouped the expenses he has properly incurred as plaintiff; and he is allowed his costs *as between solicitor and client*, because he has been at the trouble of recovering the fund for all the parties entitled to it." This rule applies also to cases where a creditor obtains the conduct of an action instituted by a legatee or next-of-kin (*k*). Ordinarily, where the assets are sufficient for payment of the debts, the creditor plaintiff is paid only his party and party costs (*l*); but where a fund had been realised by the diligence of the plaintiff, and the assets were more than sufficient for payment of the debts, the costs of the plaintiff as between party and party were ordered to be paid out of the general fund, and the extra costs of the plaintiff were directed to be paid *pro ratâ* by all the creditors who partook of the benefit of the suit (*m*).

<small>Creditor plaintiff, when entitled to solicitor and client costs.</small>

It was at one time the practice to insert in decrees for administration in creditors' suits, a direction that creditors " before coming in to prove should contribute their pro-

<small>No contribution now ordered from creditors towards plaintiff's costs.</small>

(*j*) 1 Dr. & S. 134, approved in *Richardson* v. *Richardson*, 14 C. D. 611; and see *Henderson* v. *Dodds*, 2 Eq. 532.
(*k*) *Richardson* v. *Richardson*, *loc.* cit.; *Joseph* v. *Goode*, 23 W. R. 225.
(*l*) *Lechmere* v. *Brazier*, 1 Russ. 81.
(*m*) *Stanton* v. *Hatfield*, 1 Ke. 358.

portion of the expenses of the suit" (n), but it would seem that this condition was never enforced (o), and this direction is now omitted (p).

Costs of mortgagee, plaintiff in an administration action. There is some conflict of authority as to the costs of a mortgagee who, as a creditor, brings an action for administration. It has been held that as by a sale of the mortgaged property under the order of the Court he obtains an advantage outside his contract, the costs of the executors of the mortgagor will come out of the proceeds of sale in priority to his debt and costs (q), but in *Pinchard* v. *Fellows* (r), Bacon, V.-C., ordered the plaintiff's mortgage-debt, interest, and costs of suit to be paid out of the proceeds of sale in priority to the costs of the executors. It has been held, where a mortgaged estate is sold in a creditors' action, by consent of the mortgagee, not a party to the action, that he is entitled to have his principal and interest, and the expenses of the actual sale (*but no more*) paid in priority out of the proceeds of sale, his other costs and expenses being left to be defrayed out of the general estate, and the plaintiff's costs of the sale being paid out of the balance of the proceeds (s); but in *Ward* v. *Mackinlay* (t) a doubt is expressed by Turner, L. J., as to

---

(n) *Thompson* v. *Cooper*, 2 Coll. 87.

(o) See *Shortley* v. *Selby*, 5 Madd., p. 448; *Leehmere* v. *Brazier*, 1 Russ., p. 76.

(p) Seton, 832; where it is suggested that as the taxed costs are paid before the fund in Court is distributed, the plaintiff receives contribution in effect; but if the fund be insufficient even to pay the plaintiff's costs, it would seem that creditors who by coming in under the judgment have approved and adopted the action, ought to contribute to make up the deficiency; see, however, *Stanton* v. *Hatfield*, 1

(q) *Armstrong* v. *Storer*, 14 Beav. 535; *Spensley* v. *Harrison*, 15 Eq. 16.

(r) 17 Eq. 421; see also *Aldridge* v. *Westbrook*, 5 Beav. 188; *Carr* v. *Henderson*, 11 Beav. 415; *Tuckley* v. *Thompson*, 1 J. & H. 126, where the plaintiff, an equitable mortgagee, was not allowed his costs of the sale; and *Henderson* v. *Dodds*, 2 Eq. p. 533.

(s) *Berry* v. *Hebblethwaite*, 4 K. & J. 80; notwithstanding *Hepworth* v. *Heslop*, 3 Ha. 485.

(t) 2 De G. J. & S. 358.

COSTS OF ADMINISTRATION ACTIONS.   155

the propriety of this practice, as being calculated to prevent mortgagees from consenting to a sale being made free from incumbrances, and a distinction is drawn between such cases and those where the mortgagee is plaintiff (*u*).

The case of a legatee's costs (whether of a pecuniary or residuary legatee) remains to be considered. *Costs of legatee plaintiff, where fund deficient;*

The assets may of course be sufficient for payment of the debts, but not of the legacies, or for debts and legacies, without leaving any surplus for the residuary legatee, or they may be insufficient even for payment of debts.

The costs as between party and party of the plaintiff, a pecuniary or residuary legatee, and of the residuary legatee when made a defendant, are paid out of the estate in priority to debts, if the action has enabled the Court to administer the assets (*x*). *when paid in priority to debts, but as between party and party only,* Where there are creditors and legatees upon a fund which is capable of paying them all, leaving a balance, as the fund does not belong to the creditors *alone*, but to the residuary and general legatees as well, there is no reason for giving one residuary legatee more than any other his costs as between solicitor and client (*y*); and where there is a common legatee's suit as to a fund belonging to creditors and legatees, and it turns out that there is not sufficient to pay the creditors in full, the legatee plaintiff would not (*z*) be allowed his costs as between solicitor and client, because in fact the fund did not belong to the legatees but to the creditors, and he had no right to be paid extra costs out of a fund belonging to another class of claimants (*a*); but where there is a surplus after payment of debts, but not sufficient for payment of

---

(*u*) See also *Dighton* v. *Withers*, 31 Beav. 423; *Threlfall* v. *Harrison*, W. N., 1877, 192.

(*x*) *Wetenhall* v. *Dennis* or *Davis*, 33 Beav. 285.

(*y*) *Thomas* v. *Jones*, 1 Dr. & Sm. 134.

(*z*) This was allowed in *Burrell* v. *Smith*, 9 Eq. 443; but see *Richardson* v. *Richardson*, 14 C. D. 611, where this case is questioned.

(*a*) *Thomas* v. *Jones*; *Weston* v. *Clowes*, 15 Sim. 610.

legacies (*b*), and where and so far as the estate, though insufficient to pay the plaintiff anything, has been increased by his exertions (*c*), and so far as the plaintiff's costs have been incurred in getting in and realising the estate (*d*), a legatee plaintiff is allowed solicitor and client costs. Where the funds are insufficient even to pay the costs, the plaintiff is not entitled to priority for any costs ordered to be paid between party and party: all such costs are paid *pari passu* (*e*).

except as to the costs of getting in and realization.

Next of kin plaintiffs have no priority.

It appears that the next of kin, bringing an action for administration, have no priority for their costs over the debts, they being entitled only to *undisposed* of personal estate (*f*).

Executor's right of retainer paramount to costs of all other persons.

It should be remembered, before a legatee's action is instituted, that the executor's right of retainer for his own debt (*g*), is paramount to the right of both creditor and beneficiary to the payment of their costs (*h*).

The general personalty the primary fund for costs;

Unless the testator has otherwise directed, the general personalty, that is, in ordinary cases, the residuary personal estate, after specific and pecuniary legatees have been satisfied, is the fund for the payment of the costs of administering the personal estate; and notwithstanding the cases of *Scott* v. *Cumberland* (*i*), and *Gowan* v. *Broughton* (*k*), it is well settled that there is no ascertained residue divisible amongst the beneficiaries until the debts, funeral and testamentary expenses, and costs of administering the estate have been paid, and that the costs are to be

(*b*) *Thomas* v. *Jones*, 1 Dr. & Sm. 130; *Cross* v. *Kennington*, 11 Beav. 89.
(*c*) *Wroughton* v. *Colquhoun*, 1 De G. & Sm. 357.
(*d*) *Wetenhall* v. *Dennis* or *Davis*, 33 Beav. 285.
(*e*) *Wetenhall* v. *Dennis*, approved in *Thompson* v. *Harris*, 19 C. D.

552.
(*f*) *Newbegin* v. *Bell*, 23 Beav. 386.
(*g*) See *post*, p. 166.
(*h*) *Chissum* v. *Dewes*, 5 Russ. 29; *Richmond* v. *White*, 12 C. D. 361.
(*i*) 18 Eq. 578.
(*k*) 19 Eq. 77.

paid out of the whole residue, before it is divided, and not out of any lapsed share thereof (*l*). The same rule applies where a mixed fund is created of realty and personalty (*m*).

Where, however, the residuary personalty is insufficient, the pecuniary legacies, and demonstrative legacies so far as payable out of the same fund (*n*), are first resorted to *pro ratâ* (*o*), and after them the real estate not disposed of by the will (*p*); if there still be a deficiency, the specifically bequeathed personalty, and the specifically devised realty (including realty comprised in a residuary devise) (*q*), contribute rateably to make it up (*r*). then the pecuniary legacies,
next the undisposed of realty,
lastly, specific gifts.

The costs so falling on the residuary personalty as a whole, include the costs of getting in a specific legacy (*s*), of ascertaining what persons are entitled as members of classes among whom the estate is to be divided, and that, too, although some of the classes are more numerous than others (*t*), and of severing, appropriating, and securing a legacy (*u*), but where a legacy had been appropriated and the residue had been divided, the costs of a suit by a reversioner to secure it, were ordered to be borne out of the legacy (*v*). What costs included.

Where there is real estate only to be administered, if it is disposed of in favour of a class, and some of the shares Costs of administration of real estate only

---

(*l*) *Trethewy* v. *Helyar*, 4 C. D. 53 ; *Fenton* v. *Wills*, 7 C. D. 33 ; *Blann* v. *Bell*, 7 C. D. 382.
(*m*) *Luckcraft* v. *Pridham*, 48 L. J. Ch. 636.
(*n*) *Sellon* v. *Watts*, 9 W. R. 847.
(*o*) *Tomkins* v. *Colthurst*, 1 C. D. 626 ; *Farquharson* v. *Floyer*, 3 C. D. 109, notwithstanding *Hensman* v. *Fryer*, 3 Ch. 420.
(*p*) *Wood* v. *Ordish*, 3 Sm. & G. 125 ; *Stead* v. *Hardaker*, 15 Eq. p. 177.
(*q*) *Hensman* v. *Fryer* ; *Lance-*

field v. *Iggulden*, 10 Ch. 136.
(*r*) *Jackson* v. *Pease*, 19 Eq. 96.
(*s*) *Perry* v. *Meddowcroft*, 4 Beav. 204.
(*t*) *Shuttleworth* v. *Howarth*, Cr. & Ph. 228 ; *Re Reeve's Trusts*, 4 C. D. 841 ; and see *Bland* v. *Daniell*, W. N., 1867, 169.
(*u*) *Handley* v. *Davis*, 28 L. J. Ch. 873 ; and see *Attorney-General* v. *Lawes*, 8 Ha. 32, and *Wilson* v. *Squire*, 13 Sim. 212, cited *ante*, p. 137.
(*v*) *Governesses' Benevolent Institution* v. *Rusbridger*, 18 Beav. 467.

lapse, the costs are nevertheless payable out of the whole, and not out of the lapsed shares (*x*). Where, however, different estates are specifically devised, and part of the realty is undisposed of, or some of the specific devises lapse, the costs will, as a general rule, fall on the undisposed of or lapsed estates (*y*); but in *Bagot* v. *Legge* (*z*), where the questions related entirely to the rights of the devisees *inter se*, and to the rights of the devisees and heir at law, the costs were ordered to be paid *pro ratâ* out of the descended and devised estates. It must be remembered that a residuary devise which takes effect, is in law specific (*a*), and specific devisees contribute *pro ratâ*, according to the net value of their interests (*b*).

Apportionment between real and personal estate.
Where both the real and personal estates are administered, the costs will be apportioned between them (*c*), as also is the case where the realty and personalty form a mixed fund (*d*), or two estates, or a testator's estate and another fund are administered in one action (*e*); but in some such cases the costs have been ordered to be borne in equal shares though the funds are unequal (*f*); and the Court often declines to apportion costs minutely (*g*). It would seem that the apportioned part of the costs thrown upon the real estate should be borne by it in the same manner as the costs of the action where there is real estate only to be administered; see *supra*.

(*x*) *Eyre* v. *Marsden*, 4 M. & Cr. 231; *Maddison* v. *Pye*, 32 Beav. 658; and see *Fisher* v. *Fisher*, 2 Ke. 610.

(*y*) *Sanders* v. *Miller*, 25 Beav. 154.

(*z*) 2 Dr. & S. 259.

(*a*) See *ante*, p. 157 (*q*).

(*b*) *Barnewell* v. *Iremonger*, 1 Dr. & S. 255.

(*c*) *Patching* v. *Barnett*, 51 L. J. Ch. 74; *Thompson* v. *Harris*, 19 C. D. 552; the cases to the contrary must now be taken to be overruled. Only the costs, "so far as they have been increased by the administration of the realty" are paid thereout.

(*d*) *Christian* v. *Foster*, 2 Ph. 161.

(*e*) *Young* v. *Martin*, 2 Y. & C. C. C. 582; *Irby* v. *Irby*, 24 Beav. 525.

(*f*) *Dean* v. *Morris*, 5 W. R. 345; *Mayd* v. *Field*, 24 W. R. 660.

(*g*) *Knott* v. *Cottee*, 16 Beav. p. 81; *Coates* v. *Coates*, 3 N. R. 355.

When a charitable gift fails as to impure personalty, the costs are apportioned between the pure and impure personalty (*h*), unless the pure personalty be given specifically to the charity (*i*), when the costs will be borne by the impure personalty. Apportionment between pure and impure personalty.

Where costs are ordered to be paid out of a particular fund, that does not necessarily determine that this fund is ultimately to bear them (*k*), and accordingly, where costs had been ordered to be paid out of income instead of out of corpus, it was held that the order did not preclude the matter from being afterwards set right (*l*). Adjustment after payment of costs out of a fund not chargeable therewith.

The testator may of course alter the order in which the different classes of assets are resorted to for payment of costs, whether for the benefit of a charity (*m*), or the persons entitled to the general personalty (*n*), and it is now well settled, contrary to the former rule, that the words "testamentary expenses" (*o*) in a will include the costs of an administration action (*p*); and as in a creditors' action the costs come out of the same funds as the debts, the costs will be paid out of any fund charged with the debts (*q*). Marshalling of assets by testator. Costs of administration action included in "testamentary expenses."

Where costs had been thus paid out of *equitable* assets, upon the falling in of a reversion, which was *legal* assets, an apportionment of the costs between the legal and Apportionment between legal and equitable assets.

(*h*) *Taylor* v. *Linley*, 5 Jur. N. S. 701.

(*i*) *Shepheard* v. *Bentham*, 6 C. D. 597; *Young* v. *Dolman*, 44 L. T. 499.

(*k*) But an order to pay over a fund to persons by name is incidentally a determination that other persons, who are not named, are not entitled, *Sheppard* v. *Sheppard*, 33 Beav. 129.

(*l*) *Ibid*.

(*m*) *Miles* v. *Harrison*, 9 Ch. 316.

(*n*) *Harloe* v. *Harloe*, 20 Eq. 471.

(*o*) "Testamentary expenses" thrown by the testator upon one fund include the costs of an administration action properly instituted by legatees of another fund, *Young* v. *Dolman*. For the meaning of "executorship expenses," see *Sharp* v. *Lush*, 10 C. D. 468.

(*p*) *Penny* v. *Penny*, 11 C. D. 440.

(*q*) *Wilson* v. *Heaton*, 11 Beav. 492.

equitable assets was ordered, in the interests of simple contract creditors (r).

For further information as to costs, the reader is referred to Morgan and Wurtzburg's Costs, 165—204; Seton, 826, 827, 832, 845, 846, and 875—880; Pemb., 175—178; and Lewin, 7th ed., 844—852.

(r) *Mutlow* v. *Mutlow*, 4 De G. & J. 539. For the distinction between legal and equitable assets, see *post*, p. 167.

CHAPTER XIII.

OF THE ORDER IN WHICH ASSETS ARE ADMINISTERED.

IT does not fall within the scope of this work to discuss the old law in respect of the administration of assets by the Court of Chancery, which itself was a partial amelioration, in the interests of simple contract creditors, of the rules of the Common Law. The reader is referred to the text-books of Mr. Joshua Williams and Mr. Eddis (*a*), for a historical sketch of the steps by which the various classes of creditors have one after another obtained recognition of their just rights. In this chapter we shall consider only the cases which fall under the two recent enactments, 32 & 33 Vict. c. 46, and the Judicature Act, 1875, sec. 10, as the estates administered under the old law must necessarily be few and continually decreasing in number (*b*). *The old law not here discussed.* *The Act of 1869, and the Judicature Act, 1875.*

By the first of these enactments it was provided that in the administration of the estate of every person who should die on or after the 1st January, 1870, no debt or liability of such person should be entitled to any priority or *The Act of 1869.* *Specialty creditors have*

(*a*) Williams on Real Assets, Ch. i. and ix.; Eddis on Administration of Assets, Ch. vi.

(*b*) It will be sufficient here to enumerate the order in which the various kinds of debts were paid before the Act of 1869; (1.) Debts due to the Crown by record or specialty. (2.) Debts to which particular statutes give priority. (3.) Debts on judgments obtained against the deceased, duly registered, payable *pari passu*. (4.) Debts on judgments obtained against the personal representative, payable in order of date. (5.) Recognisances and statutes. (6.) Debts by specialty, for valuable consideration, arrears of rent, and moneys payable under sec. 75 of the Companies Act, 1862. (7.) Debts by simple contract and unregistered judgments (see *Van Gheluwe* v. *Nerinckx*, 21 C. D. 189). (8.) Voluntary obligations not assigned for value; (Williams' Exors., Ch. ii.; Comp. Exors. 157—161; Seton, 815; Eddis on Assets, 14—24; Snell, 6th Ed. 255.)

M

no priority over simple contract creditors. preference by reason merely that the same is secured by or arises under a bond, deed, or other instrument under seal, or is otherwise made or constituted a specialty debt (c); but that all the creditors of such person, as well specialty as simple contract, should be treated as standing in equal degree, and be paid accordingly out of the assets of such deceased person, whether such assets are legal or equitable, any statute or other law to the contrary notwithstanding; but it was thereby provided that the Act should not prejudice or affect any lien, charge, or other security, which any creditor might hold or be entitled to for the payment of his debt.

The Judicature Act, 1875, imports the rules of Bankruptcy in administering insolvent estates. By the Judicature Act, 1875, sec. 10, to which we have already referred (d), it is enacted that, in the administration *by the Court* (e) of the assets of any person who may die after the 1st November, 1875 (f), and whose estate may prove to be insufficient for the payment in full of his debts and liabilities, the same rules shall prevail and be observed as to the respective rights of secured (g) and unsecured creditors, and as to debts and liabilities provable, and as to the valuation of annuities and future and contingent liabilities respectively, as may be in force for the time being under the Law of Bankruptcy, with respect to the estates of persons adjudged bankrupt; and all persons who in any such case would be entitled to prove for and receive dividends out of the estate of any such deceased

---

(c) Including rent; *Shirreff* v. *Hastings*, 6 C. D. 610.

(d) *Ante*, p. 107.

(e) It would therefore appear that there is now one rule when an estate is administered by the Court, and another when it is administered out of Court; see Eddis on Assets, 111. Under sec. 91 of the Judicature Act, 1873, County Courts will in the administration of assets follow the same rules as the High Court.

(f) See sec. 2, and *Sherwin* v. *Selkirk*, 12 C. D. 68.

(g) Before this Act a mortgagee might realize his security, and yet prove for and receive dividends upon the whole of his debt, until it should be fully discharged (*Mason* v. *Bogg*, 2 My. & Cr. 443). For the effect of this enactment upon mortgagees whose security is deficient, see *post*, p. 171. As to who is a secured creditor, see *post*, p. 169.

person, may come in under the decree or order for the administration of such estate, and make such claims against the same as they may respectively be entitled to by virtue of the Act. The rules of the Law of Bankruptcy with regard to the payment of debts and distribution of assets are contained in the Bankruptcy Act, 1869 (*h*), ss. 31—40.

Though, however, the Legislature has thus placed specialty and simple contract creditors upon the same footing, it has not altered the priority of Crown debts over all others of equal degree, the Crown not being named in the Statute of 1869 (*i*), nor that of certain debts to which particular statutes give priority (*j*), nor has it deprived a creditor who has obtained and registered (*k*) judgment against the deceased, or one who has obtained judgment (*l*) against the executor, whether it be or be not registered, of his right to be paid his debt in full in priority over all other creditors of equal degree (*m*) ; nor, lastly, has it taken from the executor his right of retainer, either expressly or by implication, *e.g.*, by abolishing the distinction between legal and equitable assets, or by regarding him as a secured creditor (*n*).

What debts still have priority.

With these exceptions, all unsecured creditors, and

(*h*) 32 & 33 Vict. c. 71.

(*i*) See Seton, 816 ; *Re Henley*, 9 C. D. 469 ; *Ex parte Postmaster-General*, 10 *ibid.* 595.

(*j*) *Moors* v. *Marriott*, 7 C. D. 543 ; *Fisher* v. *Shirley*, W. N. 1879, 103.

(*k*) See 23 & 24 Vict. c. 38, and *Van Gheluwe* v. *Nerinckx*, 21 C. D. 189. If the sheriff has seized under a *fi. fa.*, he is a secured creditor (*Ex parte Williams*, 7 Ch. 314) ; *quære*, whether, if the fruits of his execution prove insufficient to satisfy his judgment, he is entitled to priority for the deficiency, or whether, under the Judicature Act, 1875, sec. 10, he must prove for it with the other creditors.

(*l*) But a creditor who has obtained an order *nisi* to sign judgment against an executor, if judgment be not signed before, *i.e.*, at latest, the day before (*Parker* v. *Bingham*, 33 Beav. 535), a judgment for administration has been obtained in the Chancery Division, has no priority over the other creditors (*Hanson* v. *Stubbs*, 8 C. D. 154).

(*m*) *Williams* v. *Williams*, 15 Eq. 270 ; *Smith* v. *Morgan*, 5 C. P. D. 337 ; *Winehouse* v. *Winehouse*, 20 C. D. 545.

(*n*) *Lee* v. *Nuttall*, 12 C. D. 61 ; *Crowder* v. *Stewart*, 16 *ibid.* 368.

secured creditors, so far as their securities are deficient, now stand on an equal footing.

Costs and debts payable out of the same fund.
It will be seen that, subject to Locke King's Acts (*n*), and to any special disposition by the testator, the order in which resort is had to his assets for payment of debts corresponds closely to that in which they are taken for payment of costs: it is as follows:—

Order in which assets are resorted to.
1. The general residuary personalty.
1. The general residue of the personal (*o*) estate not specifically bequeathed, after providing for pecuniary legacies, subject, in the case of lapsed shares, to the rules stated *ante*, p. 156. This general personal estate being the primary fund for payment of debts, it requires strong words to exonerate it (*p*).

2. Real estate devised in trust to pay debts.
II. Real estates (*q*) devised in trust to pay debts (*r*), when the personalty is not expressly exonerated, and the devise is construed to be in aid only of the primary fund (*s*).

3. Real estate descended.
III. Real estates descended (*t*).

4. Specific devises and
IV. Real or personal estate specifically given, but (*u*)

(*n*) *Post*, p. 174.

(*o*) Including land in India (9 Geo. IV. c. 33; *Story* v. *Fry*, 1 Y. & C. C. 603) and in the West Indies (5 Geo. II. c. 7, s. 4; *Thomson* v. *Grant*, 1 Russ. 540 n.).

(*p*) *Bootle* v. *Blundell*, 1 Mer. p. 220; and see the notes to *Duke of Ancaster* v. *Mayer*, Wh. & Tud. i. 4th ed. 630, *et seq.*; for a case of exoneration, see *Forrest* v. *Prescott*, 10 Eq. 545.

(*q*) It may here be mentioned that a judgment recovered against executors is *primâ facie* evidence of the debt against persons interested in the realty, who may, however, have an inquiry; *Harvey* v. *Wilde*, 14 Eq. 438.

(*r*) Not including the costs incurred in defending actions by creditors, though resulting in a reduction of their claims; see *Lovat* v.

Fraser, L. R. 1 Sc. Ap. pp. 31, 38.

(*s*) *Phillips* v. *Parry*, 22 Beav. 279.

(*t*) *Donne* v. *Lewis*, 2 Bro. C. C. p. 263; *Harmood* v. *Oglander*, 8 Ves. pp. 124, 125.

(*u*) As to what amounts to a charge of debts or legacies, a question too wide for this treatise, see Wh. & Tud. ii., 130—133; *Bailey* v. *Bailey*, 12 C. D. 268; *R. Tanqueray-Willaume* and *Landau*, 20 *ibid.* 465. A direction to pay debts out of rents and profits of real estate, *primâ facie*, and unless the context is inconsistent, charges them on the corpus, not merely on the annual rents and profits; *Metcalfe* v. *Hutchinson*, 1 C. D. 591. If there was a trust of land for payment of debts, a creditor was formerly not barred by lapse of time, unless barred at the testator's death

ARE ADMINISTERED.

charged generally with the payment of debts (*u*); and if a share of such an estate lapse, the whole estate, and not primarily the lapsed share, is liable (*v*).

V. General pecuniary legacies, and demonstrative legacies (*w*), so far as the specified fund is insufficient, *pro ratâ* (*x*).

VI. Real estates specifically devised or comprised in a residuary devise, and specific bequests, (including the specified fund (*y*) for payment of demonstrative legacies), *pro ratâ* (*z*).

VII. Real and personal estate appointed under a general power (*a*), but, *semble*, if the appointment should lapse for the benefit of the heir or of the general personal estate of the appointor, the appointed estate would be liable for debts in the same order, if realty, as descended estates, or, if personalty, as the general personal estate (*b*).

Marginal notes:
5. General pecuniary legacies.
6. Specific devises and bequests.
7. Real of personal estate appointed.

(*Hughes* v. *Wynne*, T. & R. 307; *O'Connor* v. *Haslam*, 5 H. L. C. 170), *secus*, if there was a charge only (*Dickenson* v. *Teasdale*, 1 De G. J. & S. 52), or if the charge was on the personalty only (*Scott* v. *Jones*, 4 Cl. & F. 382); and the same rule applied to legacies (*Thomson* v. *Eastwood*, 2 App. Cas. 215), but now, by 37 & 38 Vict. c. 57, s. 10, it is provided (repealing, it is presumed, sec. 25 (2) of the Judicature Act, 1873) that after the 1st January, 1879, no action, suit, or other proceeding shall be brought to recover any sum of money or legacy charged upon or payable out of any land or rent and secured by an express trust, except within the time (in general, twelve years) within which the same would be recoverable if there were not any such trust. It is presumed that this will not apply if the money has been raised and is in the hands of the trustee or executor (*Philippo* v. *Munnings*, 2 M. & Cr. 309); but see *Sutton* v. *Sutton*,

W. N. 1882, 172, *Fearnside* v. *Flint*, 31 W. R. 318.

(*u*) *Donne* v. *Lewis*, 2 Bro. C. C. 263; *Harmood* v. *Oglander*, 8 Ves. 125.

(*v*) *Fisher* v. *Fisher*, 2 Keen, 610; *Wood* v. *Ordish*, 3 Sm. & G. 125.

(*w*) *Sellon* v. *Watts*, 9 W. R. 847.

(*x*) *Tomkins* v. *Colthurst*, 1 C. D. 626; *Farquharson* v. *Floyer*, 3 ibid. 109; notwithstanding *Hensman* v. *Fryer*, 3 Ch. 420.

(*y*) *Sellon* v. *Watts*.

(*z*) *Tombs* v. *Roch*, 2 Col. 490; *Hensman* v. *Fryer*; *Lancefield* v. *Iggulden*, 10 Ch. 136.

(*a*) *Fleming* v. *Buchanan*, 3 De G. M. & G. 976; *Godfrey* v. *Harben*, 13 C. D. 216. It is presumed that such personal estate is equitable assets; see *post* (*l*).

(*b*) *Sperling* v. *Rochfort*, 16 C. D. 18; *Hinsley* v. *Ickeringill*, 17 ibid. 151; and see *Freme* v. *Clement*, 18 ibid. 499.

When it is said that the testator's debts are payable out of his assets in the foregoing order, it is not, of course, suggested that creditors must wait until the various funds are successively realized; they are entitled to sue the executor at once, and the executor is entitled to pay them out of any funds in his hands. The rights of the persons interested in the assets must be subsequently adjusted (c), and it must not be forgotten that until judgment for administration is obtained, and, *semble*, unless the action is registered as a *lis pendens*, the heir or devisee of real estate not charged with or devised in trust to pay debts can defeat the creditors of the deceased, by ante-nuptial settlement or other *bonâ fide* alienation for value, whether legal or equitable (d); and the same rule has been applied in the case of personal estate, where there was no imputation as to the honesty with which the assets had been dealt with, the claim against the assets being for a breach of covenant subsequent to the alienation (e); otherwise, *semble*, the interest under the settlement of the person liable to discharge the debt might have been reached (f).

As has been already stated (g), the distinction between legal and equitable assets still prevails, and it is still open to an executor as against creditors of equal degree (h), to retain out of legal assets for his own debt, whether it be legal or equitable (i). Legal assets, as the term is applied

Marginal notes: Adjustment when debts paid out of property not chargeable therewith. Alienation by heir or devisee. Retainer by executor for his own debt, out of legal assets only.

(c) See *post*, p. 174.

(d) *Spackman* v. *Timbrell*, 8 Sim. 253; *Richardson* v. *Horton*, 7 Beav. 112; *British Mutual Investment Co.* v. *Smart*, 10 Ch. 567.

(e) *Dilkes* v. *Broadmead*, 2 De G. F. & J. 566; see also *Corser* v. *Cartwright*, L. R. 7 H. L. 731.

(f) *London and Provincial Bank* v. *Bogle*, 7 C. D. 773.

(g) *Ante*, p. 163.

(h) See *Talbot* v. *Frere*, 9 C. D. 568.

(i) Including debts of the deceased for which the executor is surety (*Wildes* v. *Dudlow*, 19 Eq. 198), though he has not been called upon to pay them (*Ferguson* v. *Gibson*, 14 Eq. 379; *Skinner* v. *M. of Anglesey*, Kay, J., 1882); debts due to him as one of two joint creditors (*Crowder* v. *Stewart*, 16 C. D. 368) including partners, (*Morris* v. *Morris*, 10 Ch. 68), or as a *cestui qui trust* of the actual creditor (*Loomes* v. *Stotherd*, 1 S. & S. p. 461), when the executor's right of retainer (*k*) is in question, are such parts of the property of a deceased person as may be reached or made available by an executor *virtute officii* (*l*), and consist only of the personal estate, whether in itself legal or equitable (*m*). If, however, an executor should resort to personalty specifically bequeathed, the legatee would have the right to compensation out of any fund properly chargeable with the debt in priority to his bequest (*n*).

The rest of the assets are equitable (*o*), and out of these there is no right of retainer (*p*).

or as executor or administrator of another person (*Thompson* v. *Cooper*, 1 Coll. 85), or as trustee by devolution (*Sander* v. *Heathfield*, 19 Eq. 21). See also Comp. Exors., 163—170; Set. 893; and Pemb. 68).

(*k*) By 3 & 4 Will. IV. c. 104, all real estate not by will charged with or devised subject to the payment of debts is made assets *to be administered in equity* (at the suit of any person interested whether as creditor, heir, or next of kin, or under a will, *Price* v. *Price*, 15 Sim. 484; *Rodney* v. *Rodney*, 16 *ibid.* 307), for the payment of the debts of the person seised thereof or entitled thereto at his death; and although in *Foster* v. *Handley*, 1 Sim. N. S. 200, and *Burrell* v. *Smith*, 9 Eq. 443, it was decided that, under the proviso in the Act saving the rights of specialty creditors, real estate affected by the Act was made legal assets, yet, now that specialty and simple contract creditors are paid *pari passu* (*ante*, p. 162), the express direction that such real estate shall be assets to be administered in equity will prevail, and it is no longer in any sense legal assets; and *semble*, the heir or devisee of land not made equitable assets by the testator may no longer retain his own debts out of the proceeds, as in

Loomes v. *Stotherd*, 1 S. & S. 458. In *Walters* v. *Walters*, 18 C. D. 182, in which *Foster* v. *Handley* was not cited, it was held to be equitable assets so as to deprive an executor of his (alleged) right of retainer. The distinction between the sense in which the term "legal assets" was applied to real estate descended (*i.e.*, for the benefit of specialty creditors), and that in which it is applied to personal estate in the hands of an executor, and subject to his right of retainer, is pointed out in Williams, Real Assets, 14.

(*l*) *Cook* v. *Gregson*, 3 Dr. 286; including land in the West Indies, *Thomson* v. *Grant*, cited *ante*, p. 164 (*o*).

(*m*) *Morris* v. *Morris*, 10 Ch. 68.

(*n*) See *post*, p. 174.

(*o*) So also was the separate estate of a married woman (*Owens* v. *Dickenson*, Cr. & Ph. 48; *Thompson* v. *Bennett*, 6 C. D. 739); but whether this will be so under the Married Women's Property Act, 1882, *quære*. An executor has no right of retainer out of the purchase-money of real estate contracted to be sold by the testator, paid into Court in an administration action (*Duignan* v. *Croome*, 41 L. T. 672).

(*p*) A mortgagee, though he be executor of his mortgagor, after

Besides executors, administrators (whether creditors (q) or not), and executors of surviving executors, have the right of retainer (r), but not executors *de son tort*, though they may prefer one creditor to another, and may even pay debts for which they are sureties (s).

Rule of hotchpot where part of debt retained or paid out of legal assets in priority to other creditors.

The executor having no right of retainer out of equitable assets, will, if he retains part only of his debt out of legal assets, be postponed to the other creditors in the distribution of equitable assets, until they have received thereout sums equal in proportion to the amount of the executor's debt retained by him, after which the remaining assets

Marshalling.

will be distributed *pro ratâ* (t). The same rule applies where judgment (or, formerly, where specialty) creditors are paid in part out of the legal assets in priority to simple contract creditors (u), and where one creditor has received part of his debts in preference to others of like degree he will not receive any more, either out of legal or equitable assets, until they have received their proper proportion (x).

The Judicature Act, 1875, and the rules of Bankruptcy.

Most of the decisions upon sect. 10 of the Judicature Act, 1875 (y), have been given upon questions arising in the winding up of companies, which are similarly affected by this enactment, and it is impossible to state with any confidence in which way many questions which must arise upon this difficult section will be determined.

It will be seen that in three particulars the rules of equity are, in the administration of an insolvent estate (z),

realising his security, and retaining the mortgage-debt, must hand over the surplus to creditors of higher degree than himself (*Talbot* v. *Frere*, 9 C. D. 568).

(q) In practice this right is taken away by the terms of the administration bond (*Coombs* v. *Coombs*, 1 P. & M. 193, 288; *In the Goods of Brackenbury*, 2 P. D. 272).

(r) W. & Tud. ii. 128.

(s) *Skinner* v. *M. of Anglesey*, Kay, J., 1882.

(t) W. & Tud. ii. 129; *Bain* v. *Sadler*, 12 Eq. 570.

(u) *Davies* v. *Topp*, 1 Bro. C. C. 525; and see *post*, p. 174.

(x) *Mitchelson* v. *Piper*, 8 Sim. 64.

(y) See *ante*, p. 162.

(z) It has been decided that it is not necessary in the administration

to give way to those of bankruptcy (a); (1), as to the respective rights of secured and unsecured creditors, (2), as to the debts and liabilities provable, and (3), as to the valuation of annuities and future and contingent liabilities.

As to (1); by sect. 16 (5) of the Bankruptcy Act, 1869 (b), a secured creditor is defined as "any creditor holding any mortgage charge or lien on the bankrupt's estate or any part thereof, as security for any debt due to him," and the following, amongst others, have been held to be secured creditors within this definition; a plaintiff in whose action a sum of money had, before the bankruptcy of the defendant, been paid into Court to abide the event (c); a judgment creditor who has *served* a garnishee order *nisi* before the bankruptcy of the judgment debtor, although it had not then been made absolute (d); a judgment creditor taking a transfer of a legal mortgage, and, in an action for sale of the property and payment of both mortgage and judgment debts, obtaining an order appointing a receiver for both debts (e); an execution creditor on whose behalf the sheriff has actually seized the debtor's goods (f), and sect. 87 of the Bankruptcy Act, under which the execution may be defeated, if the debtor be a trader and the sheriff be directed to sell

1. As to secured and unsecured creditors.

judgment to direct that if the estate prove insolvent the rules of bankruptcy shall apply (*Woods* v. *Greenwell*, 30 W. R. 283; notwithstanding *Hipkins* v. *Hildick*, 29 ibid. 733).

(a) By sec. 80 (sub-sec. 9) of the Bankruptcy Act, 1869, it is provided that where a debtor who has been adjudicated a bankrupt dies, the Court may order that the proceedings in the matter be continued as if he were alive; but this enactment does not apply to the case of a debtor filing a petition for liquidation and dying (*Re Obbard*, 19 W. R. 563).

(b) 32 & 33 Vict. c. 71.

(c) *Re Keyworth*, 9 Ch. 379.

(d) *Ex parte Joselyne*, 8 C. D. 327; *Re Stanhope Silkstone Collieries Co.*, 11 ibid. 160.

(e) *Ex parte Evans*, 13 C. D. 252.

(f) *Ex parte Rocke*, 6 Ch. 795; *Ex parte Williams*, 7 ibid. 314.

for an amount exceeding £50 (*g*), is not incorporated by sect. 10 of the Judicature Act, 1875 (*h*). In addition to these, mortgagees whether legal or equitable, persons having by law or custom a lien on the debtor's property, pawnees, and pledgees, are within the definition, but not a creditor who, after serving a writ of foreign attachment in an action in the Lord Mayor's Court, has not obtained judgment before the bankruptcy (*i*); nor is it enough merely to issue a writ of sequestration against a defendant, and serve it on a debtor to him or a trustee of a fund for him (*j*); nor does a banker become a secured creditor by making advances on bills of exchange indorsed to him to be discounted, and held by him pending discount (*k*).

Mortgagees.

In *Lee* v. *Nuttall* (*l*), James, L. J., said, "the sole object of the section, as it appears to me, was to get rid of the rule in Chancery (*m*), under which a secured creditor could prove for the full amount of his debt and realise his security afterwards, and to put him on the same footing as in bankruptcy, where he was only entitled to prove for the balance after realizing or valuing his security," and accordingly it has been held that it is not the object of the section to increase the assets; so that an unregistered bill of sale is not thereby avoided (*n*); nor are the rules of bankruptcy as to reputed ownership and fraudulent preference thereby incorporated (*o*), and, as has been pointed out by Bacon, V.-C., there is no power to disclaim a lease or onerous contract (*p*).

Object of the enactment.

(*g*) *Turner* v. *Bridgett*, 8 Q. B. D. 392.
(*h*) *Re Withernsea Brickworks*, 16 C. D. 337.
(*i*) *Levy* v. *Lovell*, 14 C. D. 234.
(*j*) *Ex parte Nelson*, 14 C. D. 41.
(*k*) *Ex parte Schofield*, 12 C. D. 337.
(*l*) 12 C. D. p. 65; but see per Jessel, M. R., in *Mersey Steel and Iron Co.* v. *Naylor*, 9 Q. B. D. p. 662.
(*m*) *I.e.*, the rule in *Mason* v. *Bogg*, see ante, p. 162 (*g*).
(*n*) *Re Knott*, 7 C. D. 549 n.; *Tudman* v. *D'Epineuil*, 20 C. D. 217.
(*o*) *Re Crumlin Viaduct Works Co.*, 11 *ibid.* 755.
(*p*) *Re Westbourne Grove Drapery Co.*, 5 C. D. 248.

But a secured creditor must in an administration action *Courses open to secured creditors.* strictly follow out the rules of bankruptcy, under which he may either (1) give up his security and prove for the whole debt, or (2) realize (*q*) his security and prove for the balance, or (3) value his security and prove for the balance (*r*). If he does not comply with one or other of these conditions, he will be excluded from all share in any dividend (*s*), and if he votes in respect of (or, *semble*, proves for) the whole debt, he thereby forfeits his security for the benefit of the estate (*t*), but *semble*, a mistake may be rectified (*u*), unless the rights of other creditors have been altered (*v*); but where a creditor of a company, believing himself fully secured, made no claim in respect of his debt, he was allowed (notwithstanding r. 101) to prove for the balance by which his security ultimately turned out deficient, on the terms of his not disturbing any past dividend (*x*).

If he values his security, the trustee (and now, pre- *Redemption by executor at creditor's valuation.* sumably, the executor) may redeem it at the amount of the valuation, and if, after valuation, it is sold and produces more than the valuation, the balance must be paid into Court as part of the assets of the deceased (r. 100); while if it produces less, the creditor cannot increase his proof, and must bear the loss (*y*). If the debtor (and now,

(*q*) The right of a secured creditor to realize his security is preserved by sec. 12 of the Bankruptcy Act; and see sec. 40, and r. 78 of 1870; and *Ex parte Punnell*, 6 C. D. 335; *Waddell* v. *Toleman*, 9 *ibid.* 212; *Ex parte Hirst*, 11 *ibid.* 278. Under rr. 78—81, the mortgagee may have the mortgaged property sold by the Court, and the proceeds will be dealt with in the same way as if he had sold. The mortgagee will, therefore, be, as formerly, at liberty to bring an action for foreclosure against the representatives of his deceased insolvent mortgagor.

(*r*) Bankruptcy Act, sec. 40.

(*s*) Sec. 40; and see *Ex parte Good*, 14 C. D. 82.

(*t*) *Ex parte Ashworth*, 18 Eq. 705.

(*u*) *Ex parte Bagshaw*, 13 C. D. 304; see *Williams* v. *Hopkins*, (2), 44 L. T. 773.

(*v*) *Couldery* v. *Bartrum*, 19 C. D. 394.

(*x*) *Ex parte Williams*, 16 C. D. 590.

(*y*) *Williams* v. *Hopkins*, 18 C. D. 370; r. 101.

presumably, the executor) puts a value on the security, the creditor is not bound, but may realize and prove for the actual balance (z), and if the trustee or another creditor be dissatisfied with the value put on it by the creditor, he may require it to be realized (a).

2. Debts and liabilities provable.

As to (2) the debts and liabilities provable; under sect. 31 of the Bankruptcy Act, all debts and liabilities, present or future, certain or contingent, (except demands in the nature of unliquidated damages arising otherwise than by reason of a contract or promise, and debts and liabilities contracted after notice of an act of bankruptcy available for adjudication) may be proved, and the definition of "liability" is extremely wide (b).

No priority for rates or wages,

Sect. 32 provides that certain debts (including a year's rates and taxes, certain wages, and moneys in the hands of a bankrupt officer of a friendly society) must be paid in priority to other debts, and it has been held that in the winding up of companies such priority is given by sect. 10 of the Judicature Act, 1875 (c), but in three other cases (d) the contrary was decided, and it is submitted

or rent.

that this is the correct view (e). Again, under sect. 34 of the Bankruptcy Act, a landlord may distrain for one year's rent, and for that only; but as it has been decided that the Judicature Act gives him no such priority as is so

Semble, right to distrain unaffected.

given by the Bankruptcy Act (f), it is not probable that it will be held that his common-law right to distrain, as

(z) *Ex parte Bestwick*, 2 C. D. 485.
(a) R. 136; but see *Ex parte Good*, 14 C. D. 42.
(b) See *Ex parte Neal*, 14 C. D. 579, a very strong case, and the cases there cited, and compare *Re Westbourne Grove Drapery Co.*, 5 ibid. 248.
(c) *Re Norton Ironworks Co.* (M. R.), 26 W. R. 53; *Re Association of Land Financiers* (V.-C. M.), 16 C. D. 373.

(d) *Re Albion Steel and Wire Co.* (M. R.), 7 C. D. 547; *Re Regent United Service Stores* (V.-C. M.), 38 L. T. 130; and *Re Wearmouth Crown Glass Co.* (Kay, J.), 19 C. D. 640.
(e) See *Thomas* v. *Patent Lionite Co.*, 17 C. D. p. 257.
(f) *Re Coal Consumers' Association*, 4 C. D. 625; *Re Bridgwater Engineering Co.*, 12 ibid. 181; *Thomas* v. *Patent Lionite Co.*

modified by 3 & 4 Will. 4, c. 27, s. 42, is limited, where the lessee's estate is being administered by the Court. On the other hand, it has been decided that the bankruptcy rules as to mutual credits (*g*) are now to be applied in the winding up of companies (*h*); but not so as to set off a debt against calls made in the liquidation (*i*); and it would seem that a creditor whose debt is barred by the Statute of Limitations can no longer prove against the estate of a deceased insolvent, the debt not being provable in bankruptcy (*k*); and that, as, in bankruptcy, creditors upon voluntary bonds are paid *pari passu* with other creditors (*l*) they should now be placed in the same category in administration, instead of being postponed to all other creditors and being only paid in priority to legatees (*m*): but there is not yet any decision on these points.

Mutual credits.

Statute-barred debts.

Voluntary bonds.

It has, however, been held that interest on debts is to be calculated only to the date of the administration judgment, that being equivalent to the adjudication in bankruptcy mentioned in r. 77 (*n*).

No interest on debts from date of administration judgment.

As to (3) valuation of annuities and future and contingent liabilities; it is believed that there are only two decisions on this point (*o*), in which, as already pointed out (*p*) contingent claims, ripening into debts during the administration or winding up, were treated as in bankruptcy.

3. Valuation of annuities and future and contingent liabilities.

(*g*) See sec. 39 of the Bankruptcy Act, *Booth* v. *Hutchinson*, 15 Eq. 30, and *Peat* v. *Jones*, 8 Q. B. D. 147.

(*h*) *Mersey Steel and Iron Co., Limited* v. *Naylor*, 9 Q. B. D. 648.

(*i*) *Gill's Case*, 12 C. D. 755; *Ex parte Branwhite*, 48 L. J. Ch. 463.

(*k*) *Ex parte Dewdney*, 15 Ves. 479.

(*l*) *Ex parte Pottinger*, 8 C. D. 621.

(*m*) *Dawson* v. *Kearton*, 3 Sm. & G. 186; *ante*, p. 107.

(*n*) *Boswell* v. *Gurney*, 13 C. D. 136.

(*o*) *Macfarlane's Claim*, 17 C. D. 337; and *Hill* v. *Bridges*, 17 *ibid*. 342; see also *Re Great Britain Mutual Life Assurance Society*, 19 *ibid*. 43, affirmed, 20 *ibid*. 351; and *Ex parte Neal*, 14 *ibid*. 579.

(*p*) *Ante*, p. 107.

Locke King's Acts.

Mortgaged estate now taken by devisee *cum onere.*

Under Locke King's Act (*q*), and the two amending statutes (*r*) passed in the interest, not of creditors, but of the persons entitled to the general personal estate of the deceased, the primary fund for the payment of any sum of money charged upon any land or other hereditaments of whatever tenure, of or to which a testator or intestate shall die seised or entitled, whether such charge be by way of mortgage or be equitable only (including any lien for unpaid purchase money), is the mortgaged property itself, unless the deceased (if a testator) has by will expressly directed to the contrary; and this direction is not sufficiently indicated by creating a charge or giving a direction for payment of debts upon or out of residuary real and personal estate or residuary real estate (*s*).

Specific legatee of mortgaged personal estate, other than leaseholds, may have it redeemed.

Where, however, real and leasehold estates are comprised in one mortgage, or real or leasehold estate is comprised with other personal estate, the mortgage debt must be borne rateably by both (*t*), and it may be mentioned that the specific legatee of any personalty except leaseholds which is in pledge or subject to any mortgage lien or charge is entitled to have it discharged therefrom at the cost of the general personalty (*u*).

Marshalling:

The right of marshalling, to which reference has several times been made (*x*) arises under the equitable prin-

---

(*q*) 17 & 18 Vict. 113.

(*r*) 30 & 31 Vict. c. 69, and 40 & 41 Vict. c. 34. The latest enactment applies in the case of all persons dying after the 31st December, 1877; as to the conflicting decisions before that Act, see Eddis on Assets, pp. 93—95, and the notes to *Duke of Ancaster* v. *Mayer*, Wh. & Tud. i. 630, *et seq.* For the curious fatality attending the obvious intentions of the legislature in this respect, see Eddis, *loc. cit.*

(*s*) See *Newmarch* v. *Storr*, 9 C. D. 12; *Rossiter* v. *Rossiter*, 13 *ibid.* 353, where the words "in exoneration of my real estate" (the mortgaged estate) were held insufficient.

(*t*) *Trestrail* v. *Mason*, 7 C. D. 655; *Leonino* v. *Leonino*, 10 C. D. 460.

(*u*) *Knight* v. *Davis*, 3 M. & K. 358; *Bothamley* v. *Sherson*, 20 Eq. 304.

(*x*) *Ante*, pp. 166, 167.

ciple (y), that a person having two funds to satisfy his demands, shall not by his election disappoint a person who has only one. Therefore, whatever may be the order in which the testator's assets have been actually distributed in payment of debts and legacies, the rights of the parties must eventually be adjusted so as, if possible (z), to discharge the claim of every person interested, although the fund out of which alone one or other had a right to be paid, may have been exhausted by the claims of persons having rights not only against that fund but against others. Marshalling in favour of simple contract creditors, under which they were paid out of real estate when the personalty had been exhausted by specialty creditors, is of course now no longer necessary (a); but as between legatees and creditors, if executors to avoid litigation pay mortgage debts out of the personalty instead of out of the real or leasehold estate which by Locke King's Acts (b) is the primary fund for the purpose, the specific devisees or legatees must refund for the benefit of the persons interested in the personalty (c); so if debts or legacies charged on land are paid out of the personalty, to the detriment of legatees or annuitants whose legacies or annuities are not so charged, they may marshal the assets in order to obtain payment (d). Similarly, persons disappointed by the election of an heir to take against the will have been allowed to prove against his estate for sums received by him under it (e).

against devisees of mortgaged estates;

against real estate in favour of legatees having no charge upon it.

(y) *Aldrich* v. *Cooper*, 8 Ves. 308; and see the notes thereto, Wh. & Tud. ii. 91—110.

(z) But the Court will not marshal the assets for the benefit of a creditor whose debt is statute-barred as against the realty, but has been kept alive by admissions of the executor as against the personalty (*Fordham* v. *Wallis*, 10 Ha. 217); and see Set. 833.

(a) See *ante*, p. 162.
(b) *Ante*, p. 174.
(c) *Wythe* v. *Henniker*, 2 M. & K. 635; *Lord Lilford* v. *Powys-Keck*, 1 Eq. 347.
(d) *Paterson* v. *Scott*, 1 De G. M. & G. 531; *Scales* v. *Collins*, 9 Ha. 656.
(e) *Greenwood* v. *Penny*, 12 Beav. 403; *Howells* v. *Jenkins*, 1 De G. J. & S. 617.

No marshalling in favour of charities :

There is, however, one important exception to the rule, for the Court will not marshal assets in favour of a charity, without a clear expression of the testator's intention (*f*), so that if a charitable legacy be given out of a mixed fund of real and personal estate, or of pure and impure personalty (*g*), it only takes effect in the proportion which the pure personalty bears to the whole fund at the testator's death (*h*), and though the testator directs it to be paid out of the pure personalty, that fund must bear its proportion with the impure personalty of the debts, funeral and testamentary expenses and costs (*i*), and the residue of the pure personalty may then be insufficient to pay the charitable legacy in full. But in a recent case (*k*) it was held that the whole of the (pure) personal estate was specifically given to a charity, and therefore that these charges (except costs of probate) must be borne by the real estate.

except by direction of testator.

Priority between legatees :

If after applying the doctrine of marshalling the assets are insufficient for payment of all the pecuniary legacies and annuities in full, questions often arise whether any of the legatees or annuitants are entitled to priority.

none in general ;

"*Primâ facie*," said Lord Langdale, M. R., "a testator must be presumed to intend that all his legacies should be equally paid, and the *onus* is upon those who contend for a priority to show that the testator meant to give a prefer-

---

(*f*) *Williams* v. *Kershaw*, 1 Ke. 274 n.

(*g*) If given *simpliciter*, it is considered to be given rateably out of the whole of the personalty, pure and impure (*Robinson* v. *Geldard*, 3 Mac. & G. p. 746).

(*h*) *Williams* v. *Kershaw* ; *Sparling* v. *Parker*, 9 Beav. 450, cited in Seton, 588. It is sometimes said that the charitable legacy fails in the proportion which the impure bears to the pure personalty, but this is only the other way of stating the proposition. If the pure and impure personalty be respectively £100 and £50, and the charitable legacy £60, the legatee will receive £40, and the gift takes effect as to two thirds, the proportion of £100 to £150; or it may be said that the amount which fails is to that which takes effect as £50 to £100, or £20 to £40.

(*i*) *Beaumont* v. *Oliveira*, 4 Ch. 309.

(*k*) *Shepheard* v. *Beetham*, 6 C. D. 597 ; and see *Miles* v. *Harrison*, 9 Ch. 316.

ence to a particular legatee" (*l*), and such directions as "in the first place," "in the next place" do not give any priority(*m*), nor is there any for an executor's legacy, even though given him for his trouble (*n*) ; nor, where there are annuitants, *with power of distress and entry*, and legatees, whose annuities and legacies are charged on real estate, have the former any priority (*o*) ; but a widow, if her husband has at his death land out of which she is dowable under the Dower Act (*p*), and not otherwise (notwithstanding sec. 12 of the Act, which provides that nothing in the Act contained shall interfere with any rule of equity or of any ecclesiastical Court by which legacies bequeathed to widows in satisfaction of dower are entitled to priority over other legacies ; *Roper* v. *Roper*) has priority for a legacy or annuity, though it may greatly exceed the amount of any dower to which she would be entitled ; and it has been held (*q*) that where a testator bequeathed to his wife certain specific articles " together with the legacy or sum of £500, which I direct to be paid to her immediately after my decease," this legacy is to be paid in priority to all others, and that where there was a direction to raise and invest two sums of money and to pay the interest to life tenants, and after their decease that these sums should fall into the residue, followed by a gift of other legacies *simpliciter*, the two sums given for life have priority over all others ; and where the Court has found an indication that a legacy is intended to be given only if there are funds to meet it, it will of course be postponed to the others (*r*).

but widow has priority, if entitled to dower, and given a legacy in satisfaction thereof.

Where an annuity is given by will, a question often Annuities, whether

(*l*) *Brown* v. *Brown*, 1 Ke. 275.
(*m*) See *Wells* v. *Borwick*, 17 C. D. 798.
(*n*) *Duncan* v. *Watts*, 16 Beav. 204.

(*o*) *Roper* v. *Roper*, 3 C. D. 714.
(*p*) 3 & 4 Will. IV. c. 108.
(*q*) *Wells* v. *Borwick*.
(*r*) *Stammers* v. *Halliley*, 12 Sim. 42.

178   OF THE ORDER IN WHICH ASSETS

payable out of capital or income only. arises between the annuitant and the residuary legatee, whether it is in fact a bequest of an annuity or of the income of a sum of money which the testator believes can and directs to be set apart to meet it. In the former case, the annuitant must be paid in full (s) before the residuary legatee takes anything (t) : in the latter, he will receive only the actual income of the fund (u), and at his death
Abatement of legacies and annuities. the whole fund will go to the residuary legatee. But, in general, if the assets are insufficient to pay the annuitants and legatees in full, they abate rateably, and the value of the annuities must be ascertained as at the testator's death, allowance being made for payments already made. If there is no provision in the will to the contrary (x), the annuitant will (subject to the provisions of Sec. 10 of the Judicature Act, 1875, as to which see *ante*, p. 173) receive the value of the annuity, less its proper rateable proportion (y) ; if there is, the apportioned sum will be invested in the purchase of a government annuity in the names of trustees (z). It is submitted that the order made in *Hankin* v. *Kilburn* (a), for the apportionment of the

(s) In some cases by annual payments of the whole annuity, part of the *corpus* being sold (*Wright* v. *Callander*, 2 De G. M. & G. 652); in others, out of rents and income only, to be applied until satisfaction of arrears (*Graves* v. *Hicks*, 11 Sim. 551 ; and see *Taylor* v. *Taylor*, 17 Eq. 324).

(t) *Gee* v. *Mahood*, 11 C. D. 891, sub nom., *Carmichael* v. *Gee*, 5 App. Cas. 588 ; *Wormald* v. *Muzeen*, 17 C. D. 167 ; but see S. C. 50 L. J. Ch. 776.

(u) *Baker* v. *Baker*, 6 H.L.C. 616.

(x) See *Hatton* v. *May*, 3 C. D. 148.

(y) *Wroughton* v. *Colquhoun*, 1 De G. & Sm. 357.

(z) *Carr* v. *Ingleby*, 1 De G. & Sm.

362.

(a) 2 C. D. 628. In this case certain legacies and annuities were bequeathed, funds were directed to be invested, to produce an income sufficient to meet the annuities, and the residue, "including the fund set apart to answer the said annuities when and so soon as such annuities shall respectively cease," was disposed of ; the estate being insufficient, it was ordered that the values of the annuities as at the death of the testatrix should be ascertained, and the amounts invested, and that the dividends only of *these investments* should be paid to the annuitants. Upon the death of an annuitant, it was held by the Court of Appeal, reversing Bacon,

residue amongst legatees and annuitants was incorrect.

It follows from what has been already stated (*b*), that specific legacies, though subject to be adeemed by the testator, in which case they fail altogether (*c*), are not liable to contribute towards the payment of pecuniary legacies: while demonstrative legacies, which, so far as the fund pointed out for their payment (in respect of which they are specific) proves insufficient, are mere pecuniary legacies, have no priority.

V.-C., that the residuary legatee could take nothing until the arrears of the annuity had been fully paid to the annuitant's representatives, which, under the circumstances of the case, would probably amount to a perpetual right to receive the dividends; but it is submitted that an annuity ought to have been bought with the amount which was so invested.

(*b*) *Ante*, pp. 164, 165.

(*c*) See *Ashburner* v. *Macguire*, Wh. & Tud. ii. 267.

CHAPTER XIV.

PROCEEDINGS AFTER FURTHER CONSIDERATION.

Assets generally distributed on further consideration.

As has been already stated (*a*), the Court will, on further consideration, if possible, and except in creditors' actions (*b*), determine all questions and distribute the assets, but it frequently happens that owing to the necessity for further accounts and inquiries, the action must come on for a second further consideration; in other cases, owing to tenancies for life, infancy of persons entitled, incumbrances created by beneficiaries, the possibility of the birth of other persons who would be entitled to shares, or other causes, the assets cannot be distributed.

If not, shares usually carried over to separate accounts.

Under these circumstances, the Court will order any share, the amount of which can be ascertained, to be carried over to the separate account (*c*) of the beneficiary contingently on attaining 21 years, or of the beneficiary and his incumbrancers, or as the case may be, in order that the subsequent proceedings by petition or summons may be simplified (*d*).

Subsequent application for payment out.

So soon as any person becomes absolutely entitled to a fund so retained in Court, he may apply in the action by

---

(*a*) *Ante*, p. 130.

(*b*) *Ante*, p. 51 (*g*).

(*c*) For a collection of forms of headings of separate accounts see 12 Beav. 212 n.; the heading is important, as in all subsequent dealings with the fund it is treated as being severed from the rest of the assets, and only those persons need be served who appear therefrom to be interested. See Dan. 1646, 1647.

(*d*) It was the invariable rule of the late and present Masters of the Rolls only to allow £10 for the costs of a petition for payment out of a fund carried over to the separate account of the petitioner, in which he alone was interested. See Dan. 1160.

petition (or, where liberty to apply at Chambers has been expressly given, or the fund is small (*e*), by summons) for payment out. A married woman may present a petition to enforce her equity to a settlement to a fund in Court, which she and her husband had joined in assigning to a purchaser while still reversionary only, the purchaser having obtained a stop order on the fund (*f*).

Petitions may also be presented for declarations as to the amount of duty payable (*g*). By 16 & 17 Vict. c. 51, s. 53, the Court is required to provide out of any property which may be in its possession or control, for the payment of Legacy and Succession Duty thereon, and under Cons. Ord. XXIII., r. 9 (*h*), the words "subject to duty" are added to the title of every separate account unless payment of the duty is provided for by the order under which the fund is carried over to such separate account. *Payment of duty.*

It has been recently said, that the leaning of the Court is now rather to get rid of a fund where there are proper trustees to take care of it (*i*), but not where there is but one trustee (*k*). *Payment out to trustees.*

Funds have been ordered to be paid out, notwithstanding a remote contingency of other persons being born and becoming entitled, upon security being given to refund (*l*), or without security, in the case of a woman being past child-bearing. This has, under special circumstances, *Payment out on security being given to refund, or when woman past child-bearing.*

(*e*) See Dan. 1649; *Winkworth* v. *Winkworth*, 32 Beav. 233; *Petty* v. *Petty*, 12 ib. 171.

(*f*) *Scott* v. *Spashett*, 3 Mac. & G. 599.

(*g*) As in *Skottowe* v. *Young*, 11 Eq. 474.

(*h*) See also County Court Rules, 1875, Ord. II. r. 14, under which the Registrar, before making any payment out of Court, requires a certificate of or receipt for the payment of duty.

(*i*) *Braithwaite* v. *Wallis*, 21 C. D. p. 122; and see *Buller* v. *Withers*, 1 J. & H. 332 (where the balance was handed over to the executor to distribute), and *Re Cope's Trusts*, W. N. 1877, 87.

(*k*) *Gouldsmith* v. *Luntley*, 32 L. T. N. S. 535; *Samson* v. *Samson*, 39 L. J. Ch. 582: but see *Bradford* v. *Nettleship*, 10 W. R. 264, and *Ibberson* v. *Warth*, 1 Jur. N. S. 440.

(*l*) *Parkin* v. *Proudfoot*, Sel. 974.

been refused at the age of 54½ (m), and allowed at 47 (n).

Payment out pending inquiries.

If it clearly appeared that a surplus would remain, after discharging the debts, although the exact amount of such surplus could not be ascertained for a considerable time, the Court would, by anticipation, direct proportional payments to be made to pecuniary legatees, so far as that could be done with safety to the creditors (o); and although by 15 & 16 Vict. c. 86, s. 57, if the Court is satisfied that the assets will be more than sufficient to answer all the claims which ought to be provided for in the action, it may, at any time after the commencement of the action, allow any of the parties interested therein, the whole or part of the income of the realty, or a part of the personalty, or a part of the whole of the income thereof up to such time as the Court shall direct, yet it has been held that this enactment only applies where assets are admitted or the debts are all shown to have been paid (p), and not without good cause being shown (q). As to payments and transfers out of Court generally, see Dan. Ch. XLI.

Chattels bequeathed for life.

Where chattels are bequeathed for life only, they are ordered to be given up to the tenant for life upon signing an inventory which will be deposited in Court (r).

Legatees now not called upon to give security to refund.

It seems to have been at one time the practice, when legacies were paid, to oblige the legatee to give security to refund, in case any other debts were discovered (s), but although the legatee's liability remains (t), security is now

---

(m) *Croxton* v. *May*, 9 C. D. 388.

(n) *Re Summer*, 22 W. R. 639, and see Set. 976.

(o) *Thomas* v. *Montgomery*, 1 R. & M. 729; and see *Coster* v. *Coster*, 1 Ke. 199.

(p) *Knight* v. *Knight*, 16 Beav. 358; *Chubb* v. *Carter*, W. N. 1867, 179.

(q) *Rowley* v. *Burgess*, 2 W. R. 652.

(r) *Foley* v. *Burnell*, 1 Bro. C. C. p. 279.

(s) See *March* v. *Russell*, 3 My. & Cr. p. 41.

(t) See *ante*, p. 116.

no longer required. The executors are sufficiently in-demnified by the orders of the Court, and (*u*) no part of the estate ought to be set apart to meet possible claims in respect of leaseholds subject to onerous covenants sold by the Court (*v*), but where the estate consisted partly of mining shares, the Court ordered the residuary legatees to undertake to answer all liability in respect thereof (*x*). *No assets now retained to meet claims in respect of leaseholds. Executors liable for distributing assets out of Court with notice of contingent claims.*

Where an order has been made directing Consols to be sold and the proceeds to be paid to the person declared to be entitled thereto, and an appeal is brought, it is of course to stay the payment out; but if the Consols have been actually sold, the proceeds must be reinvested, and the appellant must undertake, in case of failure, to make good the amount of interest falling short of 4 per cent., and must pay the costs of the sale and reinvestment (*y*), and except under special circumstances (*z*) must pay the costs of the application to stay the payment out (*a*). *Stay of payment out pending an appeal.*

(*u*) Per Romilly, M. R., *Waller* v. *Barrett*, 24 Beav. 413; and see *Ross* v. *Tatham*, 38 L. J. Ch. 577.

(*v*) But in a subsequent case, the same Judge held that the landlord's consent was necessary before payment out of a fund which had been so set apart; *Bunting* v. *Marriott*, 7 Jur. N. S. 565.

(*x*) *Williams* v. *Headland*, 4 Giff. 505; and see *Taylor* v. *Taylor*, 10 Eq. 477, where executors who had paid a legacy with notice of a liability upon bank shares were ordered to pay calls to the extent of the legacy. As to the executor's right to call upon residuary legatees to refund, see *ante*, p. 120.

(*y*) *Brewer* v. *Yorke*, 20 C. D. 669.

(*z*) *Adair* v. *Young*, 11 C. D. 136.

(*a*) *Merry* v. *Nickalls*, 8 Ch. 205.

CHAPTER XV.

OF THE JURISDICTION OF COUNTY COURTS AND DISTRICT REGISTRARS.

Concurrent jurisdiction of County Courts up to £500.

A CONCURRENT jurisdiction in the administration of the estates of deceased persons is by 28 & 29 Vict. c. 99, given to County Courts (*a*), where the personal or real, or personal and real estate does not exceed in amount or value £500 (*b*); but it should be noted that, probably by an accidental omission, the jurisdiction is confined to cases where the action is brought by creditors, legatees, devisees (in trust or otherwise), heirs-at-law or next of kin (*c*), so that the legal personal representatives, *as such*, are apparently excluded from the right to commence proceedings for general administration in the County Court (*d*).

In what Court proceedings to be commenced.

By sec. 10 (3) the proceedings must be taken in the Court within the district of which the deceased had his last place of abode in England or in which the executors or administrators or any of them have their or his place of abode [nothing is said of the place of abode of the trustees or other persons in whom the real estate may be vested];

(*a*) By sec. 1 the County Court has, in the matters mentioned in the Act, "all the power and authority of the High Court of Justice" (see *Martin* v. *Bannister*, 4 Q. B. D. 491); and therefore a County Court before which an administration action is pending cannot now restrain creditors' actions ; *Cobbold* v. *Pryke*, 4 Ex. D. 315.

(*b*) Sec. 1 (1).

(*c*) Including (as under the Chancery Improvement Act, see *ante*, p. 2) assignees and representatives of these classes of persons (*Turner* v. *Reunoldson*, 16 Eq. 37).

(*d*) Sec. 1 (1).

but if the defendant is an officer of a County Court, the action may (e) be brought in the district of which he is an officer, or in any adjoining district the judge of which is not the judge of a Court of which the defendant is an officer (f).

By sec. 3 it is provided that a Judge in Chambers may on an application of any party to the action, then and there, or, if he shall think fit, after hearing a summons served upon the other party or parties, transfer the same to the Chancery Division, upon such terms, if any, as to security for costs or otherwise as he may think fit (g) ; and by sec. 9, if during the progress of the action it shall be made to appear to the Court that the subject-matter exceeds the limit in point of amount to which the jurisdiction of the County Courts is limited, it shall not affect the validity of any order or decree already made, but it shall be the duty of the Court to direct the action to be transferred to the Chancery Division, and thereupon it shall proceed before such one of the Judges of that Division as the Lord Chancellor may by general order direct (h) ; and such Judge shall have power to regulate the whole of the procedure therein when it is so transferred ; but it is provided that it shall be lawful for any party to apply to the Judge at Chambers for an order authorizing and directing the action to be carried on and prosecuted in the County Court, notwithstanding such excess, and the Judge, if he shall deem it right to summon the other parties or any of them to appear before him for that purpose, after hearing such parties, or on default of the appearance of all or any of them, shall have full power to make such order. And

<small>Transfer to Chancery Division.</small>

<small>Provisions for a re-transfer.</small>

(e) Under 19 & 20 Vict. c. 108, s. 21.
(f) Linford v. Gudgeon, 6 Ch. 359.
(g) This power is to be exercised in the discretion of the Judge irrespectively of the amount or value of the property in question ; for an instance of an order made under this section, see Baker v. Wait, 9 Eq. 103.
(h) See Seton, 328, 3a.

When action transferred and when dismissed.

although under 30 & 31 Vict. c. 142, s. 14, whenever an action is brought in a County Court which the Court has no jurisdiction to try, the Judge must order the cause to be struck out, unless the parties consent to the Court having jurisdiction to try it, the provisions of sec. 9 of the Act of 1865 (*h*) are not thereby repealed, and the action can only be struck out under the Act of 1867, where the fact of want of jurisdiction appears upon the plaint; where it appears during the progress of the action, it should be transferred to the Chancery Division under the earlier Act (*i*).

Where an action is struck out under sec. 14 of the Act of 1867, the Judge may award costs as if the Court had jurisdiction and the plaintiff had not appeared, or had appeared and failed (*j*), but after an action has been transferred to the High Court under sec. 9 of the Act of 1865, the jurisdiction of the County Court is gone, and the Judge cannot make any order as to costs (*k*), but upon the hearing in the High Court, if the plaintiff has made a mistake in bringing the action in a Court which has no jurisdiction, he must pay the costs of the hearing in the County Court (*l*).

Counter-claim. By sec. 90 of the Judicature Act, 1873, it is provided that, where in any proceeding before an inferior Court any defence or counter-claim of the defendant involves matter beyond the jurisdiction of the Court, such defence or counter-claim shall not affect the competence or the duty of the Court to dispose of the whole matter in controversy, so far as relates to the demand of the plaintiff and the defence thereto (*m*), but no relief exceeding that

(*h*) 28 & 29 Vict. c. 99.
(*i*) *Birks* v. *Silverwood*, 14 Eq. 101; *Thomson* v. *Flinn*, 17 *ibid.* 415.
(*j*) Sec. 14.
(*k*) *Hares* v. *Lea*, 10 Eq. 683.

(*l*) *Ward* v. *Wyld*, 5 C. D. 779.
(*m*) And therefore the inferior Court may deal with a counterclaim arising out of matters entirely outside its jurisdiction, to the extent of answering the plaintiff's claim,

which the Court has jurisdiction to administer shall be given to the defendant upon any such counter-claim; but it is provided that in such case it shall be lawful for High Court, or any Division or Judge thereof, if it shall be thought fit, on the application (*n*) of any party to the proceeding, to order that the whole proceeding be transferred from such inferior Court to the High Court, or to any Division thereof; and in such case the record in such proceeding shall be transmitted by the registrar, or other proper officer, of the inferior Court, to the High Court; and the same shall thenceforth be continued and prosecuted in the High Court as if it had been originally commenced therein (*o*).

As the equitable jurisdiction of the County Court is not exclusive, and there is no such provision as to costs as is contained with respect to common-law actions in 30 & 31 Vict. c. 142, s. 5, a plaintiff who proceeds in the High Court in a case where there is jurisdiction in the County Court is entitled to his full costs, and apparently the Judge has no discretion to refuse them (*p*); but under the provisions of sec. 8 of the last-mentioned Act, upon the application in Chambers of any of the parties to an action which might have been brought in the County Court under the Act of 1865, or, *ex mero motu*, the Judge may order the proceedings to be carried on in the County Court, or one of the County Courts in which the same might have been commenced, and thereupon the proceedings shall be so carried on, and the parties shall have the same right of appeal as if the

Costs.

Transfer to County Court.

---

but not further; *Davis* v. *Flagstaff Mining Co.*, 3 C. P. D. 228.

(*n*) The application should be by summons, not *ex parte*; see W. N., 1876, 12.

(*o*) So that the plaintiff is not entitled to discovery and production till after delivery of statement of claim; *Davies* v. *Williams*, 13 C. D. 550.

(*p*) *Brown* v. *Rye*, 17 Eq. 343, notwithstanding *Simons* v. *McAdam*, 6 Eq. 324.

action had been commenced in the County Court; and the Court of Appeal will not lightly interfere with the exercise of his discretion (*q*).

Appeals.

By sec. 18 of the Act of 1865, a right of appeal in all equity actions to such one of the Vice-Chancellors as the Lord Chancellor shall appoint is given, irrespectively of the amount or value of the property in question, to any party dissatisfied with the determination or direction of the Judge on any matter of law (*r*) or equity, or on the admission or rejection of any evidence, upon giving notice of appeal within 30 days (*s*) to the opposite party or his solicitor, and depositing £10 with the Registrar of the County Court as security for the costs of the appeal, and it is provided that such appeal shall be final; but by sec. 45 of the Judicature Act, 1873, all such appeals (*t*) lie to a Divisional Court of the High Court, consisting of such of the Judges thereof as may from time to time be assigned for that purpose, as therein mentioned, and under O. LVIII. r. 19 (*u*), every Judge of the High Court is a Judge to hear and determine such appeals, which are to be entered in one list by the officers of the Crown Office of the Queen's Bench Division, and to be heard by a Divisional Court of that

(*q*) *Linford* v. *Gudgeon*, 6 Ch. p. 361. For forms of transfer to and from County Courts, see Seton, 327—329; Pemb. 96; and see County Court Rules, 1875, Ord. XX.

(*r*) See *Williams* v. *Williams*, 37 L. J. Ch. 854.

(*s*) This limit of time may be waived by the parties, and their consent to the signature of the special case by the County Court Judge is evidence of such waiver (*Ward* v. *Raw*, 15 Eq 83).

(*t*) See also sec. 34 (2), which excepts "appeals from County Courts" from the causes and matters assigned to the Chancery Division in consequence of having been formerly by Act of Parliament within the exclusive jurisdiction of the Court of Chancery or any Judge or Judges thereof. The right of appeal, by consent of the respondents, to the Vice-Chancellor of the County Palatine of Lancaster, given by sec. 19 of the Act of 1865, where the cause arose within the County Palatine, seems to be unaffected by the Judicature Acts; see sec. 95 of the Act of 1873.

(*u*) Rules of December, 1876.

Division as the President thereof shall direct. By the above-mentioned sec. 45 the determination of the Divisional Court is final unless special leave to appeal to the Court of Appeal be given by the Divisional Court. See also the County Court Rules, 1875, Order XXIX., regulating the practice upon appeals by special case; and 38 & 39 Vict. c. 50, s. 6, under which an appeal may be made *ex parte* within eight days (*w*) by motion instead of by special case to a Divisional Court sitting to hear appeals from inferior courts, or, if such a Divisional Court be not sitting (and only in that event (*x*)), to a Judge in Chambers (*y*). Except by special leave (*z*) such a motion can only be made upon production of a copy of the notes of the County Court Judge, which, at the request, *at the trial or hearing* (*a*), of either party, he is by the last-mentioned Act required to make of any question of law then raised, and of the facts in evidence in relation thereto, and of his decision thereon, and of his decision of the cause, suit, or proceeding, such copy to be signed by the Judge.

This enactment gives no *new* right of appeal (*b*), and although it is not a condition precedent of the right to appeal by motion that the Judge should have been requested to make such a note, if he has actually done so and signed it (*c*), or, if, in an equity appeal, he

Appeal by motion.

(*w*) Whether an extension of time may be obtained, *quære*; see *Tennant v. Rawlings*, 4 C. P. D. 133; *Mason v. Wirral Highway Board*, 4 Q. B. D. 459.

(*x*) *Brown v. Shaw*, 1 Ex. D. 425.

(*y*) The Judge in Chambers must hear and determine the motion, and cannot adjourn it to the next sitting of the Divisional Court; *Button v. Woolwich Building Society*, 5 Q. B. D. 83.

(*z*) See Orders of Court, January, 1877, 1; and *Morgan v. Davies*, 3 C. P. D. 260.

(*a*) *Pierpoint v. Cartwright*, 5 C. P. D. 139.

(*b*) *Cousins v. Lombard Bank*, 1 Ex. D. 404.

(*c*) *Seymour v. Coulson*, 5 Q. B. D. 359. But where there has not been any sufficient "request" under the Act, he will not be ordered to sign a copy of a note actually made, if he states that it is rough and incom-

has compiled a note after the trial from affidavits used at the trial (*d*), yet no appeal will lie unless the point of law has been in fact raised in the County Court (*e*); but the judgment may be affirmed on other grounds than those on which the County Court Judge proceeded, if they appear and are admitted in his notes (*f*).

The form of order made upon a motion under sec. 6 of the Act of 1875 is that the judgment appealed from be reversed, unless cause be shown within a specified time (*g*), and upon the application of counsel the Court will order a stay of proceedings under the judgment, which, in the absence of such order and of an order by the County Court Judge, may be enforced; see County Court Rules, 1875, Order XXIX. r. 4. When the appeal comes on, the rule *nisi* is either discharged or made absolute.

The costs of an administration action in the County Court may be taxed in the Chancery Division (*h*).

It is believed that the expense of administration actions in County Courts is as great as in the High Court, if not greater, and the jurisdiction is not often exercised, although, as District Registrars, the Registrars of the County Courts frequently take accounts and make inquiries in such actions.

District Registries.

Under the Judicature Acts, the District Registrars have jurisdiction to issue writs in the High Court, and if the defendant or all the defendants appear in the District Registry the action will proceed there (*i*); and even if the action proceeds in London, by sec. 66 of the Judicature Act, 1873, the Court or a Judge may order

plete, and not such as he would have taken if he had been requested in the terms of the Act; *Morgan* v. *Rees*, 6 Q. B. D. 508.
(*d*) *Hill* v. *Peyssé*, 25 W. R. 275.
(*e*) *Clarkson* v. *Musgrave*, 9 Q. B. D. 386.
(*f*) *Chapman* v. *Knight*, 5 C. P. D. 308.
(*g*) *Eccles* v. *Eccles*, 24 W. R. 39.
(*h*) *Re Worth*, 18 C. D. 521.
(*i*) Ord. XII. r. 4.

any books or documents to be produced or any accounts taken or inquiries made in the District Registry, and in the latter case the report in writing of the District Registrar (*j*) shall be acted upon by the Court as to the Court shall seem meet, and an action may be removed to or from a District Registry by the Court or a Judge (*k*).

Under Order XXXV., r. 1, which (as modified by the Rules of June, 1876), provides that where an action proceeds in a District Registry all proceedings, except where by the rules it is otherwise provided, or a Court or Judge otherwise orders, are to be taken in the District Registry down to and (except in Chancery actions, which ought to be tried in London before the Judge of the Chancery Division to whom they have been assigned (*l*)), including final judgment, and every order for an account by reason of the default of the defendant, or by consent, is to be entered in the District Registry, and r. 4, which confers on the District Registrar in such an action all the authority and jurisdiction of a Judge at Chambers (except such as a Master of the Queen's Bench Division is precluded from exercising), a District Registrar can make an order for an account under Order XV., r. 1, and if the order so directs (but not otherwise) can then proceed to take the account himself; but he cannot make an order for accounts in an administration action on the footing of wilful default (*m*).

If a sale of real estate is ordered in such an action, it is in the absolute discretion of the Judge whether it shall take place in the District Registry or in Chambers,

(*j*) In making the report he should adopt the form of a Chief Clerk's certificate, and state the persons who were present before him, and the materials on which he proceeded (*Bennett* v. *Bowen*, 20 C. D. 538).

(*k*) Judicature Act,'1873, sec. 65, and Ord. XXXV. rr. 11—13.
(*l*) *Hutchinson* v. *Ward*, 6 C. D. 692.
(*m*) *Bennett* v. *Bowen*.

but it would seem that in general it should take place in the District Registry (*n*), but costs will not, except under very special circumstances, be ordered to be taxed otherwise than in London (*o*).

A motion made in the Chancery Division, in an action begun in a District Registry, has the effect of removing the action to London (*p*).

Limitation of authority of District Registrars. District Registrars have no power to appoint receivers, direct banking accounts to be opened or money to be paid into those accounts (*q*), and money ordered to be paid into Court by receivers cannot in such actions be paid into a bank to the credit of the District Registrar (*r*).

(*n*) *Macdonald* v. *Foster*, 6 C. D. 193.
(*o*) *Day* v. *Whittaker*, 6 C. D. 734.
(*p*) *Dyson* v. *Pickles*, 27 W. R. 376.
(*q*) *Hutchinson* v. *Ward*, 6 C. D. 692.
(*r*) *Finlay* v. *Davis*, 12 C. D. 735.

APPENDIX.

1 (*a*) FORM OF ADMINISTRATION SUMMONS UNDER 15 & 16
VICT. c. 86, ss. 45, 47.

Cons. Ord., Schedule (K.), No. II.

In the High Court of Justice.
Chancery Division.   1882, T., No. .
Vice-Chancellor Bacon,
    or,
Mr. Justice [———].

        In the matter of the estate of John Thomas, late of the Parish of A. in the County of B., Esq., deceased.

            Between Joseph Wilson (*b*), Plaintiff,
                        and
            William Jackson, Defendant.

    Upon the application of Joseph Wilson, of Russell Square, in the county of Middlesex, Esq., who claims to be a creditor upon the estate of the above-named John Thomas, let William Jackson, the executor of the said John Thomas, attend at my chambers at the Royal Courts of Justice on   the   day of   , at   of the clock in the   noon, and show cause, if he can, why an order for the administration of the personal [*or*, real and personal] estate of the said John Thomas by the High Court of Justice should not be granted.

    Dated the   day of   , 188 .
                        W. X., Vice-Chancellor,
                            or,
                        Y. Z., Justice.

(*a*) The numbers refer to the pages, *ante*.
(*b*) Add, if so intended, "on behalf of himself and all other creditors of John Thomas, deceased;" see *ante*, p. 9; and see Daniell, Forms, 3rd Edition, No. 946.

This summons was taken out by A. & B., of Lincoln's Inn, in the County of Middlesex, solicitors for the above-named Joseph Wilson.

The following Note to be added to the original summons; and when the time is altered by indorsement, the indorsement to be referred to as below.

NOTE.—If you do not attend, either in person or by your solicitor, at the time and place above-mentioned [*or*, at the place above-mentioned at the time mentioned in the indorsement hereon], such order will be made and proceedings taken as the Judge may think just and expedient.

13   CONS. ORD. VII., r. 1.

"In suits to execute the trusts of a will, it shall not be necessary to make the heir-at-law a party; but the plaintiff shall be at liberty to make the heir-at-law a party, where he desires to have the will established against him."

14   THE COURT OF PROBATE ACT, 1857 (20 & 21 VICT. c. 77), s. 64.

In any action at law or suit in equity, where, according to the existing law, it would be necessary to produce and prove an original will in order to establish a devise or other testamentary disposition of or affecting real estate, it shall be lawful for the party intending to establish in proof such devise or other testamentary disposition to give to the opposite party, ten days at least before the trial or other proceeding in which the said proof shall be intended to be adduced, notice that he intends at the said trial or other proceeding to give in evidence as proof of the devise or other testamentary disposition the probate of the said will, or the letters of administration with the will annexed, or a copy thereof stamped with any seal of the Court of Probate; and in every such case such probate or letters of administration, or copy thereof respectively, stamped as aforesaid, shall be sufficient evidence of such will and of its validity and contents, notwithstanding the same may not have been proved in solemn form, or have been otherwise declared valid in a contentious cause or matter, as herein provided, unless the party receiving such notice shall, within four days after such receipt, give notice that he disputes the validity of such devise or other testamentary disposition.

47   FORM OF INDORSEMENT ON NOTICE OF JUDGMENT OR ORDER.

Cons. Ord. XXIII., r. 20.

"Take notice, that, from the time of the service of this notice, you [*or, as the case may be,* the infant, or person of unsound mind] will be bound by the proceedings in the above action in the same manner as if you [*or,* the said infant, or person of unsound mind] had been originally made a party thereto; and that you [*or,* the said infant, or person of unsound mind] may, by an order of course, have liberty to attend the proceedings under the within-mentioned judgment [*or,* order]; and that you [*or,* the said infant, or person of unsound mind] may, within one month after the service of this notice, apply to the Court to add to the judgment [*or,* order]."

---

50   MINUTES OF ORDINARY ADMINISTRATION JUDGMENTS.

I.

Creditors' Action.—Personal Estate.—General Accounts.

Let the following accounts and inquiry be taken and made, that is to say:—1. An account of what is due to the plaintiff and all other the creditors of A. deceased, the intestate [*or,* testator] in the plaintiff's action named. 2. An account of the intestate's [*or,* testator's] funeral expenses. 3. An account of the intestate's [*or,* testator's] personal estate come to the hands of the defendants   , the administrators of his estate [*or,* executors of his will], or of [any or] either of them, or to the hands of any other person or persons by or for their or [any or] either of their order or use. 4. An inquiry what parts (if any) of the intestate's [*or,* testator's] personal estate are outstanding or undisposed of. Let the intestate's [*or,* testator's] personal estate be applied in payment of his debts and funeral expenses in a due course of administration.—Adjourn further consideration.—Liberty to apply.

II.

Creditors' Action.—Real and Personal Estate.—General Accounts.

Let the following accounts and inquiries be taken and made: – An account of what is due and owing, &c., and accounts of personal estate [see order, *supra*]. Let the intestate's [*or*, testator's] personal estate be applied in payment of his debts and funeral expenses in a due course of administration. And in case the intestate's [*or*, testator's] personal estate shall be insufficient for payment of his debts and funeral expenses, let the following further inquiries and accounts be made and taken. An inquiry what real estate the intestate [*or*, testator] was seised of or entitled to at the time of his death. An inquiry what incumbrances (if any) affect the intestate's [*or*, testator's] real estate, or any and what parts thereof [and their priorities]. An account of what is due to such of the incumbrancers (if any) as shall consent (*c*) to the sale hereinafter directed in respect of their incumbrances. Let the intestate's [*or*, testator's] real estate, or a sufficient part thereof to make good the deficiency of his personal estate, be sold with the approbation of the judge, free from the incumbrances (if any) of such of the incumbrancers as shall consent to the sale, and subject to the incumbrances of such of them as shall not consent. Let the money to arise by the sale of such real estate be paid into Court to the credit of this action; and if such money or any part thereof shall arise from real estate sold with the consent of the incumbrancers, the same is to be applied in the first place in payment of what shall appear to be due to such incumbrancers according to their priorities—Adjourn further consideration.—Liberty to apply (*d*).

(*c*) If the mortgagee be a party, he may be put to his election whether he will have a sale or not, and the order will be framed accordingly (*Wickenden* v. *Rayson*, 6 De G. M. & G. 210), but no sale can be made without his express consent (*Langton* v. *Langton*, 1 Jur. N. S. 1078). If he consents, he must do everything necessary to facilitate the sale (*Livesey* v. *Harding*, 1 Beav. 343); and he is only entitled to six months' interest from the date of his consent to be paid off out of the purchase-money (*Day* v. *Day*, 31 Beav. 270).

If the mortgagee consents to the sale, the purchaser may be directed to pay him the amount due to him on taking the account and the balance into Court, or to pay the whole purchase-money into Court, when the mortgagee may apply for payment by summons or petition (Seton, 821, 822).

If a mortgagee be the plaintiff, and desire to realize his security and to charge the general assets with the deficiency, the action should be brought "on behalf of himself and all other the creditors," &c. (*Skey* v. *Bennett*, 2 Y. & C. C. 405; and see Seton, 823—825; Pemb. 179).

(*d*) It will be seen that no account of *rents* is ordered in the original judgment; this can, of course, be

III.

Creditors' Action.—Real and Personal Estate.—Inquiry as to Heir.

Let the following accounts and inquiries be taken and made :—An account of what is due and owing, &c., and accounts of personal estate, as in first order.—Let the intestate's personal estate be applied, &c.—Let the following further inquiries and accounts be made and taken :—An inquiry who at the time of the death of the said intestate was his heir-at-law, and whether such heir is living or dead, and if dead who, by devise, descent, or otherwise, is now entitled to such real estate (if any) of the intestate as descended to such heir-at-law. Inquiries as to real estate, rents, and profits, and incumbrances, as in preceding order. And if it shall appear that such heir-at-law of the said intestate, or the person so entitled as aforesaid, is a party to this action, let the intestate's real estate, or a sufficient part thereof to make good any deficiency, be sold, &c.—Usual directions. *Pickering* v. *Backhouse* (V.-C. B.), Feb. 17, 1873 ; see also *Chatham* v. *Higginbottom* (V.-C. W.), Feb. 11, 1860.

IV.

Creditors' Action for General Account.—Personalty.—Payment of Plaintiff's Debt.

The defendant B., the executor [*or*, administrator] of A., the testator [*or*, intestate], by his defence [*or*, counsel or solicitor] admitting assets of the said A. for the purposes of this action, and that the said A. was at the time of his death indebted to the plaintiff in the sum of £ , and that the sum of £ is now due for principal and interest in respect of such debt ; Let the defendant B. (within one month from the date of this order) pay to the plaintiff C. the said sum of £ , with subsequent interest on the principal sum of £ , part of the said £ , at the rate of £ per cent. per annum from the day of to the day of payment.—Liberty to apply. See *Woodyate* v. *Field*, 2 Hare, 211.

V.

Action by Next-of-Kin.—Personalty.

Let the following inquiries and accounts be made and taken :—
1. An inquiry who were the next-of-kin according to the statutes

obtained on further consideration, desire (Seton, 822).
if necessary, and if the creditors so

for the distribution of intestate's estates of A. deceased, the intestate in the pleadings [*or*, summons] named living at the time of his death, and whether any of them are since dead, and if dead, who are their respective legal personal representatives [*if required*; And whether the intestate left a widow, and if so, whether she is living or dead, and if dead, who is or are her legal personal representative or representatives]. 2. An account of the personal estate of the said intestate come to the hands of the defendants   , the administrators of his estate, or any [or either] of them, or to the hands of any other person or persons by or for the order or use of the defendants or any [or either] of them. 3. An account of the intestate's debts. 4. An account of the intestate's funeral expenses. 5. An inquiry what parts, if any, of the intestate's personal estate are outstanding or undisposed of. Let the intestate's personal estate be applied in payment of his debts and funeral expenses in a due course of administration.—Adjourn further consideration.—Liberty to apply (*e*).

VI.

Will Established.

Declare (*f*) that the will of   , the testator [is well proved, and that the same] ought to be established, and the trusts thereof performed and carried into execution.

If will admitted: The defendant B., the heir-at-law of   , the testator, &c., by his defence [counsel] admitting the due execution of the testator's will, dated, &c., this Court doth declare, &c.

Infant heir not asking issue: And counsel for the infant defendant B. not asking for an issue upon a will of the testator, and the Court being of opinion that it will not be for the benefit of the said infant to direct such issue, Declare, &c.

If will proves itself: Upon reading the will of the testator   , dated, &c., Declare that the same ought to be established, &c.

VII.

Action by Legatee, by Trustees, or Executors, or Beneficiary.—Personal Estate.—General Accounts.

Declare that the trusts of the will of   , the testator, &c., ought to be performed and carried into execution, and order and adjudge

---

(*e*) As to an inquiry as to advances to children, see *Waterton* v. *Ennis*, W. N., 1880, 154.

(*f*) Unnecessary in creditors' actions, see *ante*, p. 13.

the same accordingly. [And the plaintiffs (g) by their counsel submitting to account,] Let the following accounts and inquiries be taken and made, that is to say :—1. An account of the personal estate not specifically bequeathed of   , the testator, come to the hands of the plaintiffs, the executors of his will, or [any or] either of them, or to the hands of any other person or persons by or for the order or use of the defendants or [any or] either of them. 2. An account of the testator's debts. 3. An account of the testator's funeral expenses. 4. An account of the legacies [and annuities] given by the testator's will. 5. An inquiry what parts (if any) of the testator's personal estate are outstanding or undisposed of. Let the testator's personal estate not specifically bequeathed be applied in payment of his debts and funeral expenses in a due course of administration, and then in payment of the legacies and annuities given by his will.—Adjourn further consideration.—Liberty to apply.

VIII.

Action by Trustees, Executors, or Beneficiaries.—Real and Personal Estate.—General Accounts.

Declare that the trusts of the will of   , the testator, &c., ought to be performed and carried into execution, and order and adjudge the same accordingly. [And the plaintiffs (g) by their counsel submitting to account,] Let the following accounts and inquiries be taken and made : Accounts of personal estate, as in last order, with inquiry as to heir-at-law if real estate be sold. Let the testator's personal estate not specifically bequeathed be applied, &c. Let the following further inquiries and accounts be made and taken :—6. An inquiry what real estate the testator was seised of or entitled to at the time of his death. *If ordered :* 7. An account of the rents and profits of the testator's real estate received by the plaintiffs [or, defendants] or [any or] either of them, or by any other person or persons by their or [any or] either of their order, or for their or [any or] either of their use. 8. An inquiry what incumbrances (if any) affect the testator's real estate, or any and what parts thereof. 9. An account of what is due to such of the incumbrancers as shall consent to the sale hereinafter directed in respect of their incumbrances. 10. An inquiry what are the priorities of such last-mentioned incumbrances. *If ordered :* Let the testator's real estate be sold with the approbation of the judge free from the incumbrances (if any) of

(g) If executors or trustees be plaintiffs.

such of the incumbrancers as shall consent to the sale, and subject to the incumbrances of such of them as shall not consent. Let the money to arise by the sale of the testator's real estate be paid into Court to the credit of this [matter and] action to an account to be intituled "Proceeds of Testator's Real Estates." And if such money or any part thereof shall arise from real estate sold with the consent of the incumbrancers, the money so arising is to be applied in the first place in payment of what shall appear due to such incumbrancers according to their priorities.—Adjourn further consideration.—Liberty to apply.

102 FORM OF ADVERTISEMENT FOR CREDITORS.

Pursuant to a judgment [or, an order] of the High Court of Justice, made In the matter of the estate of A. B., and in an action S. against P., the creditors of A. B., late of   , in the County of   , who died in the month of   , 18 , are, on or before the   day of   , 18 , to send by post prepaid to E. F., of   , the solicitor of the defendant, C. D., the executor [or, administrator] of the deceased [or, as may be directed], their christian and surnames, addresses and descriptions, the full particulars of their claims, a statement of their accounts, and the nature of the securities (if any) held by them ; or, in default thereof, they will be peremptorily excluded from the benefit of the said judgment [or, order]. Every creditor holding any security is to produce the same before Mr. Justice   at his chambers, situated at the Royal Courts of Justice, on the   day of   , 18 , at   o'clock in the   noon, being the time appointed for adjudicating on the claims.

Dated this   day of   , 18 .

G. H.,
Chief Clerk.

103 NOTICE TO CREDITOR TO PROVE HIS CLAIM.

(*Short Title.*)

You are hereby required to prove the claim sent in by you against the estate of A. B., deceased. You are to file such affidavit as you may be advised in support of your claim, and give notice thereof to me, on or before the   day of   next, and to attend, by your solicitor, at the chambers of the Vice-Chancellor, Sir James Bacon [or,   , J.], situate at, &c., on the   day of   , 18   , at   o'clock in the   noon, being the time appointed for adjudicating on the claim.

Dated this   day of   , 18 .

G. R., of, &c., solicitor for the plaintiff
[or, defendant, or as may be].

To Mr. S. T.

---

104 NOTICE TO CREDITOR TO PRODUCE DOCUMENTS.

(*Short title.*)

You are hereby required to produce, in support of the claim sent in by you against the estate of A. B., deceased [*describe any probate, administration, deed, or document required*], before Mr. Justice   at his chambers, situate at, &c., on the   day of   , 18   , at   o'clock in the   noon.

Dated this   day of   , 18 .

G. R., of, &c., solicitor for plaintiff
[or, defendant, or as may be].

To Mr. S. T.

---

118 FORM OF ADVERTISEMENT FOR CLAIMANTS, OTHER THAN CREDITORS.

CONS. ORD., SCHEDULE (L.).

Pursuant to a judgment [*or*, order] of the High Court of Justice, made in [the matter of the estate of   , and in] an action against the persons claiming to be next of kin to [*or*, the heir of, *as the case may be*]   , late of   , in the County of   , who died in or about the month of   , 18   , are, by their solicitors, on or before the   day of   , 18   , to come in and prove their claims at the chambers of Mr. Justice   , at the Royal Courts of Justice, or in default thereof they will be peremptorily excluded from the benefit of the said judgment [*or*, order].

[Monday], the   day of   , 18   , at   o'clock in the   noon, at the said chambers, is appointed for hearing and adjudicating upon the claims.

Dated this   day of   , 18 .

A. B.,
Chief Clerk.

INDEX.

ABATEMENT,
   of legacies and annuities, 176, 178

ACCOUNT, ACCOUNTS,
   adopting, taken in another cause, 74
   assets, admission of, precludes, 50
   beneficiary's action, of personal estate, 50, 51 (*g*) ; Appendix, 197—199
         real estate, Appendix, 199
   chambers, how taken in, 90
   costs of, how borne, 143
   creditors' action, of personal estate, 50, 51 (*g*) ; Appendix, 195—197
         real estate, 9, 29 (*u*) ; Appendix, 196, 197
   debts under Turner's Act, 4
   district registry, may be taken in, 191
   evidence on taking, 90
   further, and inquiries, when and how added, 50—52
   judgment for, 23 ; Appendix, 195—199
   liability to, sole issue in administration action, 12
   real estate, not directed in action by single creditor, 9, 29 (*u*)
         rents of, not directed until deficiency shown which requires them,
            Appendix, 196 (*d*)
   separate, carrying over to, 51 (*g*), 180
         title of, 180
   summons in Chambers for usual, 22
   usual, 22 ; Appendix, 195—199
   wilful default, 5, 15, 17, 52
         not directed on summons, 5

ACTION,
   against executor, after administration judgment, only by leave of the Court, 16
                                      how stayed, 69—85. *See*
                                                 STAYING PROCEEDINGS.
         administration by the Court, 37, 183
                  out of Court, 4, 37
   before probate, 27, 32
   by executor after administration judgment, 126, 127
      improper, after administration by the Court, 126 (*k*)

ADDITIONAL ACCOUNTS AND INQUIRIES,
   when and how ordered, 50—52, 132

ADJOURNMENT,
   of summons to Judge in Chambers, 87
      vary chief clerk's certificate, 100

ADJOURNMENT—*continued.*
    right of suitor to have case adjourned to Judge, 88
        how qualified, 88

ADJUDICATION,
    on claims of creditors, 105
        other claimants, 118

ADMINISTRATION. *See* ASSETS, COSTS, EXECUTOR, JUDGMENT, PARTIES, RULES AND ORDERS, STATUTES, &c.

ADMINISTRATOR,
    ad litem, insufficient in action for administration of estate, 34
        costs of, 151 (*y*)
    creditor, grant of administration to, 108 (*l*), 168 (*q*)
    durante minore ætate, when a necessary party, 38
    feme covert cum testamento annexo, of, 35
    de bonis non, proof of title of, 14
    proof of title of, 13
    revocation of letters of administration, 28, 141
    right to costs, as between solicitor and client, 149
        generally, 141—149
        in priority to all other parties, 151
    indemnity of the Court, 142 (*n*)
    order for account under Turner's Act, 4
    retainer for his debt, 168
    sue before grant of administration, 27
    summons, cannot obtain order for administration upon, 4
  And *see* COSTS, EXECUTOR.

ADMISSION OF ASSETS,
    assent of executor to a legacy, when, 50, 137
    effect of, in dispensing with account, 50
        entitling to order for payment, 50
    in summons action, cannot be acted on, 5

ADMISSION, ADMISSIONS,
    for purposes of ordering payment into Court, what, 64
    judgment upon, for administration, 12, 18
        for payment of debt or legacy, 50, 137 (*l*) ; Appendix, 197
    order for payment into Court, upon, 60—68

ADVANCES,
    inquiry as to, by intestate, Appendix, 198

ADVERTISEMENTS,
    for claimants other than creditors, 117
    for creditors, 102

AFFIDAVIT,
    of documents by executors, 108
    verifying claims, by executors, 104
  See EVIDENCE.

ALIENATION
    by heir or devisee, when good against creditors of deceased, 166

INDEX.

AMENDMENT,
of indorsement on writ, when necessary, 9

ANNUITANT,
administration action may be brought by, 24, 29
costs of, 138

ANNUITY, *arrears, with —, Re Salwey (19— ? L.C.?)*
abatement of, 178
fund, distributable after death of annuitant, when, 178
income only, when applicable to pay, 178
valued for purposes of administration, if estate deficient, and abates accordingly, 178

APPEAL.
chambers, from, 89
      time, 89
costs, for, 140, 149
whether any, from refusal of administration order on summons, 6

APPEARANCE,
default of, judgment in, 3, 22
entry of, 3

APPLICATION,
of assets, order of, *inter se*, 159, 166, 168, 174
   in payment of costs, 156
        debts, 164

APPOINTMENT,
power of, if exercised, property is assets, 165

APPORTIONMENT,
of costs, between real and personal estate, 158
       pure and impure personalty, 159
   and debts, between legal and equitable assets, 159, 168
payment to creditor, after, 114
And *see* MARSHALLING, 159, *et seq.*

APPROPRIATION,
of assets, to answer contingent liabilities, not now made, 183
   loss after, 120

ASSENT,
of executor to a legacy, what judgment obtained after, 50, 137

ASSETS,
administration of, 161—179
admission of, 50, 137
appropriation of, 120, 183
deficient, for payment of costs, 154 (*p*)
       debts, 162, 168—173
equitable, what, 167. *See* EQUITABLE ASSETS.

ASSETS—*continued.*
    legal and equitable, distinction between, 167
        what, 167
    marshalling, 159, 166, 168, 174. *See* MARSHALLING.
    order of application of, in payment of costs, ~~161~~ 156
                                        debts, ~~156~~
    payment of, into Court, 60—68
    personal, including lands in India and the West Indies, 164 (*a*)
            property subject to power of appointment, if exercised, 165. And
            see PERSONAL ESTATE.
    real,
        by descent, 164
        by devise or charge, 164, 165
        by statute 3 & 4 Wm. 4, c. 104, 13, 167
            equitable assets, 167 (*h*)
        their priority and order of application, 164
        realisation of, under the administration, 95. And *see* REAL ESTATE.
    receipt of, by co-executor, effect of, 37
    securing, in Court, on admissions, 60—68

ASSIGNEE,
    of creditor, legatee, &c., entitled to administration judgment, 2, 30, 184 (*c*)
        costs of, 150

BANKRUPT,
    debtor to estate, set-off against legacy to, 146
    executor or trustee, costs of, 144
    one of co-executors or trustees, costs of, 146

BANKRUPTCY RULES. *See* INSOLVENT ESTATE, (168—173) ; RULES AND
    ORDERS, *post*, 227.

BENEFICIARY. *See* DEVISEE, LEGATEE.

BOND,
    proof of, in chambers, 106
    voluntary, preferred to legacies, postponed to debts, 167, 173

BREACH OF TRUST,
    summons action not applicable for, 5
    liability for, 16, 17, 65, 132

CARRYING OVER,
    residue to separate accounts on further consideration, 180

CERTIFICATE,
    of chief clerk, 96—101
            application to discharge or vary, 93, 133
            Chancery Paymaster, to be acted on by, 100
            error in, 99, 101, 134
            filing of, 97
            form of, 96
            general or separate, 98

INDEX. 207

CERTIFICATE—continued.
 irregularity in, 99, 134
 opinion of Judge on, how taken, 88
 proof of debts, after, 113
 result of accounts, how stated in, 96
 signature and adoption of, by Judge, 98
 variation of, generally on further consideration, 100, 133
    time within which application for, may be made, 98
 of counsel, that cause is fit to be heard " short," 12

CHAMBERS,
 account ordered in, where writ indorsed under O. iii., r. 8, 22
 accounts, how taken in, 90, 104
  of personal estate, order for, under Turner's Act, 4
 administration in, 1—10
 appeal from, 89
 applications for, conduct made in, 126
   payment out, in, 181
 costs of proceedings in, 93, 111
 creditors establishing debts in, 103—117
  costs of, 111
 evidence in, 90—92
 inquiries, how made in, 104
  conduct of, in, 124
 judge, opinion of, taken in, 88, 89
 legatees and others proving claims in, 118
 proceedings in, generally, 86—101
 sales under judgments conducted in, 95
 And See CONDUCT.

CHANCERY DIVISION,
 jurisdiction in administration of assets, 1 (e)
 transfers from, to County Court, 185, 187
  to, after judgment for administration, 84
  from County Court, 185

CHANCERY FUNDS RULES. See RULES AND ORDERS, post, 227.

CHANCERY PAYMASTER,
 certificate to be acted on by, 100

CHARGE,
 of real estate, with payment of debts, 164 (u)

CHARITY,
 apportionment of costs, &c., between pure and impure personalty, 159, 176
 no marshalling in favour of, 176

CHIEF CLERK,
 certificate of (quod vide), 96—101
 powers of, 91
 And see CHAMBERS.

CHILDREN,
    interest on legacies to, when payable, 119

CLAIMS,
    allowance of, 112
        after expiration of time limited, 113
        after apportionment, 114
    proof of, in Chambers, 102—121
    unliquidated damages, for, 106
    And see CREDITORS.

CLASS,
    inquiry as to, 117
    one of a, suing or being sued for all, 44

CONCURRENT ACTIONS, 69—85
    costs of applications to stay, 75
        stayed actions, 84
    Court may interfere *ex mero motu*, in, 72
    creditor's action in Q. B. D., stay of, 80
        transfer of to Chancery Division, 84
    for co-extensive relief, 70
    foreign action for same or like purpose, 79, 82, 83
    how stayed, 70
    judgment in, 74, 75
    staying one of two, after judgment in the other, 69
        on whose application, 69
    transfer of one of two, 77
    when relief not co-extensive, 72
        stay will be ordered, 69
    which will be stayed, 71
        transferred, 78

CONDUCT
    of action for administration, 122—127
    alleged creditor found a debtor, conduct given to another, 125
    application for, to be made in Chambers, 126
    costs of plaintiff deprived of, 93
    death of creditor plaintiff, 125
    of different inquiries, when given to different parties, 125
    discretion of Judge in questions of, final, 122
    plaintiff entitled to, unless good cause be shown, 122
        when deprived of, 123
    proceedings external to the administration, executors generally entitled to conduct of, 127
    of sale, trustees entitled to, 124

CoNFLICT of interests, 93(y)

CONSENT,
    administration judgment by, 23

CONSOLIDATED ORDERS. *See* RULES AND ORDERS, *post*, 227.

CONSOLIDATION OF CONCURRENT ACTIONS, 79

CONTINGENT DEBTS AND LIABILITIES,
    proof in respect of, where estate insolvent, 107, 173
    setting aside funds to meet, not usual, 183
    whether a ground for obtaining judgment for administration, 26

CONTINGENT INTERESTS,
    insufficient to entitle plaintiff to administration judgment, when, 24

CONTRIBUTION,
    to costs of action, by creditors, not now ordered, 153
        by devisees in aid of personalty, 95 (*k*)
And *see* MARSHALLING, 159 *et seq.*

CORPUS,
    annuity paid out of, when, 178
    apportionment of, amongst annuitants and legatees, 178

COSTS IN ADMINISTRATION ACTIONS, 135—160
    administrator *ad litem*, of, 151
    accounts, of taking, 143
    annuitants', 138
    appeal for, 140, 149
    apportionment, between legal and equitable assets, 159
                   pure and impure personalty, 159
                   real and personal estate, 158
    assignees or mortgagees of beneficiaries, of, 150
    bankrupt executor or trustee, of, 144, 146
    concurrent actions, of, 75, 76
    contribution towards, not now ordered, 153
    County Court, in, 187, 190
    creditors', 111, 140, 153
    defaulting executor or trustee, of, 144
    deficient estate, rules in case of, 151—156
    disclaiming trustee's, 152
    executor or administrator, of, 141—145, 146—149
                          as between solicitor and client, 149
                          not out of real estate, 152
                          when a solicitor, 147
                          when deprived of, 139, 142—144
                          when jointly liable for, though not equally guilty, 147
    first charge on assets, 135
    further consideration, costs of persons unnecessarily appearing on, 129
                                questions as to costs, disposed of on, 131
    heir's, in creditors' actions, 151
    higher and lower scale, 135
    legatees', 137, 138, 155
    liability for, of creditors or beneficiaries needlessly bringing administration actions, 136, 138, 140
                      executors or trustees improperly causing or bringing administration actions, 142—144

P

COSTS IN ADMINISTRATION ACTIONS—*continued.*
    mortgagee, where mortgage created by testator, costs of, 154
        of beneficiary, costs of, 150
    next-of-kin, of, 139, 156
    persons attending the proceedings, of, 93—95
    plaintiffs', how payable, 149, 153, 155, 156
    priority for, over debts, 155
        except debts for which executor or administrator may retain, 156
        also as to costs of next-of-kin, 156
    probate proceedings, whether costs of, payable in priority, 151
        out of realty, 152
    real estate, apportionment of costs of administration of, 153
    residuary legatees, costs of, 139
    set-off of, against debt to estate, 145
    solicitor, when executor or trustee, costs of, 147
        and client, executors and trustees entitled to costs as between, 149
        heir entitled to costs as between, when, 151
        plaintiff in creditors' action, when so entitled, 153
        beneficiary's action, when so entitled, 155
        residuary legatees not so entitled, 139
    summons, costs of, 87
    " testamentary expenses" include, 159
    trustees', how payable, 141—145, 146—149
        when severing in defence, 147
    unnecessary parties, of, 92, 94, 130
    what they include, 157

COUNTY COURTS,
    appeal from, 188—190
    concurrent jurisdiction of, when, 184
    taxation of costs in, may be in Chancery Division, 190
    transfer from, to Chancery Division, 185
        to, from High Court, 187

COUNTY COURT RULES. *See* RULES AND ORDERS, *post*, 228.

COURT. *See* CHANCERY DIVISION.

COVENANT,
    contingent breach of, will not support creditors' action, 26
    testator's, indemnity against, 183
    voluntary, will support creditors' action, 25
        debt on, order of payment in administration, 107, 173

CREDITOR, CREDITORS,
    abandonment of action for administration by, before judgment, 9
    advertisements for, 102
    affidavit by, when necessary, 103
    apportionment, proof after, 114
    certificate, proof after, 113
    contingent liabilities, 107

INDEX.

CREDITOR, CREDITORS—*continued*.
  costs of, when plaintiff, 140, 153
  cross-examination of, 108
  dominus litis until judgment for administration, 9
  evidence on behalf of, 103—105
  notice to, of allowance or disallowance of claim, 112
          to produce documents, 104, Appendix, 201
          prove his claim, 103, Appendix, 200
  payment to, on further consideration, 133
  priorities amongst, 161—164, 166, 169, 172. *See* PRIORITIES, RETAINER.
  proof of claims in chambers by, 102—116
          costs of, 111
  secured, when estate insolvent, 169—172. *See* MORTGAGEE.
  suing legatees, 116
  unliquidated damages, in respect of, 106
  verification of claim of, 104
  when entitled to take out administration, 108
  And *see* CREDITORS' ACTION ; DEBTS ; RETAINER, 166 ; STATUTE OF LIMITATIONS, 108

CREDITORS' ACTION,
  accounts. *See* INQUIRIES.
  costs of, 140, 153
  creditor, assignee of, may be plaintiff in, 2, 30
        personal representative of, may be plaintiff in, 2
  debt to support action, what sufficient, 25
              what insufficient, 26
  evidence in, 13
  form of, by single creditor, 9 ; and *see* Appendix, 197, (iv.)
      on behalf of all creditors, 9 ; and *see* Appendix, 195—197
  inquiries, less wide than in beneficiaries' actions, 51
      personal estate, Appendix, 195
      real estate, Appendix, 196, 197
          rents and profits of, 196 (*d*)
  judgment in, at the hearing, 51 ; Appendix, 195—197
      on further consideration, 135
      right to, 25
  marshalling assets in, 166—168, 174. *See* MARSHALLING.
  parties in, against personal estate, 31
      against real and personal estate, 39
  personal estate, against, 1, 9 (*l*), 31
  plaintiff in, found debtor to estate, 125
      must prove his debt again in Chambers, 105
  proof of debts in, costs of, added to debt, 111
  real estate, against, 9, 29
  sale of real estate, when ordered, 95, Appendix, 196
  single creditor, by, 9 (*l*)
  Statute of Limitations must be pleaded against plaintiff's claim *before* judgment in, 109
  summons, instituted by, 1
  theory of, 1 (*a*)

CROWN,
debts to, still entitled to priority, 161, 163
summons against Crown solicitor for administration, 3 (*i*)

DAMAGES,
unliquidated, proof for, in Chambers, 106, 172
inquiry as to, 131

DEATH,
of creditor plaintiff, procedure on, 125
of one trustee insolvent after judgment for administration, 39
of one executor before action for administration, whether his representatives should be parties, 37

DEBTS,
account of under Turner's Act, 4
charge of, on real estate, does not now exonerate mortgaged estates, 174
    per se exonerate personalty, 164
    effect of, in administration of assets, 164
creditors' action, what will support, 25
Crown, priority of, 161, 163
executor's, deemed to be assets in his hands, 63
exoneration of mortgaged estate from, 174
    personal estate from, 164
illegal, no ground for administration judgment, 26
interest on, 107, 110, 173
judgment, order of payment of, 161, 163
mortgage, now primarily charged on mortgaged estate, 174
order of liability of assets to, 164
payable *in futuro*, will support creditor's action, 25
payment of, before judgment, 55, 58
    on further consideration, 133
priorities of, under present law, 163
real estate is assets for payment of, 164 (*k*)
recognizance, of, 161, 163
of record, order of payment of, 161, 163
rent, for, now equivalent to simple contract debt, 162, 172
retainer for executor's or administrator's, 55, 58, 166. *See* RETAINER.
specialty, has no longer any priority, 162
special statutes, by, order of payment, 163
trust for payment of, does not generally exonerate mortgaged estates, 174
    does exonerate the other estates, 164
    not now a bar to the Statute of Limitations, 165
And *see* CREDITORS, EQUITABLE ASSETS, LEGAL ASSETS, PRIORITIES.

DECLARATION
of right, not made until accounts taken, 130
that will is well proved, and ought to be established and executed, Appendix, 198

DEFAULT,
of appearance, 3, 22
pleading, 19, 21

DEFAULT—*continued.*
   wilful, not chargeable in summons actions, 5
      how chargeable, at the hearing, 16
            by additional inquiries, 52
            by amendment, 17
            evidence for judgment on footing of, 17
            in a fresh action, 16
            on further consideration, 16

DELAY,
   of plaintiff in prosecuting judgment, remedy for, 122
   or refusal of co-plaintiff to appoint solicitor, remedy for, 124

DESCENDED ESTATES,
   alienation of, for value, as against creditors, 166
   order in which liable for costs, 157, 158
                   debts, 164

DEVISEE,
   alienation by, for value, as against creditors, 166
   contribution by, in aid of personalty, 95 (k)
   entitled as of course to account of testator's estate, 7, 29
   proof of title of, 14
   And *see* REAL ESTATE.

DISCOVERY
   of documents relating to claims, 108

DISCRETION
   of Judge, to refuse administration judgment on summons, 4, 6
   of executors and trustees, when controlled by Court, 54—59

DISTRESS,
   whether right of, affected by s. 10 of Judicature Act, 1875, 172

DISTRIBUTION,
   final, of the estate, 130, 180, 181

DISTRICT REGISTRAR,
   powers of, 191, 192

DISTRICT REGISTRY,
   accounts and inquiries in, 191
   actions in, 190, 191
   production of documents in, 190
   removal of actions to and from, 191, 192
   sale of real estate in, 191
   taxation of costs in, 192
   writs issued out of, 190

DOWER,
   priority of legacy in satisfaction of, 177

DUTY, 181

EQUITABLE ASSETS, 167
    apportionment of debts and costs between, and legal assets, 159, 168
    distinction between legal and equitable, 167
    real estate under 3 & 4 Will. IV. c. 104, 167 (k)
    separate estate of married women, 167 (o)

EQUITABLE CHARGE, 174
    See LOCKE-KING'S ACTS.

ESTABLISHING WILL,
    against heir, not now *necessary*, 13, Appendix, 194
        order for, Appendix, 198

EVIDENCE,
    account, in actions for, 12. And *see* ACCOUNT.
    application to vary certificate, on, 99
    bond debt, of, 106
    chambers, in, 90—92
    claims, corroborative, required of, 105
    common administration judgment, for, 15
    cross-examination, 90
    debt, of, in creditors' action, 13, 105
    documents which prove themselves, 15 (*f*)
    examiners, evidence before, 91
    further consideration, on, 131
    hearing, at the, 12
    special judgment, for, 15
    subpœna ad testificandum, no leave to serve now necessary, 91
    title of devisee, 14
        heir, 15
        legal personal representatives, 13
    wilful default, in case of, 15
    will, of, 14

EXAMINATION OF WITNESSES,
    by chief clerk, 92
    by examiner, 91

EXAMINER,
    examination of witnesses by, 91

EXECUTOR,
    account at suit of, 4, 26
            not before proving, 27
            under Turner's Act, 4
    account against, 1, 31
    accounts, duty of, to set out, 60 (*a*)
    acting, before probate, 27, 33
    actions by and against (*quod vide*), 4, 16, 27, 32, 34, 37, 69—85, 126, 127, 183
    administration by Court, no liability after, 142, 183
            summons for, by, 4
    admission by, of moneys in hand, what sufficient, 64
    advertisements for creditors and other claimants, 102, 117, Appendix, 200, 201
            when protected by, 4, 37

INDEX. 215

EXECUTOR—*continued*.
affidavit of documents by, 108
    verification of claims by, 104
agent of co-executor, no account against, 33
annuity to, for his trouble, cesser of, 55 (*e*)
assent by, to legacy, 50, 137
assets, admission of, by, 50, 137
balances in hands of, interest on, 16
before probate, action by and against, 27, 32
cannot obtain administration judgment on summons, 4
co-executors, liability for acts of, 65
conduct of proceedings arising out of administration action, generally given to, 126
contingent liabilities, setting aside sum to answer, 183
costs of—
    administration actions, in, 141—149, 151, 152. *See* COSTS.
    bankrupt executor, 144, 146
        receiver appointed against, 58
    charges and expenses, right to, 149. *See* TRUSTEE.
    priority of, 151
    severing in defence, 147
    solicitor himself an executor, 147
        and client, right to, as between, 149
costs, ordered to pay, when, 142—144
debt owing by, regarded as assets, 62
debts, preferring one to another, before judgment for administration, 55
    payment of, by, 55, 58
deceased, account against estate of, waived, 38
de son tort, no action against, for general administration, 38
    no right of retainer by, 168
discretion of, how affected by administration action, 54—59
indemnity to, after advertisements, 4, 37
    against contingent liabilities of testator, 183
interest on balances of, 16
legacy, admission of assets for, 50, 137. And *see* LEGACIES.
    prematurely paying, executor held liable for debts, 117
    action against legatee to refund, when, 120
legal and equitable assets, 166, 167
Limitations, Statute of, when legacy barred by, 164 (*n*)
management, powers of, after judgment, 54
mortgage by, 56
outstanding estate, when legatee may sue as to, 126
parties to administration actions, 24—49. *See* PARTIES.
partner of, moneys in hands of, 63
payment into Court by, when ordered, 60—68
    out of Court to, 181
preference of one creditor over another, 55
probate, before obtaining, 27, 32. *See* PROBATE.
production of documents by, 108
receipt of trust fund by co-executor, 65
receiver appointed against, when, 58
refunding by, in favour of creditors, when, 117

EXECUTOR—*continued.*
    retainer, right to, 55, 166
        no right against receiver, 58
        not affected by recent statutes, 56, 163
        only out of legal assets, 166
        waiver of right, 55 (*r*)
        what debts may be retained, 166 (*i*)
    sale by, 58
    set-off by, 145
    statute-barred debt, retainer of, 55 (*i*)
    staying actions against, 69—85
    surviving executor, account against, 38
    title of, how proved, 13
    Turner's Act (13 & 14 Vict. c. 35, s. 15), 4
    wilful default by, directions as to, 15—17. And *see* TRUSTEE, WILFUL
        DEFAULT.
        evidence required in case of, 15, 17
        not chargeable in summons action, 5
            unless charged by testator or plaintiff, 18
        special case must be made for, 17

EXONERATION,
    by devise to pay debts, 164
    of mortgaged or pledged property by general personal estate, when, 174
        land, by personal estate, none in general, 174
    personal estate from costs and debts, 156, 164
    purchased estate from purchase-money, none, 174
    pure personalty, of, in favour of charity, 159, 176
    real estate appointed, by the other assets, 165
        charged, by descended real estate, 157, 164
        descended, by devise for payment of debts, 157, 164
        and personal estate specifically given, by the other assets, 165
And *see* MARSHALLING.

EXPENSES,
    executor's or trustee's, first charge on assets, 151
    testamentary, costs of administration action included in, 159

FEME COVERT,
    action by or against, 31, 37
    equity to a settlement, how asserted by, 181
    next friend of, 31
    separate account of, transfer to, 180
        estate of, administration of, 35
            whether equitable assets, 167 (*o*)
    service on, 45
    testamentary appointment of, administration of assets on summons, 6

FILING,
    chief clerk's certificate, 97

FORECLOSURE,
action for, will not be stayed, 81, 171

FOREIGN COUNTRIES,
lands in what, personal assets, 164
stay of action after judgment in, 79
concurrent actions in, 83

FOREIGN EXECUTOR,
action against, 35, 36

FORMS,
Appendix, 193—201. *See* CONTENTS, xiv.

FUNDS IN COURT,
duty upon, 181
investment of, 68
payment out of, 180
    pending inquiries, 182
    stay of, pending appeal, 183
    to trustees, 181
    upon giving security, 181, 182

FURTHER CONSIDERATION,
appearances on, 129
certificate, when conclusive on, 134
distribution of fund on, by consent, 10 (o)
evidence on, 131
interest computed on, 132
notice of setting down action on, 129
payment of debts on, 133
proceedings on, 128—134
    after, 180—183
questions not pleaded not raised on, 132
    of costs disposed of on, 131
setting down action on, 128
summons to vary certificate usually adjourned until, 100
wilful default, inquiries as to, added on, 17

GUARDIAN *AD LITEM*, 48

HEARING,
evidence at the, 12

HEIR,
administration at suit of, 29
alienation for value by, as against creditors, 166
costs, right to, 151
election of, right to marshal by persons disappointed by, 175
establishing will against, 13, Appendix, 194
inquiry as to, Appendix, 197
proof of title of, 15
when and how bound by probate of will, 14, Appendix, 194

HEIRLOOMS,
delivery of, to tenant for life, 182

HOTCHPOT,
    rule of, in distribution of equitable assets, 168

IDIOT. *See* LUNATIC.

ILLEGAL DEBT,
    no ground for administration, 26

INCUMBRANCERS,
    costs of, 150
    inquiries as to, and their priorities, Appendix, 196, 199
    sale, with concurrence of, Appendix, 196, 199
            or, if not, subject to the incumbrances, Appendix, 196, 199

INDEMNITY,
    of executors after advertisements for creditors, 4, 37
            against testator's covenants in a lease, 183
            and trustees, by administration in Court, 142, 183

INDIA,
    land in, is personal assets, 164 (*o*)

INDORSEMENT ON WRIT, 8, 9

INFANT,
    actions by, by next friend, 31
    birth of beneficiary, after action brought, 46
    concurrent actions by, inquiry as to, 71
    fund carried to account of, 180
    interest on legacy to, 119
    service on, 44
    guardian *ad litem* of, 48

INQUIRY, INQUIRIES,
    additional, when and how ordered, 50—52, 132
    advances, as to, 198
    class, 117
    creditors' action, less extensive in, 51
    further consideration, on, 132
    incumbrances, as to, and their priorities, Appendix, 196, 199
    official referee, before, 51
    personal estate, as to, 51, Appendix, 195, 198
    real estate, as to, Appendix, 196, 197, 199
    usual, 22. *See* APPENDIX, 195—199.
    which action more beneficial to infant plaintiff, 71
    And *see* ACCOUNTS, CHAMBERS.

INSOLVENT ESTATE,
    administered by Bankruptcy Court, when, 169 (*a*)
            under rules of Bankruptcy, 107
    annuities, valuation of, 173
    contingent and future liabilities, valuation of, 173
    debts and liabilities provable, 172

INDEX.

INSOLVENT ESTATE—*continued.*
  form of judgment for administration of, 168 (z)
  interest only up to date of administration judgment, 107, 173
  mutual credits, 173
  priority for rates and wages, none, 172
  secured creditors, rights of, 169
  statute-barred debts, 173
  voluntary bonds, 173

INTEREST,
  executors charged with, on balances, 16, 132
  on debts, 110, 133
      where estate insolvent, 107, 111, 173
  on legacies, 119
      mortgage debt, when mortgagee consents to sale, 196
  rate of, what, charged against trustees, 132 (*l*)
  subsequent, computation of, 133

INTESTACY,
  as to real estate, summons action inapplicable, 7
  And *see* ADMINISTRATOR, HEIR.

INVESTMENT,
  to answer abated annuity, 178
  discretion of trustees in matters of, after administration judgment, 54
  of moneys paid into Court, 63

JUDGE,
  adjournment to, 87
  rehearing by, in Court, 89
  right of suitor to decision of, in Chambers, 88
  taking opinion of, as to certificate, 98

JUDGMENT,
  adding to, 52, 53
  administration, for, how obtained, 11—23
      forms of, Appendix, 195—200
  creditors under registered, priority of, 161, 163
      unregistered, 161, 163
  declaration in, establishing will, Appendix, 198
  District Registry, in, 191
  effect of, on actions by or against executor, 69—85. *See* CONCURRENT ACTIONS, STAYING PROCEEDINGS.
      on discretion of executor or trustee, 54—59
  evidence, what, necessary for administration judgment, 12—18
  for administration, how obtained on summons, 1, 7
      by writ, at the trial, 1
      on motion, 18—22
      by summons, 22
      by consent, 23
  on further consideration, 130
  reversal of, for administration, on revocation of probate or letters of administration, 28, 141

JURISDICTION,
    administration of real estate on summons, when, 7
    none to administer real estate of intestate on summons, 7
    service out of the, 6, 47
                effect of, unless set aside, 36

LAPSED SHARES,
    not primary fund for costs and debts, 156, 164

LEASE,
    contingent breach of covenant in, 26, 183
                      proof for, 107, 173
    power to, control of, by Court after administration judgment, 59

LEASEHOLDS,
    now within Locke-King's Act, 174

LEGACIES,
    abatement of, 178
    admission of assets for, what constitutes, 50, 137 (*l*)
    appropriation for, loss after, 120
    assent to, 50
    assignee of, action by, 2, 30
    charged on real estate, 164 (*u*)
    charitable, abatement of, 176
    dower, in lieu of, have priority, 177
    duty, payment of, 181
    general, order of payment, 176
    interest on, 119
    marshalling, 174
    order of payment, 176, 179
    payment of, before debts, when executor liable personally, 117, 183
    priority of, *inter se*, 176, 179
    refunding, 117, 183
    residuary, what composes, 156
    specific, order of payment of, 179
    Statute of Limitations, 164 (*u*).
    And *see* LEGATEE.

LEGAL ASSETS,
    distinguished from equitable, 167
    retainer only out of, 166
    And *see* EQUITABLE ASSETS.

LEGATEE,
    action by, for administration, 1, 24, 29
               recovery of assets, 126
        by summons, 1
        by writ, 24
    assignee of, plaintiff, 2
    costs of, when plaintiff, 137, 138, 155
    marshalling in favour of, 174
    refunding by, 116, 117, 120

LEGATEE—*continued.*
  residuary, costs of, 130
    refunding by, 120
    undertaking by, to answer contingent liability, 183
  And *see* LEGACIES.

LIMITATIONS, STATUTE OF,
  after judgment for administration, how and by whom set up, 109
                        executor may not pay debt barred by, 55, 108
  creditors' action, whether statute runs after institution of, 110
  debt charged on land, application to, 164 (*u*)
    trust for payment of, application to, 164 (*u*)
  executor, payment or retainer of debt by, notwithstanding, 55
  express trust, whether new Act applies to, 164 (*u*)
  how and when set up, 109
  legacy charged on land, application to, 164 (*u*)
    trust for payment of, application to, 164 (*u*)
  marshalling, none where debts barred against land but kept alive against personalty, 175
  plaintiff's debt, not set up against, after judgment, 109
  recent enactments (37 & 38 Vict. c. 57, s. 10), effect of, 164 (*u*)
    (Jud. Act, 1875, s. 10), 109, 173
  residuary legatee may set up, 109
  trust to pay debts and legacies, application to, 164 (*u*)
  who may set up, in creditors' actions, 109
    in beneficiaries' actions, 109

LOCKE-KING'S ACTS, 174. *See* EXONERATION.

LUNATIC,
  action for administration by, 31
  action by creditor of, for costs of inquisition, 25
  service on, or person of unsound mind, 44

MANAGEMENT,
  powers of, when controlled by the Court, 54

MARRIED WOMAN, 6, 31, 37, 45, 167 (*o*). *See* FEME COVERT.

MARSHALLING,
  assets among creditors and legatees, principle of, 174
  in favour of classes of creditors, 168
    legatees, against mortgaged estates, 175
      against real estate charged with debts and legacies, 175
  not ordered in favour of charities, 176
      except by direction of testator, 159
      creditors whose debts are statute-barred against realty, 175

MISCONDUCT,
> not chargeable in summons action, 5

MORTGAGE
> debt payable primarily out of mortgaged estate, 174
>> payment of, out of purchase-money of estate, 196 (c)
>
> inquiries as to, Appendix, 196, 199
> power of executor to, after administration action instituted, 56
And *see* MORTGAGEE.

MORTGAGEE,
> action by, to realise security, 9 (i), 154, 196
>> will not be stayed, 81, 171
>
> costs of, in administration of mortgagor's assets, 154
> creditors' action by, 154, 196
> party to administration action must elect whether he will join in sale or not, 196 (c)
> rules of bankruptcy applicable to, when estate insolvent, 162, 169—171
> sale cannot be ordered without his consent, except subject to the mortgage, 196 (c)

NEW TRUSTEES,
> discretion as to appointment of, after administration judgment, 54

NEXT OF KIN,
> action by, for administration, by summons, 1
>> by writ, 24
>> costs of, 119, 156
>> inquiries as to, Appendix, 197

NOTICE,
> further consideration, of, 129
> motion, of, 23
> short cause, of, 12
> to creditor, how given, 104
>> of allowance of claim, 112
>> to produce documents, 103, Appendix, 201
>>> prove debt, 103, Appendix, 200

OFFICIAL REFEREE,
> inquiries before, 51

ORDERS OF COURT. *See* RULES AND ORDERS, *post*, 228.

OUTSTANDING ESTATE,
> inquiry as to, 51, Appendix, 195—199
> recovery of, conduct of proceedings for, 126

PALATINE COURT,
  appeal to, from County Court, 188
  concurrent jurisdiction of, 72

PARTIES,
  adding, 32, 146
  administrator *durante minore ætate*, 38
  assignees, 2, 30, 184
  Attorney-General, 38
  deceased executor's representatives, when made, 2, 37
  defendants, 31—40
  executors, all must be, 30
      de son tort, 38
  feme covert, 31, 37, 45
  generally, 24—49
  infants, 31, 44, 48
  legal personal representative, necessity for, 34, 39
  lunatic, 31, 45
  new, coming into existence after judgment, 46
  personal estate, in administration of, 1, 24, 42
  plaintiffs, 24—31
  real and personal estate, in administration of, 7, 29, 30, 43
  representation of *cestuis que trustent* by trustees, 40
      class by one or more members, 44
      persons interested in personalty by executor, 42
  served with notice of decree, who should be, 40
  service dispensed with, 45
  trustees, all must be, 39
      how far they represent *cestuis que trustent*, 40
  want of, no demurrer for, 40
  See FEME COVERT, INFANT, LUNATIC.

PARTNER,
  creditor of deceased's firm may obtain administration judgment, 25
  moneys in hands of executor's, payment into Court of, 63

PAYMASTER-GENERAL,
  certificates to be acted on by, 100

PAYMENT,
  into Court in administration action, 60—68
      after what deductions by executor, 63
      investment after, 68
      order for, on admissions, 60
          when made, 65
          when refused, 61
  of costs, legacies, and debts, 131, 133
      duty, 181
  out of Court on further consideration, 133
      petition for, after further consideration, 180
  unnecessary, in and out of Court, prevented, 62

PERSONAL ESTATE,
    accounts of, 51, Appendix, 195—199
    administration of, by writ, 24—28
                      on summons, 1—6. *See* CREDITORS' ACTION, PARTIES.
    appointed, is liable to debts, 165
    apportionment of costs between, and realty, 158
    exoneration of, from mortgage debts, 174
                  generally, 156, 164
    outstanding, inquiry as to, 51, Appendix, 195—199
    parties in administration of, 1, 24, 42
    primarily liable to costs and debts, 156, 164
    pure and impure, apportionment between, 159, 176
    summons for administration of, 1—6

PERSONAL REPRESENTATIVE,
    necessary party to action for administration of assets, 34
    proof of title of, 13
    And *see* ADMINISTRATOR, EXECUTOR.

PETITION,
    after further consideration, 180

PLAINTIFF. *See* PARTIES.

PLEADINGS,
    default of, judgment in, 19, 21

PLEDGE,
    redemption of, specifically bequeathed, 174

POWERS
    of appointment, exercise of, makes property assets, 165
        chief clerk, 91
        executors and trustees, how far controlled by Court, 54—59

PRACTICE. *See* ACCOUNT, ADMINISTRATION, CHAMBERS, INQUIRIES, SUMMONS, &c.

PREFERENCE,
    by executor between creditors, 55, 58
    And *see* PRIORITIES.

PRIORITIES,
    application of assets, *inter se*, 164
    costs of parties, *inter se*, 151—156
    creditors have none out of equitable assets, 168
    Crown debts, 163
    debts, *inter se*—
        Crown, 163
        judgment, registered and unregistered, 163
        rates and taxes, none for, 172
        rent, none for, 162, 172

PRIORITIES—*continued.*
    debts *inter se,*
        simple contract and specialty, *pari passu,* 162
        voluntary bonds and covenants, 107, 173
        wages, none for, 172
    legacies, generally, 176
    old law, under, 161
    And *see* EXONERATION, MARSHALLING, PERSONAL ESTATE, REAL ESTATE.

PROBATE,
    conclusive, how made against heir, 14, Appendix, 194
    must be obtained before judgment, 27

PROCEDURE. *See* ACCOUNT, ADMINISTRATION, CHAMBERS, INQUIRIES, SUMMONS, &c.

PROCEEDINGS,
    costs of persons attending, 92—95
    order of course to attend, 48

PROOF,
    of claims, 117—121. *See* CLAIMS.
        debts, 102—117. *See* CREDITOR, DEBTS.
        will, 13.

RATES,
    no priority for payment of, 172

REAL ESTATE,
    administration of, 7, 29, Appendix, 196, 197, 199
            not in single creditor's action, 9, 29
            not without administration of personalty, 29 (*n*)
    appointed, is liable to debts, 165
    apportionment of costs between, and personalty, 158
    assets for payment of debts, 167 (*k*)
    charged with debts, 164
    creditor, not administered at suit of single, 9, 29
    contribution by devisees of, 95 (*k*)
    costs of administration of, 158
    descended, liable to debts, 164, 167 (*k*)
            and aliened for value, 166
    devised, liable to debts, 164, 167 (*k*)
            in trust for payment of debts, 164
            is specific, though residuary, as against legatees, 157, 165
    equitable assets, 167 (*k*)
    Indian, is personal assets, 164 (*o*)
    inquiry as to, and incumbrances, Appendix, 196, 197, 199
    mortgaged, sale of, 154, 196 (*c*)
    order of liability of, for payment of debts, 164
            payment of debts out of, 163
    parties in administration of, 7, 29, 39
    rents of, account of, not ordered at the hearing, 196 (*d*)
    residuary devise of, is specific, 157, 165

Q

REAL ESTATE—*continued.*
  sale of, by consent of mortgagee, 196 (*o*)
    conditional order for, in creditors' action, 196
    conduct of, 124
    in District Registry, 191
    ordered on summons, when, 7
    under judgment or order, 95
  specifically devised, how far liable to debts, 165
  summons to administer, when applicable, 7
  who may sue for administration of, 7, 29. *See* PARTIES.
  And *see* ASSETS, CREDITORS' ACTION.

RECEIVER,
  appointed before legal personal representative constituted, 32
  claim for, 8
  not appointed, when administrator *ad litem* appointed by Probate Division, 34
  when appointed against executor, 58

RECOVERY OF LAND,
  what claim may be joined in action for, 29 (*r*)

REDEMPTION,
  of mortgage at creditor's valuation, 171

REFUNDING,
  when ordered for payment of debts, 116, 119

REGISTRATION,
  of judgment, priority secured by, 163

RELEASE,
  question of, cannot be tried in summons action, 5

RENT, RENTS,
  account of, not directed until deficiency shown, 196 (*d*),
  debt for, has no priority, 162, 172
  distress for, whether allowed where estate insolvent, 172

REPRESENTATION,
  of *cestuis que trustent* by trustee, 40, 43
    class by one or more members, 44
    persons interested in personalty by executor, 42

REPRESENTATIVE,
  appointment of one to represent a class, 44
  dispensed with, 39
  And *see* ADMINISTRATOR, EXECUTOR, PERSONAL REPRESENTATIVE.

RESIDUARY LEGATEE,
  administration at suit of, 1, 21
  costs of, 139
  refunding by, 116, 120

INDEX. 227

RESIDUE,
  costs payable out of, 130, 156
  debts payable out of, 164
  of real estate, devise of, is specific, 157, 165

RETAINER
  of his debt by executor or administrator, right of, 55, 156, 163, 166
    by heir or devisee, whether any, 167 (k)

REVOCATION *[handwritten annotation]*

RULES AND ORDERS,
  BANKRUPTCY RULES, 1870
    r. 77 : 173
    rr. 78—81, 101 : 171
    r. 136 : 172

  CHANCERY FUNDS RULES, 1874
    r. 10 : 133
    rr. 36, 61—67 : 68

  CONSOLIDATED ORDERS OF THE HIGH COURT OF JUSTICE, 1860
    Ord. VII. (Persons under disability)
      r. 1 : 13, Appendix, 194
      r. 5 : 45
      r. 6 : 49
      r. 7 : 49
    Ord. XXI. (Setting down and hearing)
      r. 10 : 128, 129
    Ord. XXIII. (Judgments and orders)
      rr. 2, 9 : 181
      r. 14 : 51
      r. 18 : 49
      r. 19 : 46
      r. 20 : 47, Appendix, 195
    Ord. XXXV. (Proceedings in Chambers)
      rr. 7—9 : 3
      r. 13 : 96
      r. 15 : 86
      r. 16 : 87, 93
      r. 18 : 45
      r. 19 : 52, 53
      r. 20 : 94
      r. 22 : 86, 123
      r. 23 : 124
      rr. 26—28 : 90
      r. 29 : 91
      r. 30 : 92
      rr. 33, 34 : 90
      rr. 35, 36 : 103
      rr. 37, 38 : 118
      r. 39 : 103, 118
      r. 40 : 105, 118
      r. 41 : 118

RULES AND ORDERS—*continued.*
  CONSOLIDATED ORDERS OF THE HIGH COURT OF JUSTICE, 1860
    Ord. XXXV. (Proceedings in Chambers)
        rr. 43, 44 : 119
        r. 45 : 100
        rr. 46, 48 : 97
        rr. 49, 50 : 88, 100
        rr. 51, 52 : 98, 100
        rr. 53, 54 : 100
        r. 55 : 98
        r. 56 : 100
    Ord. XXXVII. (Time)
        r. 10 : 49
    Ord. XL. (Costs)
        rr. 24, 25 : 111
    Ord. XLII. (Miscellaneous)
        rr. 9, 10 : 110
        r. 11 : 119
    Sched. K., No. II. : Appendix, 193
    Sched. L. : Appendix, 201
    Ord., May 27, 1865 : 102—105, 112, 113, 118, 133

  COUNTY COURT RULES, 1875
    Ord. II., r. 14 : 181
    Ord. XX. : 188
    Ord. XXIX. : 189
        r. 4 : 190

  REGISTRARS' NOTICE, 1877 : 19—21

  REGISTRARS' REGULATIONS, 1860 : 129

  REGULATIONS, August 8, 1857 : 45, 86, 96

  RULES OF THE SUPREME COURT, 1875
    Ord. I. (Commencement of Action)
        r. 1 : 8
    Ord. II. (Writ of Summons)
        r. 1 : 8
    Ord. III. (Indorsements of Claim)
        r. 2 : 8
        r. 4 : 9
        r. 8 : 8, 22
    Ord. V. (Issue of Writ of Summons)
        rr. 4, 4a : 8
    Ord. IX. (Service of Writ of Summons)
        rr. 4, 5 : 45
    Ord. XI. (Service out of the Jurisdiction) : 6
        rr. 1, 1a : 36
    Ord. XII. (Appearance)
        r. 4 : 190
    Ord. XIII. (Default of Appearance)
        r. 9 : 22

INDEX. 229

RULES AND ORDERS—*continued*
  RULES OF THE SUPREME COURT, 1875
    Ord. XV. (Application for Account) : 8, 23
      r. 1 : 22, 191
      r. 2 : 22
    Ord. XVI. (Parties)
      r. 7 : 43
      rr. 9, 9a : 44
      r. 12 : 41
      r. 12a : 45
      r. 12b : 93
      r. 17 : 116
    Ord. XVII. (Joinder of Causes of Action)
      r. 2 : 29
    Ord. XXIX. (Default of Pleading)
      r. 10 : 19
      r. 11 : 20
    Ord. XXXIII. (Inquiries and Accounts) : 23, 52
    Ord. XXXV. (District Registries)
      rr. 1, 4, 11—13 : 191
    Ord. XL. (Motion for Judgment)
      r. 1 : 21
      r. 11 : 18, 66, 68
    Ord. L. (Change of Parties)
      r. 4 : 46
    Ord. LI. (Transfers and Consolidation)
      rr. 1, 3 : 77
      r. 2a : 84
      r. 4 : 79
    Ord. LII. (Interlocutory Orders)
      r. 6a : 124
    Ord. LIII. (Motions)
      r. 4 : 19, 20
    Ord. LVIII. (Appeals)
      r. 15 : 88
      r. 19 : 188
    App. A. II., s. 1 : 9
  Add. Rules, 12 August, 1875
    Ord. VI., 1 : 135
  Add. Rules, 1875 (Costs)
    r. 21 : 95
  Orders of Court, 1877
    r. 1 : 189

SALE,
  of real estate in administration action, 95
              auction, by, in general, 96
              authority of Court, to order, 95 (*k*)
              conduct of, 124
              devised, how prevented, 95 (*k*)
              in District Registry, 191
              mortgaged, how obtained, 196 (*e*)
              when directed, 95 (*k*), Appendix, 196

SALE—*continued.*
powers of, controlled by Court after judgment, 58
summons action when executors have, 7

SECURED CREDITOR,
rights of, when estate insolvent, 169—172

SECURING ASSETS,
by payment into Court, 60—68

SECURITY
for costs, 113
repayment by legatees unusual, 182

SEPARATE ACCOUNT,
fund carried to, 180

SERVICE,
dispensing with, 45
entry of memorandum of, 46
of administration summons, 3
copy of judgment, 47
notice of judgment, 40—49
binds persons served, 47
out of the jurisdiction, 6, 36, 47
substituted, 45
upon infants, lunatics, and married women, 44, 45
And *see* NOTICE.

SET-OFF,
costs or debt, of, against legacy, 145
mutual credits, of, when estate insolvent, 81, 173

SHORT CAUSE,
further consideration, on, 129
setting down, 12, 20

SIMPLE CONTRACT DEBTS,
order of payment of, 161

SOLICITOR,
and client, when costs paid as between, 149, 151, 153, 155
costs of, when executor or trustee, 147
nomination of one, by Judge, to represent a class, 94

SPECIALTY DEBT,
priority of, none under present law, 161. And *see* DEBTS.

SPECIFIC
bequests, no account of, ordered in beneficiary's action, 51 (*g*)
and devises, order in which resorted to for costs, 157
debts, 164, 165
devise, residuary, is, 157, 165

STATEMENT OF CLAIM,
copy to be left at chambers, 86
when necessary, 21

INDEX. 231

STATUTES, TABLE OF,
  5 Geo. 2, c. 7 (Land in Colonies), s. 4 : 164
  36 Geo. 3, c. 52 (Legacy Duty), 68
  37 Geo. 3, c. 135 (Legacy Duty), 68
  38 Geo. 3, c. 87 (Executors), ss. 1—3 : 37
  9 Geo. 4, c. 33 (Land in India) : 164
  3 & 4 Will. 4, c. 27 (Limitation of Actions), s. 42 : 119, 173
  —— —— c. 104 (Real Estate made Assets) : 13, 167
  —— —— c. 108 (Dower Act) : 177
  4 & 5 Will. 4, c. 82 (Repealed by 42 & 43 Vict. c. 59) : 6
  13 & 14 Vict. c. 35 (Turner's Act),
          s. 19 : 4
          s. 28 : 132
  15 & 16 Vict. c. 80 (Masters in Chancery Abolition),
          s. 26 : 126
          s. 30 : 91
          s. 33 : 88
          s. 34 : 98
  15 & 16 Vict. c. 86 (Chancery Procedure Act, 1852),
          s. 42, r. 1 : 24 ; rr. 2, 3 : 29 ; r. 6 : 26 ; r. 8 : 40, 44,
              47, 48, 49 ; r. 9 : 40, 43
          s. 44 : 34
          s. 45 : 1, Appendix, 193
          s. 46 : 3
          s. 47 : 7, Appendix, 193
          s. 52 : 46
          s. 54 : 75
          s. 55 : 95
          s. 57 : 182
  16 & 17 Vict. c. 51 (Succession Duty Act), s. 53 : 181
  17 & 18 Vict. c. 113 (Locke-King's Act), 174, 175
  19 & 20 Vict. c. 108 (County Courts), s. 21 : 185
  20 & 21 Vict. c. 77 (Probate Act),
          s. 64 : 14, Appendix, 194
          s. 74 : 37
          ss. 81—83 : 26
  20 & 21 Vict. c. 85 (Divorce Court Act), ss. 21, 25, 26 : 37
  22 & 23 Vict. c. 35 (Lord St. Leonards' Act), ss. 27—32 : 4, 37, 102
  23 & 24 Vict. c. 38 (Lord St. Leonards' Act, 1860), s. 14 : 4
  25 & 26 Vict. c. 89 (Companies Act, 1862),
          s. 75 : 161
          s. 105 : 25
  28 & 29 Vict. c. 99 (County Courts Equitable Jurisdiction),
          s. 1 : 80, 184
          s. 3 : 185
          s. 9 : 187
          ss. 18, 19 : 188
  30 & 31 Vict. c. 69 (Locke-King's Act Amendment), 174, 175
  30 & 31 Vict. c. 142 (County Courts),
          ss. 5, 8 : 187
          s. 14 : 186
          s. 31 : 172
          s. 80 (9) : 169

STATUTES, TABLE OF—*continued*.
  32 & 33 Vict. c. 46 (Assets) : 56, 141, 161
        s. 12 : 171
        s. 16 (5) : 169
  32 & 33 Vict. c. 71 (Bankruptcy Act, 1869),
        ss. 31—40 : 163, 171
        s. 87 : 169
  35 & 36 Vict. c. 44 (Chancery Funds Act, 1872), ss. 14, 15 : 68
  36 & 37 Vict. c. 66 (Judicature Act, 1873),
        s. 16 (1) : 1
        s. 24 (5) : 80
        s. 25 (2) : 165
        s. 25 (6) : 31
        s. 34 (2) : 188
        s. 34 (3) : 1, 8, 22
        s. 45 : 188, 189
        s. 49 : 140, 149
        s. 66 : 190
        s. 90 : 186
        s. 91 : 162
        s. 95 : 188
  37 & 38 Vict. c. 57 (Limitation of Actions) : 109
        ss. 8, 10 : 119, 165
  38 & 39 Vict. c. 50 (County Courts), s. 6 : 189, 190
  ———— c. 77 (Judicature Act, 1875), s. 10 : 56, 107, 111, 161, 162,
        168, 172, 178
  40 & 41 Vict. c. 34 (Locke-King's Act Amendment) : 174, 175
  44 & 45 Vict. c. 68 (Judicature Act, 1881), s. 2 : 1
  45 & 46 Vict. c. 75 (Married Women's Property Act, 1882), 167
        s. 1 (2) : 45
        ss. 2, 5, 12 : 31

STAYING DISTRIBUTION OF FUNDS,
  for benefit of creditors after certificate, 114
  pending an appeal, 183

STAYING PROCEEDINGS, 69—85
  after administration judgment, 69
        foreign judgment, 79
  concurrent actions (*quod vide*), 69—77
  consolidation with a view to, 72
  costs, 75
  executor, against, 80
  foreign Courts, in, 79, 82
  High Court, in, not now by Chancery Division, 80
        not in, may still be stayed by Chancery Division, 82
  Palatine Court, in, 72
  upon whose application, 69
  when plaintiff's title gone, 48
  which action will be stayed, 70

INDEX. 233

SUMMONS,
    for administration, under 15 & 16 Vict. c. 86,
                                      personal estate, 1
                                      real estate, 7
    form of, Appendix, 193
    in what cases applicable, 2—7
    parties to, 1, 7
    usual order only will be made, 2, 5

TAXES
    no priority for, 172

TESTAMENTARY EXPENSES, 159

TIME
    for appeal from Chambers, 89
    appearance to administration summons, 3
    applications to vary certificate, 98
    claims in Chambers, 112
    signature of certificate by Judge. 98, 100
    taking Judge's opinion on certificate, 88

TRANSFER,
    from Chancery Division to Queen's Bench Division, 50 (*b*)
    County Court to High Court, 185
    one branch of Chancery Division to another, 77
    Queen's Bench Division to Chancery Division, 84
    High Court to County Court, 185, 187
    District Registry to London, 192
    when transfer and when dismissal the proper course, 186
  And *see* PAYMENT INTO COURT, STAYING PROCEEDINGS.

TRUST,
    breach of, executor made liable for, on further consideration, 16, 17, 132
    of co-executor, liability for, 65
    not chargeable in summons action, 5
    for payment of debts and legacies, 164 (*u*)

TRUSTEE,
    appeal for costs by, 149
    breach of trust by, not chargeable in summons action, 5
    costs charges and expenses, right to, 149
    costs of suit, entitled to, in priority to all other parties, 151
                    when deprived of, 141
    disclaiming, costs of, 152
    discretion of, when controlled by Court, after administration judgment, 54
                                                generally, 57
                                                not before judgment, 56, 58
    heir, when regarded as, 151
    severing in defence, costs of, 147
    And *see* EXECUTOR.

TURNER'S (SIR G.) ACT (13 & 14 Vict. c. 35), 4, 132

VOLUNTARY
  assignment of debt, whether now sufficient to support creditors' action, 3
  bond or covenant, whether postponed to other debts, 107, 161 (*b*), 173
  covenant sufficient to support creditors' action, 25

WAGES,
  no priority for payment of, 172

WIFE. *See FEME COVERT.*

WILFUL DEFAULT,
  account for, not ordered on summons, 5
    on further consideration, when ordered, 16, 17, 132
    only on special case made, 15—18

WILL,
  evidence of, what, 13, 14

WITNESS,
  in Chambers, 91
  refusing to answer, 92

WRIT FOR ADMINISTRATION,
  indorsement on, 8, 9, 22
  title of, 8

THE END.

BRADBURY, AGNEW, & CO., PRINTERS, WHITEFRIARS.

A CATALOGUE

OF

LAW WORKS

PUBLISHED AND SOLD BY

STEVENS & HAYNES,

Law Publishers, Booksellers & Exporters,

13, BELL YARD, TEMPLE BAR,

LONDON.

BOOKS BOUND IN THE BEST BINDINGS.

Works in all Classes of Literature supplied to Order.

FOREIGN BOOKS IMPORTED.

LIBRARIES VALUED FOR PROBATE, PARTNERSHIP, AND OTHER PURPOSES.

LIBRARIES OR SMALL COLLECTIONS OF BOOKS PURCHASED.

A large Stock of Reports of the various Courts of England, Ireland, and Scotland, always on hand.

Catalogues and Estimates Furnished, and Orders Promptly Executed.

NOTE.—*To avoid confusing our firm with any of a similar name, we beg to notify that we have no connexion whatever with any other house of business, and we respectfully request that Correspondents will take special care to direct all communications to the above names and address.*

INDEX OF SUBJECTS.

ADMINISTRATORS—
  Walker 6
ADMIRALTY LAW—
  Jones 14
  Kay 17
  Smith 23
ARTICLED CLERKS—
  See STUDENTS.
ARTIZANS AND LABOURERS'
  DWELLINGS—Lloyd 13
ASSAULTS—
  See MAGISTERIAL LAW.
BALLOT ACT—
  Bushby 33
BANKRUPTCY—
  Baldwin 15
  Ringwood 15
BAR EXAMINATION JOURNAL 39
BIBLIOGRAPHY 40
BILLS OF LADING—
  Campbell 9
  Kay 17
BILLS OF SALE—
  Baldwin 15
  Indermaur 28
  Ringwood 15
BIRTHS AND DEATHS REGISTRATION—
  Flaxman 43
BUILDING LEASES AND CONTRACTS—
  Emden 8
CAPACITY—
  See PRIVATE INTERNATIONAL LAW.
CAPITAL PUNISHMENT—
  Copinger 42
CARRIERS—
  See RAILWAY LAW.
  ,, SHIPMASTERS.
CHANCERY DIVISION, Practice of—
  Brown's Edition of Snell . . . 22
  Griffith and Loveland 6
  Indermaur 25
  Williams 7
  And *See* EQUITY.
CHARITABLE TRUSTS—
  Cooke 10
  Whiteford 20
CHURCH AND CLERGY—
  Brice 9
CIVIL LAW—*See* ROMAN LAW.
CODES—Argles 32
COLLISIONS AT SEA—Kay . . 17
COLONIAL LAW—
  Canada 18
  Cape Colony 38
  Forsyth 14
  New Zealand Jurist 18
  New Zealand Statutes 18
  Tarring 41

COMMERCIAL AGENCY—
  Campbell 9
COMMON LAW—
  Indermaur 24
COMMON PLEAS DIVISION, Practice of—
  Griffith and Loveland 6
COMPANIES LAW—
  Brice 16
  Buckley 17
  Reilly's Reports 29
  Smith 39
  Watts 47
  See MAGISTERIAL LAW.
COMPENSATION—
  Browne 19
  Lloyd 13
COMPULSORY PURCHASE—
  Browne 19
CONSTABLES—
  See POLICE GUIDE.
CONSTITUTIONAL LAW AND HISTORY—
  Forsyth 14
  Taswell-Langmead 21
  Thomas 28
CONTRACTS—
  Kay 17
CONVEYANCING—
  Copinger, Title Deeds 45
  Copinger, Precedents in . . . 40
  Deane, Principles of 23
  Williams 7
COPYRIGHT—
  Copinger 45
CORPORATIONS—
  Brice 16
  Browne 19
COSTS, Crown Office—
  Short 41
COVENANTS FOR TITLE—
  Copinger 45
CREW OF A SHIP—
  Kay 17
CRIMINAL LAW—
  Copinger 42
  Harris 27
  See MAGISTERIAL LAW.
CROWN LAW—
  Forsyth 14
  Hall 30
  Kelyng 35
  Taswell-Langmead 21
  Thomas 28
CROWN PRACTICE—
  Corner 10
CUSTOM AND USAGE—
  Browne 19
  Mayne 38
CUSTOMS—
  See MAGISTERIAL LAW.

INDEX OF SUBJECTS—continued.

	PAGE		PAGE
DAMAGES—		GAME LAWS—Locke	32
Mayne	31	See MAGISTERIAL LAW.	
DICTIONARIES—		HACKNEY CARRIAGES—	
Brown	26	See MAGISTERIAL LAW.	
DIGESTS—		HINDU LAW—	
Law Magazine Quarterly Digest	37	Coghlan	28
Menzies' Digest of Cape Reports	38	Cunningham	38 and 42
DISCOVERY—		Mayne	38
Griffith's Judicature Acts	6	Michell	44
DISTRICT REGISTRIES—		HISTORY—	
Simmons	6	Braithwaite	18
DIVORCE—Harrison	23	Taswell-Langmead	21
DOMICIL—		HYPOTHECATION—	
See PRIVATE INTERNATIONAL LAW.		Kay	17
DUTCH LAW	38	INDEX TO PRECEDENTS—	
ECCLESIASTICAL LAW—		Copinger	40
Brice	9	INFANTS—	
Smith	23	Simpson	43
EDUCATION ACTS—		INJUNCTIONS—	
See MAGISTERIAL LAW.		Joyce	11
ELECTION LAW and PETITIONS—		INSTITUTE OF THE LAW—	
Bushby	33	Brown's Law Dictionary	26
Hardcastle	33	INTERNATIONAL LAW—	
O'Malley and Hardcastle	33	Clarke	44
Seager	47	Foote	36
EQUITY—		Law Magazine	37
Choyce Cases	35	INTERROGATORIES AND DISCOVERY—	
Pemberton	32	Griffith and Loveland's Edition of the Judicature Acts	6
Snell	22		
Williams	7	INTOXICATING LIQUORS—	
EVIDENCE—		See MAGISTERIAL LAW.	
See USAGES AND CUSTOMS.		JOINT STOCK COMPANIES—	
EXAMINATION OF STUDENTS—		See COMPANIES.	
Bar Examination Journal	39	JUDICATURE ACTS—	
Indermaur	24 and 25	Cunningham and Mattinson	7
EXECUTORS—		Griffith	6
Walker	6	Indermaur	25
EXCHEQUER DIVISION, Practice of—		Kelke	6
Griffith and Loveland	6	JURISPRUDENCE—Forsyth	14
EXTRADITION—		JUSTINIAN'S INSTITUTES—	
Clarke	44	Campbell	47
See MAGISTERIAL LAW.		Harris	20
FACTORIES—		LANDS CLAUSES CONSOLIDATION ACT—	
See MAGISTERIAL LAW.			
FISHERIES—		Lloyd	13
See MAGISTERIAL LAW.		LAND, IMPROVEMENT OF, by Buildings—	
FIXTURES—			
Brown	33	Emden	8
FOREIGN LAW		LATIN MAXIMS	28
Argles	32	LAW DICTIONARY—	
Dutch Law	38	Brown	26
Foote	36	LAW MAGAZINE and REVIEW	37
Harris	47	LEADING CASES—	
FORGERY—		Common Law	25
See MAGISTERIAL LAW.		Constitutional Law	28
FRAUDULENT CONVEYANCES—		Equity and Conveyancing	25
May	29	Hindu Law	28
GAIUS INSTITUTES—		LEADING STATUTES—	
Harris	20	Thomas	28

B 2

INDEX OF SUBJECTS—*continued.*

	PAGE
LEASES—	
Copinger	45
LEGACY AND SUCCESSION—	
Hanson	10
LEGITIMACY AND MARRIAGE—	
See PRIVATE INTERNATIONAL LAW.	
LICENSES—	
See MAGISTERIAL LAW.	
LIFE ASSURANCE—	
Buckley	17
Reilly	29
LIMITATION OF ACTIONS—	
Banning	42
LIQUIDATION with CREDITORS—	
Baldwin	15
Ringwood	15
And *see* BANKRUPTCY.	
LLOYD'S BONDS	14
LUNACY—	
Williams	7
MAGISTERIAL LAW—	
Greenwood and Martin	46
MALICIOUS INJURIES—	
See MAGISTERIAL LAW.	
MARRIAGE and LEGITIMACY—	
Foote	36
MARRIED WOMEN'S PROPERTY ACTS—	
Bromfield's Edition of Griffith	40
MASTER AND SERVANT—	
See SHIPMASTERS & SEAMEN.	
MASTERS AND SERVANTS—	
See MAGISTERIAL LAW.	
MERCANTILE LAW	32
Campbell	9
See SHIPMASTERS and SEAMEN.	
,, STOPPAGE IN TRANSITU.	
MERCHANDISE MARKS—	
Daniel	42
MINES—	
Harris	47
See MAGISTERIAL LAW.	
MORTMAIN—	
See CHARITABLE TRUSTS.	
NATIONALITY—	
See PRIVATE INTERNATIONAL LAW.	
NEGLIGENCE—	
Campbell	40
NEW ZEALAND—	
Jurist Journal and Reports	18
Statutes	18
OBLIGATIONS—	
Brown's Savigny	20
PARLIAMENT—	
Taswell-Langmead	21
Thomas	28

	PAGE
PARLIAMENTARY PRACTICE—	
Browne	19
PARTITION—	
Walker	43
PASSENGERS—	
See MAGISTERIAL LAW.	
,, RAILWAY LAW.	
PASSENGERS AT SEA—	
Kay	17
PATENT CASES—	
Higgins	12
PAWNBROKERS—	
See MAGISTERIAL LAW.	
PERSONATION AND IDENTITY—	
Moriarty	14
PETITIONS IN CHANCERY AND LUNACY—	
Williams	7
PILOTS—	
Kay	17
POLICE GUIDE—	
Greenwood and Martin	46
POLLUTION OF RIVERS—	
Higgins	30
PRACTICE BOOKS—	
Bankruptcy	15
Companies Law	29 and 39
Compensation	13
Compulsory Purchase	19
Conveyancing	45
Damages	31
Ecclesiastical Law	9
Election Petitions	33
Equity	7, 22 and 32
High Court of Justice	6 and 25
Injunctions	11
Judicature Acts	6 and 25
Magisterial	46
Pleading, Precedents of	7
Privy Council	44
Railways	14
Railway Commission	19
Rating	19
Supreme Court of Judicature	6 and 25
PRECEDENTS OF PLEADING—	
Cunningham and Mattinson	7
PRIMOGENITURE—	
Lloyd	13
PRINCIPLES—	
Brice (Corporations)	16
Browne (Rating)	19
Deane (Conveyancing)	23
Harris (Criminal Law)	27
Houston (Mercantile)	32
Indermaur (Common Law)	24
Joyce (Injunctions)	11
Ringwood (Bankruptcy)	15
Snell (Equity)	22

INDEX OF SUBJECTS—continued.

	PAGE
PRIORITY—	
Robinson	32
PRIVATE INTERNATIONAL LAW—	
Foote	36
PRIVY COUNCIL—	
Michell	44
PROBATE—	
Hanson	10
Harrison	23
PROMOTERS—	
Watts	47
PUBLIC WORSHIP	
Brice	9
QUARTER SESSIONS—	
Smith (F. J.)	6
QUEEN'S BENCH DIVISION, Practice of—	
Griffith and Loveland	6
Indermaur	25
QUESTIONS FOR STUDENTS—	
Aldred	21
Bar Examination Journal	39
Indermaur	25
Waite	22
RAILWAYS -	
Browne	19
Godefroi and Shortt	14
Goodeve	29
See MAGISTERIAL LAW.	
RATING—	
Browne	19
REAL PROPERTY—	
Deane	23
Tarring	26
REGISTRATION—	
Flaxman (Births and Deaths)	43
Seager (Parliamentary)	47
REMINISCENCE—	
Braithwaite	18
REPORTS—	
Bellewe	34
Brooke	35
Choyce Cases	35
Cooke	35
Cunningham	34
Election Petitions	33
Finlason	32
Gibbs, Seymour Will Case	10
Kelyng, John	35
Kelynge, William	33
Reilly	29
Shower (Cases in Parliament)	34
ROMAN DUTCH LAW—	
Van Leeuwen	38
ROMAN LAW—	
Brown's Analysis of Savigny	20
Campbell	47
Harris	20

	PAGE
SALVAGE—	
Jones	14
Kay	17
SANITARY ACTS—	
See MAGISTERIAL LAW.	
SEA SHORE—	
Hall	30
SHIPMASTERS AND SEAMEN—	
Kay	17
SOCIETIES—	
See CORPORATIONS.	
STAGE CARRIAGES—	
See MAGISTERIAL LAW.	
STAMP DUTIES -	
Copinger	40 and 45
STATUTE OF LIMITATIONS—	
Banning	42
STATUTES—	
Hardcastle	9
New Zealand	18
Thomas	28
STOPPAGE IN TRANSITU—	
Campbell	9
Houston	32
Kay	17
STUDENTS' BOOKS	20—28, 39, 47
SUCCESSION DUTIES—	
Hanson	10
SUCCESSION LAWS	
Lloyd	13
SUPREME COURT OF JUDICATURE, Practice of—	
Cunningham and Mattinson	7
Griffith and Loveland	6
Indermaur	25
TELEGRAPHS—	
See MAGISTERIAL LAW.	
TITLE DEEDS—	
Copinger	45
TOWNS IMPROVEMENTS-	
See MAGISTERIAL LAW.	
TRADE MARKS—	
Daniel	42
TREASON—	
Kelyng	35
Taswell-Langmead	21
TRIALS—Queen *v.* Gurney	32
ULTRA VIRES—	
Brice	16
USAGES AND CUSTOMS—	
Browne	19
Mayne	38
VOLUNTARY CONVEYANCES—	
May	29
WATER COURSES—	
Higgins	30
WILLS, CONSTRUCTION OF—	
Gibbs, Report of Wallace *v.* Attorney-General	10

In Royal 12mo, price 20s., cloth,

QUARTER SESSIONS PRACTICE,

A Vade Mecum

OF GENERAL PRACTICE IN APPELLATE AND CIVIL CASES
AT QUARTER SESSIONS.

By FREDERICK JAMES SMITH,

OF THE MIDDLE TEMPLE, BARRISTER-AT-LAW, AND RECORDER OF MARGATE.

"Mr. Smith's book will, we are sure, be found to afford much assistance to the magistrates forming the Court, and to those who practice before them."—*Law Magazine.*

"This book will, we think, obtain a high place amongst the books which deal with this branch of the law."—*Law Journal.*

In one volume, 8vo, price 21s., cloth,

A COMPENDIUM OF THE LAW RELATING TO EXECUTORS AND ADMINISTRATORS, With an Appendix of

Statutes, Annotated by means of References to the Text. By W. GREGORY WALKER, B.A., of Lincoln's Inn, Barrister-at-Law, Author of "The Partition Acts, 1868 and 1876; A Manual of the Law of Partition and of Sale in Lieu of Partition," &c.

"We highly approve of Mr. Walker's arrangement. . . . The Notes are full, and as far as we have been able to ascertain, carefully and accurately compiled. . . . We can commend it as bearing on its face evidence of skilful and careful labour, and we anticipate that it will be found a very acceptable substitute for the ponderous tomes of the much esteemed and valued Williams."—*Law Times.*

"Mr. Walker is fortunate in his choice of a subject, and the power of treating it succinctly, for the ponderous tomes of Williams, however satisfactory as an authority, are necessarily inconvenient for reference as well as expensive. . . . . . On the whole we are inclined to think the book a good and useful one."—*Law Journal.*

In one thick volume, 8vo, price 30s., cloth lettered,

THE SUPREME COURT OF JUDICATURE ACTS,

1873, 1875, and 1877; the Appellate Jurisdiction Act, 1876, and the Rules, Orders, and Costs thereunder; Edited with Notes, References, and a Copious Analytical Index. Second Edition. Embodying all the Reported Cases to Michaelmas Sittings, 1877, and a Time Table. BY WILLIAM DOWNES GRIFFITH, of the Inner Temple, Barrister-at-Law, and a Judge of County Courts; and RICHARD LOVELAND LOVELAND, of the Inner Temple, Barrister-at-Law, Editor of "Hall's Essay on the Rights of the Crown in the Seashore," &c.

In royal 12mo, price 4s., cloth,

A DIGEST OF THE LAW OF

PRACTICE UNDER THE JUDICATURE ACTS AND RULES,

AND THE CASES DECIDED IN THE CHANCERY AND COMMON LAW DIVISIONS
FROM NOVEMBER 1875, TO AUGUST 1880.

BY W. H. HASTINGS KELKE, M.A., Barrister-at-Law.

In royal 12mo, price 3s. 6d., cloth,

THE PRESENT PRACTICE IN

DISTRICT REGISTRIES OF THE COMMON LAW DIVISION

OF THE HIGH COURT OF JUSTICE.

BY FRANK SIMMONS.

In 8vo, price 6s., cloth,

THE NEW CONVEYANCING ACTS.
INCLUDING
THE CONVEYANCING AND LAW OF PROPERTY ACT, 1881, AND THE SOLICITORS REMUNERATION ACT, 1881.
WITH AN INTRODUCTION, NOTES, AND FORMS.
By SYDNEY E. WILLIAMS, of Lincoln's Inn, Barrister-at-Law,
Author of "Petitions in Chancery and Lunacy."

In one volume, 8vo, price 18s., cloth,
THE LAW AND PRACTICE RELATING TO
PETITIONS IN CHANCERY AND LUNACY,
INCLUDING
THE SETTLED ESTATES ACT, LANDS CLAUSES ACT, TRUSTEE ACT, WINDING-UP PETITIONS, PETITIONS RELATING TO SOLICITORS, INFANTS, ETC., ETC.
WITH AN APPENDIX OF FORMS AND PRECEDENTS.
By SYDNEY E. WILLIAMS, of Lincoln's Inn, Barrister-at-Law.

"Mr. Williams' arrangement of the procedure under his various headings, which include Payment out, Trustee Relief Act, Lands Clauses Act, Settled Estates Act, and many other subjects of jurisdiction which have from time to time been conferred on the Court of Chancery or the Lunacy jurisdiction by special statutes, is very convenient. The chapter on the Lands Clauses Act is especially good."—*Law Times*.

"The book is furnished with a selection of Forms and Precedents; the arrangement of matter seems convenient; and we have found it easy to consult. We have not observed any important omission within the scope of the Treatise, and the writer deserves the praise of having put together with some skill an unpretending work, which is at least more useful than certain larger law books we know of."—*Solicitors' Journal*.

In 8vo, price 28s., cloth,
A SELECTION OF PRECEDENTS OF PLEADING
UNDER THE JUDICATURE ACTS IN THE COMMON LAW DIVISIONS.
With Notes explanatory of the different Causes of Action and Grounds of Defence: and an Introductory Treatise on the Present Rules and Principles of Pleading as illustrated by the various Decisions down to the Present Time.

By JOHN CUNNINGHAM, of the Middle Temple, Barrister-at-Law,
Author of the "Law Relating to Parliamentary and Municipal Elections;" and
MILES WALKER MATTINSON, of Gray's Inn, Barrister-at-Law.

REVIEWS.

"The notes are very pertinent and satisfactory: the introductory chapters on the present system of pleading are excellent, and the precedents will be found very useful."—*Irish Law Times*.

"For pupils, also, and beginners at the bar, the book will be very useful; because these, never having served an apprenticeship to the old system, are very apt to omit allegations, essential in certain cases to the validity of a pleading. The authors of the book before us have introduced their collection of forms to the reader by an essay on pleading under the new rules; and we think that a perusal of this essay, which is written in an attractive style, would do a great deal of good both to barristers and masters. . . . We think that the authors have deserved well of the profession, and that they have produced a book likely to grow in favour even among those who at first might conceive a prejudice against a work of this kind."—*Law Journal*.

"A work which, in the compass of a single portable volume, contains a brief Treatise on the Principles and Rules of Pleading, and a carefully annotated body of Forms which have to a great extent gone through the entirely separate sifting processes of Chambers, Court, and Judges' Chambers, cannot fail to be a most useful companion in the Practitioner's daily routine."—*Law Magazine and Review*.

The work contains a treatise on the new rules of pleading which is well written, but would bear compression. To most of the precedents there are notes referring to the decisions which are most useful to the pleader in connection with the particular cause of action involved. We are disposed to think that this is the most valuable portion of the work. It is extremely convenient to have some work which collects notes of this sort in connection with pleading."—*Solicitors' Journal*.

In royal 12mo, price 20s., cloth.

EMDEN'S LAW RELATING TO

BUILDING LEASES & BUILDING CONTRACTS,

THE IMPROVEMENT OF LAND BY, AND THE CONSTRUCTION OF, BUILDINGS.

WITH A FULL COLLECTION OF **PRECEDENTS** OF ARRANGEMENTS FOR BUILDING LEASES, BUILDING LEASES, CONTRACTS FOR BUILDING, BUILDING GRANTS, MORTGAGES, AND OTHER FORMS WITH RESPECT TO MATTERS CONNECTED WITH BUILDING.

TOGETHER WITH THE

STATUTES RELATING TO BUILDING,

WITH NOTES AND THE LATEST CASES UNDER THE VARIOUS SECTIONS.

And a Glossary of Architectural and Building Terms.

By ALFRED EMDEN,

OF THE INNER TEMPLE, ESQ., BARRISTER-AT-LAW.

"The present treatise of Mr. Emden deals with the subject in an exhaustive manner, which leaves nothing to be desired."—*The Times.*

"It is obvious that the number of persons interested in the subject of building is no small one. To supply the wants of this class by providing a treatise devoted exclusively to the law of building and kindred matters has been accordingly the main object of Mr. Emden's labours. We are able on the whole to say with confidence that his efforts deserve reward. His arrangement of the subject is clear and perspicuous. . . . . It may be said without hesitation that they have been dealt with in a manner which merits high commendation."—*Law Times.*

"This is a careful digest of a branch of the law which, so far as we know, has not yet been fully treated. . . . . The book seems to us a very complete and satisfactory manual, alike for the lawyer as for the architect and the builder."—*Solicitors' Journal.*

"Mr. Emden has obviously given time and labour to his task, and therefore will save time and labour to those who happen to be occupied in the same field of enquiry."—*Law Journal.*

"In this work Mr. Emden has collected and systematically arranged a mass of legal lore relating to Building Leases, Building Contracts, and generally to the improvement of land by buildings and their construction. The lawyer, the architect, and the contractor will here find brought into a focus and readily available, information which would, but for this convenient volume, have to be sought for in various quarters."—*Law Magazine.*

"It may safely be recommended as a practical text-book and guide to all people whose fortune or misfortune it is to be interested in the construction of buildings and other works."—*Saturday Review.*

"In such cases it is serviceable to possess a book like Mr. Emden's on 'the Law of Building Leases, Building Contracts, and Buildings.' The subjects, it is needless to say, are difficult, but the exposition of them is sufficiently plain to be comprehended by every intelligent layman. Mr. Emden's book is incomparably the best among those which are professedly intended for the use of architects, builders, agents, as well as lawyers . . . . . throughout the pages there is not a paragraph to be discovered which is not perfectly clear."—*The Architect.*

"Mr. Emden's very useful handbook, which supplies a desideratum long felt by lawyers, architects, and others engaged in preparing leases, contracts, and in building operations generally. The work is well printed, and marginal references are given throughout."—*Building News.*

"To supply this want is the writer's object in publishing this work, and we have no hesitation [in expressing our opinion that it will be found valuable by several distinct classes of persons . . . . it seems to us a good and useful book, and we recommend the purchase of it without hesitation."—*The Builder.*

"We are aware of no other work which deals exclusively with the law relating to buildings and contracts to build. Mr. Emden writes in an unusually clear style for the compiler of a law book, and has not failed to note the latest decisions in the law courts. His list of precedents is very full."—*The Field.*

"From the point of view of practical utility the work cannot fail to be of the greatest use to all who require a little law in the course of their building operations. They will find both a sound arrangement and a clear sensible style, and by perusing it with ordinary attention many matters of which they were before doubtful will become quite comprehensible."—*City Press.*

Now ready, royal 12mo, price 2s. 6d., cloth.

EMDEN'S METROPOLIS MANAGEMENT AND BUILDINGS ACTS (AMENDMENT) ACT, 1882.

With Notes to the Sections, and an Index. Forming a Supplement to the "Law Relating to Building Leases, Building Contracts," &c. By ALFRED EMDEN, of the Inner Temple, Barrister-at-Law.

"There is a copious index to the work, and the architect and surveyor who require to be well informed up to present date in the Statute Law will obtain this Supplement to Mr. Emden's valuable handbook."—*Building News.*

In one volume, royal 8vo, price 30s., cloth,

THE LAW RELATING TO THE
SALE OF GOODS AND COMMERCIAL AGENCY.
By ROBERT CAMPBELL, M.A.,
OF LINCOLN'S INN, BARRISTER-AT-LAW; ADVOCATE OF THE SCOTCH BAR;
AUTHOR OF THE "LAW OF NEGLIGENCE," ETC.

"His book will, we are convinced, prove of great service as a thoughtful and clear exposition of a branch of law of practical interest, not only to the legal profession, but also to the merchant, the shipper, the underwriter and the broker, and to the mercantile community in general. The Table of Contents is analytical and remarkably full; being, in fact, almost an Index within an Index."—*Law Magazine.*
"Notwithstanding the existence of the works referred to by the author in his preface, he has produced a treatise which cannot fail to be of utility to practising lawyers, and to increase his own reputation."—*Law Times.*

In one volume, 8vo, 1879, price 20s., cloth,

A TREATISE ON THE RULES WHICH GOVERN
THE CONSTRUCTION AND EFFECT OF STATUTORY LAW.
WITH AN APPENDIX
OF CERTAIN WORDS AND EXPRESSIONS USED IN STATUTES, WHICH HAVE BEEN JUDICIALLY OR STATUTABLY CONSTRUED.

By HENRY HARDCASTLE,
OF THE INNER TEMPLE, BARRISTER-AT-LAW;
EDITOR OF "BUSHBY'S ELECTION LAW," "HARDCASTLE'S ELECTION PETITIONS," AND JOINT-EDITOR OF "ELECTION PETITION REPORTS."

"We should be doing less than justice, however, to the usefulness of Mr. Hardcastle's book if we did not point out a valuable special feature, consisting of an appendix devoted to the collection of a list of words which have been judicially or statutably explained, with reference to the cases in which they are so explained. We believe this is a feature peculiar to Mr. Hardcastle's Treatise, and it is one which cannot fail to commend itself to the profession."—*Law Magazine and Review.*
"A vast amount of information will be found in its pages—much of it arranged so as to be got at without much difficulty; the chapters and sections being headed with lines of indication. We can only hope Mr. Hardcastle will receive that measure of success to which the amount of labour which he has evidently bestowed upon the work entitles him."—*Law Times.*
"Its method and object are excellent, and it appears to be the fruit of much careful study."—*Daily News.*

In one volume, 8vo, price 28s., cloth,

THE LAW RELATING TO PUBLIC WORSHIP;
WITH SPECIAL REFERENCE TO

𝔐atters of 𝔑itual and 𝔒rnamentation,

AND THE MEANS OF SECURING THE DUE OBSERVANCE THEREOF,

AND CONTAINING IN EXTENSO,

WITH NOTES AND REFERENCES,
THE PUBLIC WORSHIP REGULATION ACT, 1874; THE CHURCH DISCIPLINE ACT; THE VARIOUS ACTS OF UNIFORMITY; THE LITURGIES OF 1549, 1552, AND 1559,
COMPARED WITH
THE PRESENT RUBRIC; THE CANONS; THE ARTICLES; AND THE INJUNCTIONS, ADVERTISEMENTS, & OTHER ORIGINAL DOCUMENTS OF LEGAL AUTHORITY.

By SEWARD BRICE, LL.D.,
OF THE INNER TEMPLE, BARRISTER-AT-LAW.

"*To the vast number of people who in various ways are interested in the working of the Act, Mr. Brice's volume cannot fail to be welcome. It is well conceived and carefully executed.*"—THE TIMES.

Now ready, in 8vo, price 6s. 6d., cloth.

THE CUSTOMS AND INLAND REVENUE ACTS,
1880 and 1881
(43 Vict. Cap. 14, and 44 Vict. Cap. 12.)

So far as they Relate to the Probate, Legacy, and Succession Duties, and the Duties on Accounts. With an Introduction and Notes. By ALFRED HANSON, Esq., Comptroller of Legacy and Succession Duties.

** This forms a Supplement to the Third Edition of the Probate, Legacy, and Succession Duty Acts, by the same Author.

Third Edition, in 8vo, 1876, price 25s., cloth.

THE ACTS RELATING TO PROBATE, LEGACY, AND SUCCESSION DUTIES.
Comprising the 36 Geo. III. c. 52 ; 45 Geo. III. c. 28 ; 55 Geo. III. c. 184; and 16 & 17 Vict. c. 51 : with an Introduction, Copious Notes, and References to all the Decided Cases in England, Scotland, and Ireland. An Appendix of Statutes, Tables, and a full Index. By ALFRED HANSON, of the Middle Temple, Esq., Barrister-at-Law, Comptroller of Legacy and Succession Duties. Third Edition. Incorporating the Cases to Michaelmas Sittings, 1876.

" It is the only complete book upon a subject of great importance.
" Mr. Hanson is peculiarly qualified to be the adviser at such a time. Hence a volume without a rival."—*Law Times.*
" His book is in itself a most useful one; its author knows every in and out of the subject, and has presented the whole in a form easily and readily handled, and with good arrangement and clear exposition."—*Solicitors' Journal.*

In royal 8vo, 1877, price 10s., cloth,

LES HOSPICES DE PARIS ET DE LONDRES.

THE CASE OF LORD HENRY SEYMOUR'S WILL
(WALLACE v. THE ATTORNEY-GENERAL).
Reported by FREDERICK WAYMOUTH GIBBS, C.B., Barrister-at-Law,
LATE FELLOW OF TRINITY COLLEGE, CAMBRIDGE.

In preparation, and to be published shortly,

CORNER'S CROWN PRACTICE :
Being the Practice of the Crown Side of the Queen's Bench Division of the High Court of Justice; with an Appendix of Rules, Forms, Scale of Costs and Allowances, &c.
SECOND EDITION.
By FREDERICK H. SHORT, of the Crown Office, and M. D. CHALMERS,
OF THE INNER TEMPLE, BARRISTER-AT-LAW, AUTHOR OF "DIGEST OF THE LAW OF BILLS OF EXCHANGE."

In 8vo, 1867, price 16s., cloth,

CHARITABLE TRUSTS ACTS, 1853, 1855, 1860;
THE CHARITY COMMISSIONERS JURISDICTION ACT, 1862;
THE ROMAN CATHOLIC CHARITIES ACTS:

Together with a Collection of Statutes relating to or affecting Charities, including the Mortmain Acts, Notes of Cases from 1853 to the present time, Forms of Declarations of Trust, Conditions of Sale, and Conveyance of Charity Land, and a very copious Index. Second Edition.

By HUGH COOKE and R. G. HARWOOD, of the Charity Commission.

"Charities are so numerous, so many persons are directly or indirectly interested in them, they are so much abused, and there is such a growing desire to rectify those abuses and to call in the aid of the commissioners for a more beneficial application of their funds, and we are not surprised to receive a second edition of a collection of all the statutes that regulate them, admirably annotated by two such competent editors as Messrs. Cooke and Harwood, whose official experience peculiarly qualifies them for the task."—*Law Times.*

In one volume, royal 8vo, 1877, price 30s., cloth,

THE DOCTRINES & PRINCIPLES OF THE LAW OF INJUNCTIONS.

By WILLIAM JOYCE,
OF LINCOLN'S INN, BARRISTER-AT-LAW.

"Mr. Joyce, whose learned and exhaustive work on 'The Law and Practice of Injunctions,' has gained such a deservedly high reputation in the Profession, now brings out a valuable companion volume on the 'Doctrines and Principles' of this important branch of the Law. In the present work the Law is enunciated in its abstract rather than its concrete form, as few cases as possible being cited; while at the same time no statement of a principle is made unsupported by a decision, and for the most part the very language of the Courts has been adhered to. Written as it is by so acknowledged a master of his subject, and with the conscientious carefulness that might be expected from him, this work cannot fail to prove of the greatest assistance alike to the Student—who wants to grasp principles freed from their superincumbent details—and to the practitioner, who wants to refresh his memory on points of doctrine amidst the oppressive details of professional work."—*Law Magazine and Review.*

BY THE SAME AUTHOR.

In two volumes, royal 8vo, 1872, price 70s., cloth,

THE LAW & PRACTICE OF INJUNCTIONS.

EMBRACING

ALL THE SUBJECTS IN WHICH COURTS OF EQUITY AND COMMON LAW HAVE JURISDICTION.

By WILLIAM JOYCE,
OF LINCOLN'S INN, BARRISTER-AT-LAW.

REVIEWS.

"A work which aims at being so absolutely complete, as that of Mr. Joyce upon a subject which is of almost perpetual recurrence in the Courts, cannot fail to be a welcome offering to the profession, and, doubtless, it will be well received and largely used, for it is as absolutely complete as it aims at being. . . . . This work is, therefore, eminently a work for the practitioner, being full of practical utility in every page, and every sentence, of it. . . . . We have to congratulate the profession on this new acquisition to a digest of the law, and the author on his production of a work of permanent utility and fame."—*Law Magazine and Review.*

"Mr. Joyce has produced not a treatise but a complete and compendious *exposition* of the Law and Practice of Injunctions both in equity and common law.

"Part III. is devoted to the practice of the Courts. *Contains an amount of valuable and technical matter nowhere else collected.*

"From these remarks it will be sufficiently perceived what elaborate and painstaking industry, as well as legal knowledge and ability, has been necessary in the compilation of Mr. Joyce's work. No labour has been spared to save the practitioner labour, and no research has been omitted which could tend towards the elucidation and exemplification of the general principles of the Law and Practice of Injunctions."—*Law Journal.*

"He does not attempt to go an inch beyond that for which he has express written authority; he allows the cases to speak, and does not speak for them.

"The work is something more than a treatise on the Law of Injunctions. It gives us the general law on almost every subject to which the process of injunction is applicable. Not only English, but American decisions are cited, the aggregate number being 3,500, and the statutes cited 160, whilst the index is, we think, the most elaborate we have ever seen—occupying nearly 200 pages. The work is probably entirely exhaustive."—*Law Times.*

"This work, considered either as to its matter or manner of execution, is no ordinary work. It is a complete and exhaustive treatise both as to the law and the practice of granting injunctions. It must supersede all other works on the subject. The terse statement of the practice will be found of incalculable value. We know of no book as suitable to supply a knowledge of the law of injunctions to our common law friends as Mr. Joyce's exhaustive work. It is alike indispensable to members of the Common Law and Equity Bars. Mr Joyce's great work would be a casket without a key unless accompanied by a good index. His index is very full and well arranged. We feel that this work is destined to take its place as a standard text-book, and *the* text-book on the particular subject of which it treats. The author deserves great credit for the very great labour bestowed upon it. The publishers, as usual, have acquitted themselves in a manner deserving of the high reputation they bear."—*Canada Law Journal.*

HIGGINS'S DIGEST OF PATENT CASES.

Price 21s.,

A DIGEST OF THE REPORTED CASES

RELATING TO THE

LAW AND PRACTICE OF LETTERS PATENT FOR INVENTIONS,

Decided from the passing of the Statute of Monopolies to the present time;

Together with an Appendix, giving the Reported Cases from June, 1875, to March, 1880, as also some Cases not reported elsewhere.

By CLEMENT HIGGINS, M.A., F.C.S.,

OF THE INNER TEMPLE, BARRISTER-AT-LAW.

"Mr. Higgins s work will be useful as a work of reference. Upwards of 700 cases are digested : and, besides a table of contents, there is a full index to the subject-matter ; and that index, which greatly enhances the value of the book, must have cost the author much time, labour and thought."—*Law Journal.*

"'This is essentially,' says Mr. Higgins in his preface, 'a book of reference.' It remains to be added whether the compilation is reliable and exhaustive. It is only fair to say that we think it is; and we will add, that the arrangement of subject-matter (chronological under each heading, the date, and double or even treble references being appended to every decision) and the neat and carefully-executed index (which is decidedly above the average), are such as no reader of 'essentially a book of reference' could quarrel with."—*Solicitors' Journal.*

"On the whole Mr. Higgins's work has been well accomplished. It has ably fulfilled its object by supplying a reliable and authentic summary of the reported patent law cases decided in English courts of law and equity, while presenting a complete history of legal doctrine on the points of law and practice relating to its subject."—*Irish Law Times.*

"Mr. Higgins has, with wonderful and accurate research, produced a work which is much needed, since we have no collection of patent cases which does not terminate years ago. We consider, too, if an inventor furnishes himself with this Digest and a little treatise on the law of patents, he will be able to be as much his own patent lawyer as it is safe to be."—*Scientific and Literary Review.*

"Mr. Higgins's object has been to supply a reliable and exhaustive summary of the reported patent cases decided in English courts of law and equity, and this object he appears to have attained. The classification is excellent, being as Mr. Higgins very truly remarks, that which naturally suggests itself from the practical working of patent law rights. The lucid style in which Mr. Higgins has written his Digest will not fail to recommend it to all who may consult his book ; and the very copious index, together with the table of cases, will render the work especially valuable to professional men."—*Mining Journal.*

"The appearance of Mr. Higgins's Digest is exceedingly opportune. The plan of the work is definite and simple. We consider that Mr. Higgins, in the production of this work, has met a long-felt demand. Not merely the legal profession and patent agents, but patentees, actual or intending inventors, manufacturers, and their scientific advisers will find the Digest an invaluable book of reference."—*Chemical News.*

"The arrangement and condensation of the main principles and facts of the cases here digested render the work invaluable in the way of reference."—*Standard.*

"The work constitutes a step in the right direction, and it is likely to prove of much service as a guide, a by no means immaterial point in its favour being that it includes a number of comparatively recent cases."—*Engineer.*

"From these decisions the state of the law upon any point connected with patents may be deduced. In fine, we must pronounce the book as invaluable to all whom it may concern."—*Quarterly Journal of Science.*

In 8vo, price 6s., sewed,

A DIGEST OF THE REPORTED CASES

RELATING TO THE

LAW AND PRACTICE OF LETTERS PATENT FOR INVENTIONS

DECIDED BETWEEN JUNE, 1875, AND MARCH, 1880:

TOGETHER WITH SOME UNREPORTED CASES

FORMING

AN APPENDIX TO DIGEST OF PATENT CASES.

By CLEMENT HIGGINS,

BARRISTER-AT-LAW.

In 8vo, price 25s., cloth,

THE LAW OF COMPENSATION FOR LANDS, HOUSES, &c.

UNDER THE LANDS CLAUSES, RAILWAY CLAUSES CONSOLIDATION AND METROPOLITAN ACTS,

THE ARTIZANS AND LABOURERS' DWELLINGS IMPROVEMENT ACT 1875.

WITH A FULL COLLECTION OF FORMS AND PRECEDENTS.

FIFTH EDITION, ENLARGED, WITH ADDITIONAL FORMS, INCLUDING PRECEDENTS OF BILLS OF COSTS.

By EYRE LLOYD,

OF THE INNER TEMPLE, BARRISTER-AT-LAW.

"The work is eminently a practical one, and is of great value to practitioners who have to deal with compensation cases."—*Solicitors' Journal*.

"*A fourth edition of Mr. Lloyd's valuable treatise has just been published. Few branches of the law affect so many and such important interests as that which gives to private individuals compensation for property compulsorily taken for the purpose of public improvements. The questions which arise under the different Acts of Parliament now in force are very numerous and difficult, and a collection of decided cases epitomised and well arranged, as they are in Mr. Lloyd's work, cannot fail to be a welcome addition to the library of all who are interested in landed property, whether as owners, land agents, public officers or solicitors.*"—MIDLAND COUNTIES HERALD.

"It is with much gratification that we have to express our unhesitating opinion that Mr. Lloyd's treatise will prove thoroughly satisfactory to the profession, and to the public at large. Thoroughly satisfactory it appears to us in every point of view—comprehensive in its scope, exhaustive in its treatment, sound in its exposition."—*Irish Law Times*.

"In providing the legal profession with a book which contains the decisions of the Courts of Law and Equity upon the various statutes relating to the Law of Compensation, Mr. Eyre Lloyd has long since left all competitors in the distance,' and his book may now be received as the standard work upon the subject. The plan of Mr. Lloyd's book is generally known, and its lucidity is appreciated; the present quite fulfils all the promises of the preceding editions, and contains in addition to other matter a complete set of forms under the Artizans and Labourers Act, 1875, and specimens of Bills of Costs, which will be found a novel feature, extremely useful to legal practitioners."—JUSTICE OF THE PEACE.

"The work is one of great value. It deals with a complicated and difficult branch of the law, and it deals with it exhaustively. It is not merely a compilation or collection of the statutes bearing on the subject, with occasional notes and references. Rather it may be described as a comprehensive treatise on, and digest of, the law relating to the compulsory acquisition and purchase of land by public companies and municipal and other local authorities, and the different modes of assessment of the compensation. All the statutes bearing on the subject have been collated, all the law on the subject collected, and the decisions conveniently arranged. With this comprehensiveness of scope is united a clear statement of principles, and practical handling of the points which are likely to be contested, and especially of those in which the decisions are opposed or differently understood."—*Local Government Chronicle*.

In 8vo, price 7s., cloth,

THE SUCCESSION LAWS OF CHRISTIAN COUNTRIES,

WITH SPECIAL REFERENCE TO

THE LAW OF PRIMOGENITURE AS IT EXISTS IN ENGLAND.

By EYRE LLOYD, B.A.,

OF THE INNER TEMPLE, BARRISTER-AT-LAW; AUTHOR OF "THE LAW OF COMPENSATION UNDER THE LANDS CLAUSES CONSOLIDATION ACTS," ETC.

"Mr. Lloyd has given us a very useful and compendious little digest of the laws of succession which exist at the present day in the principal States of both Europe and America; and we should say it is a book which not only every lawyer, but every politician and statesman, would do well to add to his library."—*Pall Mall Gazette*.

"Mr. Eyre Lloyd compresses into little more than eighty pages a considerable amount of matter both valuable and interesting; and his quotations from Diplomatic Reports by the present Lord Lytton, and other distinguished public servants, throw a picturesque light on a narrative much of which is necessarily dry reading. We can confidently recommend Mr. Eyre Lloyd's new work as one of great practical utility, if, indeed, it be not unique in our language, as a book of reference on Foreign Succession Laws."—*Law Magazine and Review*.

"Mr. Eyre Lloyd has composed a useful and interesting abstract of the laws on the subject of succession to property in Christian countries, with special reference to the law of primogeniture in England."—*Saturday Review*.

"This is a very useful little handy book on foreign succession laws. It contains in an epitomised form information which would have to be sought through a great number of scattered authorities and foreign law treatises, and will be found of great value to the lawyer, the writer, and the political student."—*Standard*.

In one volume, royal 8vo, price 30s., cloth,

CASES AND OPINIONS ON CONSTITUTIONAL LAW,

AND VARIOUS POINTS OF ENGLISH JURISPRUDENCE.

Collected and Digested from Official Documents and other Sources; with Notes. By WILLIAM FORSYTH, M.A., M.P., Q.C., Standing Counsel to the Secretary of State in Council of India, Author of "Hortensius," "History of Trial by Jury," "Life of Cicero," etc., late Fellow of Trinity College, Cambridge.

From the CONTEMPORARY REVIEW.

"We cannot but regard with interest a book which, within moderate compass, presents us with the opinions or *responsa* of such lawyers and statesmen as Somers, Holt, Hardwicke, Mansfield, and, to come down to our own day, Lyndhurst, Abinger, Denman, Cranworth, Campbell, St. Leonards, Westbury, Chelmsford, Cockburn, Cairns, and the present Lord Chancellor Hatherley. At the end of each chapter of the 'Cases and opinions,' Mr. Forsyth has added notes of his own, containing a most excellent summary of all the law bearing on that branch of his subject to which the 'Opinions' refer."

From the LAW MAGAZINE and LAW REVIEW.

"Mr. Forsyth has largely and beneficially added to our legal stores. His work may be regarded as in some sense a continuation of 'Chalmers's Opinions of Eminent Lawyers.' . . . The constitutional relations between England and her colonies are becoming every day of more importance. The work of Mr. Forsyth will do more to make these relations perfectly clear than any which has yet appeared. Henceforth it will be the standard work of reference in a variety of questions which are constantly presenting themselves for solution both here and in our colonies."

From the LAW TIMES.

"This one volume of 560 pages or thereabouts is a perfect storehouse of law not readily to be found elsewhere, and the more useful because it is not abstract law but the application of principles to particular cases. Mr. Forsyth's plan is that of classification. He collects in separate chapters a variety of opinions bearing upon separate branches of the law . . . This is a book to be read, and therefore we recommend it not to all lawyers only, but to every law student. The editor's own notes are not the least valuable portion of the volume."

In one thick volume, 8vo, price 32s., cloth,

THE LAW OF RAILWAY COMPANIES.

Comprising the Companies Clauses, the Lands Clauses, the Railways Clauses Consolidation Acts, the Railway Companies Act, 1867, and the Regulation of Railways Act, 1868; with Notes of Cases on all the Sections, brought down to the end of the year 1868; together with an Appendix giving all the other material Acts relating to Railways, and the Standing Orders of the Houses of Lords and Commons; and a copious Index. By HENRY GODEFROI, of Lincoln's Inn, and JOHN SHORTT, of the Middle Temple, Barristers-at-Law.

"The title of this book is the best possible explanation of its contents. Here we have all the statutes affecting Railway Companies, with the standing orders of Parliament, in a volume exquisitely printed, and of most convenient size and form. . . . We believe that we have said enough to show that this book will prove to be of pre-eminent value to practitioners, both before Parliamentary committees and in the Courts of Law and Equity."—*Law Journal.*

In 8vo, price 2s. 6d.,

MORIARTY ON PERSONATION AND DISPUTED IDENTITY

AND THEIR TESTS.

In a handy volume, crown 8vo, 1870, price 10s. 6d., cloth,

THE LAW OF SALVAGE,

As administered in the High Court of Admiralty and the County Courts; with the Principal Authorities, English and American, brought down to the present time; and an Appendix, containing Statutes, Forms, Table of Fees, etc. By EDWYN JONES, of Gray's Inn, Barrister-at-Law.

"This book will be of infinite service to lawyers practising in the maritime law courts and to those engaged in shipping. In short, Mr. Jones's book is a complete guide, and is full of information upon all phases of the subject, tersely and clearly written."—*Liverpool Journal of Commerce.*

In 8vo, 1867, price 1s., sewed,

LLOYD'S BONDS: THEIR NATURE AND USES.

By HENRY JEFFERD TARRANT, of the Middle Temple, Barrister-at-Law.

Second Edition, in 8vo, price 10s., cloth,

THE PRINCIPLES OF BANKRUPTCY.

WITH AN APPENDIX,

CONTAINING

THE GENERAL RULES OF 1870, 1871, 1873, & 1878, SCALE OF COSTS, AND THE BILLS OF SALE ACTS, 1878 & 1882, AND THE RULES OF DECEMBER 1882.

By RICHARD RINGWOOD, B.A.,

OF THE MIDDLE TEMPLE, ESQ., BARRISTER-AT-LAW; LATE SCHOLAR OF TRINITY COLLEGE, DUBLIN.

"This edition is a considerable improvement on the first, and although chiefly written for the use of Students, the work will be found useful to the practitioner."—*Law Times*.

"The author of this convenient handbook sees the point upon which we insist elsewhere in regard to the chief aim of any system of Bankruptcy Law which should deserve the title of National. . . . . There can be no question that a sound measure of Reform is greatly needed, and would be welcomed by all parties in the United Kingdom. Pending this amendment it is necessary to know the Law as it is, and those who have to deal with the subject in any of its practical legal aspects will do well to consult Mr. Ringwood's unpretending but useful volume."—*Law Magazine*.

"The above work is written by a distinguished scholar of Trinity College, Dublin. Mr. Ringwood has chosen a most difficult and unattractive subject, but he has shown sound judgment and skill in the manner in which he has executed his task. His book does not profess to be an exhaustive treatise on bankruptcy law, yet in a neat and compact volume we have a vast amount of well-digested matter. The reader is not distracted and puzzled by having a long list of cases flung at him at the end of each page, as the general effect of the law is stated in a few well-selected sentences, and a reference given to the leading decisions only on the subject. . . . An excellent index, and a table of cases, where references to four sets of contemporary reports may be seen at a glance, show, the industry and care with which the work has been done."—*Daily Paper*.

Third Edition, in royal 12mo, price 18s., cloth,

A CONCISE TREATISE UPON

THE LAW OF BANKRUPTCY.

WITH AN APPENDIX,

CONTAINING

The Bankruptcy Act, 1869; General Rules of 1870, 1871, 1873, & 1878;

Forms of 1870 and 1871; Scale of Costs; the Debtors Act, 1869; Debtors Act, 1878; and Bills of Sale Acts, 1878 and 1882.

By EDWARD T. BALDWIN, M.A.,

OF THE INNER TEMPLE, BARRISTER-AT-LAW.

"This is an excellent book . . . . It is an eminently practical treatise, and at once concise and exact . . . . We have no doubt that Mr. Baldwin's book will be found, alike as a guide and as a work of reference, most useful to both branches of the profession."—*Law Magazine*.

"This edition is a praiseworthy effort to reduce the Law of Bankruptcy within moderate limits. It refers to all the important cases on the Act of 1869, and concludes with an excellent Index."—*Law Times*.

"This treatise is certainly the most readable book on the subject, and so carefully is the text annotated, that it is perfectly reliable."—*Law Journal*.

THE LAW OF CORPORATIONS.

In one volume of One Thousand Pages, royal 8vo, price 42s., cloth,

A TREATISE ON THE DOCTRINE OF

ULTRA VIRES:

BEING

An Investigation of the Principles which Limit the Capacities, Powers, and Liabilities of

CORPORATIONS,

AND MORE ESPECIALLY OF

JOINT STOCK COMPANIES.

SECOND EDITION.

By SEWARD BRICE, M.A., LL.D. LONDON,

OF THE INNER TEMPLE, BARRISTER-AT-LAW.

REVIEWS.

"*Despite its unpromising and cabalistic title, and the technical nature of its subject, it has so recommended itself to the profession that a second edition is called for within three years from the first publication; and to this call Mr. Brice has responded with the present volume, the development of which in excess of its predecessor is remarkable even in the annals of law books. Sixteen hundred new cases have been introduced, and, instead of five hundred pages octavo, the treatise occupies a thousand very much larger pages. This increase in bulk is partly due to the incorporation with the English law on the subject of the more important American and Colonial doctrines and decisions—a course which we think Mr. Brice wise in adopting, since the judgments of American tribunals are constantly becoming more frequently quoted and more respectfully considered in our own courts, particularly on those novel and abstruse points of law for which it is difficult to find direct authority in English reports. In the present speculative times, anything relating to Joint-Stock Companies is of public importance, and the points on which the constitution and operation of these bodies are affected by the doctrine of Ultra Vires are just those which are most material to the interests of the shareholders and of the community at large. . . . . . . Some of the much disputed questions in regard to corporations, on which legal opinion is still divided, are particularly well treated. Thus with reference to the authority claimed by the Courts to restrain corporations or individuals from applying to Parliament for fresh powers in breach of their express agreements or in derogation of private rights, Mr. Brice most elaborately and ably reviews the conflicting decisions on this apparent interference with the rights of the subject, which threatened at one time to bring the Legislature and the Courts into a collision similar to that which followed on the well-known case of Ashby v. White. . . . Another very difficult point on which Mr. Brice's book affords full and valuable information is as to the liability of Companies on contracts entered into before their formation by the promoters, and subsequently ratified or adopted by the Company, and as to the claims of promoters themselves for services rendered to the inchoate Company. . . . The chapter on the liabilities of corporations ex delicto for fraud and other torts committed by their agents within the region of their authority seems to us remarkably well done, reviewing as it does all the latest and somewhat contradictory decisions on the point. . . . On the whole we consider Mr. Brice's exhaustive work a valuable addition to the literature of the profession.*"—SATURDAY REVIEW.

"The doctrine which forms the subject of Mr. Seward Brice's elaborate and exhaustive work is a remarkable instance of rapid growth in modern Jurisprudence. His book, indeed, now almost constitutes a Digest of the Law of Great Britain and her Colonies and of the United States on the Law of Corporations—a subject vast enough at home, but even more so beyond the Atlantic, where Corporations are so numerous and powerful. Mr. Seward Brice relates that he has embodied a reference in the present edition to about 1600 new cases, and expresses the hope that he has at least referred to 'the chief cases.' We should think there can be few, even of the Foreign Judgments and Dicta, which have not found their way into his pages. The question what is and what is not Ultra Vires is one of very great importance in commercial countries like Great Britain and the United States. Mr. Seward Brice has done a great service to the cause of Comparative Jurisprudence by his new recension of what was from the first a unique text-book on the Law of Corporations. He has gone far towards effecting a Digest of that Law in its relation to the Doctrine of Ultra Vires, and the second edition of his most careful and comprehensive work may be commended with equal confidence to the English, the American, and the Colonial Practitioner, as well as to the scientific Jurist."—*Law Magazine and Review.*

"It is the Law of Corporations that Mr. Brice treats of (and treats of more fully, and at the same time more scientifically, than any work with which we are acquainted), not the law of principal and agent; and Mr. Brice does not do his book justice by giving it so vague a title."—*Law Journal.*

"A guide of very great value. Much information on a difficult and unattractive subject has been collected and arranged in a manner which will be of great assistance to the seeker after the law on a point involving the powers of a company."—*Law Journal.* (Review of First Edition.)

"On this doctrine, first introduced in the Common Law Courts in *East Anglian Railway Co.* v. *Eastern Counties Railway Co.*, BRICE ON ULTRA VIRES may be read with advantage."—*Judgment of* LORD JUSTICE BRAMWELL, *in the Case of Evershed* v. *L. & N. W. Ry. Co.* (L. R., 3 Q. B. Div. 141.)

Now Ready, Fourth Edition, in royal 8vo, price 32s. cloth,

BUCKLEY ON THE COMPANIES ACTS.

FOURTH EDITION BY THE AUTHOR.

THE LAW AND PRACTICE UNDER THE COMPANIES ACTS, 1862 TO 1880,

THE JOINT STOCK COMPANIES ARRANGEMENT ACT, 1870,

AND

THE LIFE ASSURANCE COMPANIES ACTS, 1870 TO 1872.

A Treatise on the Law of Joint Stock Companies.

Containing the Statutes, with the Rules, Orders, and Forms, regulating Proceedings in the Chancery Division of the High Court of Justice By H. BURTON BUCKLEY, M.A., of Lincoln's Inn, Barrister-at-Law, late Fellow of Christ's College, Cambridge.

"We have no doubt that the present edition of this useful and thorough work will meet with as much acceptance as its predecessors have."—*Scottish Journal of Jurisprudence.*

"The mere arrangement of the leading cases under the successive sections of the Acts, and the short explanation of their effect, are of great use in saving much valuable time, which would be otherwise spent in searching the different digests; but the careful manner in which Mr. Buckley has annotated the Acts, and placed the cases referred to under distinct headings, renders his work particularly useful to all who are required to advise in the complications in which the shareholders and creditors of companies frequently find themselves involved. . . . . The Index, always an important part of a law book, is full and well arranged."—*Scottish Journal of Jurisprudence.*

In two volumes, royal 8vo, 70s. cloth,

THE LAW RELATING TO

SHIPMASTERS AND SEAMEN.

THEIR APPOINTMENT, DUTIES, POWERS, RIGHTS, LIABILITIES, AND REMEDIES.

By JOSEPH KAY, Esq., M.A., Q.C.,

OF TRIN. COLL. CAMBRIDGE, AND OF THE NORTHERN CIRCUIT;

SOLICITOR-GENERAL OF THE COUNTY PALATINE OF DURHAM; ONE OF THE JUDGES OF THE COURT OF RECORD FOR THE HUNDRED OF SALFORD;

AND AUTHOR OF "THE SOCIAL CONDITION AND EDUCATION OF THE PEOPLE IN ENGLAND AND EUROPE."

REVIEWS OF THE WORK.

From the **NAUTICAL MAGAZINE**, July, 1875.

"It is rarely that we find a book fulfilling the requirements of both classes—full and precise enough for the lawyer, and at the same time intelligible to the non-legal understanding. *Yet the two volumes by Mr. Kay on the law relating to shipmasters and seamen will, we venture to say, be of equal service to the captain, the lawyer, and the Consul, in their respective capacities*, and even of interest to the public generally, written as it is in a clear and interesting style, and treating of a subject of such vast importance as the rights and liabilities and relative duties of all, passengers included, who venture upon the ocean ; more than that, we think that any able-seaman might read that chapter on the crew with the certainty of acquiring a clearer notion of his own position on board ship.

"We can make no charge of redundancy or omission against our author : but if we were called upon to select any one out of the fifteen parts into which the two volumes are divided as being especially valuable, we should not hesitate to choose that numbered three, and entitled 'The Voyage.'

There the master will find a succinct and compendious statement of the law respecting his duties general and particular, with regard to the ship and its freight from the moment when, on taking command, he is bound to look to the seaworthiness of the ship, and to the delivery of her log at the final port of destination. In Part IV. his duties are considered with respect to the cargo, this being a distinct side of his duplicate character, inasmuch as he is agent of the owner of the cargo just as much as the owner of the ship.

"Next in order of position come 'Bills of Lading' and 'Stoppage in Transitu.' We confess that on first perusal we were somewhat surprised to find the subject of the delivery of goods by the master given priority over that of bills of lading ; the logical sequence, however, of these matters was evidently sacrificed, and we think with advantage, to the author's desire for unity in his above-mentioned chapters on 'The Voyage.' That this is so is evidenced by the fact that after his seventh chapter with the heading of the former and a reference

THE LAW RELATING TO SHIPMASTERS AND SEAMEN.

REVIEWS OF THE WORK—*continued.*

ante, "The power of the master to bind the owner by his personal contracts,' 'Hypothecation,' and 'The Crew,' form the remainder of the contents of the first volume, of which we should be glad to have made more mention, but it is obviously impossible to criticize in detail a work in which the bare list of cited cases occupies forty-four pages.
"The question of compulsory pilotage is full of difficulties, which are well summed up by Mr. Kay.
"In conclusion, we can heartily congratulate Mr. Kay upon his success."

From the LIVERPOOL JOURNAL OF COMMERCE.

"'The law relating to Shipmasters and Seamen' such is the title of a voluminous and important work which has just been issued by Messrs. Stevens and Haynes, the eminent law publishers, of London. The author is Mr. Joseph Kay, Q.C., and while treating generally of the law relating to shipmasters and seamen, he refers more particularly to their appointment, duties, rights, liabilities, and remedies. It consists of two large volumes, the text occupying nearly twelve hundred pages, and the value of the work being enhanced by copious appendices and index, and by the quotation of a mass of authorities. . . . *The work must be an invaluable one to the shipowner, shipmaster, or consul* at a foreign port. The language is clear and simple, while the legal standing of the author is a sufficient guarantee that he writes with the requisite authority, and that the cases quoted by him are decisive as regards the points on which he touches."

From the LAW JOURNAL.

"The author tells us that for ten years he has been engaged upon it. . . . Two large volumes containing 1181 pages of text, 81 pages of appendices, 98 pages of index, and upwards of 1800 cited cases, attest the magnitude of the work designed and accomplished by Mr. Kay.
"Mr. Kay says that he has 'endeavoured to compile a guide and reference book for masters, ship agents, and consuls.' He has been so modest as not to add lawyers to the list of his pupils; but *his work will, we think, be welcomed by lawyers who have to do with shipping transactions, almost as cordially as it undoubtedly will be by those who occupy their business in the great waters.*"

In 8vo, price 1s.,

THE "SIX CLERKS IN CHANCERY;"

Their SUCCESSORS IN OFFICE, and the "HOUSES" they lived in.

A Reminiscence.

By THOMAS W. BRAITHWAITE, of the Record and Writ Clerks' Office.

"The removal of the Record and Writ Office to the new building has suggested the publication of an interesting and opportune little piece of legal history."—*Solicitors' Journal.*

---

2 vols. 4to, 1876—77. 5*l*. 5*s*. calf,

THE

PRACTICAL STATUTES OF NEW ZEALAND.

WITH NOTES AND INDEX.

EDITED BY G. B. BARTON, of the Middle Temple, Barrister-at-Law.

In royal 8vo, price 30*s*., half calf,

THE CONSTITUTION OF CANADA.

THE BRITISH NORTH AMERICA ACT, 1867;

ITS INTERPRETATION, GATHERED FROM THE DECISIONS OF COURTS, THE DICTA OF JUDGES, AND THE OPINIONS OF STATESMEN AND OTHERS;

To which is added the Quebec Resolutions of 1864, and the Constitution of the United States.

By JOSEPH DOUTRE, Q.C., of the Canadian Bar.

In one thick volume, 8vo, 1875, price 25s., cloth,

THE PRINCIPLES OF

THE LAW OF RATING OF HEREDITAMENTS
IN THE OCCUPATION OF COMPANIES.

By J. H. BALFOUR BROWNE,

OF THE MIDDLE TEMPLE, BARRISTER-AT-LAW, AND REGISTRAR TO THE RAILWAY COMMISSIONERS.

"The tables and specimen valuations which are printed in an appendix to this volume will be of great service to the parish authorities, and to the legal practitioners who may have to deal with the rating of those properties which are in the occupation of Companies, and we congratulate Mr. Browne on the production of a clear and concise book of the system of Company Rating. There is no doubt that such a work is much needed, and we are sure that all those who are interested in, or have to do with, public rating, will find it of great service. Much credit is therefore due to Mr. Browne for his able treatise—a work which his experience as Registrar of the Railway Commission peculiarly qualified him to undertake."—*Law Magazine.*

In 8vo, 1875, price 7s. 6d., cloth,

THE LAW OF USAGES & CUSTOMS:
A Practical Law Tract.

By J. H. BALFOUR BROWNE,

OF THE MIDDLE TEMPLE, BARRISTER-AT-LAW, AND REGISTRAR TO THE RAILWAY COMMISSIONERS.

"We look upon this treatise as a valuable addition to works written on the Science of Law."—*Canada Law Journal.*

"As a tract upon a very troublesome department of Law it is admirable—the principles laid down are sound, the illustrations are well chosen, and the decisions and *dicta* are harmonised so far as possible and distinguished when necessary."—*Irish Law Times.*

"As a book of reference we know of none so comprehensive dealing with this particular branch of Common Law. . . . In this way the book is invaluable to the practitioner."—*Law Magazine.*

In one volume, 8vo, 1875, price 18s., cloth,

THE PRACTICE BEFORE THE RAILWAY COMMISSIONERS
UNDER THE REGULATION OF RAILWAY ACTS, 1873 & 1874;

With the Amended General Orders of the Commissioners, Schedule of Forms, and Table of Fees : together with the Law of Undue Preference, the Law of the Jurisdiction of the Railway Commissioners, Notes of their Decisions and Orders, Precedents of Forms of Applications, Answers and Replies, and Appendices of Statutes and Cases.

By J. H. BALFOUR BROWNE,

OF THE MIDDLE TEMPLE, BARRISTER-AT-LAW, AND REGISTRAR TO THE RAILWAY COMMISSIONERS.

"Mr. Browne's book is handy and convenient in form, and well arranged for the purpose of reference ; its treatment of the subject is fully and carefully worked out : it is, so far as we have been able to test it, accurate and trustworthy. It is the work of a man of capable legal attainments, held by official position intimate with his subject ; and we therefore think that it cannot fail to meet a real want and to prove of service to the legal profession and the public."—*Law Magazine.*

In 8vo, 1876, price 7s. 6d., cloth,

ON THE COMPULSORY PURCHASE OF THE UNDERTAKINGS OF COMPANIES BY CORPORATIONS,

And the Practice in Relation to the Passage of Bills for Compulsory Purchase through Parliament. By J. H. BALFOUR BROWNE, of the Middle Temple, Barrister-at-Law ; Author of "The Law of Rating," "The Law of Usages and Customs," &c., &c.

"This is a work of considerable importance to all Municipal Corporations, and it is hardly too much to say that every member of these bodies should have a copy by him for constant reference. Probably at no very distant date the property of all the existing gas and water companies will pass under municipal control, and therefore it is exceedingly desirable that the principles and conditions under which such transfers ought to be made should be clearly understood. This task is made easy by the present volume. The stimulus for the publication of such a work was given by the action of the Parliamentary Committee which last session passed the preamble of the 'Stockton and Middlesborough Corporations Water Bill, 1876.' The volume accordingly contains a full report of the case as it was presented both by the promoters and opponents, and as this was the first time in which the principle of compulsory purchase was definitely recognised, there can be no doubt that it will long be regarded as a leading case. As a matter of course, many incidental points of interest arose during the progress of the case. Thus, besides the main question of compulsory purchase, and the question as to whether there was or was not any precedent for the Bill, the questions of water compensations, of appeals from one Committee to another, and other kindred subjects were discussed. These are all treated at length by the Author in the body of the work, which is thus a complete legal compendium on the large subject with which it so ably deals."

In 8vo, 1878, price 6s., cloth,
THE
LAW RELATING TO CHARITIES,
ESPECIALLY WITH REFERENCE TO THE VALIDITY AND CONSTRUCTION OF
CHARITABLE BEQUESTS AND CONVEYANCES.
By FERDINAND M. WHITEFORD, of Lincoln's Inn, Barrister-at-Law.

"The Law relating to Charities by F. M. Whiteford contains a brief but clear exposition of the law relating to a class of bequests in which the intentions of donors are often frustrated by unacquaintance with the statutory provisions on the subject. Decisions in reported cases occupy a large portion of the text, together with the explanations pertinent to them. The general tenor of Mr. Whiteford's work is that of a digest of Cases rather than a treatise, a feature, however, which will not diminish its usefulness for purposes of reference."—*Law Magazine and Review.*

In 8vo, 1872, price 7s. 6d., cloth,
AN EPITOME AND ANALYSIS OF
SAVIGNY'S TREATISE ON OBLIGATIONS IN ROMAN LAW.
By ARCHIBALD BROWN, M.A.
EDIN. AND OXON., AND B.C.L. OXON., OF THE MIDDLE TEMPLE, BARRISTER-AT-LAW.

"Mr. Archibald Brown deserves the thanks of all interested in the science of Law, whether as a study or a practice, for his edition of Herr von Savigny's great work on 'Obligations.' Mr. Brown has undertaken a double task—the translation of his author, and the analysis of his author's matter. That he has succeeded in reducing the bulk of the original will be seen at a glance; the French translation consisting of two volumes, with some five hundred pages apiece, as compared with Mr. Brown's thin volume of a hundred and fifty pages. At the same time the pith of Von Savigny's matter seems to be very successfully preserved, nothing which might be useful to the English reader being apparently omitted.
"The new edition of Savigny will, we hope, be extensively read and referred to by English lawyers. If it is not, it will not be the fault of the translator and epitomiser. Far less will it be the fault of Savigny himself, whose clear definitions and accurate tests are of great use to the legal practitioner."—*Law Journal.*

THE ELEMENTS OF ROMAN LAW.
In 216 pages 8vo, 1875, price 10s., cloth.
A CONCISE DIGEST OF THE
INSTITUTES OF GAIUS AND JUSTINIAN.
With copious References arranged in Parallel Columns, also Chronological and Analytical Tables, Lists of Laws, &c. &c.
Primarily designed for the Use of Students preparing for Examination at Oxford, Cambridge, and the Inns of Court.
By SEYMOUR F. HARRIS, B.C.L., M.A.,
OF WORCESTER COLLEGE, OXFORD, AND THE INNER TEMPLE, BARRISTER-AT-LAW
AUTHOR OF "UNIVERSITIES AND LEGAL EDUCATION."

"*Mr. Harris's digest ought to have very great success among law students both in the Inns of Court and the Universities. His book gives evidence of praiseworthy accuracy and laborious condensation.*"—LAW JOURNAL.

"*This book contains a summary in English of the elements of Roman Law as contained in the works of Gaius and Justinian, and is so arranged that the reader can at once see what are the opinions of either of these two writers on each point. From the very exact and accurate references to titles and sections given he can at once refer to the original writers. The concise manner in which Mr. Harris has arranged his digest will render it most useful, not only to the students for whom it was originally written, but also to those persons who, though they have not the time to wade through the larger treatises of Poste, Sanders, Ortolan, and others, yet desire to obtain some knowledge of Roman Law.*"—OXFORD AND CAMBRIDGE UNDERGRADUATES' JOURNAL.

"*Mr. Harris deserves the credit of having produced an epitome which will be of service to those numerous students who have no time or sufficient ability to analyse the Institutes for themselves.*"—LAW TIMES.

In Crown 8vo, price 3s.; or Interleaved for Notes, price 4s.

CONTRACT LAW.

QUESTIONS ON THE LAW OF CONTRACTS. WITH NOTES TO THE ANSWERS. *Founded on "Anson," "Chitty," and "Pollock."*

By PHILIP FOSTER ALDRED, D.C.L., Hertford College and Gray's Inn; late Examiner for the University of Oxford.

"This appears to us a very admirable selection of questions, comparing favourably with the average run of those set in examinations, and useful for the purpose of testing progress."—*Law Journal.*

For the Preliminary Examinations before Entering into Articles of Clerkship to Solicitors under the Solicitors Act, 1877.

In a handsome 4to volume, with Map of the World, price 10s., cloth,

THE STUDENTS' REMINDER & PUPILS' HELP
IN PREPARING FOR A PUBLIC EXAMINATION.

By THOMAS MARSH,
PRIVATE TUTOR, AUTHOR OF AN "ENGLISH GRAMMAR," &c.

"We welcome this compendium with great pleasure as being exactly what is wanted in this age of competitive examinations. It is evidently the work of a master hand, and could only be compiled by one thoroughly experienced in the work of teaching. Mr. Marsh has summarised and analysed the subjects required for the preliminary examinations of law students, as well as for the University and Civil Service examinations. He has paid special attention to mathematics, but the compendium also includes ancient and modern languages, geography, dictation, &c. It was a happy idea to make it quarto size, and the type and printing are clear and legible."—*Irish Law Times.*

Now ready, Second Edition, in 8vo, price 21s., cloth,

ENGLISH CONSTITUTIONAL HISTORY.

FROM THE TEUTONIC INVASION TO THE PRESENT TIME.

Designed as a Text-book for Students and others.

By T. P. TASWELL-LANGMEAD, B.C.L.,
OF LINCOLN'S INN, BARRISTER-AT-LAW, LATE TUTOR ON CONSTITUTIONAL LAW AND LEGAL HISTORY TO THE FOUR INNS OF COURT, AND FORMERLY VINERIAN SCHOLAR IN THE UNIVERSITY OF OXFORD.

Second and Enlarged Edition, revised throughout, and in many parts rewritten.

"The work before us it would be hardly possible to praise too highly. In style, arrangement, clearness, and size, it would be difficult to find anything better on the real history of England, the history of its constitutional growth as a complete story, than this volume."—*Boston (U.S.) Literary World.*

"As it now stands, we should find it hard to name a better text-book on English Constitutional History."—*Solicitors' Journal.*

"That the greatest care and labour have been bestowed upon it is apparent in every page, and we doubt not that it will become a standard work not likely soon to die out."—*Oxford and Cambridge Undergraduates' Journal.*

"As a text-book for the lecturer it is most valuable. It does not always observe a strict chronological sequence, but brings together all that has to be said on a given subject at the point when that subject happens to possess a special importance."—*Contemporary Review.*

"Mr. Taswell-Langmead's compendium of the rise and development of the English Constitution has evidently supplied a want. . . . The present Edition is greatly improved. . . . We have no hesitation in saying that it is a thoroughly good and useful work."—*Spectator.*

"We think Mr. Taswell-Langmead may be congratulated upon having compiled an elementary work of conspicuous merit."—*Pall Mall Gazette.*

"For students of history we do not know any work which we could more thoroughly recommend."—*Law Times.*

"It is a safe, careful, praiseworthy digest and manual of all constitutional history and law."—*Globe.*

"The volume on English Constitutional History, by Mr. Taswell-Langmead, is exactly what such a history should be."—*Standard.*

"As a text-book for students, we regard it as an exceptionally able and complete work."—*Law Journal.*

"Mr. Taswell-Langmead has thoroughly grasped the bearings of his subject. It is, however, in dealing with that chief subject of constitutional history—parliamentary government—that the work exhibits its great superiority over its rivals."—*Academy.*

Sixth Edition, in 8vo, 1882, price 25s., cloth,

THE PRINCIPLES OF EQUITY.

INTENDED FOR THE USE OF STUDENTS AND THE PROFESSION.

By EDMUND H. T. SNELL,
OF THE MIDDLE TEMPLE, BARRISTER-AT-LAW.

SIXTH EDITION.

TO WHICH IS ADDED

AN EPITOME OF THE EQUITY PRACTICE.

THIRD EDITION.

By ARCHIBALD BROWN, M.A., EDIN. & OXON., & B.C.L. OXON.,
OF THE MIDDLE TEMPLE, BARRISTER-AT-LAW; AUTHOR OF "A NEW LAW DICTIONARY,"
"AN ANALYSIS OF SAVIGNY ON OBLIGATIONS," AND THE "LAW OF FIXTURES."

REVIEWS.

"On the whole we are convinced that the Sixth Edition of Snell's Equity is destined to be as highly thought of as its predecessors, as it is, in our opinion, out and out the best work on the subject with which it deals."—*Gibson's Law Notes.*

"Rarely has a text-book attained more complete and rapid success than Snell's 'Principles of Equity,' of which a fifth edition has just been issued."—*Law Times.*

"Seldom does it happen that a work secures so great a reputation as this book, and to Mr. Brown is due the credit of keeping it up with the times. . . . . It is certainly the most comprehensive as well as the best work on Equity Jurisprudence in existence."—*Oxford and Cambridge Undergraduates' Journal.*

"The changes introduced by the Judicature Acts have been well and fully explained by the present edition of Mr. Snell's treatise, and everything necessary in the way of revision has been conscientiously accomplished. We perceive the fruitful impress of the 'amending hand' in every page; the results of the decisions under the new system have been carefully explained, and engrafted into the original text; and in a word, Snell's work, as edited by Mr. Brown, has proved the fallacy of Bentham's description of Equity as 'that capricious and inconsistent mistress of our fortunes, whose features no one is able to delineate.'"—*Irish Law Times.*

"*We know of no better introduction to the Principles of Equity.*"—CANADA LAW JOURNAL.

"Within the ten years which have elapsed since the appearance of the first edition of this work, its reputation has steadily increased, and it has long since been recognised by students, tutors, and practitioners, as the best elementary treatise on the important and difficult branch of the law which forms its subject."—*Law Magazine and Review.*

In Crown 8vo, price 2s. 6d., sewed.

QUESTIONS ON EQUITY.

FOR STUDENTS PREPARING FOR EXAMINATION,

FOUNDED ON

SNELL'S "PRINCIPLES OF EQUITY,"

By W. T. WAITE,
BARRISTER-AT-LAW, HOLT SCHOLAR OF THE HONOURABLE SOCIETY OF GRAY'S INN.

Second Edition, in one volume, 8vo, nearly Ready,

PRINCIPLES OF CONVEYANCING.

AN ELEMENTARY WORK FOR THE USE OF STUDENTS.

By HENRY C. DEANE,

OF LINCOLN'S INN, BARRISTER-AT-LAW, SOMETIME LECTURER TO THE INCORPORATED LAW SOCIETY OF THE UNITED KINGDOM.

"Mr. Deane is one of the Lecturers of the Incorporated Law Society, and in his elementary work intended for the use of students, he embodies some lectures given at the hall of that society. It would weary our readers to take them over the ground necessarily covered by Mr. Deane. The first part is devoted to Corporeal Hereditaments, and the second to Conveyancing. The latter is prefaced by a very interesting 'History of Conveyancing,' and for practical purposes the chapter (Ch. 2, Part II.) on Conditions of Sale is decidedly valuable."—*Law Times.*

"*We hope to see this book, like Snell's Equity, a standard class-book in all Law Schools where English law is taught.*"—CANADA LAW JOURNAL.

"It seems essentially the book for young conveyancers, and will, probably, in many cases supplant Williams. It is, in fact, a modern adaptation of Mr. Watkin's book on conveyancing, and is fully equal to its prototype."—*Irish Law Times.*

"Extremely useful to students, and especially to those gentlemen who are candidates for the various legal examinations. There are so many questions set now on case law that they would do well to peruse this treatise of Mr. Deane's, and use it in conjunction with a book of questions and answers. They will find a considerable amount of equity case law, especially in the second part of Mr. Deane's book, which comprises in substance some lectures delivered by the author at the Law Institution."—*Law Journal.*

Second Edition, in 8vo, price 10s. 6d., cloth,

A SUMMARY OF THE

LAW & PRACTICE IN ADMIRALTY.

FOR THE USE OF STUDENTS.

By EUSTACE SMITH,

OF THE INNER TEMPLE; AUTHOR OF "A SUMMARY OF COMPANY LAW."

"The book is well arranged, and forms a good introduction to the subject.—*Solicitor's Journal.*"
"It is however, in our opinion, a well and carefully written little work, and should be in the hands of every student who is taking up Admiralty Law at the Final."—*Law Students' Journal.*
"Mr. Smith has a happy knack of compressing a large amount of useful matter in a small compass. The present work will doubtless be received with satisfaction equal to that with which his previous 'Summary' has been met."—*Oxford and Cambridge Undergraduates' Journal.*

Second Edition, in 8vo, price 7s., cloth,

A SUMMARY OF THE

LAW AND PRACTICE IN THE ECCLESIASTICAL COURTS.

FOR THE USE OF STUDENTS.

By EUSTACE SMITH,

OF THE INNER TEMPLE; AUTHOR OF "A SUMMARY OF COMPANY LAW," AND "A SUMMARY OF THE LAW AND PRACTICE IN ADMIRALTY."

"His object has been, as he tells us in his preface, to give the student and general reader a fair outline of the scope and extent of ecclesiastical law, of the principles on which it is founded, of the Courts by which it is enforced, and the procedure by which these Courts are regulated. We think the book well fulfils its object. Its value is much enhanced by a profuse citation of authorities for the propositions contained in it."—*Bar Examination Journal.*

In 8vo, price 6s., cloth,

AN EPITOME OF THE LAWS OF PROBATE AND DIVORCE,

FOR THE USE OF STUDENTS FOR HONOURS EXAMINATION.

By J. CARTER HARRISON, SOLICITOR.

Third Edition. In one volume, 8vo, price 20s., cloth,

PRINCIPLES OF THE COMMON LAW.

INTENDED FOR THE USE OF STUDENTS AND THE PROFESSION.

SECOND EDITION.

By JOHN INDERMAUR, Solicitor,

AUTHOR OF "A MANUAL OF THE PRACTICE OF THE SUPREME COURT," "EPITOMES OF LEADING CASES," AND OTHER WORKS.

"The work is acknowledged to be one of the best written and most useful elementary works for Law Students that has been published."—*Law Times.*

"The praise which we were enabled to bestow upon Mr. Indermaur's very useful compilation on its first appearance has been justified by a demand for a second edition."—*Law Magazine.*

"We were able, four years ago, to praise the first edition of Mr. Indermaur's book as likely to be of use to students in acquiring the elements of the law of torts and contracts. The second edition maintains the character of the book."—*Law Journal.*

"Mr. Indermaur renders even law light reading. He not only possesses the faculty of judicious selection, but of lucid exposition and felicitous illustration. And while his works are all thus characterised, his 'Principles of the Common Law' especially displays those features. That it has already reached a second edition, testifies that our estimate of the work on its first appearance was not unduly favourable, highly as we then signified approval; nor needs it that we should add anything to that estimate in reference to the general scope and execution of the work. It only remains to say, that the present edition evinces that every care has been taken to insure thorough accuracy, while including all the modifications in the law that have taken place since the original publication; and that the references to the Irish decisions which have been now introduced are calculated to render the work of greater utility to practitioners and students, *both* English and Irish."—*Irish Law Times.*

"*This work, the author tells us in his Preface, is written mainly with a view to the examinations of the Incorporated Law Society; but we think it is likely to attain a wider usefulness. It seems, so far as we can judge from the parts we have examined, to be a careful and clear outline of the principles of the common law. It is very readable; and not only students, but many practitioners and the public might benefit by a perusal of its pages.*"—Solicitors' Journal.

"Mr. Indermaur has very clear notions of what a law student should be taught to enable him to pass the examinations of the Incorporated Law Society. In this, his last work, the law is stated carefully and accurately, and the book will probably prove acceptable to students."—*Law Times.*

"The practising solicitor will also find this a very useful compendium. Care has evidently been taken to note the latest decisions on important points of law. A full and well-constructed index supplies every facility for ready reference."—*Law Magazine.*

WORKS FOR LAW STUDENTS.

Second Edition, in 8vo, price 10s. 6d., cloth,

A MANUAL OF THE PRACTICE OF THE SUPREME COURT OF JUDICATURE,
In the Queen's Bench and Chancery Divisions. Intended for the use of Students.
By JOHN INDERMAUR, Solicitor.

"The second edition has followed quickly upon the first, which was published in 1873. This fact affords good evidence that the book has been found useful. It contains sufficient information to enable the student who masters the contents to turn to the standard works on practice with advantage."—*Law Times.*

"This is a very useful student's book. It is clearly written, and gives such information as the student requires, without bewildering him with details. The portion relating to the Chancery Division forms an excellent introduction to the elements of the practice, and may be advantageously used, not only by articled clerks, but also by pupils entering the chambers of equity draftsmen."—*Solicitors' Journal.*

Fifth Edition, in 8vo, price 6s., cloth,

AN EPITOME OF LEADING COMMON LAW CASES;
WITH SOME SHORT NOTES THEREON.
Chiefly intended as a Guide to "SMITH'S LEADING CASES." By JOHN INDERMAUR, Solicitor (Clifford's Inn Prizeman, Michaelmas Term, 1872).

"We have received the third edition of the 'Epitome of Leading Common Law Cases,' by Mr. Indermaur, Solicitor. The first edition of this work was published in February, 1873, the second in April, 1874, and now we have a third edition dated September, 1875. No better proof of the value of this book can be furnished than the fact that in less than three years it has reached a third edition."—*Law Journal.*

Fourth Edition, in 8vo, 1881, price 6s., cloth,

AN EPITOME OF LEADING CONVEYANCING AND EQUITY CASES;
WITH SOME SHORT NOTES THEREON, FOR THE USE OF STUDENTS.
By JOHN INDERMAUR, Solicitor, Author of "An Epitome of Leading Common Law Cases."

"We have received the second edition of Mr. Indermaur's very useful Epitome of Leading Conveyancing and Equity Cases. The work is very well done."—*Law Times.*

"The Epitome well deserves the continued patronage of the class—Students—for whom it is especially intended. Mr. Indermaur will soon be known as the 'Students' Friend.' "—*Canada Law Journal.*

Third Edition, in 8vo, 1880, price 5s., cloth,

SELF-PREPARATION FOR THE FINAL EXAMINATION.
CONTAINING A COMPLETE COURSE OF STUDY, WITH STATUTES, CASES AND QUESTIONS;
And intended for the use of those Articled Clerks who read by themselves.
By JOHN INDERMAUR, Solicitor.

"In this edition Mr. Indermaur extends his counsels to the whole period from the intermediate examination to the final. His advice is practical and sensible: and if the course of study he recommends is intelligently followed, the articled clerk will have laid in a store of legal knowledge more than sufficient to carry him through the final examination."—*Solicitors' Journal.*

"This book contains recommendations as to how a complete course of study for the above examination should be carried out, with reference to the particular books to be read *seriatim*. We need only remark that it is essential for a student to be set on the right track in his reading, and that anyone of ordinary ability, who follows the course set out by Mr. Indermaur, ought to pass with great credit."—*Law Journal.*

Second Edition, in 8vo, price 6s., cloth,

SELF-PREPARATION FOR THE INTERMEDIATE EXAMINATIONS,
As it at present exists on Stephen's Commentaries. Containing a complete course of Study, with Statutes, Questions, and Advice as to portions of the book which may be omitted, and of portions to which special attention should be given; also the whole of the Questions and Answers at the nine Intermediate Examinations which have at present been held on Stephen's Commentaries, and intended for the use of all Articled Clerks who have not yet passed the Intermediate Examination. By JOHN INDERMAUR, Author of "Principles of Common Law," and other works.

In 8vo, 1875, price 6s., cloth,

THE STUDENTS' GUIDE TO THE JUDICATURE ACTS,
AND THE RULES THEREUNDER:
Being a book of Questions and Answers intended for the use of Law Students.
By JOHN INDERMAUR, Solicitor.

Second Edition. In 8vo, price 26s., cloth,

A NEW LAW DICTIONARY,

AND INSTITUTE OF THE WHOLE LAW;

EMBRACING FRENCH AND LATIN TERMS AND REFERENCES TO THE AUTHORITIES, CASES, AND STATUTES.

SECOND EDITION, revised throughout, and considerably enlarged.

By ARCHIBALD BROWN,

M.A. EDIN. AND OXON., AND B.C.L. OXON., OF THE MIDDLE TEMPLE, BARRISTER-AT-LAW; AUTHOR OF THE "LAW OF FIXTURES," "ANALYSIS OF SAVIGNY'S OBLIGATIONS IN ROMAN LAW," ETC.

Reviews of the Second Edition.

"*So far as we have been able to examine the work, it seems to have been most carefully and accurately executed, the present Edition, besides containing much new matter, having been thoroughly revised in consequence of the recent changes in the law; and we have no doubt whatever that it will be found extremely useful, not only to students and practitioners, but to public men, and men of letters.*"—IRISH LAW TIMES.

"*Mr. Brown has revised his Dictionary, and adapted it to the changes effected by the Judicature Acts, and it now constitutes a very useful work to put into the hands of any student or articled clerk, and a work which the practitioner will find of value for reference.*"—SOLICITORS' JOURNAL.

"*It will prove a reliable guide to law students, and a handy book of reference for practitioners.*"—LAW TIMES.

In Royal 8vo., price 5s., cloth,

ANALYTICAL TABLES

OF

THE LAW OF REAL PROPERTY;

Drawn up chiefly from STEPHEN'S BLACKSTONE, with Notes.

By C. J. TARRING, of the Inner Temple, Barrister-at-Law.

CONTENTS.

TABLE I. Tenures.	TABLE V. Uses.
,, II. Estates, according to quantity of Tenants' Interest.	,, VI. Acquisition of Estates in land of freehold tenure.
,, III. Estates, according to the time at which the Interest is to be enjoyed.	,, VII. Incorporeal Hereditaments.
,, IV. Estates, according to the number and connection of the Tenants.	,, VIII. Incorporeal Hereditaments.

"Will supply the law student with help of a kind found very generally useful. The tables, which are based on Stephen's Blackstone, have gone through the practical test of being employed as aids to the mental arrangement of the knowledge of the subject required for examinations, and will no doubt be appreciated by the large and increasing classes whose requirements they are intended to meet."—*Law Magazine*.

"Great care and considerable skill have been shown in the compilation of these tables, which will be found of much service to students of the Law of Real Property."—*Law Times*.

Second Edition, in 8vo, price 20s., cloth,

PRINCIPLES OF THE CRIMINAL LAW.
INTENDED AS A LUCID EXPOSITION OF THE SUBJECT FOR THE USE OF STUDENTS AND THE PROFESSION.

By SEYMOUR F. HARRIS, B.C.L., M.A. (Oxon.),

AUTHOR OF "A CONCISE DIGEST OF THE INSTITUTES OF GAIUS AND JUSTINIAN."

SECOND EDITION.

REVISED BY THE AUTHOR AND F. P. TOMLINSON, M.A.,
OF THE INNER TEMPLE, BARRISTER-AT-LAW.

REVIEWS.

" *The favourable opinion we expressed of the first edition of this work appears to have been justified by the reception it has met with. Looking through this new Edition, we see no reason to modify the praise we bestowed on the former Edition. The recent cases have been added and the provisions of the Summary Jurisdiction Act are noticed in the chapter relating to Summary Convictions. The book is one of the best manuals of Criminal Law for the student.*"—SOLICITORS' JOURNAL.

" *There is no lack of Works on Criminal Law, but there was room for such a useful handbook of Principles as Mr. Seymour Harris has supplied. Accustomed, by his previous labours, to the task of analysing the law, Mr. Harris has brought to bear upon his present work qualifications well adapted to secure the successful accomplishment of the object which he had set before him. That object is not an ambitious one, for it does not pretend to soar above utility to the young practitioner and the student. For both these classes, and for the yet wider class who may require a book of reference on the subject, Mr. Harris has produced a clear and convenient Epitome of the Law. A noticeable feature of Mr. Harris's work, which is likely to prove of assistance both to the practitioner and the student, consists of a Table of Offences, with their legal character, their punishment, and the statute under which it is inflicted, together with a reference to the pages where a Statement of the Law will be found.*"—LAW MAGAZINE AND REVIEW.

"This work purports to contain 'a concise exposition of the nature of crime, the various offences punishable by the English law, the law of criminal procedure, and the law of summary convictions,' with tables of offences, punishments, and statutes. The work is divided into four books. Book I. treats of crime, its divisions and essentials; of persons capable of committing crimes; and of principals and accessories. Book II. deals with offences of a public nature; offences against private persons; and offences against the property of individuals. Each crime is discussed in its turn, with as much brevity as could well be used consistently with a proper explanation of the legal characteristics of the several offences. Book III. explains criminal procedure, including the jurisdiction of Courts, and the various steps in the apprehension and trial of criminals from arrest to punishment. This part of the work is extremely well done, the description of the trial being excellent, and thoroughly calculated to impress the mind of the uninitiated. Book IV. contains a short sketch of 'summary convictions before magistrates out of quarter sessions.' The table of offences at the end of the volume is most useful, and there is a very full index. Altogether we must congratulate Mr. Harris on his adventure."—*Law Journal.*

" *Mr. Harris has undertaken a work, in our opinion, so much needed that he might diminish its bulk in the next edition by obliterating the apologetic preface. The appearance of his volume is as well timed as its execution is satisfactory. The author has shown an ability of omission which is a good test of skill, and from the overwhelming mass of the criminal law he has discreetly selected just so much only as a learner needs to know, and has presented it in terms which render it capable of being easily taken into the mind. The first half of the volume is devoted to indictable offences, which are defined and explained in succinct terms; the second half treats of the prevention of offences, the courts of criminal jurisdiction, arrest, preliminary proceedings before magistrates, and modes of prosecuting and trial; and a brief epitome of the laws of evidence, proceedings after trial, and summary convictions, with a table of offences, complete the book. The part on procedure will be found particularly useful. Few young counsel, on their first appearance at sessions, have more than a loose and general notion of the manner in which a trial is conducted, and often commit blunders which, although trifling in kind, are nevertheless seriously discouraging and annoying to themselves at the outset of their career. From even such a blunder as that of mistaking the order in which the speeches are made and witnesses examined they may be saved by the table of instructions given here.*"—SOLICITORS' JOURNAL.

Now Ready, in 12mo, price 5s. 6d., cloth,

A CONCISE TREATISE ON THE LAW OF BILLS OF SALE,

FOR THE USE OF LAWYERS, LAW STUDENTS, & THE PUBLIC.

Embracing the Acts of 1878 and 1882. Part I.—Of Bills of Sale generally. Part II.—Of the Execution, Attestation, and Registration of Bills of Sale and satisfaction thereof. Part III.—Of the Effects of Bills of Sale as against Creditors. Part IV.—Of Seizing under, and Enforcing Bills of Sale. Appendix, Forms, Acts, &c. By JOHN INDERMAUR, Solicitor.

"The object of the book is thoroughly practical. Those who want to be told exactly what to do and where to go when they are registering a bill of sale will find the necessary information in this little book."—*Law Journal*.

Now ready, in 8vo, price 2s. 6d., cloth,

A COLLECTION OF LATIN MAXIMS,

LITERALLY TRANSLATED.

INTENDED FOR THE USE OF STUDENTS FOR ALL LEGAL EXAMINATIONS.

"The book seems admirably adapted as a book of reference for students who come across a Latin maxim in their reading."—*Law Journal*.

"The collection before us is not pretentious, and disarms criticism by its simplicity and general correctness. Students would do well, early in their studies, to commit these maxims to memory, and subsequent reading will often be systematized and more easily remembered."—*Canada Law Journal*.

In one volume, 8vo, price 9s., cloth,

LEADING STATUTES SUMMARISED,

FOR THE USE OF STUDENTS.

By ERNEST C. THOMAS,

BACON SCHOLAR OF THE HON. SOCIETY OF GRAY'S INN, LATE SCHOLAR OF TRINITY COLLEGE, OXFORD; AUTHOR OF "LEADING CASES IN CONSTITUTIONAL LAW BRIEFLY STATED."

"Will doubtless prove of much use to students, for whom it is intended. . . . Any student who, with this brief summary as a guide, carefully studies the enactments themselves in the Revised Edition of the Statutes, cannot fail to gain a very considerable acquaintance with every branch of English law."—*Law Magazine*.

Second Edition, in 8vo, in preparation.

LEADING CASES IN CONSTITUTIONAL LAW

BRIEFLY STATED, WITH INTRODUCTION, EXCURSUSES, AND NOTES.

By ERNEST C. THOMAS,

BACON SCHOLAR OF THE HON. SOCIETY OF GRAY'S INN, LATE SCHOLAR OF TRINITY COLLEGE, OXFORD.

"Mr. E. C. Thomas has put together in a slim octavo a digest of the principal cases illustrating Constitutional Law, that is to say, all questions as to the rights or authority of the Crown or persons under it, as regards not merely the constitution and structure given to the governing body, but also the mode in which the sovereign power is to be exercised. In an introductory essay Mr. Thomas gives a very clear and intelligent survey of the general functions of the Executive, and the principles by which they are regulated; and then follows a summary of leading cases."—*Saturday Review*.

"Mr. Thomas gives a sensible introduction and a brief epitome of the familiar leading cases."—*Law Times*.

In 8vo, price 8s., cloth,

AN EPITOME OF HINDU LAW CASES. With

Short Notes thereon. And Introductory Chapters on Sources of Law, Marriage, Adoption, Partition, and Succession. By WILLIAM M. P. COGHLAN, Bombay Civil Service, late Judge and Sessions Judge of Tanna.

In a handy volume, price 5s. 6d., cloth,

RAILWAY PASSENGERS AND RAILWAY COMPANIES:
THEIR DUTIES, RIGHTS, AND LIABILITIES.
With an Appendix containing Addenda et Corrigenda to Nov. 1880.

By LOUIS ARTHUR GOODEVE,
OF THE MIDDLE TEMPLE, BARRISTER-AT-LAW.

*** *The Appendix can be had separately, price* 1s.

"Mr. Goodeve's little book is a concise epitome of the Acts, Bye-laws, and Cases relating to passengers and their personal luggage. It is clearly written, and the reader is able speedily enough to find any point upon which he desires to inform himself."—*Law Journal.*

"Mr. Goodeve has rendered a service to the public in making a digest of the law relating to railway passengers, including the respective duties, rights, and liabilities of the Companies on the one hand and passengers on the other, as laid down by the statutes and the decisions of the Superior Courts. The various points are treated in a clear yet concise manner; and it is to be hoped that this little work will be widely studied so that people may know what are their rights, and take steps to maintain them."—*Saturday Review.*

"After reading the volume with great interest, we can only say that it is clear, compact, and accurate. Passengers who want reliable information should consult this book."—*Sheffield Post.*

EUROPEAN ARBITRATION.

Part I., price 7s. 6d., sewed,

LORD WESTBURY'S DECISIONS.
REPORTED BY FRANCIS S. REILLY,
OF LINCOLN'S INN, BARRISTER-AT-LAW.

ALBERT ARBITRATION.

Parts I., II., and III., price 25s., sewed,

LORD CAIRNS'S DECISIONS.
REPORTED BY FRANCIS S. REILLY,
OF LINCOLN'S INN, BARRISTER-AT-LAW.

In 8vo, price 21s., cloth,

A TREATISE ON

THE STATUTES OF ELIZABETH AGAINST FRAUDULENT CONVEYANCES.
THE BILLS OF SALE REGISTRATION ACTS AND THE LAW OF VOLUNTARY DISPOSITIONS OF PROPERTY GENERALLY.

By H. W. MAY, B.A, (Ch. Ch. Oxford),
AND OF LINCOLN'S INN, BARRISTER-AT-LAW.

"This treatise has not been published before it was wanted. The statutes of Elizabeth against fraudulent conveyances have now been in force for more than three hundred years. The decisions under them are large in number, and not at all times consistent with each other. An attempt to reduce the mass of decisions into something like shape, and the exposition of legal principles involved in the decisions, under any circumstances, must have been a work of great labour, and we are pleased to observe that in the book before us there has been a combination of unusual labour with considerable professional skill.... We cannot conclude our notice of this work without saying that it reflects great credit on the publishers as well as the author. The facilities afforded by Messrs. Stevens and Haynes for the publication of treatises by rising men in our profession are deserving of all praise. We feel assured that they do not lightly lend their aid to works presented for publication, and that in consequence publication by such a firm is to some extent a guarantee of the value of the work published."—*Canada Law Journal.*

"Examining Mr. May's book, we find it constructed with an intelligence and precision which render it entirely worthy of being accepted as a guide in this confessedly difficult subject. The subject is an involved one, but with clean and clear handling it is here presented as clearly as it could be.... On the whole, he has produced a very useful book of an exceptionally scientific character."—*Solicitors' Journal.*

"The subject and the work are both very good. The former is well chosen, new, and interesting; the latter has the quality which always distinguishes original research from borrowed labours."—*American Law Review.*

"We are happy to welcome his (Mr. May's) work as an addition to the, we regret to say, brief catalogue of law books conscientiously executed. We can corroborate his own description of his labours, 'that no pains have been spared to make the book as concise and practical as possible, without doing so at the expense of perspicuity, or by the omission of any important points.'"—*Law Times.*

In one volume, 8vo, price 25s., cloth,

AN ESSAY ON

THE RIGHTS OF THE CROWN
AND THE PRIVILEGES OF THE SUBJECT
IN THE SEA SHORES OF THE REALM.

By ROBERT GREAM HALL,
OF LINCOLN'S INN, BARRISTER-AT-LAW.

SECOND EDITION.

REVISED AND CORRECTED, TOGETHER WITH EXTENSIVE ANNOTATIONS,
AND REFERENCES TO THE LATER AUTHORITIES IN ENGLAND,
SCOTLAND, IRELAND, AND THE UNITED STATES.

By RICHARD LOVELAND LOVELAND,
OF THE INNER TEMPLE, BARRISTER-AT-LAW.

"This is an interesting and valuable book. It treats of one of those obscure branches of the law which there is no great inducement for a legal writer to take up. .... Mr. Hall, whose first edition was issued in 1830, was a writer of considerable power and method. Mr. Loveland's editing reflects the valuable qualities of the 'Essay' itself. He has done his work without pretension, but in a solid and efficient manner. The 'Summary of Contents' gives an admirable epitome of the chief points discussed in the 'Essay,' and indeed, in some twenty propositions, supplies a useful outline of the whole law. Recent cases are noted at the foot of each page with great care and accuracy, while an Appendix contains much valuable matter; including Lord Hale's treatise *De Jure Maris*, about which there has been so much controversy, and Serjeant Merewether's learned argument on the rights in the river Thames. The book will, we think, take its place as the modern authority on the subject."—*Law Journal*.

"The treatise, as originally published, was one of considerable value, and has ever since been quoted as a standard authority. But as time passed, and cases accumulated, its value diminished, as it was necessary to supplement it so largely by reference to cases since decided. A tempting opportunity was, therefore, offered to an intelligent editor to supply this defect in the work, and Mr. Loveland has seized it, and proved his capacity in a very marked manner. As very good specimens of annotation, showing clear judgment in selection, we may refer to the subject of alluvion at page 109, and the rights of fishery at page 50. At the latter place he begins his notes by stating under what expressions a 'several fishery' has been held to pass, proceeding subsequently to the evidence which is sufficient to support a claim to ownership of a fishery. The important question under what circumstances property can be acquired in the soil between high and low water mark is lucidly discussed at page 77, whilst at page 81 we find a pregnant note on the property of a grantee of wreck in goods stranded within his liberty.

"We think we can promise Mr. Loveland the reward for which alone he says he looks—that this edition of Hall's Essay will prove a most decided assistance to those engaged in cases relating to the foreshores of the country."—*Law Times*.

"*The entire book is masterly.*"—ALBANY LAW JOURNAL.

In one volume, 8vo, price 12s., cloth,

A TREATISE ON THE LAW RELATING TO THE

POLLUTION AND OBSTRUCTION OF WATER COURSES;

TOGETHER WITH A BRIEF SUMMARY OF THE VARIOUS SOURCES OF RIVERS POLLUTION.

By CLEMENT HIGGINS, M.A., F.C.S.,
OF THE INNER TEMPLE, BARRISTER-AT-LAW.

"As a compendium of the law upon a special and rather intricate subject, this treatise cannot but prove of great practical value, and more especially to those who have to advise upon the institution of proceedings under the Rivers Pollution Preventive Act, 1876, or to adjudicate upon those proceedings when brought."—*Irish Law Times*.

"We can recommend Mr. Higgins' Manual as the best guide we possess."—*Public Health*.

"County Court Judges, Sanitary Authorities, and Riparian Owners will find in Mr. Higgins' Treatise a valuable aid in obtaining a clear notion of the Law on the Subject. Mr. Higgins has accomplished a work for which he will readily be recognised as having special fitness, on account of his practical acquaintance both with the scientific and the legal aspects of his subject."—*Law Magazine and Review*.

"The volume is very carefully arranged throughout, and will prove of great utility both to miners and to owners of land on the banks of rivers."—*The Mining Journal*.

"Mr. Higgins writes tersely and clearly, while his facts are so well arranged that it is a pleasure to refer to his book for information; and altogether the work is one which will be found very useful by all interested in the subject to which it relates."—*Engineer*.

"A compact and convenient manual of the law on the subject to which it relates."—*Solicitors' Journal*.

In 8vo, THIRD EDITION, price 25s., cloth,

MAYNE'S TREATISE
ON
THE LAW OF DAMAGES.
THIRD EDITION.
BY

JOHN D. MAYNE,
OF THE INNER TEMPLE, BARRISTER-AT-LAW;

AND

LUMLEY SMITH,
OF THE INNER TEMPLE, Q.C.

"*During the twenty-two years which have elapsed since the publication of this well-known work, its reputation has been steadily growing, and it has long since become the recognised authority on the important subject of which it treats.*"—LAW MAGAZINE AND REVIEW.

"This edition of what has become a standard work has the advantage of appearing under the supervision of the original author as well as of Mr. Lumley Smith, the editor of the second edition. The result is most satisfactory. Mr. Lumley Smith's edition was ably and conscientiously prepared, and we are glad to find that the reader still enjoys the benefit of his accuracy and learning. At the same time the book has doubtless been improved by the reappearance of its author as co-editor. The earlier part, indeed, has been to a considerable extent entirely rewritten.

"Upon the general principles, according to which damages are to be assessed in actions of contract, *Hadley* v. *Baxendale* (9 Ex. 341) still remains the leading authority, and furnishes the text for the discussion contained in the second chapter of Mr. Mayne's book. Properly understood and limited, the rule proposed in that case, although in one respect not very happily worded, is a sound one, and has been repeatedly approved both in England and America. The subsequent decisions, which are concisely summarized by Mr. Mayne, have established a more knowledge of special circumstances is not enough, unless it can be inferred from the whole transaction that the contractor consented to become liable to the extra damage. This limitation is obviously just, especially in the case of persons, such as common carriers, who have no option to refuse the contract. Mere knowledge on their part of special circumstances ought not, and, according to the *dicta* of the judges in the Exchequer Chamber in *Horne* v. *Midland Railway Company* (21 W. R. 481, L. R. 8 C. P. 131), would not involve the carrier in additional responsibility. Mr. Mayne's criticism of the numerous cases in which this matter has been considered leaves nothing to be desired, and the rules he deduces therefrom (pp. 32, 33) appear to us to exhaust the subject.

"Mr. Mayne's remarks on damages in actions of tort are brief. We agree with him that in such actions the courts are governed by far looser principles than in contracts; indeed, sometimes it is impossible to say they are governed by any principles at all. In actions for injuries to the person or reputation, for example, a judge cannot do more than give a general direction to the jury to give what the facts proved in their judgment required. And, according to the better opinion they may give damages 'for example's sake,' and mulct a rich man more heavily than a poor one. In actions for injuries to property, however, 'vindictive' or 'exemplary' damages cannot, except in very rare cases, be awarded, but must be limited, as in contract, to the actual harm sustained.

"The subject of remoteness of damage is treated at considerable length by Mr. Mayne, and we notice that much new matter has been added. Thus the recent case of *Riding* v. *Smith* (24 W. R. 487, 1 Ex. D. 91) furnishes the author with an opportunity of discussing the well-known rule in *Ward* v. *Weeks* (7 Bing. 211) that injury resulting from the repetition of a slander is not actionable. The rule has always seemed to us a strange one, if a man is to be made responsible for the natural consequences of his acts. For everyone who utters a slander may be perfectly certain that it will be repeated.

"It is needless to comment upon the arrangement of the subjects in this edition, in which no alteration has been made. The editors modestly express a hope that all the English as well as the principal Irish decisions up to the date have been included, and we believe from our own examination that the hope is well founded. We may regret that, warned by the growing bulk of the book, the editors have not included any fresh American cases, but we feel that the omission was unavoidable. We should add that the whole work has been thoroughly revised."—*Solicitors' Journal.*

"*This text-book is so well known, not only as the highest authority on the subject treated of, but as one of the best text-books ever written, that it would be idle for us to speak of it in the words of commendation that it deserves. It is a work that no practising lawyer can do without.*"—CANADA LAW JOURNAL.

In 8vo, price 2s., sewed,

TABLE of the FOREIGN MERCANTILE LAWS and CODES

in Force in the Principal States of EUROPE and AMERICA. By CHARLES LYON-CAEN, Professeur agrégé à la Faculté de Droit de Paris; Professeur à l'Ecole libre des Sciences politiques. Translated by NAPOLEON ARGLES, Solicitor, Paris.

In one volume, demy 8vo, price 10s. 6d., cloth,

PRINCIPLES OF THE LAW OF STOPPAGE IN TRANSITU, RETENTION, AND DELIVERY.

By JOHN HOUSTON, of the Middle Temple, Barrister-at-Law.

"We have no hesitation in saying that we think Mr. Houston's book will be a very useful accession to the library of either the merchant or the lawyer."—*Solicitors' Journal*.

"We have, indeed, met with few works which so successfully surmount the difficulties in the way of this arduous undertaking as the one before us; for the language is well chosen, it is exhaustive of the law, and is systematised with great method."—*American Law Review*.

In 8vo, price 10s. 6d., cloth,

A REPORT OF THE CASE OF

THE QUEEN v. GURNEY AND OTHERS,

In the Court of Queen's Bench before the Lord Chief Justice COCKBURN. With an Introduction, containing a History of the Case, and an Examination of the Cases at Law and Equity applicable to it; or Illustrating THE DOCTRINE OF COMMERCIAL FRAUD. By W. F. FINLASON, Barrister-at-Law.

"It will probably be a very long time before the prosecution of the Overend and Gurney directors is forgotten. It remains as an example, and a legal precedent of considerable value. It involved the immensely important question where innocent misrepresentation ends, and where fraudulent misrepresentation begins.

"All who perused the report of this case in the columns of the *Times* must have observed the remarkable fulness and accuracy with which that duty was discharged, and nothing could be more natural than that the reporter should publish a separate report in book form. This has been done, and Mr. Finlason introduces the report by one hundred pages of dissertation on the general law. To this we shall proceed to refer, simply remarking, before doing so, that the charge to the jury has been carefully revised by the Lord Chief Justice."—*Law Times*.

12mo, price 10s. 6d., cloth,

A TREATISE ON THE GAME LAWS OF ENGLAND AND WALES:

Including Introduction, Statutes, Explanatory Notes, Cases, and Index. By JOHN LOCKE, M.P., Q.C., Recorder of Brighton. The Fifth Edition, in which are introduced the GAME LAWS of SCOTLAND and IRELAND. By GILMORE EVANS, of the Inner Temple, Barrister-at-Law.

In royal 8vo, price 10s. 6d., cloth,

THE PRACTICE OF EQUITY BY WAY OF REVIVOR AND SUPPLEMENT.

With Forms of Orders and Appendix of Bills.

By LOFTUS LEIGH PEMBERTON, of the Chancery Registrar's Office.

"Mr. Pemberton has, with great care, brought together and classified all these conflicting cases, and has, as far as may be, deduced principles which will probably be applied to future cases.—*Solicitors' Journal*.

In 8vo, price 5s., cloth,

THE LAW OF PRIORITY.

A CONCISE VIEW OF THE LAW RELATING TO PRIORITY OF INCUMBRANCES AND OF OTHER RIGHTS IN PROPERTY.

By W. G. ROBINSON, M.A., Barrister-at-Law.

"Mr. Robinson's book may be recommended to the advanced student, and will furnish the practitioner with a useful supplement to larger and more complete works."—*Solicitors' Journal*.

In crown 8vo, price 16s., cloth,

A MANUAL OF THE PRACTICE OF PARLIAMENTARY ELECTIONS THROUGHOUT GREAT BRITAIN AND IRELAND.

Comprising the Duties of Returning Officers and their Deputies, Town Clerks, Agents, Poll-Clerks, &c., and the Law of Election Expenses, Corrupt Practices, and illegal Payments. With an Appendix of Statutes and an Index. By HENRY JEFFREYS BUSHBY, Esq., one of the Metropolitan Police Magistrates, sometime Recorder of Colchester.—Fifth Edition. Adapted to and embodying the recent changes in the Law, including the Ballot Act, the Instructions to Returning Officers in England and Scotland issued by the Home Office, and the whole of the Statute Law relating to the subject. Edited by HENRY HARDCASTLE, of the Inner Temple, Barrister-at-Law.

"We have just received at a very opportune moment the new edition of this useful work. We need only say that those who have to do with elections will find 'Bushby's Manual' replete with information and trustworthy, and that Mr. Hardcastle has incorporated all the recent changes of the law."—*Law Journal.*

"As far as we can judge, Mr. Hardcastle, who is known as one of the joint editors of O'Malley and Hardcastle's Election Reports, has done his work well....... For practical purposes, as a handy manual, we can recommend the work to returning officers, agents, and candidates; and returning officers cannot do better than distribute this manual freely amongst their subordinates, if they wish them to understand their work."—*Solicitors' Journal.*

A Companion Volume to the above, in crown 8vo, price 9s., cloth,

THE LAW AND PRACTICE OF ELECTION PETITIONS,

With an Appendix containing the Parliamentary Elections Act, 1868, the General Rules for the Trial of Election Petitions in England, Scotland, and Ireland, Forms of Petitions, &c. Second Edition. By HENRY HARDCASTLE, of the Inner Temple, Barrister-at-Law.

"Mr. Hardcastle gives us an original treatise with foot notes, and he has evidently taken very considerable pains to make his work a reliable guide. Beginning with the effect of the Election Petitions Act, 1868, he takes his readers step by step through the new procedure. His mode of treating the subject of 'particulars' will be found extremely useful, and he gives all the law and practice in a very small compass. In an Appendix is supplied the Act and the Rules. We can thoroughly recommend Mr. Hardcastle's book as a concise manual on the law and practice of election petitions."—*Law Times.*

Now ready, Vols. I., II., & III., price 73s.; and Vol. IV., Pt. I., price 2s. 6d.,

REPORTS OF THE DECISIONS OF THE

JUDGES FOR THE TRIAL OF ELECTION PETITIONS

IN ENGLAND AND IRELAND.

PURSUANT TO THE PARLIAMENTARY ELECTIONS ACT, 1868.
By EDWARD LOUGHLIN O'MALLEY AND HENRY HARDCASTLE.

In 8vo, price 12s., cloth,

THE LAW OF FIXTURES,

IN THE PRINCIPAL RELATION OF

LANDLORD AND TENANT,

AND IN ALL OTHER OR GENERAL RELATIONS.

FOURTH EDITION.

By ARCHIBALD BROWN, M.A. Edin. and Oxon., and B.C.L. Oxon.,

OF THE MIDDLE TEMPLE, BARRISTER-AT-LAW.

"The author tells us that every endeavour has been made to make this Edition as complete as possible. We think he has been very successful. For instance, the changes effected by the Bills of Sale Act, 1878, have been well indicated, and a new chapter has been added with reference to the Law of Ecclesiastical Fixtures and Dilapidations. The book is worthy of the success it has achieved."—*Law Times.*

"We have touched on the principal features of this new edition, and we have not space for further remarks on the book itself; but we may observe that the particular circumstances of the cases cited are in all instances sufficiently detailed to make the principle of law clear; and though very many of the principles given are in the very words of the judges, at the same time the author has not spared to deduce his own observations, and the treatise is commendable as well for originality as for laboriousness."—*Law Journal.*

Stevens and Haynes' Series of Reprints of the Early Reporters.

SIR BARTHOLOMEW SHOWER'S PARLIAMENTARY CASES.

In 8vo, 1876, price 4*l.* 4*s.*, best calf binding,

SHOWER'S CASES IN PARLIAMENT

RESOLVED AND ADJUDGED UPON PETITIONS & WRITS OF ERROR.

FOURTH EDITION.

CONTAINING ADDITIONAL CASES NOT HITHERTO REPORTED.

REVISED AND EDITED BY

RICHARD LOVELAND LOVELAND,

OF THE INNER TEMPLE, BARRISTER-AT-LAW; EDITOR OF "KELYNG'S CROWN CASES," AND "HALL'S ESSAY ON THE RIGHTS OF THE CROWN IN THE SEASHORE."

"Messrs. STEVENS & HAYNES, the successful publishers of the Reprints of Bellewe, Cooke, Cunningham, Brookes's New Cases, Choyce Cases in Chancery, William Kelynge and Kelyng's Crown Cases, determined to issue a new or fourth Edition of Shower's Cases in Parliament.

"The volume, although beautifully printed on old-fashioned Paper, in old-fashioned type, instead of being in the quarto, is in the more convenient octavo form, and contains several additional cases not to be found in any of the previous editions of the work.

"These are all cases of importance, worthy of being ushered into the light of the world by enterprising publishers.

"Shower's Cases are models for reporters, even in our day. The statements of the case, the arguments of counsel, and the opinions of the Judges, are all clearly and ably given.

"This new edition with an old face of these valuable reports, under the able editorship of R. L. Loveland, Esq., should, in the language of the advertisement, 'be welcomed by the profession, as well as enable the custodians of public libraries to complete or add to their series of English Law Reports.'"—*Canada Law Journal.*

BELLEWE'S CASES, T. RICHARD II.

In 8vo, 1869, price 3*l.* 3*s.*, bound in calf antique,

LES ANS DU ROY RICHARD LE SECOND.

Collect' ensembl' hors les abridgments de Statham, Fitzherbert et Brooke. Per RICHARD BELLEWE, de Lincolns Inne. 1585. Reprinted from the Original Edition.

"No public library in the world, where English law finds a place, should be without a copy of this edition of Bellewe."—*Canada Law Journal.*

"We have here a *fac-simile* edition of Bellewe, and it is really the most beautiful and admirable reprint that has appeared at any time. It is a perfect gem of antique printing, and forms a most interesting monument of our early legal history. It belongs to the same class of works as the Year Book of Edward I. and other similar works which have been printed in our own time under the auspices of the Master of the Rolls; but is far superior to any of them, and is in this respect highly creditable to the spirit and enterprise of private publishers. The work is an important link in our legal history; there are no year books of the reign of Richard II., and Bellewe supplied the only substitute by carefully extracting and collecting all the cases he could find, and he did it in the most convenient form—that of alphabetical arrangement in the order of subjects, so that the work is a digest as well as a book of law reports. It is in fact a collection of cases of the reign of Richard II., arranged according to their subjects in alphabetical order. It is therefore, one of the most intelligible and interesting legal memorials of the Middle Ages."—*Law Times.*

CUNNINGHAM'S REPORTS.

In 8vo, 1871, price 3*l.* 3*s.*, calf antique,

CUNNINGHAM'S (T.) Reports in K. B., 7 to 10 Geo. II.; to which is prefixed a Proposal for rendering the Laws of England clear and certain, humbly offered to the Consideration of both Houses of Parliament. Third edition, with numerous Corrections. By THOMAS TOWNSEND BUCKNILL, Barrister-at-Law.

"The instructive chapter which precedes the cases, entitled 'A proposal for rendering the Laws of England clear and certain,' gives the volume a degree of peculiar interest, independent the value of many of the reported cases. That chapter begins with words which ought, for the information of every people, to be printed in letters of gold. They are as follows: 'Nothing conduces more to the peace and prosperity of every nation than good laws and the due execution of them.' The history of the civil law is then rapidly traced. Next a history is given of English Reporters, beginning with the reporters of the Year Books from 1 Edw. III. to 12 Hen. VIII.,—being near 200 years—and afterwards to the time of the author."—*Canada Law Journal.*

Stevens and Haynes' Series of Reprints of the Early Reporters.

CHOYCE CASES IN CHANCERY.

In 8vo, 1870, price 2l. 2s., calf antique,

THE PRACTICE OF THE HIGH COURT OF CHANCERY.

With the Nature of the several Offices belonging to that Court. And the Reports of many Cases wherein Relief hath been there had, and where denyed.

"This volume, in paper, type, and binding (like "Bellewe's Cases") is a fac-simile of the antique edition. All who buy the one should buy the other."—*Canada Law Journal.*

In 8vo, 1872, price 3l. 3s., calf antique.

SIR G. COOKE'S COMMON PLEAS REPORTS

IN THE REIGNS OF QUEEN ANNE, AND KINGS GEORGE I. AND II.

The Third Edition, with Additional Cases and References contained in the Notes taken from L. C. J. EYRE's MSS. by Mr. Justice NARES, edited by THOMAS TOWNSEND BUCKNILL, of the Inner Temple, Barrister-at-Law.

"Law books never can die or remain long dead so long as Stevens and Haynes are willing to continue them or revive them when dead. It is certainly surprising to see with what facial accuracy	an old volume of Reports may be produced by these modern publishers, whose good taste is only equalled by their enterprise."—*Canada Law Journal.*

BROOKE'S NEW CASES WITH MARCH'S TRANSLATION.

In 8vo, 1873, price 4l. 4s., calf antique.

BROOKE'S (Sir Robert) New Cases in the time of Henry VIII., Edward VI., and Queen Mary, collected out of Brook's Abridgement, and arranged under years, with a table, together with MARCH'S (John) *Translation of* BROOKE'S New Cases in the time of Henry VIII., Edward VI., and Queen Mary, collected out of BROOKE'S Abridgement, and reduced alphabetically under their proper heads and titles, with a table of the principal matters. In one handsome volume. 8vo. 1873.

"Both the original and the translation having long been very scarce, and the misspaging and other errors in March's translation making a new and corrected edition peculiarly desirable Messrs.	Stevens and Haynes have reprinted the two books in one volume, uniform with the preceding volumes of the series of Early Reports."—*Canada Law Journal.*

KELYNGE'S (W.) REPORTS.

In 8vo, 1873, price 4l. 4s., calf antique,

KELYNGE'S (William) Reports of Cases in Chancery, the King's Bench, &c., from the 3rd to the 9th year of his late Majesty King George II., during which time Lord King was Chancellor, and the Lords Raymond and Hardwicke were Chief Justices of England. To which are added, seventy New Cases not in the First Edition. Third Edition. In one handsome volume. 8vo. 1873.

KELYNG'S (SIR JOHN) CROWN CASES.

In 8vo, 1873, price 4l. 4s., calf antique,

KELYNG'S (Sir J.) Reports of Divers Cases in Pleas of the Crown in the Reign of King Charles II., with Directions to Justices of the Peace, and others; to which are added, Three Modern Cases, viz., Armstrong and Lisle, the King and Plummer, the Queen and Mawgridge. Third Edition, *containing several additional Cases never before printed*, together with a TREATISE UPON THE LAW AND PROCEEDINGS IN CASES OF HIGH TREASON, first published in 1793. The whole carefully revised and edited by RICHARD LOVELAND LOVELAND, of the Inner Temple, Barrister-at-Law.

"We look upon this volume as one of the most important and valuable of the unique reprints of Messrs Stevens and Haynes. Little do we know of the mines of legal wealth that lie buried in the old law books. But a careful examination, either of the reports or of the treatise embodied in the volume now before us, will give the reader some idea of the	good service rendered by Messrs. Stevens and Haynes to the profession. . . . Should occasion arise, the Crown prosecutor, as well as counsel for the prisoner will find in this volume a complete *vade mecum* of the law of high treason and proceedings in relation thereto."—*Canada Law Journal.*

In one volume, 8vo, price 25s., cloth,

A CONCISE TREATISE ON

PRIVATE INTERNATIONAL JURISPRUDENCE,

BASED ON THE DECISIONS IN THE ENGLISH COURTS.

By JOHN ALDERSON FOOTE,

OF LINCOLN'S INN, BARRISTER-AT-LAW; CHANCELLOR'S LEGAL MEDALLIST AND SENIOR WHEWELL SCHOLAR OF INTERNATIONAL LAW CAMBRIDGE UNIVERSITY, 1873; SENIOR STUDENT IN JURISPRUDENCE AND ROMAN LAW, INNS OF COURT EXAMINATION, HILARY TERM, 1874.

"This work seems to us likely to prove of considerable use to all English lawyers who have to deal with questions of private international law. Since the publication of Mr. Westlake's valuable treatise, twenty years ago, the judicial decisions of English courts bearing upon different parts of this subject have greatly increased in number, and it is full time that these decisions should be examined, and that the conclusions to be deduced from them should be systematically set forth in a treatise. Moreover, Mr. Foote has done this well."—*Solicitors' Journal.*

"Mr. Foote has done his work very well, and the book will be useful to all who have to deal with the class of cases in which English law alone is not sufficient to settle the question."—*Saturday Review,* March 8, 1879.

"The author's object has been to reduce into order the mass of materials already accumulated in the shape of explanation and actual decision on the interesting matter of which he treats; and to construct a framework of private international law, not from the *dicta* of jurists so much as from judicial decisions in English Courts which have superseded them. And it is here, in compiling and arranging in a concise form this valuable material, that Mr. Foote's wide range of knowledge and legal acumen bear such good fruit. As a guide and assistant to the student of international law, the whole treatise will be invaluable: while a table of cases and a general index will enable him to find what he wants without trouble. —*Standard.*

"The recent decisions on points of international law (and there have been a large number since Westlake's publication) have been well stated. So far as we have observed, no case of any importance has been omitted, and the leading cases have been fully analysed. The author does not hesitate to criticise the grounds of a decision when these appear to him to conflict with the proper rule of law. Most of his criticisms seem to us very just. .... On the whole we can recommend Mr. Foote's treatise as a useful addition to our text-books, and we expect it will rapidly find its way into the hands of practising lawyers."—*The Journal of Jurisprudence and Scottish Law Magazine.*

"Mr. Foote has evidently borne closely in mind the needs of Students of Jurisprudence as well as those of the Practitioners. For both, the fact that his work is almost entirely one of Case-law, will commend it as one useful alike in Chambers and in Court."—*Law Magazine and Review.*

"Mr. Foote's book will be useful to the student. . . . . One of the best points of Mr. Foote's book is the 'Continuous Summary,' which occupies about thirty pages, and is divided into four parts—Persons, Property, Acts, and Procedure. Mr. Foote remarks that these summaries are not in any way intended as an attempt at codification. However that may be, they are a digest which reflects high credit on the author's assiduity and capacity. They are 'meant merely to guide the student;' but they will do much more than guide him. They will enable him to get such a grasp of the subject as will render the reading of the text easy and fruitful."—*Law Journal.*

"This book is well adapted to be used both as a text-book for students and a book of reference for practising barristers."—*Bar Examination Journal.*

"This is a book which supplies the want which has long been felt for a really good modern treatise on Private International Law adapted to the every-day requirements of the English Practitioner. The whole volume, although designed for the use of the practitioner, is so moderate in size—an octavo of 500 pages only—and the arrangement and development of the subject so well conceived and executed, that it will amply repay perusal by those whose immediate object may be not the actual decisions of a knotty point but the satisfactory disposal of an examination paper."—*Oxford and Cambridge Undergraduates' Journal.*

"Since the publication, some twenty years ago, of Mr. Westlake's Treatise, Mr. Foote's book is, in our opinion, the best work on private international law which has appeared in the English language. . . . The work is executed with much ability, and will doubtless be found of great value by all persons who have to consider questions on private international law."—*Athenæum.*

THE
Law Magazine and Review,
AND
QUARTERLY DIGEST OF ALL REPORTED CASES.

Price **FIVE SHILLINGS** each Number.

No. CCXVIII. (Vol. 1, No. I, of the New QUARTERLY Series.) November, 1875.
No. CCXIX.   (Vol. 1, 4th Series No. II.) February, 1876.

N.B.—These two Numbers are out of print.

No. CCXX.	(Vol. 1, 4th Series No. III.)	For May, 1876.
No. CCXXI.	(Vol. 1, 4th Series No. IV.)	For August, 1876.
No. CCXXII.	(Vol. 2, 4th Series No. V.)	For November, 1876.
No. CCXXIII.	(Vol. 2, 4th Series No. VI.)	For February, 1877.
No. CCXXIV.	(Vol. 2, 4th Series No. VII.)	For May, 1877.
No. CCXXV.	(Vol. 2, 4th Series No. VIII.)	For August, 1877.
No. CCXXVI.	(Vol. 3, 4th Series No. IX.)	For November, 1877.
No. CCXXVII.	(Vol. 3, 4th Series No. X.)	For February, 1878.
No. CCXXVIII.	(Vol. 3, 4th Series No. XI.)	For May, 1878.
No. CCXXIX.	(Vol. 3, 4th Series No. XII.)	For August, 1878.
No. CCXXX.	(Vol. 4, 4th Series No. XIII.)	For November, 1878.
No. CCXXXI.	(Vol. 4, 4th Series No. XIV.)	For February, 1879.
No. CCXXXII.	(Vol. 4, 4th Series No. XV.)	For May, 1879.
No. CCXXXIII.	(Vol. 4, 4th Series No. XVI.)	For August, 1879.
No. CCXXXIV.	(Vol. 5, 4th Series No. XVII.)	For November, 1879.
No. CCXXXV.	(Vol. 5, 4th Series No. XVIII.)	For February, 1880.
No. CCXXXVI.	(Vol. 5, 4th Series No. XIX.)	For May, 1880.
No. CCXXXVII.	Vol. 5, 4th Series No. XX.)	For August, 1880.
No. CCXXXVIII.	(Vol. 6, 4th Series No. XXI.)	For November, 1880.
No. CCXXXIX.	(Vol. 6, 4th Series No. XXII.)	For February, 1881.
No. CCXL.	(Vol. 6, 4th Series No. XXIII.)	For May, 1881.
No. CCXLI.	(Vol. 6, 4th Series No. XXIV.)	For August, 1881.
No. CCXLII.	(Vol. 7, 4th Series No. XXV.)	For November, 1881.
No. CCXLIII.	(Vol. 7, 4th Series No. XXVI.)	For February, 1882.
No. CCXLIV.	(Vol. 7, 4th Series No. XXVII.)	For May, 1882.
No. CCXLV.	(Vol. 7, 4th Series No. XXVIII.)	For August, 1882.
No. CCXLVI.	(Vol. 8, 4th Series No. XXIX.)	For November, 1882.
No. CCXLVII.	(Vol. 8, 4th Series No. XXX.)	For February, 1883.

An Annual Subscription of 20s., paid in advance to the Publishers, will secure the receipt of the **LAW MAGAZINE**, free by post, within the United Kingdom, or for 24s. to the Colonies and Abroad.

Third Edition, in one vol., 8vo, price , cloth, *in preparation.*

A TREATISE ON HINDU LAW AND USAGE.

By JOHN D. MAYNE, of the Inner Temple, Barrister-at-Law, Author of "A Treatise on Damages," &c.

"A new work from the pen of so established an authority as Mr. Mayne cannot fail to be welcome to the legal profession. In his present volume the late Officiating Advocate-General at Madras has drawn upon the stores of his long experience in Southern India, and has produced a work of value alike to the practitioner at the Indian Bar, or at home, in appeal cases, and to the scientific jurist.

"To all who, whether as practitioners or administrators, or as students of the science of jurisprudence, desire a thoughtful and suggestive work of reference on Hindu Law and Usage, we heartily recommend the careful perusal of Mr. Mayne's valuable treatise."
—*Law Magazine and Review.*

In 8vo, 1877, price 15s., cloth,

A DIGEST OF HINDU LAW.

AS ADMINISTERED IN THE COURTS OF THE MADRAS PRESIDENCY.

ARRANGED AND ANNOTATED

By H. S. CUNNINGHAM, M.A., Advocate-General, Madras.

DUTCH LAW.

Vol. I., Royal 8vo, price 40s., cloth,

VAN LEEUWEN'S COMMENTARIES ON THE ROMAN-DUTCH LAW. Revised and Edited with Notes in Two Volumes by C. W. DECKER, Advocate. Translated from the original Dutch by J. G. KOTZÉ, LL.B., of the Inner Temple, Barrister-at-Law, and Chief Justice of the Transvaal. With Facsimile Portrait of DECKER from the Edition of 1780.

*** Vol. II. is in course of preparation.

BUCHANAN (J.). Reports of Cases decided in the Supreme Court of the CAPE OF GOOD HOPE. 1868, 1869, 1870-73, and 74. Bound in Three Vols. Royal 8vo.
———— 1875, 1876, 1879, etc.

MENZIES' (W.), Reports of Cases decided in the Supreme Court of the CAPE OF GOOD HOPE. Vol. I., Vol. II., Vol. III.

BUCHANAN (J.), Index and Digest of Cases decided in the Supreme Court of the CAPE OF GOOD HOPE, reported by the late Hon. WILLIAM MENZIES. Compiled by JAMES BUCHANAN, Advocate of the Supreme Court. In One Vol., royal 8vo.

In 8vo, 1878, cloth,

PRECEDENTS IN PLEADING: being Forms filed of Record in the Supreme Court of the Colony of the Cape of Good Hope. Collected and Arranged by JAMES BUCHANAN.

In Crown 8vo, price 31s. 6d., boards,

THE INTRODUCTION TO DUTCH JURISPRUDENCE OF HUGO GROTIUS, with Notes by Simon van Groenwegen van der Made, and References to Van der Keesel's Theses and Schorer's Notes. Translated by A. F. S. MAASDORP, B.A., of the Inner Temple, Barrister-at-Law.

In 12mo, price 15s. *nett*, boards,

SELECT THESES ON THE LAWS OF HOLLAND & ZEELAND.

Being a Commentary of Hugo Grotius' Introduction to Dutch Jurisprudence, and intended to supply certain defects therein, and to determine some of the more celebrated Controversies on the Law of Holland. By DIONYSIUS GODEFRIDUS VAN DER KESSEL, Advocate, and Professor of the Civil and Modern Laws in the Universities of Leyden. Translated from the original Latin by C. A. LORENZ, of Lincoln's Inn, Barrister-at-Law. Second Edition, With a Biographical Notice of the Author by Professor J. DE WAL, of Leyden.

The Bar Examination Journal.

No. 36. Price 2s.

HILARY, 1883.

CONTENTS:—

SUBJECTS OF EXAMINATION.
EXAMINATION PAPERS, WITH ANSWERS.
   REAL AND PERSONAL PROPERTY.
   EQUITY.
   COMMON LAW.
   ROMAN LAW.
LIST OF SUCCESSFUL CANDIDATES.
STUDENTSHIP EXAMINATION PAPERS.

EDITED BY

A. D. TYSSEN, D.C.L., M.A.,
OF THE INNER TEMPLE, BARRISTER-AT-LAW; AND

W. D. EDWARDS, LL.B.,
OF LINCOLN'S INN, BARRISTER-AT-LAW.

⁎⁎ *It is intended in future to publish a Number of the* Journal *after each Examination.*

Now published, in 8vo, price 18s. each, cloth,

THE BAR EXAMINATION JOURNAL, VOLS. IV. & V.

Containing the Examination Questions and Answers from Easter Term, 1878, to Hilary Term, 1880, and Easter Term, 1880, to Hilary Term, 1882, with List of Successful Candidates at each examination, Notes on the Law of Property, and a Synopsis of Recent Legislation of importance to Students, and other information.
BY A. D. TYSSEN AND W. D. EDWARDS, Barristers-at-Law.

Second Edition. In 8vo, price 6s., cloth,

A SUMMARY OF JOINT STOCK COMPANIES' LAW.

BY T. EUSTACE SMITH,
OF THE INNER TEMPLE, BARRISTER-AT-LAW.

"The author of this hand-book tells us that, when an articled student reading for the final examination, he felt the want of such a work as that before us, wherein could be found the main principles of law relating to joint-stock companies . . . Law students may well read it; for Mr. Smith has very wisely been at the pains of giving his authority for all his statements of the law or of practice, as applied to joint-stock company business usually transacted in solicitor's chambers. In fact, Mr. Smith has by his little book offered a fresh inducement to students to make themselves—at all events, to some extent—acquainted with company law as a separate branch of study."—*Law Times.*

"These pages give, in the words of the Preface, 'as briefly and concisely as possible, a general view both of the principles and practice of the law affecting companies.' The work is excellently printed, and authorities are cited; but in no case is the very language of the statutes copied. The plan is good, and shows both grasp and neatness, and, both amongst students and laymen, Mr. Smith's book ought to meet a ready sale."—*Law Journal.*

"The book is one from which we have derived a large amount of valuable information, and we can heartily and conscientiously recommend it to our readers."—*Oxford and Cambridge Undergraduates' Journal.*

In 8vo, Fifth Edition, price 9s., cloth,

THE MARRIED WOMEN'S PROPERTY ACTS;
1870, 1874, and 1882,
WITH COPIOUS AND EXPLANATORY NOTES, AND AN APPENDIX OF THE ACTS RELATING TO MARRIED WOMEN.

By S. WORTHINGTON BROMFIELD, M.A., Christ Church, Oxon., and the Inner Temple, Barrister-at-Law. Being the Fifth Edition of The Married Women's Property Acts. By the late J. R. GRIFFITHS, B.A., Oxon., of Lincoln's Inn, Barrister-at-Law.

"Upon the whole we are of opinion that this is the best work upon the subject which has been issued since the passing of the recent Act. Its position as a well-established manual of acknowledged worth gives it at starting a considerable advantage over new books; and this advantage has been well maintained by the intelligent treatment of the Editor."—*Solicitor's Journal.*

"The notes are full, but anything rather than tedious reading, and the law contained in them is good, and verified by reported cases. . . . A distinct feature of the work is its copious index, practically a summary of the marginal headings of the various paragraphs in the body of the text. This book is worthy of all success."—*Law Magazine.*

In 8vo, price 12s., cloth,

THE LAW OF NEGLIGENCE.
SECOND EDITION.

By ROBERT CAMPBELL, of Lincoln's Inn, Barrister-at-Law, and Advocate of the Scotch Bar.

"No less an authority than the late Mr. Justice Willes, in his judgment in *Oppenheim v. White Lion Hotel Co.*, characterised Mr. Campbell's 'Law of Negligence' as a 'very good book;' and since very good books are by no means plentiful, when compared with the numbers of indifferent ones which annually issue from the press, we think the profession will be thankful to the author of this new edition brought down to date. It is indeed an able and scholarly treatise on a somewhat difficult branch of law, in the treatment of which the author's knowledge of Roman and Scotch Jurisprudence has stood him in good stead. We confidently recommend it alike to the student and the practitioner."—*Law Magazine.*

In royal 8vo, price 28s., cloth,

AN INDEX TO TEN THOUSAND PRECEDENTS
IN CONVEYANCING, AND TO COMMON AND COMMERCIAL

FORMS. Arranged in Alphabetical order with Subdivisions of an Analytical Nature; together with an Appendix containing an Abstract of the Stamp Act, 1870, with a Schedule of Duties; the Regulations relative to, and the Stamp Duties payable on, Probates of Wills, Letters of Administration, Legacies, and Successions. By WALTER ARTHUR COPINGER, of the Middle Temple, Barrister-at-Law.

BIBLIOTHECA LEGUM.

In 12mo (nearly 400 pages), price 2s., cloth,

A CATALOGUE OF LAW BOOKS. Including all the Reports
in the various Courts of England, Scotland, and Ireland; with a Supplement to December, 1882. By HENRY G. STEVENS and ROBERT W. HAYNES, Law Publishers.

In small 4to, price 2s., cloth, beautifully printed, with a large margin, for the special use of Librarians,

A CATALOGUE OF THE REPORTS IN THE VARIOUS COURTS OF THE UNITED KINGDOM OF GREAT BRITAIN AND IRELAND. *ARRANGED BOTH IN ALPHABETICAL & CHRONOLOGICAL ORDER.* By STEVENS & HAYNES, Law Publishers.

Just published, in 8vo, price 12s., cloth,

CHAPTERS ON THE
LAW RELATING TO THE COLONIES.

To which is appended a TOPICAL INDEX of CASES DECIDED in the PRIVY COUNCIL on Appeal from the Colonies, the Channel Islands and the Isle of Man, reported in Acton, Knapp, Moore, the Law Journal Reports, and the Law Reports, to July, 1882.

By CHARLES JAMES TARRING,
OF THE INNER TEMPLE, ESQ., BARRISTER-AT-LAW.

CONTENTS.

TABLE OF CASES CITED.
TABLE OF STATUTES CITED.
Introductory.—Definition of a Colony.
Chapter I.—The laws to which the Colonies are subject.
Chapter II.—The Executive.
   Section 1.—The Governor.
   Section 2.—The Executive Council.
Chapter III.—The Legislative power.
   Section 1.—Crown Colonies.
   Section 2.—Privileges and powers of colonial Legislative Assemblies.
Chapter IV.—The Judiciary and Bar.

Chapter V.—Appeals from the Colonies.
Chapter VI.—Section 1.—Imperial Statutes relating to the Colonies in general.
   Section 2.—Imperial Statutes relating to particular Colonies.

TOPICAL INDEX OF CASES.
INDEX OF TOPICS OF ENGLISH LAW DEALT WITH IN THE CASES.
INDEX OF NAMES OF CASES.

GENERAL INDEX.

In 8vo, price 10s. cloth,

THE TAXATION OF COSTS IN THE CROWN OFFICE.

COMPRISING A COLLECTION OF

BILLS OF COSTS IN THE VARIOUS MATTERS TAXABLE IN THAT OFFICE;

INCLUDING

COSTS UPON the PROSECUTION of FRAUDULENT BANKRUPTS, AND ON APPEALS FROM INFERIOR COURTS;

TOGETHER WITH

A TABLE OF COURT FEES,

AND A SCALE OF COSTS USUALLY ALLOWED TO SOLICITORS, ON THE TAXATION OF COSTS ON THE CROWN SIDE OF THE QUEEN'S BENCH DIVISION OF THE HIGH COURT OF JUSTICE.

By FREDK. H. SHORT,

CHIEF CLERK IN THE CROWN OFFICE.

"This is decidedly a useful work on the subject of those costs which are liable to be taxed before the Queen's Coroner and Attorney (for which latter name that of 'Solicitor' might now well be substituted), or before the master of the Crown Office ; in fact, such a book is almost indispensable when preparing costs for taxation in the Crown Office, or when taxing an opponent's costs. Country solicitors will find the scale relating to bankruptcy prosecutions of especial use, as such costs are taxed in the Crown Office. The 'general observations' constitute a useful feature in this manual."—*Law Times*.

"This book contains a collection of bills of costs in the various matters taxable in the Crown Office. When we point out that the only scale of costs available for the use of the general body of solicitors is that published in Mr. Corner's book on 'Crown Practice' in 1844, we have said quite enough to prove the utility of the work before us.

"In them Mr. Short deals with 'Perusals,' 'Copies for Use,' 'Affidavits,' 'Agency,' 'Correspondence,' 'Close Copies,' 'Counsel,' 'Affidavit of Increase,' and kindred matters ; and adds some useful remarks on taxation of 'Costs in Bankruptcy Prosecutions,' '*Quo Warranto*,' '*Mandamus*,' 'Indictments,' and 'Rules.'

"We have rarely seen a work of this character better executed, and we feel sure that it will be thoroughly appreciated."—*Law Journal*.

"The recent revision of the old scale of costs in the Crown Office renders the appearance of this work particularly opportune, and it cannot fail to be welcomed by practitioners. Mr. Short gives, in the first place, a scale of costs usually allowed to solicitors on the taxation of costs in the Crown Office, and then bills of costs in various matters. These are well arranged and clearly printed."—*Solicitors' Journal*.

In one volume, 8vo, price 16s., cloth,
A CONCISE TREATISE ON THE

STATUTE LAW OF THE LIMITATIONS OF ACTIONS.

With an Appendix of Statutes, Copious References to English, Irish, and American Cases, and to the French Code, and a Copious Index.

By HENRY THOMAS BANNING, M.A.,
OF THE INNER TEMPLE, BARRISTER-AT-LAW.

"In this work Mr. Banning has grappled with one of the most perplexing branches of our statute law. The law, as laid down by the judicial decisions on the various Statutes of Limitations, is given in thirty-three short chapters under as many headings, and each chapter treats of a sub-division of one of the main branches of the subject; thus we have ten chapters devoted to real property. This arrangement entails a certain amount of repetition, but is not without its advantages, as the subject of each chapter is tolerably exhaustively treated of within the limits of a few pages. We think that in this respect the author has exercised a wise discretion. So far as we have tested the cases cited, the effect of the numerous decisions appears to be accurately given—indeed, the author has, as we are informed in the preface, 'so far as is consistent with due brevity, employed the *ipsissima verba* of the tribunal;' and the cases are brought down to a very recent date. . . . . The substance of the book is satisfactory; and we may commend it both to students and practitioners."—*Solicitors' Journal*.

"Mr. Banning's 'Concise Treatise' justifies its title. He brings into a convenient compass a general view of the law as to the limitation of actions as it exists under numerous statutes, and a digest of the principal reported cases relating to the subject which have arisen in the English and American courts."—*Saturday Review*.

"Mr. Banning has adhered to the plan of printing the Acts in an appendix, and making his book a running treatise on the case-law thereon. The cases have evidently been investigated with care and digested with clearness and intellectuality."—*Law Journal*.

In 8vo, price 8s., cloth,

The TRADE MARKS REGISTRATION ACT, 1875,

And the Rules thereunder; THE MERCHANDISE MARKS ACT, 1862, with an Introduction containing a SUMMARY OF THE LAW OF TRADE MARKS, together with practical Notes and Instructions, and a copious INDEX. By EDWARD MORTON DANIEL, of Lincoln's Inn, Barrister-at-Law.

"The last of the works on this subject, that by Mr. Daniel, appears to have been very carefully done. Mr. Daniel's book is a satisfactory and useful guide."—*The Engineer*.

"This treatise contains, within moderate compass, the whole of the law, as far as practically required, on the subject of trade marks. The publication is opportune, the subject being one which must nearly concern a considerable portion of the public, and it may be recommended to all who desire to take advantage of the protection afforded by registration under the new legislation. It is practical, and seems to be complete in every respect. The volume is well printed and neatly got up."—*Law Times*.

In 8vo, price 1s., sewed,
AN ESSAY ON THE

ABOLITION OF CAPITAL PUNISHMENT.

Embracing more particularly an Enunciation and Analysis of the Principles of Law as applicable to Criminals of the Highest Degree of Guilt.

By WALTER ARTHUR COPINGER,
OF THE MIDDLE TEMPLE, ESQ., BARRISTER-AT-LAW;

Author of "The Law of Copyright in Works of Literature and Art," "Index to Precedents in Conveyancing," "On the Custody and Production of Title Deeds."

"We can recommend Mr. Copinger's book as containing the fullest collection we have seen of facts and quotations from eminent jurists, statistics, and general information bearing on the subject of capital punishments."—*Manchester Courier*.

In 8vo, price 31s. 6d., cloth,

THE INDIAN CONTRACT ACT, No. IX., of 1872.

TOGETHER
WITH AN INTRODUCTION AND EXPLANATORY NOTES, TABLE OF CONTENTS, APPENDIX, AND INDEX.

By H. S. CUNNINGHAM AND H. H. SHEPHERD,
BARRISTERS-AT-LAW.

Second Edition, in 8vo, price 8s., cloth,

THE PARTITION ACTS, 1868 & 1876,

A MANUAL OF THE LAW OF PARTITION AND OF SALE IN LIEU OF PARTITION.

With the Decided Cases, and an Appendix containing Judgments and Orders.

By W. GREGORY WALKER,

OF LINCOLN'S INN, BARRISTER-AT-LAW, B.A., AUTHOR OF "A COMPENDIUM OF THE LAW OF EXECUTORS AND ADMINISTRATORS."

"This is a very good manual—practical, clearly written, and complete. The subject lends itself well to the mode of treatment adopted by Mr. Walker, and in his notes to the various sections he has carefully brought together the cases and discussed the difficulties arising upon the language of the different provisions."—*Solicitors' Journal.*

"The main body of the work is concerned only with the so-called Partition Acts, which are really Acts enabling the Court in certain cases to substitute a sale for a partition. What these cases are is very well summed up or set out in the present edition of this book, which is well up to date. The work is supplemented by a very useful selection of precedents of pleadings and orders."—*Law Journal.*

"This is a very painstaking and praiseworthy little treatise. That such a work has now been published needs, in fact, only to be announced; for, meeting as it does an undoubted requirement, it is sure to secure a place in the library of every equity practitioner. . . . . We are gratified to be able to add our assurance that the practitioner will find that his confidence has not been misplaced, and that Mr. Walker's manual, compact and inexpensive as it is, is equally exhaustive and valuable."—*Irish Law Times.*

In 8vo, price 21s., cloth,
A TREATISE ON THE

LAW AND PRACTICE RELATING TO INFANTS.

By ARCHIBALD H. SIMPSON, M.A.,

OF LINCOLN'S INN, ESQ., BARRISTER-AT-LAW, AND FELLOW OF CHRIST'S COLLEGE, CAMBRIDGE.

"Mr. Simpson's book comprises the whole of the law relating to infants, both as regards their persons and their property, and we have not observed any very important omissions. The author has evidently expended much trouble and care upon his work, and has brought together, in a concise and convenient form, the law upon the subject down to the present time."—*Solicitors' Journal.*

"Its law is unimpeachable. We have detected no errors, and whilst the work might have been done more scientifically, it is, beyond all question, a compendium of sound legal principles."—*Law Times.*

"Mr. Simpson has arranged the whole of the Law relating to Infants with much fulness of detail, and yet in comparatively little space. The result is due mainly to the businesslike condensation of his style. Fulness, however, has by no means been sacrificed to brevity, and, so far as we have been able to test it, the work omits no point of any importance, from the earliest cases to the last. In the essential qualities of clearness, completeness, and orderly arrangement it leaves nothing to be desired.

"Lawyers in doubt on any point of law or practice will find the information they require, if it can be found at all, in Mr. Simpson's book, and a writer of whom this can be said may congratulate himself on having achieved a considerable success."
Law Magazine, February, 1876.

"The reputation of 'Simpson on Infants' is now too perfectly established to need any encomiums on our part: and we can only say that, as the result of our own experience, we have invariably found this work an exhaustive and trustworthy repertory of information on every question connected with the law and practice relating to its subject."—*Irish Law Times,* July 7, 1877.

In 8vo, price 8s., cloth,
THE LAW CONCERNING THE

REGISTRATION OF BIRTHS AND DEATHS

IN ENGLAND AND WALES, AND AT SEA.

Being the whole Statute Law upon the subject; together with a list of Registration Fees and Charges. Edited, with Copious Explanatory Notes and References, and an Elaborate Index, by ARTHUR JOHN FLAXMAN, of the Middle Temple, Barrister-at-Law.

"*Mr. Flaxman's unpretentious but admirable little book makes the duties of all parties under the Act abundantly clear*. . . . Lawyers *will find the book not only handy, but also instructive and suggestive. To registrars, and all persons engaged in the execution of the law, the book will be invaluable.* The index occupies thirty-five pages, and is so full that information on a minute point can be obtained without trouble. It is an index that must have cost the author much thought and time. *The statements of what is to be done, who may do it, and what must not be done, are so clear that it is well-nigh impossible for any one who consults the book to err.* Those who use Flaxman's 'Registration of Births and Deaths will admit that our laudatory criticism is thoroughly merited."—*Law Journal.*

"Mr. Arthur John Flaxman, barrister-at-law, of the Middle Temple, has published a small work on 'The Law concerning the Registration of Births and Deaths in England and Wales, and at Sea.' Mr. Flaxman has pursued the only possible plan, giving the statutes and references to cases. The remarkable feature is the index, which fills no less than 35 out of a total of 112 pages. The index alone would be extremely useful, and is worth the money asked for the work."—*Law Times.*

THE LAW OF EXTRADITION.

Second Edition, in 8vo, price 18s., cloth,

A TREATISE UPON

THE LAW OF EXTRADITION,

WITH THE

CONVENTIONS UPON THE SUBJECT EXISTING BETWEEN ENGLAND AND FOREIGN NATIONS,

AND THE CASES DECIDED THEREON.

By EDWARD CLARKE,

OF LINCOLN'S INN, Q.C.

"Mr. Clarke's accurate and sensible book is the best authority to which the English reader can turn upon the subject of Extradition."—*Saturday Review.*

"The opinion we expressed of the merits of this work when it first appeared has been fully justified by the reputation it has gained. This new edition, embodying and explaining the recent legislation on extradition, is likely to sustain that reputation. . . . There are other points we had marked for comment, but we must content ourselves with heartily commending this new edition to the attention of the profession. It is seldom we come across a book possessing so much interest to the general reader and at the same time furnishing so useful a guide to the lawyer."—*Solicitors' Journal.*

"The appearance of a second edition of this treatise does not surprise us. It is a useful book, well arranged and well written. A student who wants to learn the principles and practice of the law of extradition will be greatly helped by Mr. Clarke. Lawyers who have extradition business will find this volume an excellent book of reference. Magistrates who have to administer the extradition law will be greatly assisted by a careful perusal of 'Clarke upon Extradition.' This may be called a warm commendation, but those who have read the book will not say it is unmerited. We have so often to expose the false pretenders to legal authorship that it is a pleasure to meet with a volume that is the useful and unpretending result of honest work. Besides the Appendix, which contains the extradition conventions of this country since 1843, we have eight chapters. The first is 'Upon the Duty of Extradition;' the second on the 'Early Treaties and Cases;' the others on the law in the United States, Canada, England, and France, and the practice in those countries."—*Law Journal.*

"One of the most interesting and valuable contributions to legal literature which it has been our province to notice for a long time, is 'Clarke's Treatise on the Law of Extradition.' . . . . . Mr. Clarke's work comprises chapters upon the Duty of Extradition; Early Treaties and Cases; History of the Law in the United States, in Canada, in England, in France, &c., with an Appendix containing the Conventions existing between England and Foreign Nations, and the cases decided thereon . . . The work is ably prepared throughout, and should form a part of the library of every lawyer interested in great Constitutional or International Questions."—*Albany Law Journal.*

THE TIMES of September 7, 1874, in a long article upon "Extradition Treaties," makes considerable use of this work, and writes of it as "*Mr. Clarke's useful Work on Extradition.*"

In 8vo, 1876, price 8s., cloth,

THE PRACTICE AND PROCEDURE IN APPEALS
FROM INDIA TO THE PRIVY COUNCIL.

By E. B. MICHELL AND R. B. MICHELL,

BARRISTERS-AT-LAW.

"A useful manual arranging the practice in convenient order, and giving the rules in force in several Courts. It will be a decided acquisition to those engaged in Appeals from India."—*Law Times.*

PRACTICE OF CONVEYANCING.

In 8vo, price 2s. 6d., cloth,

TABLES OF STAMP DUTIES
FROM 1815 TO THE PRESENT TIME.

By WALTER ARTHUR COPINGER,

OF THE MIDDLE TEMPLE, ESQUIRE, BARRISTER-AT-LAW; AUTHOR OF "THE LAW OF COPYRIGHT IN WORKS OF LITERATURE AND ART," "INDEX TO PRECEDENTS IN CONVEYANCING," "TITLE DEEDS," &c.

"Conveyancers owe Mr. Copinger a debt of gratitude for his valuable Index to Precedents in Conveyancing; and we think the little book now before us will add to their obligations. Mr. Copinger gives, first of all, an abstract of the Stamp Act, 1870, with the special regulations affecting conveyances, mortgages, and settlements in full. He then presents in a tabular form the *ad valorem* stamp duties on conveyances, mortgages, and settlements, payable in England from the 1st of September, 1815, to the 10th of October, 1850, and then tables of *ad valorem* duties payable on the three classes of instruments since the last-mentioned date, and at the present time; arranged very clearly in columns. We cannot pretend to have checked the figures, but those we have looked at are correct: and we think this little book ought to find its way into a good many chambers and offices."—*Solicitors' Journal*.
"This book, or at least one containing the same amount of valuable and well-arranged information, should find a place in every Solicitor's office. It is of especial value when examining the abstract of a large number of old title deeds."—*Law Times*.
"His *Tables of Stamp Duties, from 1815 to 1878*, have already been tested in Chambers, and being now published, will materially lighten the labours of the profession in a tedious department, yet one requiring great care."—*Law Magazine and Review*.

In one volume, 8vo, price 14s., cloth,

TITLE DEEDS:
THEIR CUSTODY, INSPECTION, AND PRODUCTION, AT LAW, IN EQUITY, AND IN MATTERS OF CONVEYANCING,

Including Covenants for the Production of Deeds and Attested Copies; with an Appendix of Precedents, the Vendor and Purchaser Act, 1874, &c., &c., &c. By WALTER ARTHUR COPINGER, of the Middle Temple, Barrister-at-Law; Author of "The Law of Copyright" and "Index to Precedents in Conveyancing."

"In dealing with 'documentary evidence at law and in equity and in matters of conveyancing, including covenants for the production of deeds and attested copies,' Mr. Copinger has shown discrimination, for it is a branch of the general subject of evidence which is very susceptible of independent treatment. We are glad, therefore, to be able to approve both of the design and the manner in which it has been executed.
"The literary execution of the work is good enough to invite quotation, but the volume is not large and we content ourselves with recommending it to the profession."—*Law Times*.
"A really good treatise on this subject must be essential to the lawyer; and this is what we have here. Mr. Copinger has supplied a much-felt want, by the compilation of this volume. We have not space to go into the details of the book; it appears well arranged, clearly written, and fully elaborated. With these few remarks we recommend this volume to our readers."—*Law Journal*.

In 8vo, Second Edition, considerably enlarged, price 30s., cloth

THE LAW OF COPYRIGHT,

In Works of Literature and Art; including that of the Drama, Music, Engraving, Sculpture, Painting, Photography, and Ornamental and Useful Designs; together with International and Foreign Copyright, with the Statutes Relating thereto, and References to the English and American Decisions. By WALTER ARTHUR COPINGER, of the Middle Temple, Barrister-at-Law.

"Mr. Copinger's book is very comprehensive, dealing with every branch of his subject, and even extending to copyright in foreign countries. So far as we have examined, we have found all the recent authorities noted up with scrupulous care, and there is an unusually good index. There are merits which will, doubtless, lead to the placing of this edition on the shelves of the members of the profession whose business is concerned with copyright; and deservedly, for the book is one of considerable value."—*Solicitors' Journal*.
"Meanwhile we recommend Mr. Copinger's volume as a clear and convenient work of reference on the many knotty points concerning the existing law of Copyright, national and international."—*Notes and Queries*.

Second Edition, in One large Volume, 8vo, price 42s., cloth,

A MAGISTERIAL AND POLICE GUIDE:

BEING THE STATUTE LAW,

INCLUDING THE SESSION 43 VICT. 1880.

WITH NOTES AND REFERENCES TO THE DECIDED CASES,

RELATING TO THE

PROCEDURE, JURISDICTION, AND DUTIES OF MAGISTRATES AND POLICE AUTHORITIES,

IN THE METROPOLIS AND IN THE COUNTRY.

With an Introduction showing the General Procedure before Magistrates both in Indictable and Summary Matters, as altered by the Summary Jurisdiction Act, 1879, together with the Rules under the said Act.

By HENRY C. GREENWOOD,

STIPENDIARY MAGISTRATE FOR THE DISTRICT OF THE STAFFORDSHIRE POTTERIES; AND

TEMPLE C. MARTIN,

CHIEF CLERK OF THE LAMBETH POLICE COURT.

"A second edition has appeared of Messrs. Greenwood and Martin's valuable and comprehensive magisterial and police Guide, a book which Justices of the peace should take care to include in their Libraries."—*Saturday Review.*

"Hence it is that we rarely light upon a work which commands our confidence, not merely by its research, but also by its grasp of the subject of which it treats. The volume before us is one of the happy few of this latter class, and it is on this account that the public favour will certainly wait upon it. We are moreover convinced that no effort has been spared by its authors, to render it a thoroughly efficient and trustworthy guide."—*Law Journal.*

"Magistrates will find a valuable handbook in Messrs. Greenwood and Martin's 'Magisterial and Police Guide,' of which a fresh Edition has just been published."—*The Times.*

"A very valuable introduction, treating of proceedings before Magistrates, and largely of the Summary Jurisdiction Act, is in itself a treatise which will repay perusal. We expressed our high opinion of the Guide when it first appeared, and the favourable impression then produced is increased by our examination of this Second Edition."—*Law Times.*

"For the form of the work we have nothing but commendation. We may say we have here our ideal law book. It may be said to omit nothing which it ought to contain."—*Law Times.*

"This handsome volume aims at presenting a comprehensive magisterial handbook for the whole of England. The mode of arrangement seems to us excellent, and is well carried out."—*Solicitors' Journal.*

"The *Magisterial and Police Guide*, by Mr. Henry Greenwood and Mr. Temple Martin, is a model work in its conciseness, and, so far as we have been able to test it, in completeness and accuracy. *It ought to be in the hands of all who, as magistrates or otherwise, have authority in matters of police.*"—*Daily News.*

"This work is eminently practical, and supplies a real want. It plainly and concisely states the law on all points upon which Magistrates are called upon to adjudicate, systematically arranged, so as to be easy of reference. It ought to find a place on every Justice's table, and we cannot but think that its usefulness will speedily ensure for it as large a sale as its merits deserve."—*Midland Counties Herald.*

"The exceedingly arduous task of collecting together all the enactments on the subject has been ably and efficiently performed, and the arrangement is so methodical and precise that one is able to lay a finger on a Section of an Act almost in a moment. It is wonderful what a mass of information is comprised in so comparatively small a space. We have much pleasure in recommending the volume not only to our professional, but also to our general readers; nothing can be more useful to the public than an acquaintance with the outlines of magisterial jurisdiction and procedure."—*Sheffield Post.*

www.ingramcontent.com/pod-product-compliance
Lightning Source LLC
Chambersburg PA
CBHW030003240426
43672CB00007B/812